Table of Contents

ISBN - 978-0-9810568-14

Chapter 1 - Introduction

I discovered *Blender* back in 1999 and was immediately drawn in. I was always a fan of 3D artwork and couldn't believe I could make my own 3D creations with a piece of software that was free. *Blender* was quite different back then and the amount of work needed to accomplish anything half decent dwarfs what can be accomplished very quickly with the *Blender* of today.

My relationship with *Blender* was initially sporadic. I would follow a tutorial or two and marvel at the impressive results. I'm the kind of person who needs a project to work on before I can commit myself to something. It wasn't until I decided to write a book and use *Blender* to do the illustrations that I got serious about learning the ins and outs of *Blender*. The book I wrote was an overview of computers and I created a computer system and all of its components as *3D Models* in blender. I then used those *3D Models* to create all of my illustrations. I learned a lot about *Blender* in the years it took me to write the book (3 years or so). I used a version of *Blender* that isn't remotely as feature rich as the *Blender* of today and when I go back at look at the illustrations I think about how I would do my illustrations today and how different they would look.

As I started using *Blender* I quickly realized there was one particular aspect of the creation process that I loved much more than the others. Creating and rendering a scene requires lighting, materials etc. and I learned enough to get the job done with decent results. What excited me the most was *3D Modeling*. I loved the process of creating a *3D Model* and most tutorials I watched or read always had to do with *3D Modeling*. I was drawn in and was continuously trying to learn as many new techniques as I could. I started looking at common everyday objects and thinking about how I would go about *Modeling* them.

As I learned about different *Modeling* tools and techniques I quickly realized that I would end up forgetting all the little tips and tricks I had learned if I didn't keep track of them. I starting storing the tips and tricks in a wiki. I had sections for materials, lighting etc. but the biggest section in the wiki by far was the section on *Modeling*. I thought it was a good foundation for writing a book

As I thought about how I wanted to write this book I decided to approach it as a reference for the tools that allow you to create or facilitate the creation of *3D Models* in *Blender*. I describe all the tools and their functionality in depth and provide tips and tricks where applicable. One of the main reasons for this decision was that I found after completing one *Modeling* tutorial after another I started to get less and less value for time spent. I would often spend a few hours watching a *Modeling* tutorial only to learn one or two new techniques. I started to lean towards watching mini-tutorials that dealt with one or two topics that I was specifically interested in to help ensure I got value for time spent.

Unlike many *Blender* books on the market, this book will not walk you through a *Modeling* project from start to finish. I find that approach leads to only addressing the necessary *Modeling* techniques needed to finish a particular project. Instead, you can think of this book as a comprehensive reference with tips, tricks and mini tutorials.

Who is this book for?

This book is aimed towards all skill levels although I do assume a basic working knowledge of *Blender*. If you are an absolute beginner, I suggest doing a few beginner tutorials to help you familiarize yourself with the *Blender UI* and its basic features. You should also learn how to add *Objects* to a *Scene* and perform basic *Transform Operations* (*Grab*, *Rotate* and *Scale*). There are plenty of tutorials out there. I recommend *Blender Cookie* (https://cgcookie.com/blender/). They have many high quality tutorials for people of all levels. The *Blender Basics* course is a great place to start if you're a beginner (https://cgcookie.com/blender/cgc-courses/blender-basics-introduction-for-beginners/).

How to read this book

The book can be read in any order but if you are new to intermediate it's recommended you read it from beginning to end without skipping around. My goal was to present the topics in the order I would use if I was sitting down in front of someone with the goal of introducing them to *Blender*. I spent a lot of time thinking about how to order the chapters and probably an equal amount of time moving things around when I wasn't sure a particular section was in the right place in the book.

I use plenty of illustrations in this book. I am a very visual learner and I believe 1 illustration can demonstrate a concept that would often take several paragraphs to explain.

Blender Words

Throughout the book you will notice there are words that are capitalized and have a different color than the regular text. I will call them *Blender Words*. A *Blender Word* (at least as far as this book is concerned) is a word that is specific to *Blender*. By specific to *Blender* I mean a term that is a component or tool of *Blender* or an operation performed in *Blender* as so on. A good example is the word "select". When I *Select* an *Object* in *Blender*, that is a *Blender* operation and the word will be highlighted as a *Blender* word. If I select an item from a *Menu*, that use of the word "select" doesn't refer to a *Blender* operation and will be treated as regular text. I hope the end result is a quick and easy way to identify when I am talking about something *Blender* specific.

Operating System and Blender Version

Blender is available on Windows, Mac OSX, Linux and FreeBSD. I am writing this book on a PC running Windows 10. All of the shortcuts I reference are based on the Windows keyboard. The shortcuts may be slightly different on other operating systems. A very common example is the *Ctrl* key on Windows should be substituted with the *Command* key on Mac OSX. I imagine most people are used to substituting the proper key when performing a tutorial but if you are new to *Blender* it's something to be aware of.

Blender is always changing. By the time I finished this book I was on *Blender* version 2.76. All information and illustrations are based on a particular version of *Blender* and may differ slightly (and eventually differ greatly) as new versions of *Blender* are released.

Feedback and Corrections

I welcome all feedback. If you think I missed something, let me know. If you want a particular tool covered in a future edition, let me know. If something doesn't make sense the way it's written, let me know. If a word is misspelled or my grammar is lacking, let me know. I will take all feedback and use it to make the book as complete and error free as I possibly can.

I am human and I make mistakes. Although I made every effort to ensure the information in this book was as accurate as possible, I may have made a mistake here and there. Many of the tools have very little documentation which resulted in me having to discover how a tool works by simply using it. I didn't want to settle for not talking about a particular option on a tool because I couldn't find any information on how it works. I probably doubled my knowledge of *3D Modeling* in *Blender* by writing this book. Even though I have been using *Blender* for years and I often found myself saying "I didn't know that I could do that" or "that is a really cool option" several times as I researched various topics for this book.

I hope you enjoy reading this book and I expect it will leave you with a broader knowledge of *Blender's Tools* and functionality. As a result, you should be better prepared to tackle the challenges that arise when trying to create that perfect *3D Model*.

Chapter 2 - Blender UI

The *Blender UI* is made up of panels that can be created, merged and resized in any configuration you like. This allows for enormous flexibility allowing you to essentially create any *UI* layout you like. This chapter will revolve around some of the more useful panels and editors in *Blender*.

Tools and Properties Shelves

In the *3D View* window, you can use T and N to toggle the *Tools* and *Properties Panels* respectively. They are actually referred to as the *Tools Shelf* and the *Properties Shelf*.

The *Tools Shelf* contains commonly used tools and the contents of the shelf changes depending on what you are doing. Many of the tools on this shelf are also available through keyboard shortcuts or in the *Specials Menu* (W in *Edit Mode*), *Edges Menu* (Ctrl+E in *Edit Mode*) and *Faces Menu* (Ctrl+F in *Edit Mode*).

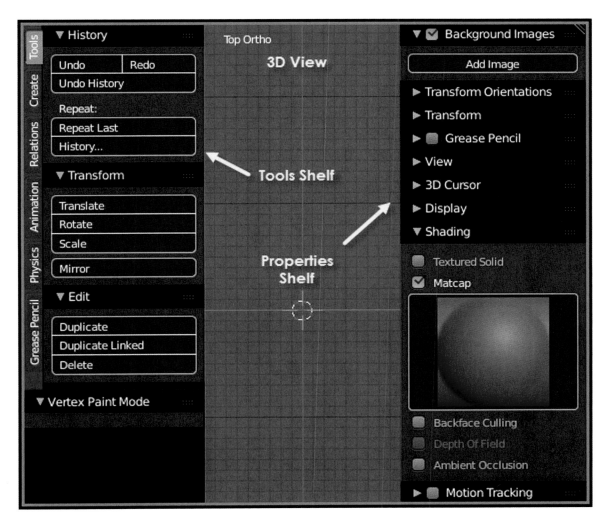

The *Properties Shelf* has panels that are useful when *Modeling* as well as panels used to change settings / options related to the *3D View* window. This includes adding a *Background Image*, the *Grease Pencil*, a *Display Panel* that allows you to toggle the grid or switch to *Quad View* and many others. I touch on several of these panels at various spots in the book but I encourage you to explore the *Properties Shelf* and play with some of the settings. You may, as I have, find something that you didn't know existed that is useful or just plain cool.

I like to keep the *Tools* and *Properties Shelves* open as I use them often, although you can decide what works best for you. I use a wide screen monitor so they don't take up too much real estate on my screen and I use them often enough that most of the time it's worth it for me to leave them open.

Outliner

I initially didn't use the *Outliner* much. I watched a tutorial one day and it opened my eyes to its power and flexibility. I actually keep 2 *Outliner Panels* open. One is the default *All Scenes View* which shows all *Objects* in your scenes. I also use the *Groups View* to help me organize my *Objects* (see **Chapter 7 – Grouping Objects**).

Blender comes with *Layers* that help you organize your *Objects* which are very useful for *Isolating* what you are working on and reducing screen clutter. The *Outliner* allows you to do the same thing and much more at a more granular level. All of your *Objects* are listed in the *All Scenes View*. Everything from mesh *Objects* to *Lamps* and *Cameras*.

The first thing you notice is there an a few icons beside each item in the *Outliner*. The first is a little eye which allows you to hide an *Object* from you *Scene*. Hiding *Objects* in your *Scene* is a great way to get a better view of the *Mesh* you are currently working on. The arrow icon allows you to lock an *Object* in place. Once locked you will no longer be able to *Select* or *Transform* the *Object* in any way. This can be helpful when you have several *Objects* in close proximity and you don't want to hide them but you don't want to accidentally keep selecting the wrong *Object*. The last icon is a *Camera*. Selecting this icon will prevent the corresponding *Object* from being *Rendered*.

Another very handy feature of the *Outliner* is the *Search* window. Not only can you use it to filter by *Object* name but you can even use it to filter by *Material* name or just about anything that has a label in the *Outliner*.

As I mentioned earlier, I also like to have a 2nd *Outliner Panel* so I can view my various *Object Groups*. I find using *Groups* is a great way to keep my *Objects* organized. I can then *Select* / *Hide* / *Lock* an entire *Group* with 1 mouse click.

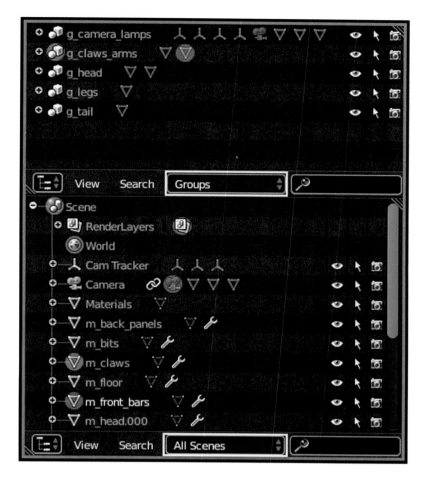

As you can see in the above illustration, by using 2 *Outliner Panels* I can quickly and easily *Select* / *Hide* / *Lock Objects* individually or in groups.

For more information on *Groups* and how to use the *Outliner* to maximize their usefulness, (see **Chapter 7 – Grouping Objects**).

Here are a few more tips for using the *Outliner*:

- Use the *Outliner* as an easy way to select *Objects* in your scene. Hit NumPad. to *Center* on the *Object* once selected.
- If there is an *Object* in the *Outliner* you don't recognize, select it and *Center* on it to quickly locate it.
- You can rename *Objects* in the *Outliner*.
- Place *Camera*, *Lights* and other related *Objects* in a group so you can quickly *Hide* or *Lock* them in place. I use *Empties* to track my *Camera* and *Lights* and like the convenience of keeping them all in in one group.

Layers

Layers are used to help organize your *Objects* so that they are more manageable. The more *Objects* you add to your *Scene*, the harder it gets to keep it all organized. If you are familiar with any graphics software then the idea of *Layers* shouldn't be foreign to you. Keep in mind that the order of the *Layers* has no effect on the *Scene* like it does in other graphics software. You can think of them as a way to hide some *Objects* allowing you to easily work on other *Objects*. Once an *Object* is moved to a *Layer*, you can then turn that *Layer* on or off and consequently toggle the visibility of all *Objects* in that *Layer*. *Layers* can be toggled on and off using the *Layer* buttons or the number keys on your keyboard.

You may have noticed that some of the *Layers* have a little dot in them. The dot is an indication that there is at least 1 *Object* on that *Layer*.

To add an *Object* to a *Layer* simply *Select* the *Object* and press M. A small dialog will appear allowing you to select which *Layer* you want to move your *Object* to. You can actually add an *Object* to multiple *Layers* by pressing M and holding down *Shift* while selecting which *Layers* to add your *Object* to.

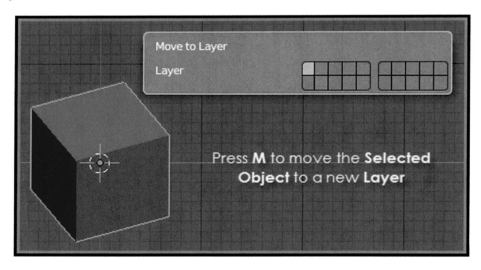

Tips:

- Put your *Camera* and *Lights* on one *Layer*. I use the same *Layer* every time so I can quickly switch to that *Layer* as needed.

- I like to reserve 1 *Layer* as a junk layer. I put any *Objects* that I no longer need into that *Layer*. You would be surprised how many times the junk *Layer* will save you hours of time because you accidentally deleted or screwed up something you were working on.
- You can *Select* all *Layers* at once by pressing the ~ key.

Themes

You can modify the look of the *User Interface* using *Themes*. I have a *Theme* that I created and will use for the majority of the screenshots in this book.

Creating your own *Theme* can be time consuming, but it can also be rewarding. I had an idea of what I was looking for when I started creating my own *Theme* and slowly, over time, it evolved into what you see in the illustrations for much of the book. I continue to tweak it when I see a something that I think can be improved.

Blender comes with a few *Themes* and there are also several downloadable *Themes* on the internet. *Themes* can be found by googling "blender themes".

Choosing or Installing a Theme

Open *User Preferences* via the *File Menu* or keyboard shortcut Ctrl + Alt + U and go to the *Themes Tab*.

- Go to the *Themes* tab.
  - To use an existing *Theme*, simply select a new *Theme* from the *Presets Menu*.
  - To install a new *Theme*, press the *Install Theme* button and browse to the location of your *Theme*. *Themes* are usually stored in an .xml file.

Change multiple sliders at once

There are times where you might want to change the value of 3 sliders at the same time. Here is how to do it:

1. Click and hold the LMB on the first field.
2. Drag down to highlight all the remaining fields.
3. Drag left or right to change all values at the same time.

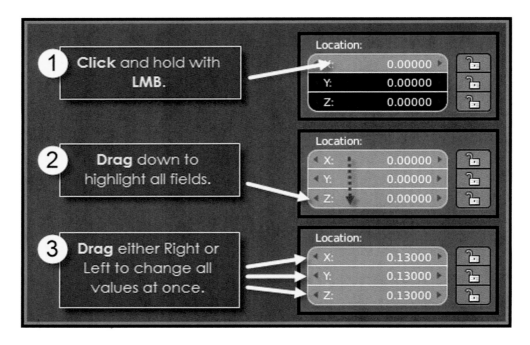

Copying and Pasting Values

You can copy and paste values from many of the fields in *Blender* including both numeric and text values. To copy a value, simply hover over a field and press Ctrl+C. To paste a copied value, hover a field and press Ctrl+V.

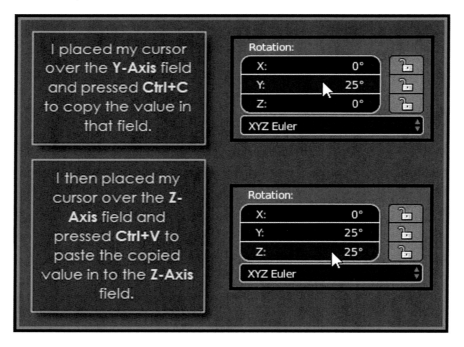

Collapse Menus

You can collapse a *Menu Bar* so that it's represented by a small icon. This gives you a little more real estate and that's always a good thing.

Simply *Right-Click* on a *Menu*, scroll up to the *Header Menu* item and select *Collapse Menus*.

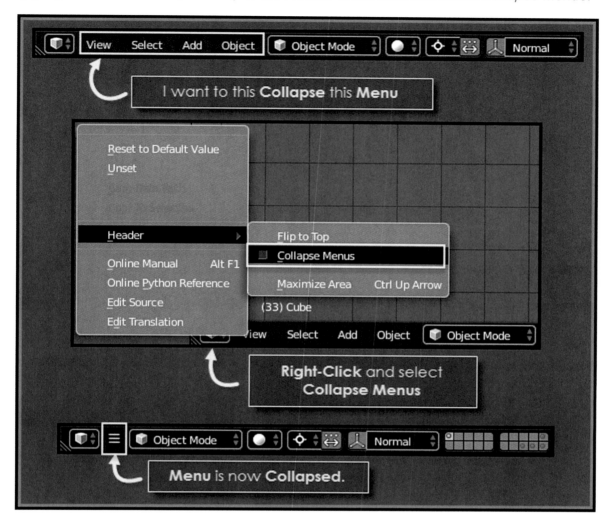

The *Menu* is now available through an icon.

Blender Preferences

There are several tweaks I make to *Preferences*. Some are personal preferences but I thought I would share them as they may be helpful, especially if you didn't know about them.

Start by opening *User Preferences* via the *File Menu* or keyboard shortcut Ctrl + Alt + U.

Interface Tab - enable *Zoom To Mouse Position*. Enabling this setting allows you to *Zoom* to any *Location* in the *3D View*. Simply point to a *Location* and use the Mouse Wheel (or Numpad + and Numpad -) to *Zoom* to that *Location*. I use this often when I am *Zoomed* out and want to *Zoom* in to certain parts of my *Model* to have a better look.

Editing Tab - set *Undo* steps to **64**. This allows you to set how many actions you can revert using Ctrl + Z. Anyone who has made mistakes knows the more you can *Undo*, the better. It has saved me on more than on occasion.

File Tab - I set the *File Paths* for *Fonts*, *Textures*, *Render Output*, *Scripts* and *Temp*. Not having to navigate to your *Fonts* folder or *Textures* folder etc. is a real time saver. I also enable the *Show Thumbnails* check box which results in all images and movies being displayed in *Thumbnail View* by default.

System Tab - I enable *Region Overlap* so that the *Properties* and *Tools* shelves don't cause the main *3D Window* to resize when I open them.

Once you have made all of your changes make sure you save your *User Settings* by pressing the *Save User Settings* button at the bottom left of the *User Preferences* window.

Pie Menus

Blender now comes with an add-on call *Pie Menus*. Once enabled, pressing any of the configured shortcut keys will cause a *Pie Menu* to appear. The *Pie Menu* is essentially a group of related functionality represented by graphical icons.

Here is what you will see if you press Q with the *Pie Menus* add-on enabled.

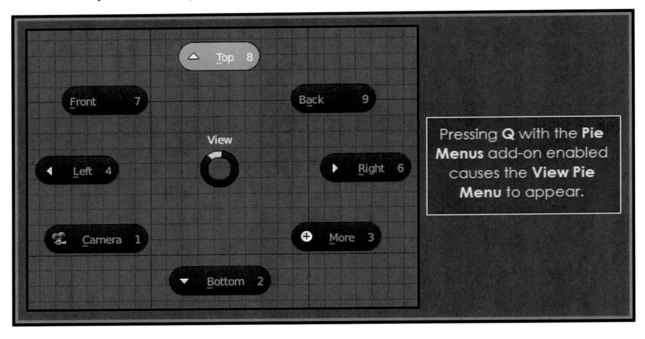

Pressing **Q** with the **Pie Menus** add-on enabled causes the **View Pie Menu** to appear.

As you can see in the above illustration, pressing Q gave me access to a *Pie Menu* that allows me to change the alignment of the *View* in the *3D View*. The *Pie Menu* mimics the functionality usually accessed through the number pad on the keyboard. I can simply move my *Mouse* to one of the icons and click it to change the *View*. Thanks to *Pie Menus*, 1 shortcut allows me to access the functionality that normally requires 6 shortcut keys. But wait, there's more. Notice at the bottom right hand corner there is an icon labeled "More". If you click on that icon you are presented with another *Pie Menu* with more options for changing your *View*. You have a total of 13 options for manipulating your *View* available by pressing 1 key.

I really encourage you to enable the *Pie Menus* add-on and give it a test drive. I think once you get used to using *Pie Menus* you won't go back. I know I did and now consider them essential to my *Modeling* flow.

To enable *Pie Menus* open *User Preferences* via the *File Menu* or keyboard shortcut Ctrl + Alt + U and go to the *Add-Ons* tab. Do a search for **Pie**. Enable the *User Interface: Pie Menus Official* radio button and click *Save User Settings*.

Context Windows

Throughout the book I will refer to what are known as *Context Windows*. A *Context Window* is another name for a *Panel* that gives you access to related functionality. *Blender* has several *Context Windows* and which ones are accessible depends on your current activity. For example, *Selecting* a *Camera* will result in several *Context Windows* like *Material* and *Texture* becoming unavailable. It will also result in 1 new *Context Window* (the *Camera Context Window*) becoming available. *Context Windows* are accessed through icons in the *Properties Panel*. Here are some of the *Context Windows* available in *Blender*.

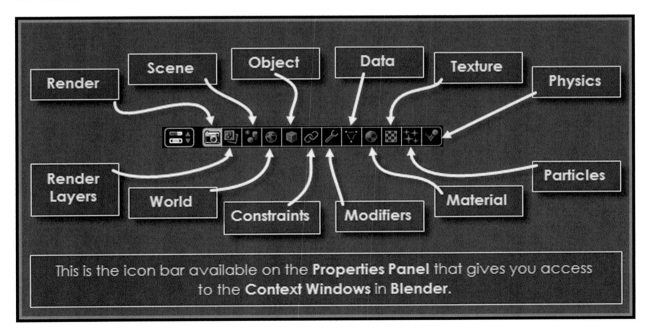

This is the icon bar available on the **Properties Panel** that gives you access to the **Context Windows** in **Blender.**

Chapter 3 - The 3D View

There are a plethora of options when it comes to manipulating the *3D View*. This includes everything from window layout, aligning the *Views*, changing the *Shading* and displaying information about the *Objects* In the *3D View* among others.

Maximize Area and Quad View

You can make any *Panel* in *Blender* occupy the full screen (or more accurately the entire *Blender* application window) using Shift + Space / Ctrl + Up Arrow / Ctrl + Down Arrow. In *Blender* this is referred to as *Maximize Area*. I use this often in the *3D View* when *Modeling*. You get more real estate when *Modeling* and as I have previously mentioned, that's always a good thing. Simply hover your cursor over any *Blender Panel* or *View* and use the shortcut to *Maximize* that particular *Panel* or *View*. Here is an example of *Maximizing* the *3D View*.

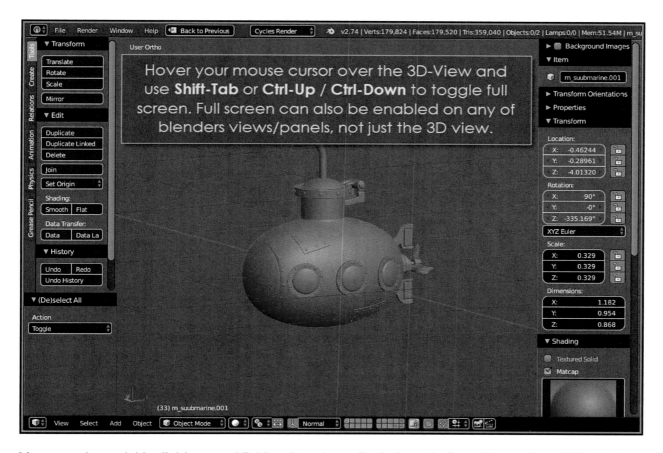

You can also quickly divide your *3D View* into 4 small windows (referred to as *Quad View*) using Ctrl + Alt + Q.

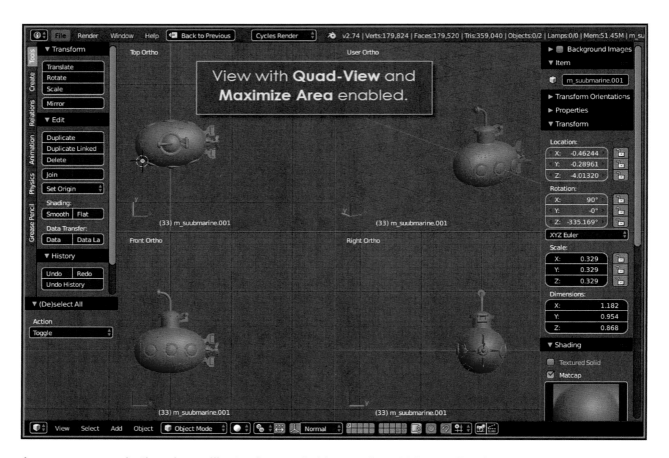

As you can see in the above illustration, switching to *Quad View* splits the *3D View* window into 4 smaller windows. One of the windows is set to *Top View*, one to *Front View* and one to *Right* (*Side*) *View*. This allows you to quickly see your model from 3 standard *Views*. The 4th window is the *User Window* and represents the *3D Window View* as it existed before you switched to *Quad View*. The *User Window* is the only window that allows you to *Rotate* the *3D View*. All of the other windows are *Locked* by default. You can still *Zoom* and *Pan* in each of the standard *View* windows.

There is an option to disable the *Lock* option for the 3 *Locked Windows*. It's available on the *Properties Shelf* in the *Display Panel*. There is also a button to toggle *Quad View* as an alternative to the keyboard shortcut.

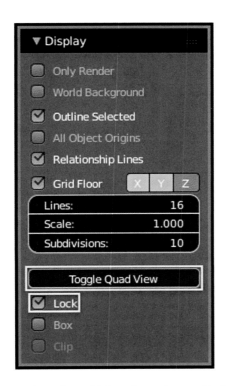

One thing to keep in mind is that using *Quad View* is not exactly the same as manually dividing the *3D View* into 4 separate *3D Windows*. In *Quad View*, there is still only 1 *3D Window* with four *Views*. That one *3D Window* has one *Window Header* for all four windows. If you want a *Window Header* for each *3D View Window*, you have to split the *3D Window* manually.

3D Window View

There are plenty of options when it comes to manipulating the *3D View*. Many of those options use the *Middle Mouse Button*. If you don't have a mouse that has a *Middle Mouse Button*, I suggest you get one. It's practically indispensable when it comes to navigating and manipulating the *3D View* and is used in many other *Blender* operations. 3 button mice are inexpensive and extremely common these days. Most Logitech mice have a scroll wheel that also acts as a *Middle Mouse Button*.

Orthographic vs. Perspective View

Blender offers 2 options that affect the *View* from any *Viewing* angle. By pressing *Numpad 5* you can toggle between either *View Mode*. First we have the *Orthographic View Mode* and this is the mode you will want to work in when *3D Modeling*. The *Orthographic View Mode* is essential during *Transform* operations or for accurately judging distance etc. The *Perspective View Mode* is essentially how we see the world. If I look at a row of corn in a field, even though the corn is the same height, it appears to get smaller the further away we look. You can easily see the difference using several *Objects*. To show the difference first I set up 3 *Objects*.

I can now switch to *Front View* to demonstrate the difference between *Orthographic* and *Perspective View Mode*.

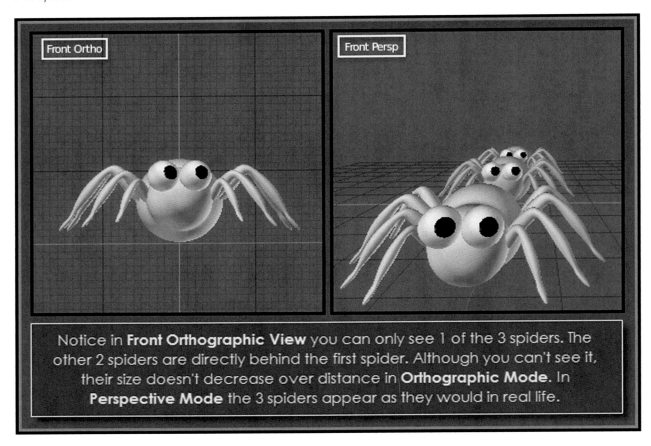

As you can see, attempting *Hard Surface Modeling* in *Perspective Mode* would probably result in *Objects* right out of the Cat in the Hat books.

The *Perspective View* is the default *View Mode* when *Rendering* your *Scene*. You can switch your *Camera* to use *Orthographic View* if you like. I rarely switch the *View Mode* on my *Camera* but it can be useful. For example, *Orthographic View* is a good choice if you use *Blender* to create buttons for a web page. *Rendering* all buttons at once in *Perspective View* will result in the buttons not appearing identical in shape. To demonstrate, first I create 4 buttons in *Blender*.

Now I *Render* the *Scene* in *Orthographic View*.

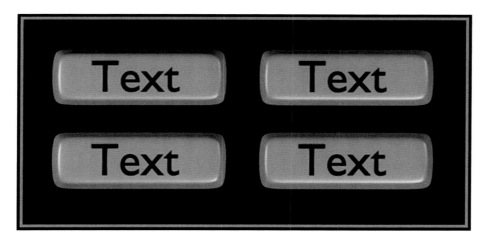

Notice the buttons are identical in size and shape. Now I *Render* the *Scene* again in *Perspective View*.

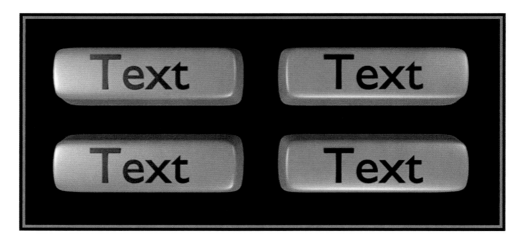

As you can see, the shape of the buttons is inconsistent as is the *Lighting*.

The majority of the time you will want to work in *Orthographic View* to ensure precision. I usually *Render* in *Perspective View* but there are situations were *Orthographic View* is a better option (the buttons above are a good example).

View Selected

The *View Selected* functionality allows you to *Zoom* in to one or more *Selected Object*(s) or *Mesh Element*(s). In *Object Mode*, *Select* one or more *Objects* and press Numpad . to *Zoom* in to the *Selected Objects*. *View Selected* behaves the same way in *Edit Mode*. You can *Zoom* in to *Selected Mesh Elements* by pressing Numpad . on the keyboard.

I intentionally put the section on the *View Selected* functionality near the top of this section of the book because I use it constantly. It is, in my opinion, the best way to focus in on an *Object* or *Mesh Element*. Another big advantage of using *View Selected* is that once completed you are perfectly positioned to *Rotate* around the *Selected Object*(s) / *Mesh Elements*.

Front, Side and Top View

In *Blender*, you can align your *View* to any of the default *Views* using the keys on the Number Pad or using the *Pie Menu* (assuming you have *Pie Menus* enabled (see **Chapter 2 – Pie Menus**). You can *Align* your *3D View* to the *Front*, *Back*, *Right Side*, *Left Side*, *Top* and *Bottom*. Here are the keyboard shortcuts for each of the *Views*.

- *Front* - Numpad 1
- *Back* – Ctrl + Numpad 1
- *Right* - Numpad 3
- *Left* – Ctrl + Numpad 3
- *Top* - Numpad 7
- *Bottom* – Ctrl + Numpad 7

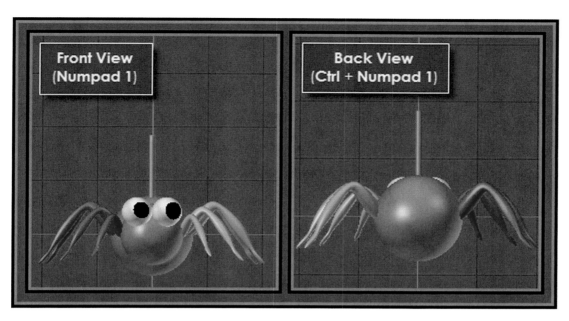

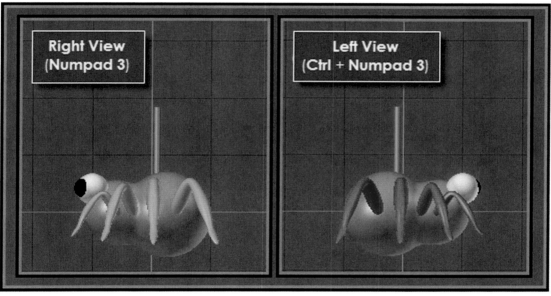

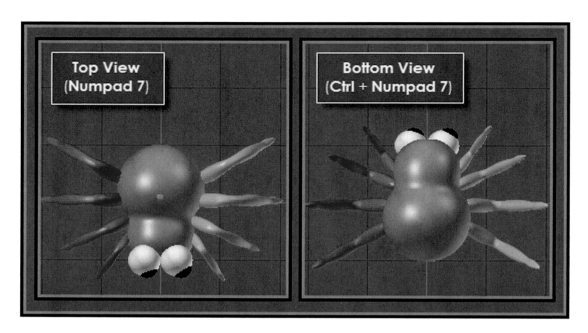

As I mentioned above, there is now a *Pie Menu* that allows you to switch *Views.*

During the course of creating a *3D Model* I switch *Views* constantly. I started using the *Pie Menu* to switch *Views* and I haven't looked back. Having the ability to switch to any *View* with 1 key press is extremely useful, especially for functionality that I use on a constant basis.

Orbiting the View

You can *Incrementally Orbit* the *View* around a point in *3D Space* using the Numpad 2, 4, 6 and 8 keys as follows.

- *Orbit Left* - Numpad 4
- *Orbit Right* - Numpad 6
- *Orbit Up* - Numpad 8
- *Orbit Down* - Numpad 2

Pressing any of the above keys will *Orbit* the *3D View* incrementally by 15 degrees (according to my math ☺). The *Rotation Point* for this operation depends on the *Active Object* as well as the position of your *3D View*. When I *Orbit* the *3D View* it's often to *Orbit* around a particular *Object*. If after initiating an *Orbit* operation the *3D View* isn't *Orbiting* the *Active Object*, you can use the *View Selected* functionality (press Numpad .) to *Zoom* to the current *Selection*. The *Orbit* operation should then work as expected.

I don't use keys to *Orbit* the *View* very often. I use the Middle Mouse but I leave it to you to try it and have it in your toolbox as an option.

Camera View

Switching to *Camera View* as one might expect gives you the *View* from the *Active Camera*.

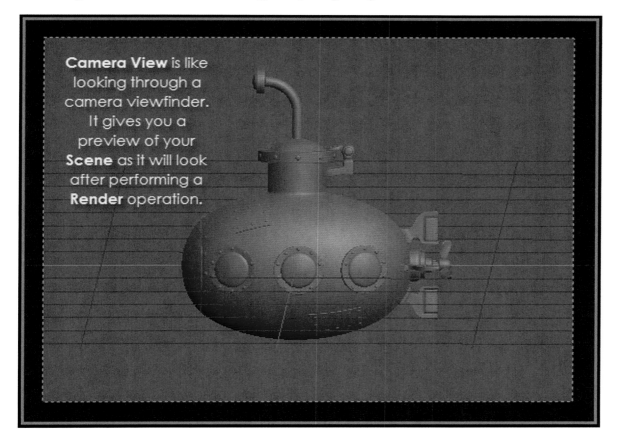

Camera View is like looking through a camera viewfinder. It gives you a preview of your Scene as it will look after performing a Render operation.

The *Camera*, like all *Objects*, can be re-positioned as desired. You can *Transform* the *Camera* in *Camera View* which can be useful for fine tuning *Camera* placement.

Rotating the View

You can *Rotate* the *View* with complete freedom using the *Middle Mouse Button*. Press the *Middle Mouse Button* and drag you *Mouse* to *Rotate* the *View* in any direction. I mentioned above that I am constantly switching to the *Default Views*. One of the reasons for that is that I am also constantly *Rotating* the *View* with my *Middle Mouse Button*. I do a little *Mesh Modeling*, I *Rotate* the *View* to see the result, I then switch back to one of the *Default Views* to continue *Modeling*. You will see this workflow frequently when watching / performing tutorials.

Similar to *Orbiting* the *View*, the *Rotation Point* isn't always what you expect or desire. If you find yourself *Rotating* the *View* and the *Rotation* operation causes the *3D View* to *Rotate* in some strange or exaggerated fashion or you become completely lost in *3D Space*, you can usually recover by using the *View Selected* functionality (press *Numpad .*). As mentioned previously, *View Selected* will allow you to *Zoom* to the currently *Selected Object*. You can also press the *Home* key which will *Zoom* out of the *3D View* allowing you to see all *Objects* in the *3D View*. Another option is to *Select* the desired *Object* in the *Outliner* and then use *View Selected* in the *3D Window* to *Zoom* in on the *Object*.

Panning

You can *Pan* the *3D View* by holding the *Shift* key followed by pressing *Middle Mouse Button* and dragging the *Mouse*. You can also *Pan* Incrementally by holding the *Ctrl Key* and pressing *Numpad 2*, *Numpad 4*, *Numpad 6* or *Numpad 8*.

If you were unaware of the *Panning* functionality I encourage you to add it to your toolbox. I don't use it as often as *Rotating* and switching to the *Default Views*, but I do use it often enough as it's ideal for quickly moving several *Objects* to the *Center* of the *3D View*.

Zooming

There are several ways to *Zoom* in and out of the *3D View*. The easiest and most convenient is using the *Mouse Wheel*. Simply scroll the *Mouse Wheel* forward and back to *Zoom* in and out of the *3D View*. If you don't have a *Mouse* with a *Wheel* I suggest you try and pick one up. You will *Zoom* in and out often and not having to do it via the keyboard will save time.

I mentioned earlier in the book that it's a good idea to enable *Zoom to Mouse Position* which is located on the *Input Tab* in the *Blender User Preferences*. This will allows you to place your *Mouse Cursor* anywhere in the *3D View* window and *Scroll* towards that point.

You can also *Zoom* in and out by holding down *Ctrl* and the *Middle Mouse button* while dragging. Using this method to *Zoom* gives you more precise control when *Zooming* compared to using the *Mouse Wheel*. If your *Mouse* has no *Wheel* or *Middle Mouse Button*, go buy one now, or you can use *Numpad +* and *Numpad -* to *Zoom* in and out of the *3D View*.

Another option for *Zooming* is the *Zoom Border Tool*. To enable the *Zoom Border Tool*, press Shift + B on the keyboard and drag your *Mouse* to create a rectangle around the area that you want to *Zoom* to. Blender will *Zoom* in so that the rectangle you defined fills the entire *3D Window*.

One of my favorite ways to *Zoom* is to use the *View Selected* functionality which I mentioned several times (see **Chapter 3 – View Selected**).

Align View to Selected

You can align your *3D View* with the *Normal* of the currently *Active Face* in *Edit Mode*. (I talk more about *Active Objects* / *Mesh Elements* here - (see **Chapter 5 – Active Element**) and *Normals* here - (see **Chapter 3 – Normals**). To *Align* the *View* to the *Normal* of the *Selected Face*, hold the Shift or Ctrl + Shift key and press one of the Numpad keys. The result will depend on the Numpad key you press but they are identical to the results you get when changing the default *Views*. As with changing the default *View*, the keys map as follows:

- *Front* - Numpad 1
- *Back* - Ctrl + Numpad 1
- *Right* - Numpad 3
- *Left* - Ctrl + Numpad 3
- *Top* - Numpad 7
- *Bottom* - Ctrl + Numpad 7

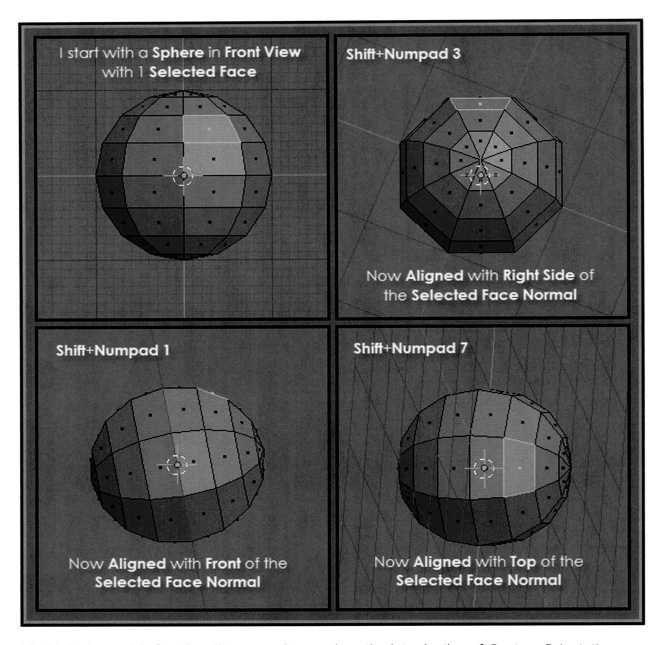

I find I don't use this functionality as much now since the introduction of *Custom Orientations* (see **Chapter 5 – Custom Orientation**).

Centering the 3D View

There are a couple of options available when you want to change the *View* so that all *Objects* in the *Scene* are visible. You can *View* all *Objects* in your *Scene* by pressing Home on the keyboard. Pressing Shift + C will also result in all *Objects* in the *Scene* coming in to *View* and will also center the *3D Cursor* back to the *Origin Point* of the *3D World*.

Global vs. Local View

There are times when you have several *Objects* in your *Scene* and would like to work on one or more *Objects* without everything in the *Scene* impeding your *View*. Using Numopad / on the keyboard, you can *Isolate* one or more *Objects* in your *Scene* allowing you to focus on the *Selected Object* or group of *Objects*. *Isolating* the *Object*(s) in this way switches the *View* to what is known as *Local View*. When you are not in *Local View* you are said to be in *Global View*. In other words, when you *Isolate* an *Object* (using Numpad /) you are in *Local View*, otherwise you are in *Global View*.

Switching to *Local View* is similar to selecting one or more *Objects* and pressing Shift + H on the keyboard to *Hide* all *Non-Selected Objects*. The one advantage with switching to *Local View* is that *Blender* will *Zoom* in and *Center* the selected *Object*(s) in the *3D View*. Once you go back to *Global View*, *Blender* will *Zoom* back out.

I constantly use *View Selected* (Numpad .) and *Local View* (Numpad /) to *Zoom* in to the *Object*(s) I am working on. Both will *Zoom* in to your *Selected Object*(s) and with *Local View* it also *Hides* any *Non-Selected Object*(s).

Shading

There are several settings that allow you to change how *Objects* are displayed and *Shaded* in the *3D Viewport*.

Viewport Shading

The *Viewport Shading Menu* has several *Shading Modes* to choose from and is located in the *3D Window Header*.

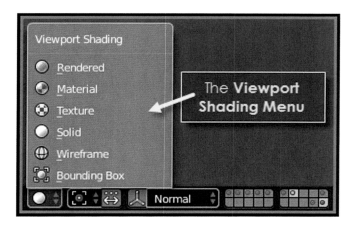

I will go through each *Menu* option using the following *Mesh Objects* as a starting point.

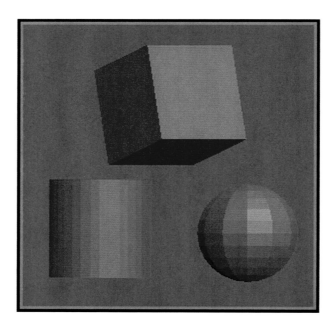

Bounding Box - this option simply shows a *Box* around each *Object* in the *3D Viewport*. This does not include *Camera*, *Lights* etc.

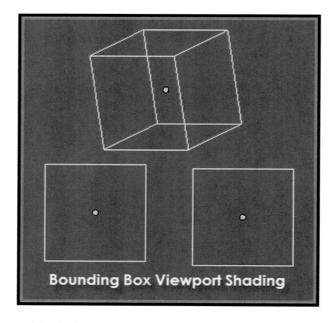

Wireframe - displays your *Mesh Objects* using a *Wireframe* that represents the *Edges* in your *Object*. The result is very similar to how a *Mesh* is displayed in *Edit Mode* with *Mesh Select Mode* set to *Edge* (see **Chapter 6 – Mesh Select Mode**).

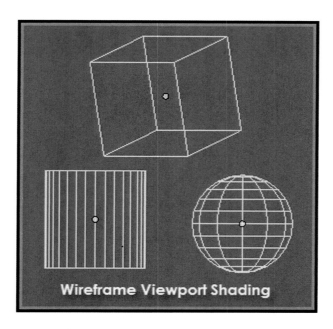

Wireframe Viewport Shading

Solid - the *Solid Shading* option is probably were you will spend most of your time. It's the default drawing mode and offers flat colors and basic shading. Setting the *Viewport Shading* to *Solid* and enabling *Matcap* (covered later in this section) is the *Shading* option I frequently go with when I am *Modeling*.

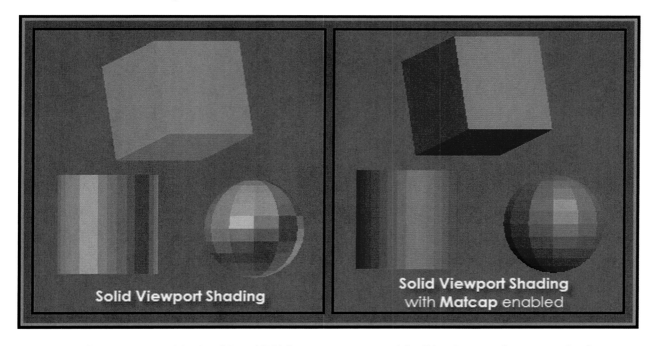

Solid Viewport Shading

Solid Viewport Shading with **Matcap** enabled

Texture - if you have a *Mesh* with a *UV Map* you can use this *Shading* mode to see the image used in that *UV Map*. *UV Maps* are outside the scope of this book so I won't go to in depth about this *Shading* option.

Material - this *Shading Mode* displays each *Mesh* with the *Material* applied to that *Mesh*. The result isn't *Render* quality but gives a decent impression of the *Material* applied to a *Mesh*.

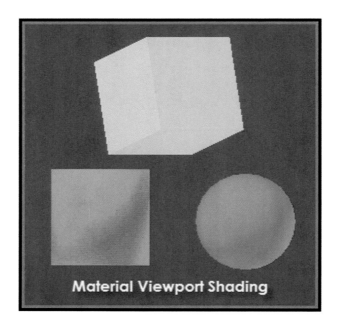

Rendered - shows a *Rendered View* of the current *Scene*. Keep in mind that you don't have to be in *Camera View* for this *Shading* option to work. Once *Rendered Shading* is enabled, you can freely move and rotate the *3D View*. Every time you finish manipulating the *3D View* the *Scene* will be *Re-Rendered*. The *Rendering* is done with the actual *Render Engine* which means the *Lights* in your *Scene* will affect the final result of the *Render*. Any *Lights* that are not visible will have no effect on the *Render* (just like a real *Render*...which is what it is).

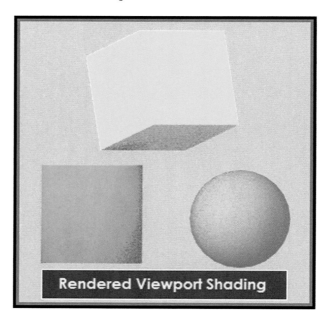

One thing to remember is that the *Rendered Shading* mode can be very slow if you don't use the correct settings. To ensure the *Rendering* time is short you can set the number of *Samples* used in the *Preview Render*. To change the samples go to the *Sampling Panel* in the *Render*

Context Window. **There are 2** *Samples*: **settings. Change the** *Preview*: **setting to something low like 10.**

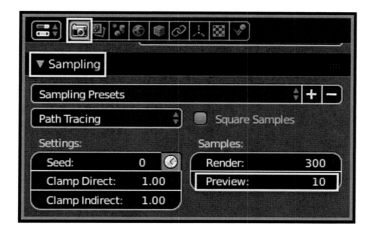

There are also shortcuts for quickly changing the *Shading*. You can switch between *Wireframe* and *Solid Shading* using the Z key, *Wireframe* and *Rendered Shading* using Shift + Z and between *Solid* and *Textured Shading* using Alt + Z. There is also a *Pie Menu* available for changing the *Shading* that puts all options in a *Pie Menu* accessed using the Z key.

As I mentioned above, I use the *Solid Shading* option with *Matcap* enabled most of the time. It's fast and clean and still provides a very good idea of how your *Mesh* is progressing without having to do a *Render*.

Flat vs Smooth

The default *Shading Mode* for any newly added Mesh Primitives (see **Chapter 8 – Mesh Primitives**) is *Flat Shaded* (assumes *Viewport Shading* is currently set to *Solid*). You can tell when a *Mesh* is *Flat Shaded* as all the *Faces* on the *Mesh* will have visible *Edges*. For lack of a better way to put it, it won't look *Smooth*.

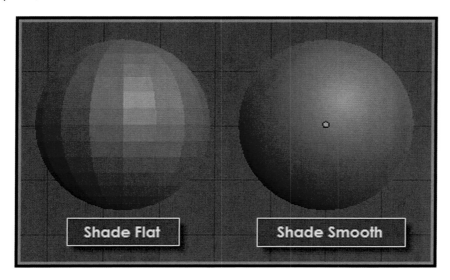

The majority of the time I set *Shading* to *Smooth* when creating a *3D Model*. You probably won't want *Flat Shading* enabled when performing a final *Render* so switching to *Smooth Shading* will give you a better preview of the final *Render*. It also just looks better.

There are a couple of ways to change between *Flat* and *Smooth Shading*. In *Object Mode* you can change between *Flat Shading* and *Smooth Shading* using buttons on the *Tools Shelf*. The *Flat / Smooth* buttons are located on the *Tools Tab* in the *Edit Panel*. In *Edit Mode* you can toggle between *Flat* and *Smooth Shading* using the *Specials Menu* which is accessed using the W key.

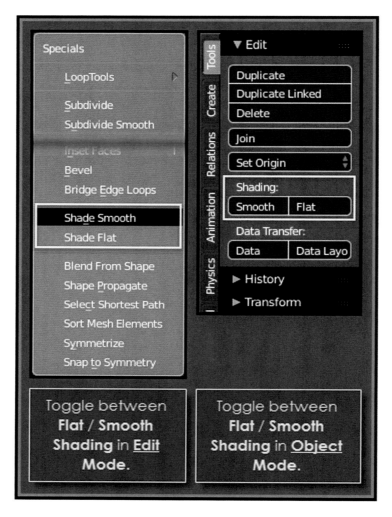

Matcap

What is *Matcap*? I had a look at the *Blender* wiki definition and thought, ok that's the technical way to put it. So why use *Matcap*? I use *Matcap* as it has 2 big advantages (personal opinion, I imagine people have other reasons). 1. It allows you to check for artifacts and other inconsistencies in your *Model* without doing a *Render* and 2. It's very fast.

Turning on *Matcap* for a model:

- You must have *Viewport Shading* set to *Solid*.

- Enable the *Matcap* checkbox in the *Properties Shelf* on the *Shading Panel*.
- Select your *Matcap Material* by clicking the *Matcap* preview window to bring up a list of available *Materials*.

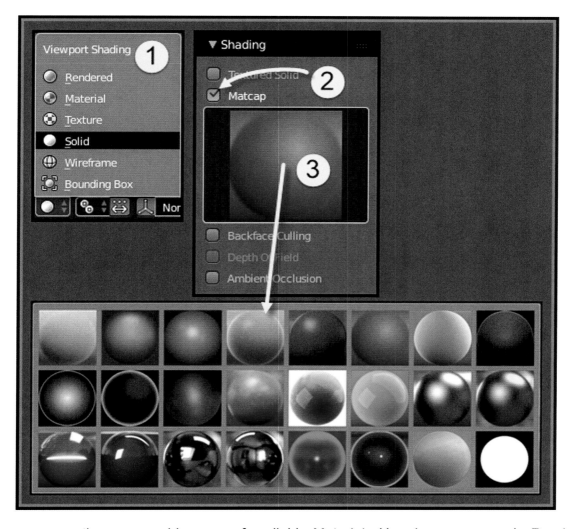

As you can see, there are a wide range of available *Materials*. Here is some example *Renders*:

I try to leave *Matcap* enabled during the *Modeling* process. The sooner I find an issue with a *Model,* the quicker I can fix it. There are times when finding an issue late in the *Modeling* process can prove to be difficult and time consuming to fix.

Here is a slightly exaggerated example to get my point across. ☺

Normals

Normals in *Blender* basically refer to the direction that a *Face* or *Vertex* is pointing. *Blender* uses *Normals* at various times to make calculations around *Lighting*, *Particles* as well as numerous other things. There are far more technical explanations of *Normals* if you care to search the internet. It's not important, generally speaking, to understand the intricacies of *Normals*. Just knowing how to recognize and fix issues with them should suffice. First, let's see a visual representation of the *Normals* for a given *Mesh*.

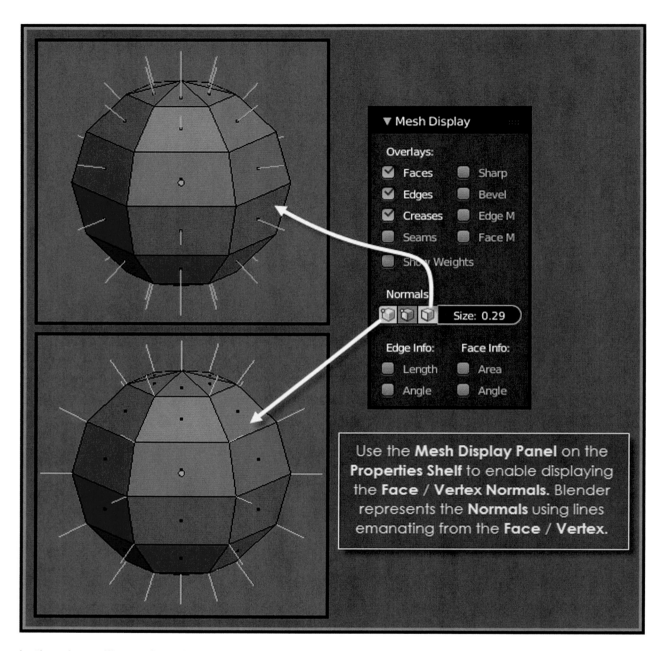

In the above illustration all the *Normals* are pointing outward which is desirable, however, this isn't always the case. During the course of *Modeling* the *Normals* may become reversed causing undesirable effects. Fortunately, *Blender* provides the means to quickly identify and fix reversed *Normals*. Displaying the *Normals* as we did above will help you identify reversed *Normals*.

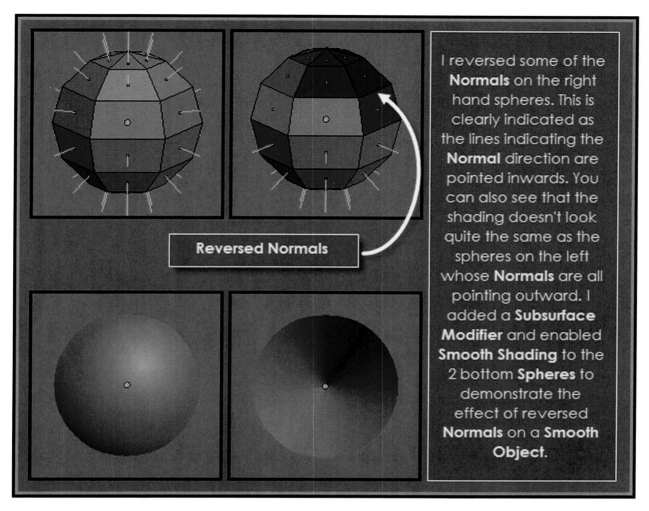

Reversed Normals

I reversed some of the **Normals** on the right hand spheres. This is clearly indicated as the lines indicating the **Normal** direction are pointed inwards. You can also see that the shading doesn't look quite the same as the spheres on the left whose **Normals** are all pointing outward. I added a **Subsurface Modifier** and enabled **Smooth Shading** to the 2 bottom **Spheres** to demonstrate the effect of reversed **Normals** on a **Smooth Object.**

Another way to identify reversed *Normals* is to enable *Backface Culling* on the *Properties Shelf*. The results are a little odd as it causes *Faces* with reversed *Normals* to disappear in such a way that all *Faces* behind that *Face* also appear to disappear.

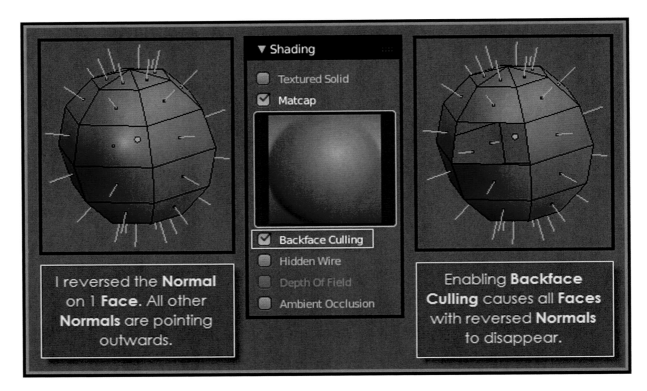

As you can see from the above illustration, enabling *Backface Culling* can give, at least in my opinion, odd looking results. That being said, it can be a good option if you want to quickly verify that your *Normals* are behaving as expected.

Fixing reversed *Normals* can be done using the keyboard shortcuts Ctrl + N and Ctrl + Shift + N. Ctrl + N will make the *Vertex* and *Face Normals* point outwards which is usually desirable. Ctrl + Shift + N will make the *Vertex* and *Face Normals* point inwards which is usually undesirable. The majority of the time, if you see issues with your *Normals*, pressing Ctrl + N will fix those issues and you can move on.

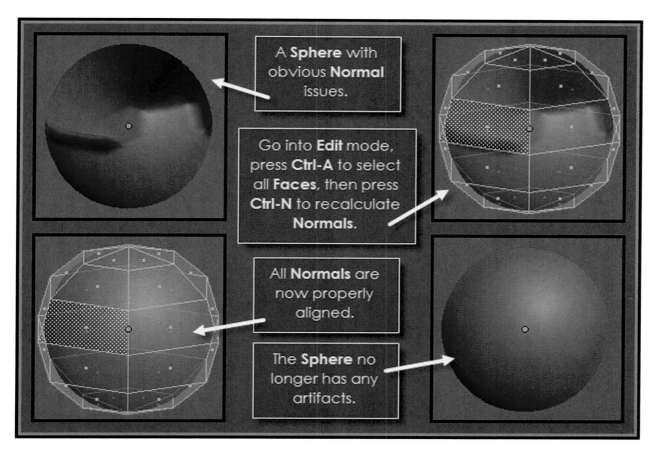

There are times, however, when using Ctrl+N actually reverses some of the *Normals*. Fortunately, the shortcuts only affect *Selected Faces / Vertices* so you can choose to flip the *Normals* on specific *Mesh Elements* if needed.

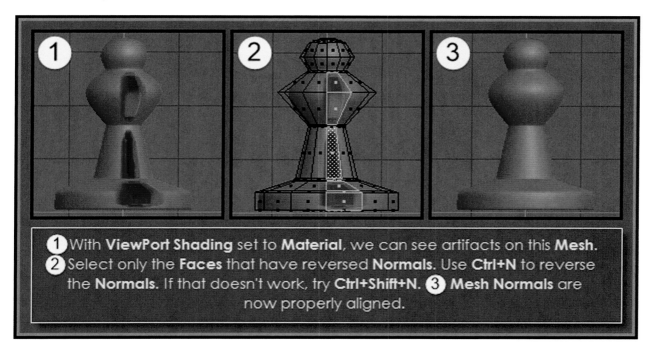

1 With **ViewPort Shading** set to **Material**, we can see artifacts on this **Mesh**. **2** Select only the **Faces** that have reversed **Normals**. Use **Ctrl+N** to reverse the **Normals**. If that doesn't work, try **Ctrl+Shift+N**. **3** **Mesh Normals** are now properly aligned.

There are also buttons on the *Shading / UVs Tab* of the *Tools Shelf* to *Recalculate* and *Flip Normals*. They can be found on the *Shading Panel*. I prefer using shortcuts but If you're a fan of using the *UI*, this option if for you.

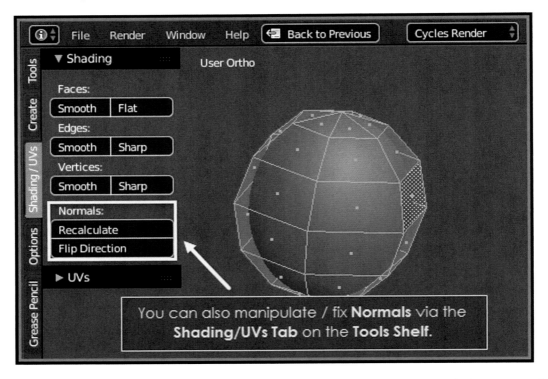

Getting in to the habit of fixing *Normals* is a good idea and you should include it as part of your *Modeling* workflow. I have watched many *Modeling* tutorials where fixing *Normals* is done frequently as part of the *Modeling* process. As you gain experience you will soon be able to quickly identify when there is an issue with your *Mesh Normals*. Generally, if you have the *Viewport Shading* set to *Material* and the *Shading* looks strange, it's a good bet you have some reversed *Normals*.

Mesh Display

The *Mesh Display Panel* is available in *Edit Mode* and can be used to toggle various options that give you information related to your *Mesh*. This includes distance and angles as well as *Normals*, *Seams*, *Sharp Edges*, *Bevel* and more. You can use this panel to do precision work in *Blender*.

To use the *Mesh Display Panel*, go into *Edit Mode* and open the *Properties Shelf*. The *Mesh Display Panel* should now be visible.

Here are examples of the kind of information that can be displayed using the *Mesh Display Panel*. The unit of measurement in the next few illustrations is the default *Blender Unit* (see **Chapter 5 – Units in Blender**).

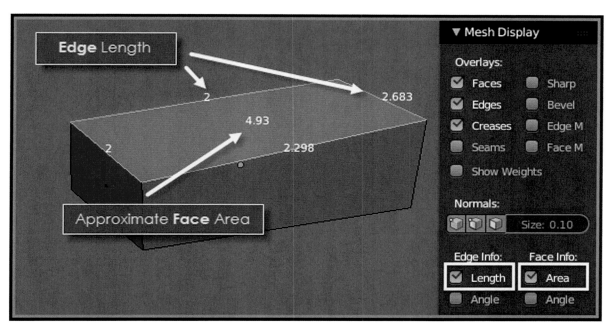

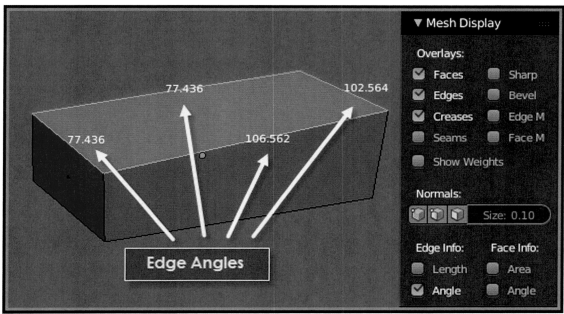

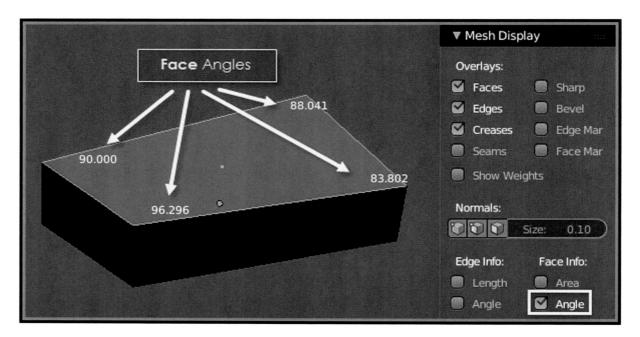

You can change the *Units* used for the measurement / angle info. You can set the units on the *Units Panel* in the *Scene Context Window*. Here are some examples using various *Unit* settings.

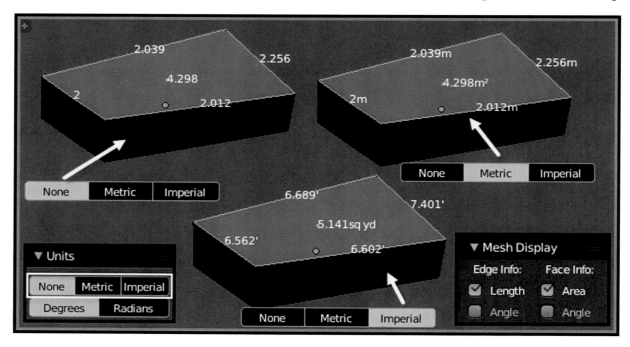

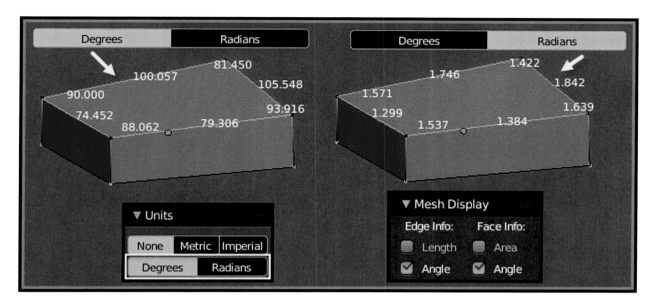

If you're interested, you can find articles on the internet that explain the *Mesh Display Panel* in far more detail than I do here. I don't use this panel often but I thought I would touch on it as these tools can help ensure accuracy when you're creating a *Mesh* that requires precision.

Object Display Sub-Panel

The *Object Context Window* contains a panel that displays details about your *Object*(s) including its *Name* and current *Axis*. There are several other options on the *Display Panel* but I will only touch on the ones I find the most useful.

The ability to display the *Object Name* is very handy. I try to stay in the habit of naming all of my *Objects* when *Modeling* as it helps keep things organized. Displaying the *Object Name* makes it easy to find various *Objects* in your *Scene* and keeps me honest in terms of ensuring I name everything in a meaningful way. I also like to name *Empties* with a descriptive name and then display the *Name* so I can quickly identify what the *Empty* does. (I talk about *Empties* here - Chapter 7 – Empties). Here is how to display the *Name* for a *Selected Object*.

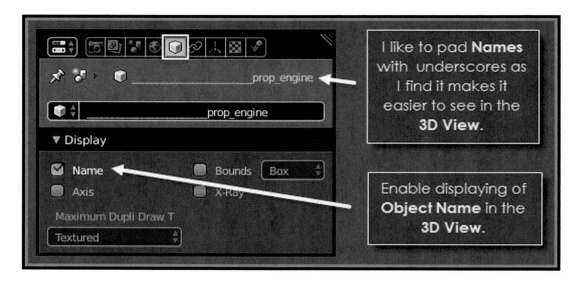

I like to pad **Names** with underscores as I find it makes it easier to see in the **3D View**.

Enable displaying of **Object Name** in the **3D View.**

Here is an example where *Naming* my *Empties* helps me quickly identify what each *Empty* is used for.

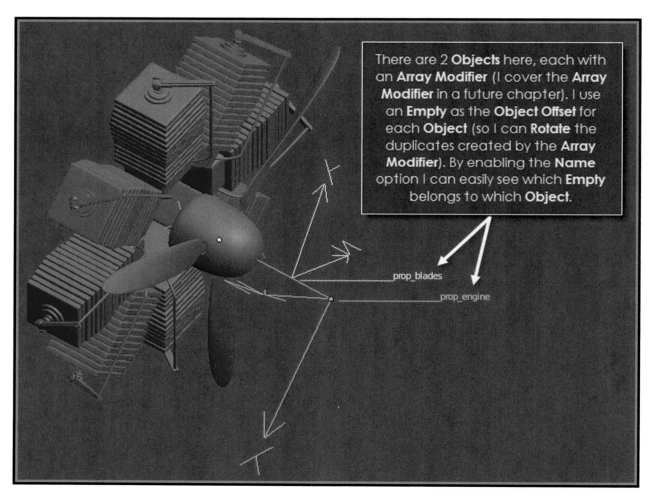

There are 2 **Objects** here, each with an **Array Modifier** (I cover the **Array Modifier** in a future chapter). I use an **Empty** as the **Object Offset** for each **Object** (so I can **Rotate** the duplicates created by the **Array Modifier**). By enabling the **Name** option I can easily see which **Empty** belongs to which **Object.**

I often use *Empties* to *Parent* (see **Chapter 7 – Parenting**) a group of *Objects* and by giving the *Empty* a descriptive name I can get a quick visual of what the *Empty* is *Parented* to.

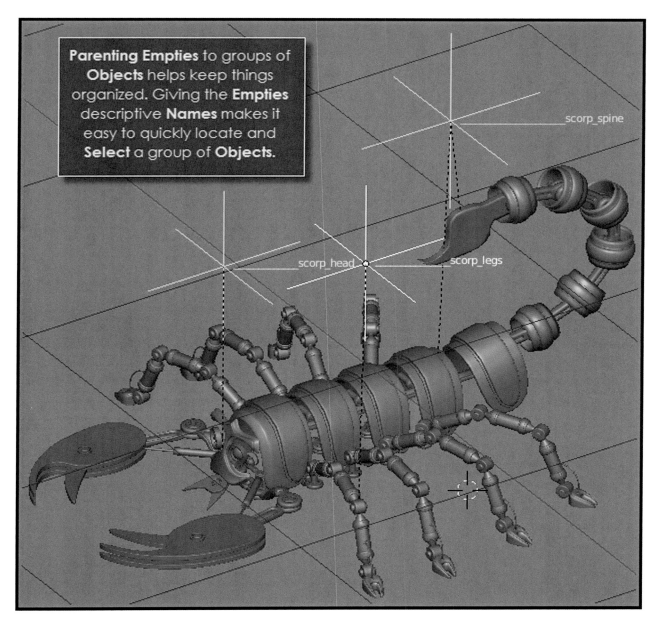

You can also enable the *Axis* checkbox to display the direction of the *X, Y* and *Z-Axis* as it relates to your *Object*. This can be very useful when you keep track of the *Local X, Y, Z-Axis* on a *Mesh* as it can change when *Rotating* in *Object Mode* vs *Edit Mode*. I talk about the effects of *Rotating* in *Object Mode* vs. *Edit Mode* in Chapter 5 - Local Transform Orientation.

Chapter 4 - Mesh Topology

Quads, Triangles, Ngons

Mesh Topology is crucial to creating good models. I have watched several tutorials where the person creating the *Model* makes liberal use of *Triangles* and *Ngons*. I usually watch *Modeling* tutorials to learn new techniques to add to my *Modeling* toolbox so when I watch a tutorial where the use of *Triangles / Ngons* isn't discouraged it makes me cringe a little. It's not my place to tell anyone how to model but based on what I have read and learned, avoiding *Triangles / Ngons* is integral to creating good models and I almost feel like the modeler is encouraging bad habits. Often the person doing the *Modeling* creates exceptional models but I know that I wouldn't be happy with the final results unless it had proper topology. I take a certain amount of pride when I finish a model with all *Quads* and good topology. *Quads* you say? Read on.

I have read several articles over the years on whether to use all *Quads* in your models or if it's ok to have *Triangles* and *Ngons*. If you are new to this terminology, a *Triangle* is a *Face* created using 3 *Vertices*, a *Quad* has 4 *Vertices* and an *Ngon* has 5 or more.

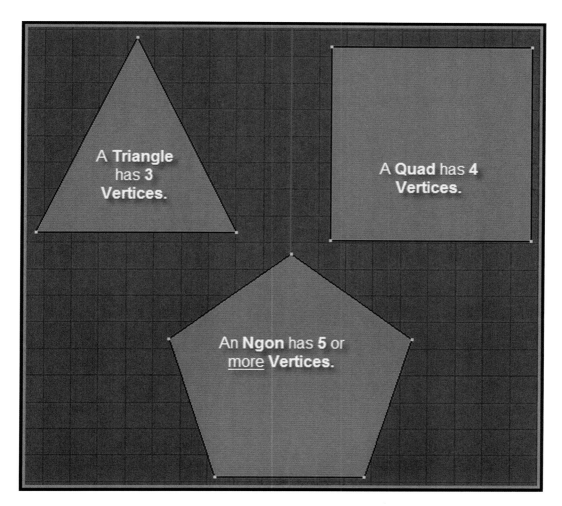

Most articles I have read state that you should always strive for all *Quads* in your *3D Models*. One of the main reasons is that *Triangles* and *Ngons* don't *Subdivide* smoothly. They can also negatively affect *Topology* flow and are not ideal for animation.

Quads on the other hand have several advantages. You get better *Subdivision Surface* results from *Quads*. *Edge Loops* behave as expected when using *Quads*. This includes adding and removing *Edge Loops* and using *Edge Slide* on *Edge / Face Loops*. *Edge Loops* are crucial when it comes to creating the type of *Topology* required to create facial features like eyes / nose / mouth etc. If you aren't familiar with *Subdivision Surface, Edge Loops, Edge Slide* etc. I cover them later in the book.

Edge / Face Loops on *Triangle / Ngon* based models can lead to strange results like stretching or the creation of artifacts and it's often not the results you are looking for. There are plenty of excellent videos around *Mesh Topology* if you want to explore the topic further. What I took from everything I learned is *Quads* are ideal and consequently I strive to achieve all *Quads* in my models. Up until now, I have never had to use a *Triangle / Ngon* in any of my models (at least to the best of my memory). I have always found a way to get all *Quads* in my *3D Models*. It can take time and experimentation to create a *Model* with all *Quads* but I believe the time spent learning pays dividends in the long run. I have also found that the more work at it the better you'll get.

Note: There are actually times when *Triangles* are ok or even desirable and that's when creating *Low Poly Models* to be used in games.

There is a great set of videos on topology at http://cgcookie.com/blender/. Do a search for "**learning mesh topology**". The videos are very thorough and cover the topic of *Mesh Topology* far more in-depth than I do here.

MeshLint Add-On

There is an excellent add-on for *Blender* called *MeshLint*. This add-on is used to ensure you produce a good quality *Mesh* by checking for bad *Topology*.

The *MeshLint* add-on checks for the following:

- **Triangles** - should be avoided as they don't *Sub-Divide* well and cause issues with flow. I strive for 0 *Triangles* in my *Meshes*.
- **Ngons** - should also be avoided for many of the same reasons as *Triangles*.
- **Nonmanifold Elements** - these are elements that aren't water tight. An *Edge* that doesn't have exactly 2 *Faces* attached to it is considered to be a *Nonmanifold Element*.
- **Interior Faces** - This one is a bit hard to explain. A good example is to add a *Cube*, do a *Loop Cut* down the center and then press F to fill the *Face*. Now apply a *Subdivision Surface Modifier*. For more on *Loop Cuts* see **Chapter 8 – The Loop Cut Tool**.

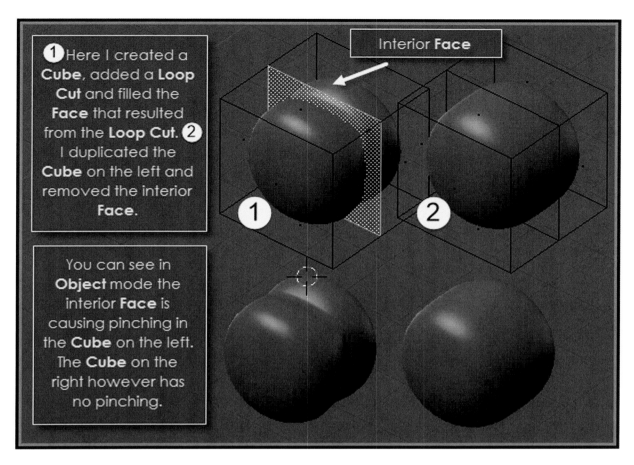

1 Here I created a **Cube**, added a **Loop Cut** and filled the **Face** that resulted from the **Loop Cut.** 2 I duplicated the **Cube** on the left and removed the interior **Face.**

You can see in **Object** mode the interior **Face** is causing pinching in the **Cube** on the left. The **Cube** on the right however has no pinching.

Interior **Face**

- **6+ edge Poles** is a *Vertex* with 6 or more attached *Edges*. These should be avoided in organic models but it's a good idea to avoid them in any *Mesh*.
- *MeshLint* will also give you other information about your *Mesh* including telling you that your *Mesh* is badly named. Apparently *"Circle.002"* is not a very good name.

Enabling Mesh Lint:

- You can enable *Mesh Lint* in the *Add-Ons* tab in the *Blender User Preferences Window.*
- Open *Blender Users Preferences* (Ctrl + Alt + U).
- Select *Add-Ons* tab.
- Search for "**lint**".
- Enable the *Mesh Lint* add-on.
- Press *Save User Settings* button.

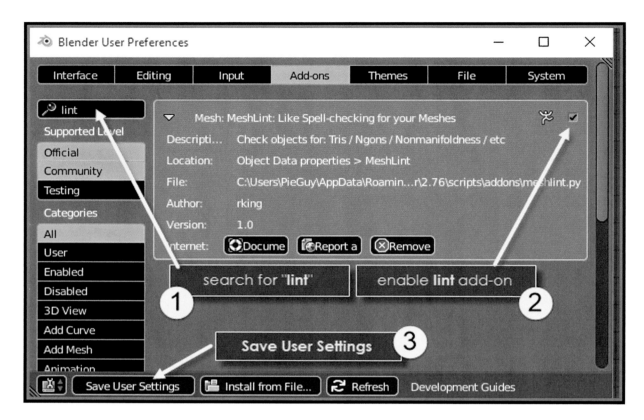

After enabling the *Mesh Lint Add-On* you can go to the *Data Context Window* and you should now see a *MeshLint Panel*. Here is an example of checking for lint in a *Mesh*.

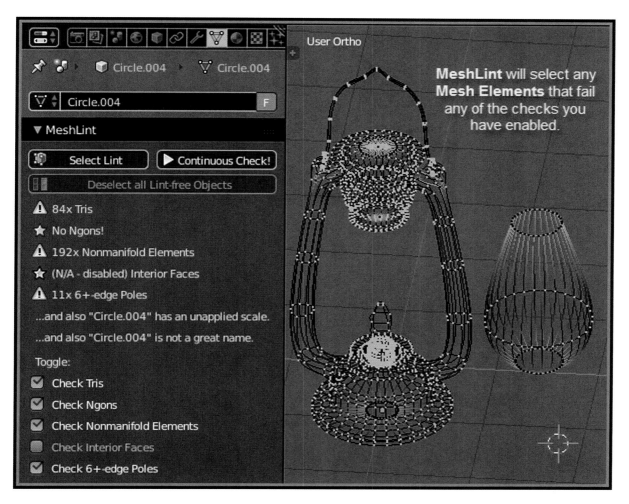

In the above illustration I performed a *Select Lint* operation and any *Mesh Elements* that failed any of the checks I have enabled are now *Selected*. You might want start by enabling all checks and to see if any *Mesh Lint* is found. If any *Lint* is detected, you can then enable each check one at a time to identify its location.

One of the things I like to do after checking for *Lint* is using Ctrl + NumPad + to *Select More Vertices* (basically expand the current selection by *Selecting* any *Vertices* connected to the currently *Selected Vertices*). Then press Shift + H to hide all *Non-Selected Elements*. Then press the *Select Lint* button again. The result is an uncluttered overview of all *Topology* issues and you may even be able to fix some of them before *Un-Hiding* all *Hidden Elements*.

1. In **Edit Mode**, press
   Select Lint
2. Press ***Ctrl-NumPad+***
3. Press ***Shift-H***
4. Press *Select Lint*
Now only the **Lint** and its
surrounding **Vertices**
are visible.

I won't go into great detail about how I fixed the various issues with my *Mesh*. You could write a whole book on that topic alone. I am no expert on the matter and often end up using a little trial and error before finding a solution to a *Topology* problem. With some practice you will get the hang of it. Watching *Modeling* tutorials to see how others deal with *Topology* issues is also helpful. There are plenty of in depth tutorials around understanding the ins and outs of mesh *Topology* if you're interested in finding out more.

I took the time to fix the lamp.

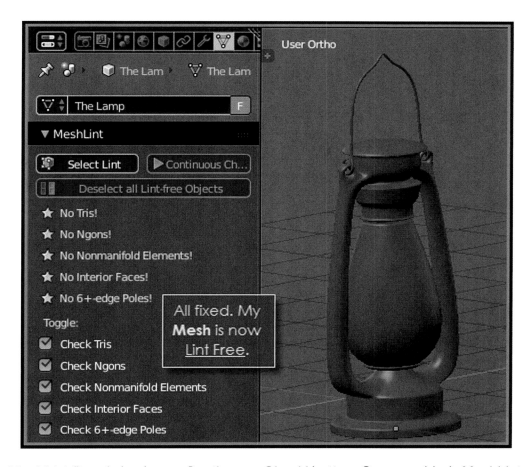

The *MeshLint Panel* also has a *Continuous Check!* button. Once enabled, *MeshLint* will alert you about the appearance of any new *Lint* via a message in the *Info Bar* at the top of the *3D View*. The info in the top bar is updated in real time as you work on your mesh.

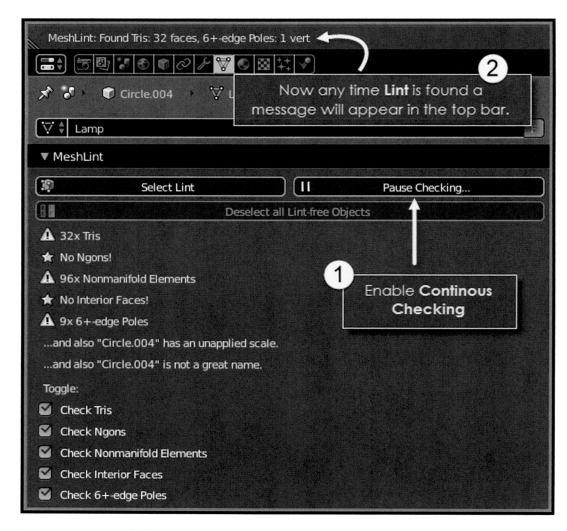

There is also a *Deselect All Lint-Free Objects* button that works as the name implies. This functionality is only available in *Object Mode* and allows you to clean up the *Scene* by hiding all non-offending *Objects*.

Edge Flow

Edge Flow is another rather large topic. I won't be going in to great depth about *Edge Flow* but it's important to know what it is and how you should be aware of it when creating a *3D Model*.

Edge Flow, as the term implies, is how the *Edges Flow* around your *3D Model*. You should always strive for good *Edge Flow*. How do you know if you have good *Edge Flow*? Well if your *3D Model* looks clean and well structured, you probably have good *Edge Flow*. If your Model is visually a mess and is disorganized, there's a good chance you have poor *Edge Flow* which will make it harder to work with.

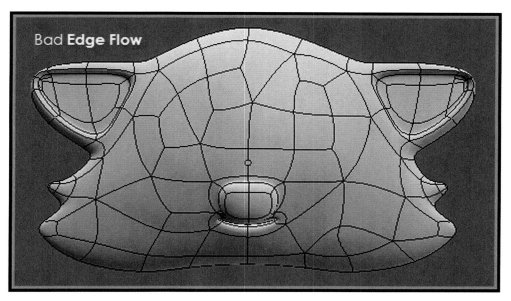

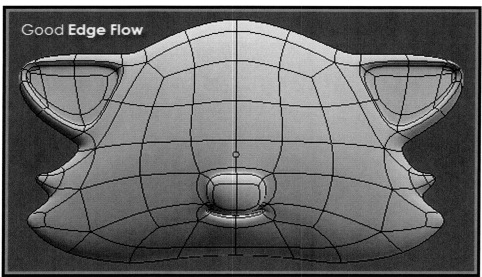

Edge Flow is particularly important when it comes to animating a *Model* and even though this book focuses on *3D Modeling*, I believe striving for good *Edge Flow* will make you a better modeler overall. Anyone who does any *3D Modeling* will immediately be able to tell if you took care to ensure good *Edge Flow* when you created your *3D Model*.

In order to achieve good *Edge Flow* you will often have to modify your *Edge Flow*. There are a few ways to do this. *Rotating Edges* is a great way to change *Edge Flow*. You use the *Loop Cut Tool* (see **Chapter 8 – The Loop Cut Tool**) to check the *Edge Flow* of your *Model*. When performing a *Loop Cut* you hover over your *Mesh Elements* and *Blender* will give you a preview of the *Loop Cut* before you apply it. That preview will follow the *Edge Flow* which means you can use the *Loop Cut Tool* to do a sort of *Edge Flow* audit on your *Mesh*.

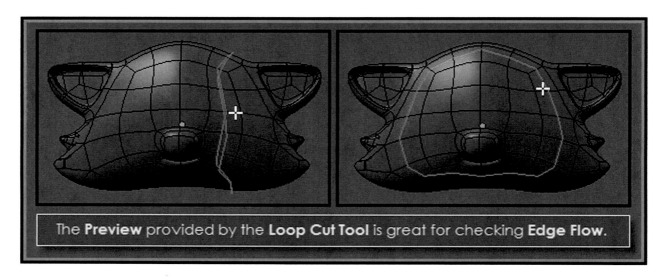

The **Preview** provided by the **Loop Cut Tool** is great for checking **Edge Flow.**

As I mentioned above, you can also change the *Edge Flow* by *Rotating Edges.* The above illustration demonstrating bad *Edge Flow* was created by *Rotating* several *Edges.* Now for an example of how *Rotating* one single *Edge* can have a big effect on *Edge Flow.*

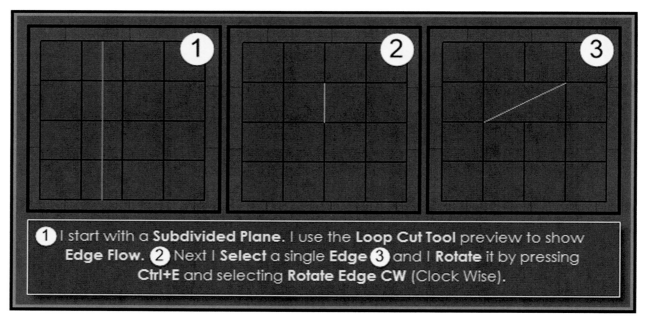

1 I start with a **Subdivided Plane.** I use the **Loop Cut Tool** preview to show **Edge Flow.** **2** Next I **Select** a single **Edge** **3** and I **Rotate** it by pressing **Ctrl+E** and selecting **Rotate Edge CW** (Clock Wise).

Now let's see how *Rotating* 1 Single *Edge* has affected *Edge Flow* using the *Loop Cut Tool* preview.

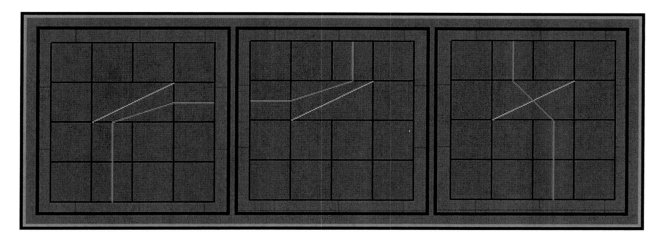

As you can see, *Edge Flow* was altered significantly with one *Edge Rotation*. Here is another basic example. Here is a *Mesh* that could represent the panel on a car or motorcycle.

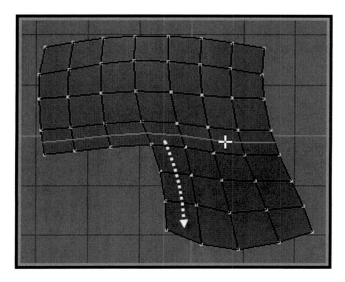

I want to change the *Edge Flow* so that it flows as indicated in the above illustration. I can accomplish this by simply *Selecting* and performing an *Edge Rotation* operation on one *Edge*.

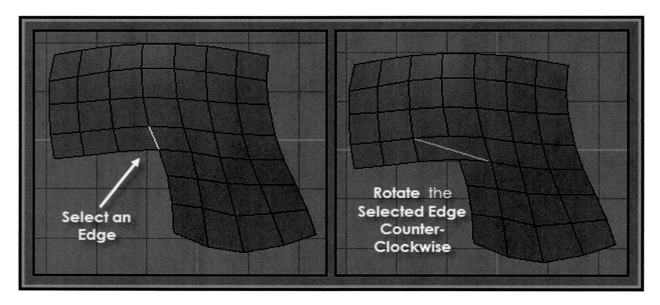

Here is the result (I cleaned up the *Vertices* so things look a little more equally distributed).

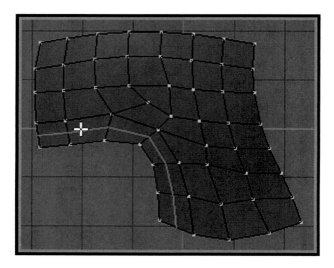

Another option for changing *Edge Flow* is the *Rip Tool*. For an example, see **Chapter 8 – The Rip Tool**.

I have barely scratched the surface when it comes to *Edge Flow* and *Mesh Topology* in general. It's an important topic when it comes to *3D Modeling* and as I have already mentioned, a whole book could be written on that topic alone. You don't have to be an expert at *Edge Flow* to identify bad *Edge Flow* and then make an attempt to fix it.

There are plenty of tutorials and articles that discuss *Edge Flow* in depth. Simply Google "blender mesh topology" and you will find all kinds of information on the topic. There is a particularly in depth discussion at https://cgcookie.com/archive/learning-mesh-topology-collection/.

As someone who loves *3D Modeling* and *3D Models* I often go to websites like Turbo Squid (http://www.turbosquid.com/) and look at the various *Models* there. Most *Models* have accompanying *Wire Frame* screenshots and you can learn a lot about how other *3D Modelers* approach *Edge Flow*. I often look at a final *Render* before looking at the *Wireframe Renders*. Often I say to myself, "I would love to know how they *Modeled* that". I then go look at the *Wireframe Renders* to find out. The models on Turbo Squid are mostly made with 3D Studio Max and other expensive *3D Modeling* software but a polygon is a polygon no matter what software you use. The *3D Modeling* software you use differs in the tools and features available but not the final result. *Blender* can do almost anything the big expensive software packages can do and it's free.

Chapter 5 - Transform Operations

Blender keeps track of the values that represent an *Objects Location, Orientation* and size or *Scale*. Those values can be modified using *Blender's Transform Tools*. There are 3 main *Transform Tools* in *Blender*. These tools allow you to *Grab, Rotate* and *Scale* your *Mesh Elements / Objects*. A very large portion of creating a *Model* will involve the *Transform Tools*. You will be *Grabbing, Rotating* and *Scaling* several times a minute during the course of creating a *Mesh*.

There are several ways to access the *Transform Tools* but I will stick with the shortcut keys for most of this chapter. I will touch on the other options for accessing the *Transform Tools* in a section below.

Units in Blender

The default *Unit* of measurement when performing *Transform* operations in *Blender* is known as a *Blender Unit*. There is no real world equivalent for a *Blender Unit*. It's up to you the user to decide what you want a *Blender Unit* to be equivalent to. The *Blender Unit* is the default unit of measurement but you can also change it to use *Imperial* or *Metric Units*. To change the *Unit* type, go to the *Units Panel* in the *Scene Context Window*. See the section on *Mesh Display* to learn more about viewing the actual unit data for an *Object* (see **Chapter 3 – Mesh Display**).

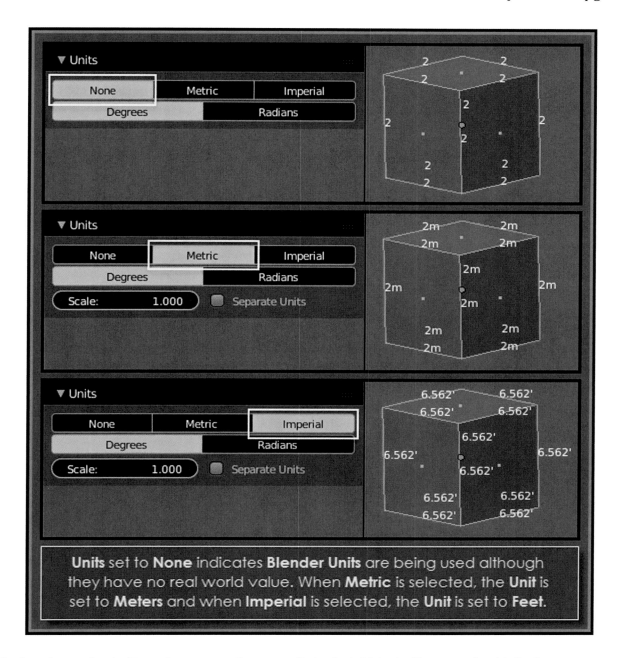

Performing a *Scale Transform* operation on a *Selected Object* will cause the *Unit* of measurement to change. This only applies when *Units* are set to *Metric* or *Imperial*. With *Metric* selected, performing a *Scale* operation will cause the *Unit* of measurement to change from micrometer to millimeters to centimeters to meters to kilometers. When set to *Imperial* the *Unit* of measurement will change from thousandths to inches to feet to yards to chains to furlongs.

There are articles that go in depth about the differences between the *Unit* types if you want to get down to the nuts and bolts of it. I included a section on it so there was some context when I talk about performing more precise *Translations* using numeric values.

I personally don't change the *Unit* type very often but it useful in situations where you are following a blueprint and you want the exact dimensions to be represented correctly in your *Scene*.

The Basics

Before I discuss each *Transform Tool* in detail I wanted to describe the basic functionality of each tool.

The *Grab Tool* (also referred to as the *Translate Tool*) allows you to move a *Mesh Element* / *Object* around in *3D Space*. You activate this tool with the keyboard shortcut G. Once activated, you can move the *Mesh Element* / *Object* around in *Free Form Mode* which means you can move it anywhere in the *3D View*. This is generally not ideal but I will detail options on how to make the *Grab Tool* operations more precise later in the chapter.

The *Rotate Tool* allows you to *Rotate* a *Mesh Element* / *Object* around a *Pivot Point*. You activate this tool with the keyboard shortcut R. You can configure the *Pivot Point* for *Rotation* operations giving it great flexibility.

Hitting R, R will enable the *Rotation Tool* in *Track Ball* mode. This allows you to *Rotate* along 2 *Axis* using your *Mouse*. This type of *Rotation* operation can produce some interesting results depending on your currently selected *Pivot Point*.

The *Scale Tool* allows you to *Scale* or resize a *Mesh Element* / *Object*. . You activate this tool with the keyboard shortcut S. The *Pivot Point* plays a role when using this *Transform Tool*.

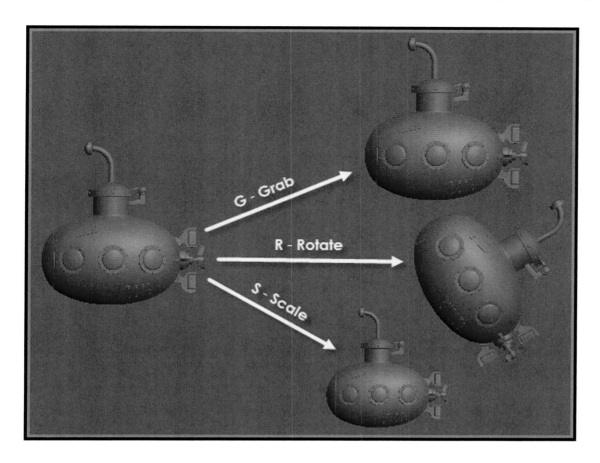

Transform operations can also be performed in *Edit Mode*.

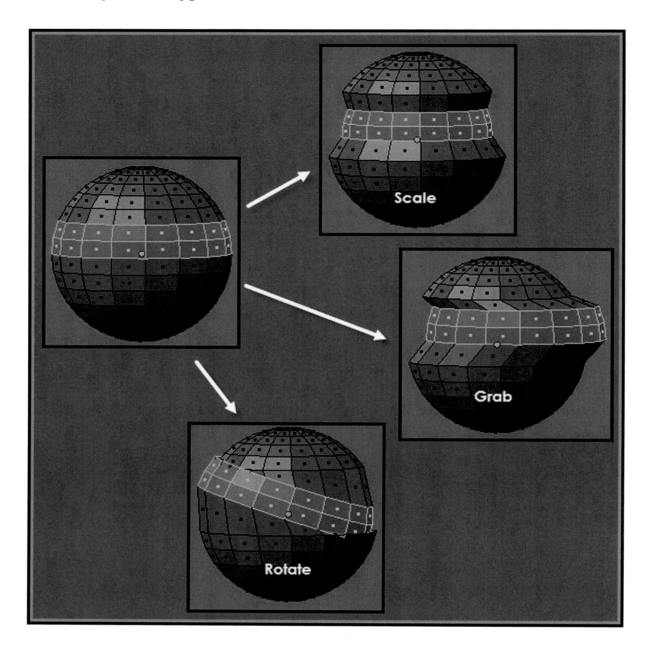

Transform Tools Operator Panels

Press F6 after performing any *Transform* operation to can gain access to the *Operator Panel* for that particular *Transform* operation (the *Operator Panels* are also visible on the *Tools Shelf* if you have it open). There you can change several options related to the current *Transform* operation.

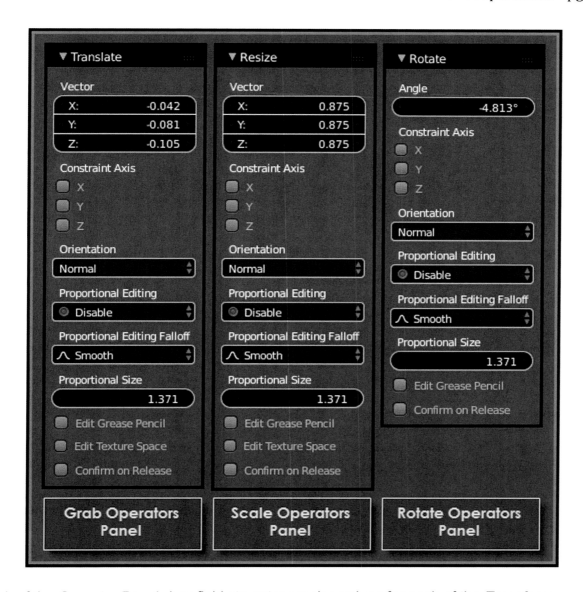

Each of the *Operator Panels* has fields to enter precise values for each of the *Transform* operations as well as the ability to *Constrain* the *Transform* operation along an *Axis*. There is also a *Menu* used to set the *Transform Orientation*. I cover all 3 options later in this chapter. There are also several settings related to *Proportional Editing* which I cover in Chapter 8 – Proportional Editing.

Pivot Point

If you decided to experiment with *Transform* operations and things didn't behave quite as expected there is a good chance it's related to your currently selected *Pivot Point*. The behavior of *Scale* and *Rotation* operations change based on the current *Pivot Point*. There are 5 options available when selecting a *Pivot Point*. I personally only use 3 of them for most of my *Modeling* projects but I will discuss all of them.

You change the *Pivot Point* via the *Pivot Point Menu*.

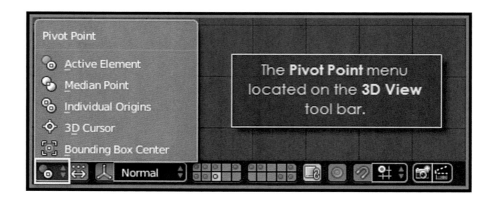

If you have *Pie Menus* enabled, you can quickly access the *Pivot Point Pie Menu* using the period key.

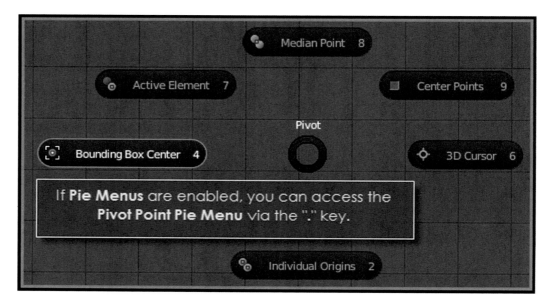

Active Element

As you start adding *Object(s)* / *Mesh Element(s)* to a *Selection*, you will notice that the last item you added has a different color than all other items in the *Selection*. This item is referred to as the *Active Object* / *Active Element*. You can find more information about the *Active Objects* and *Elements* here (**Chapter 6 – Active Objects and Elements**).

In *Object Mode*, setting the *Pivot Point* to *Active Object* will result in *Transformations* happening around the *Origin* (see **Chapter 7 – Object Origins**) of the *Active Object*.

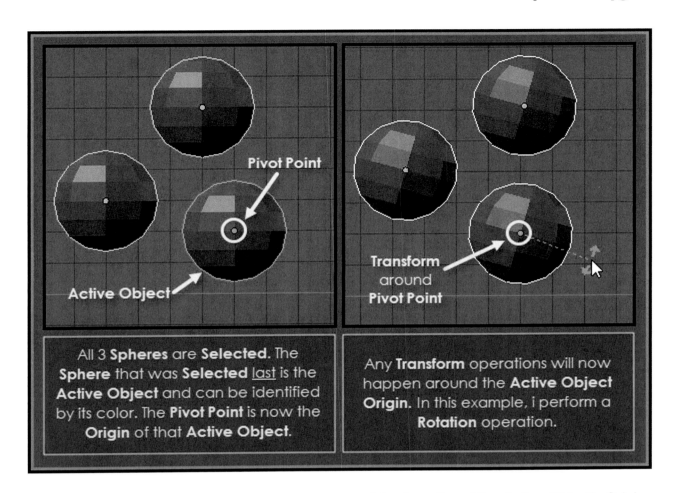

All 3 **Spheres** are **Selected**. The **Sphere** that was **Selected** last is the **Active Object** and can be identified by its color. The **Pivot Point** is now the **Origin** of that **Active Object**.

Any **Transform** operations will now happen around the **Active Object Origin**. In this example, i perform a **Rotation** operation.

An *Object's Origin* can be changed so being aware of the *Location* of the *Active Object's Origin* is essential to ensure *Transform* operations behaving as expected.

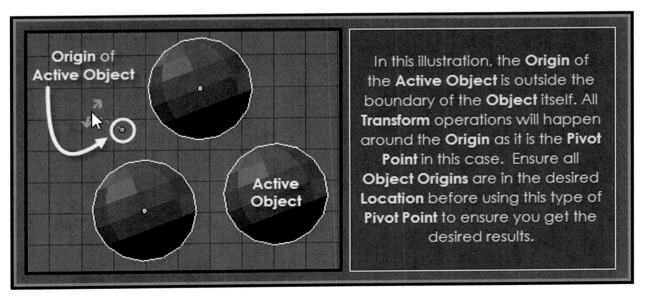

In this illustration, the **Origin** of the **Active Object** is outside the boundary of the **Object** itself. All **Transform** operations will happen around the **Origin** as it is the **Pivot Point** in this case. Ensure all **Object Origins** are in the desired **Location** before using this type of **Pivot Point** to ensure you get the desired results.

Transform operations in Edit Mode happen around the currently active Mesh Element when the Pivot Point is set to Active Object. The active Mesh Element is the last Mesh Element you selected. For example, if you are Selecting Faces, the last Face you Selected is the Active Mesh Element and can be identified by its color. As you continue to Select Mesh Elements, the last Mesh Element Selected will always be the active Mesh Element. If only 1 Mesh Element is Selected, it automatically becomes the Active Mesh Element.

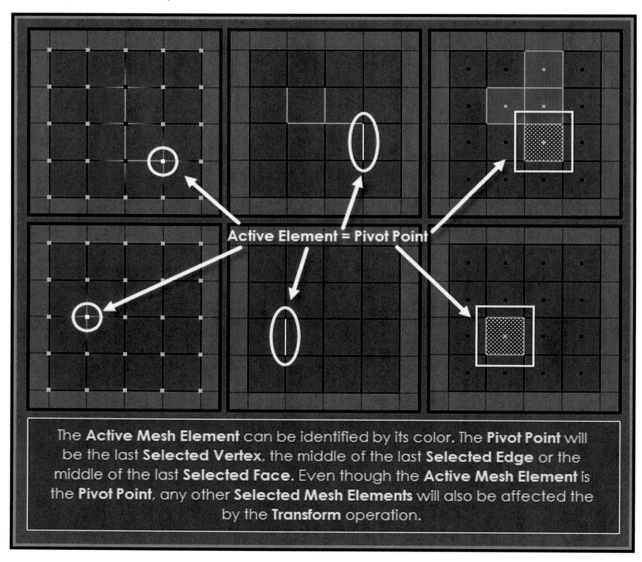

Active Element = Pivot Point

The **Active Mesh Element** can be identified by its color. The **Pivot Point** will be the last **Selected Vertex**, the middle of the last **Selected Edge** or the middle of the last **Selected Face**. Even though the **Active Mesh Element** is the **Pivot Point**, any other **Selected Mesh Elements** will also be affected the by the **Transform** operation.

It should be noted that if only 1 Vertex is selected in Edit Mode, the only Transform operation you will be able to perform is Grab. You shouldn't Rotate or Scale a single Vertex as there is no visible result and may cause issues later in the Modeling process. On the other hand, you can perform all Transform operations when a single Edge or Face is Selected.

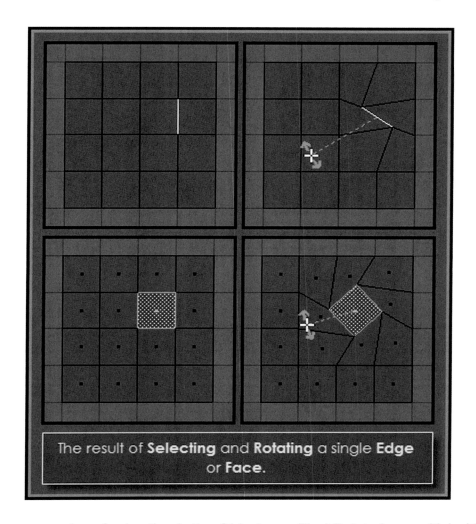

The result of **Selecting** and **Rotating** a single **Edge** or **Face.**

Here are some examples of using the *Active Object* as a *Pivot Point* when multiple *Mesh Elements* are selected.

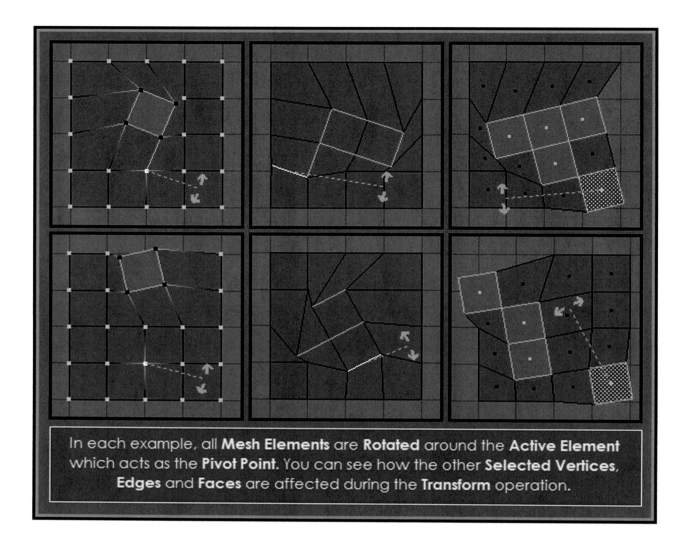

In each example, all **Mesh Elements** are **Rotated** around the **Active Element** which acts as the **Pivot Point.** You can see how the other **Selected Vertices, Edges** and **Faces** are affected during the **Transform** operation.

Median Point

You can find plenty of definitions of *Median Point* as it relates to mathematics etc. I was never good at Math! The *Median* is often considered to be the midpoint of something. In *Blender*, the *Median* is the midpoint of an *Object* or *Mesh Element*, but often not the way you would expect. This type of *Pivot Point* behaves differently in *Object* vs *Edit Mode*. Let's start with *Object Mode*.

In *Object Mode*, the *Median Point* is calculated using the *Origins* of all *Selected Objects*.

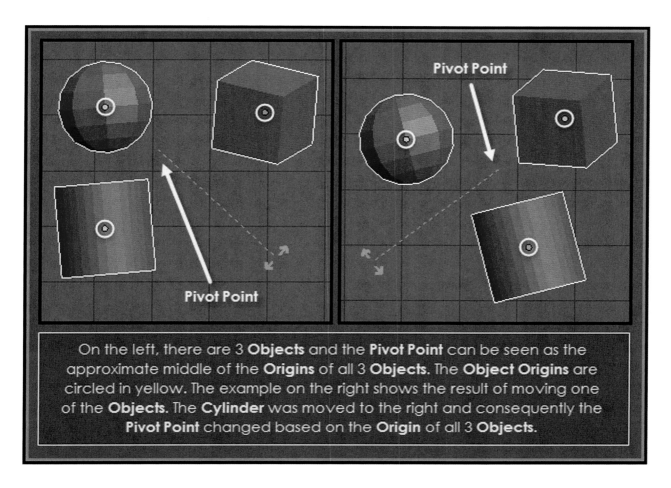

On the left, there are 3 **Objects** and the **Pivot Point** can be seen as the approximate middle of the **Origins** of all 3 **Objects**. The **Object Origins** are circled in yellow. The example on the right shows the result of moving one of the **Objects**. The **Cylinder** was moved to the right and consequently the **Pivot Point** changed based on the **Origin** of all 3 **Objects**.

As mentioned above, the *Object Origin* can be moved so you have to be aware of the *Origin* of each *Object* in order to get expected behavior.

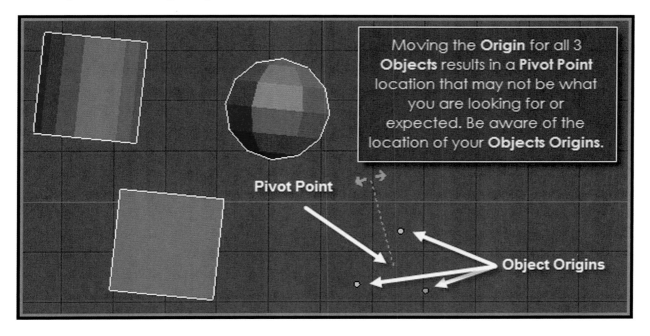

Moving the **Origin** for all 3 **Objects** results in a **Pivot Point** location that may not be what you are looking for or expected. Be aware of the location of your **Objects Origins**.

In *Edit Mode* the *Median Point* will be determined based on the number of *Vertices* that are *Selected*. The *Mesh Select Mode* plays no role here (see **Chapter 6 – Mesh Select Mode**). If you are working with *Faces* or *Edges*, *Blender* still uses the <u>Vertices</u> of the currently selected *Mesh Elements* to make its calculations. The concentration of *Vertices* also plays a role resulting in interesting results. *Blender* gives each *Vertex* the same weight or value. If you have a concentration of *Vertices* in one spot *Blender* will calculate the *Median Point* closer to that cluster of *Vertices*.

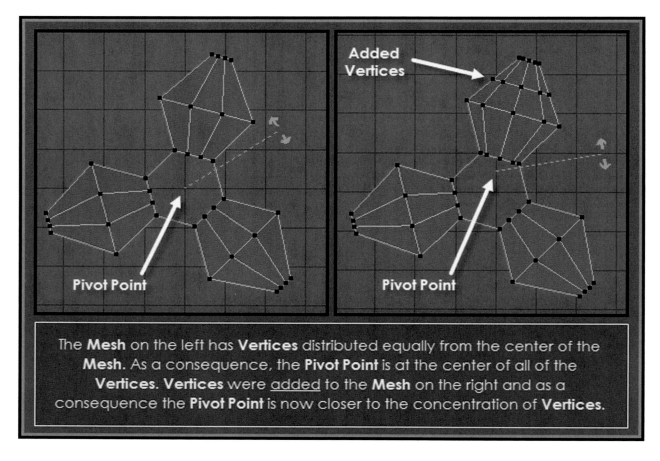

The **Mesh** on the left has **Vertices** distributed equally from the center of the **Mesh**. As a consequence, the **Pivot Point** is at the center of all of the **Vertices**. **Vertices** were <u>added</u> to the **Mesh** on the right and as a consequence the **Pivot Point** is now closer to the concentration of **Vertices**.

As you can see from the above illustration, each *Vertex* is given equal weight when calculating the *Median Pivot Point*.

I must admit I rarely use *Median* as a *Pivot Point* and have never seen it used in any tutorials I have watched or read (to the best of my memory). If I come across a good example of how this can be used, I will include it in the book.

Individual Origins

Setting the *Pivot Point* to *Individual Origins* is an option you may not use too often but is an absolute life saver when you do. It allows you to *Transform* a group of *Objects* or *Mesh Elements* independently of each other.

In *Object Mode*, each *Object* will be *Transformed* around its own *Origin Point*.

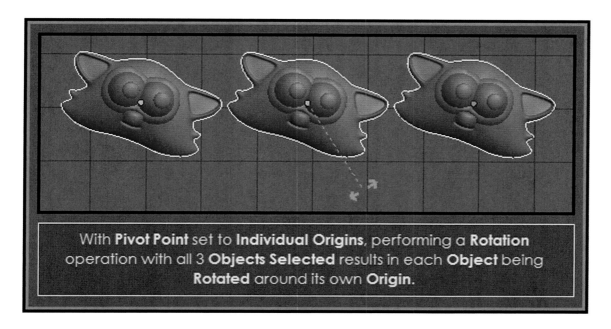

With **Pivot Point** set to **Individual Origins**, performing a **Rotation** operation with all 3 **Objects Selected** results in each **Object** being **Rotated** around its own **Origin**.

Once again, be aware of the *Origin Point* of all your *Objects* to ensure expected results.

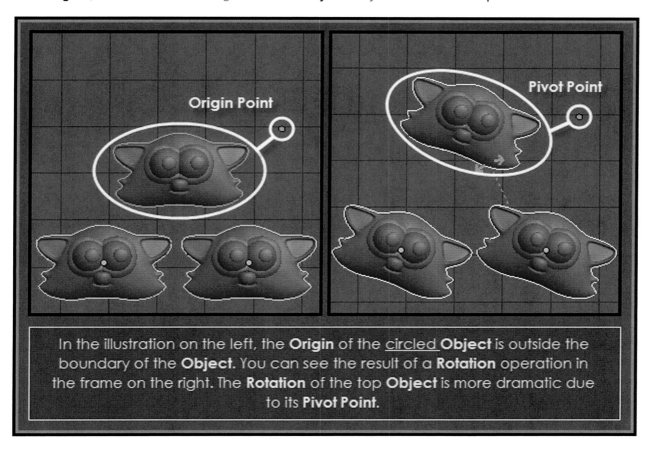

In the illustration on the left, the **Origin** of the <u>circled</u> **Object** is outside the boundary of the **Object**. You can see the result of a **Rotation** operation in the frame on the right. The **Rotation** of the top **Object** is more dramatic due to its **Pivot Point**.

This type of *Pivot Point* is used often during the *Animation* process as it allows for the *Transform* of multiple *Objects* quickly.

In *Edit Mode*, the *Median* of the selected *Mesh Elements* acts as the *Pivot Point*. You can *Transform* one or more single *Vertices* but it has no visually visible effect (and I imagine may eventually cause you issues). By single *Vertices* I mean *Vertices* that are selected but are not touching.

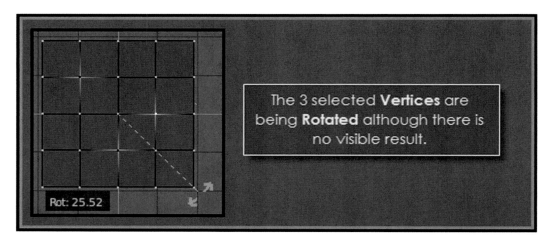

While in *Vertex Select Mode*, 2 *Vertices* that form an *Edge* behave like an *Edge* during *Transform* operations. When 3 or more *Vertices* form a *Face* they behave like a *Face* during *Transform* operations.

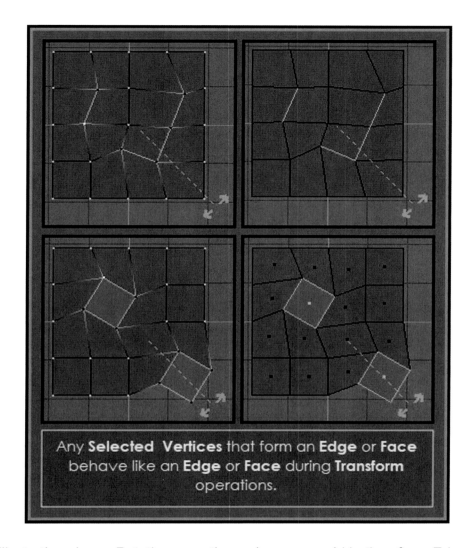

Any **Selected Vertices** that form an **Edge** or **Face** behave like an **Edge** or **Face** during **Transform** operations.

The above illustration shows *Rotation* operations where several *Vertices* form *Edges* or *Faces*. The *Transform* operations behave the same way regardless of *Mesh Select Mode*.

You may have noticed that in the above illustration, specifically the examples that use *Edges*, that the individual *Edges* were not *Transformed*. *Blender* does not *Transform* each individual *Edge* or *Face* as you might expect. Any selected *Mesh Elements* that touch each other are considered a single entity and all *Transform* operations will happen at the *Center* of that entity.

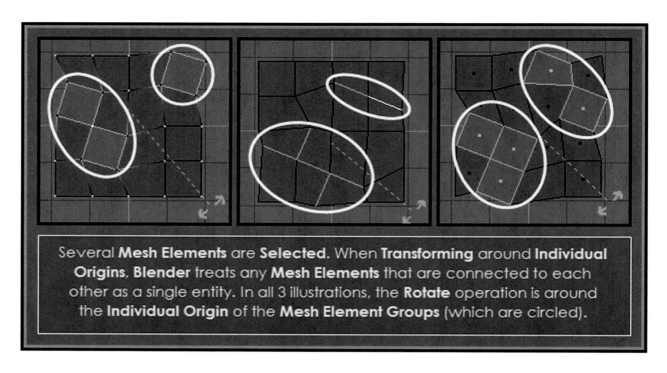

Several **Mesh Elements** are **Selected**. When **Transforming** around **Individual Origins, Blender** treats any **Mesh Elements** that are connected to each other as a single entity. In all 3 illustrations, the **Rotate** operation is around the **Individual Origin** of the **Mesh Element Groups** (which are circled).

I have been using *Rotation* in many examples but as you might expect, the same rules apply when *Scaling*.

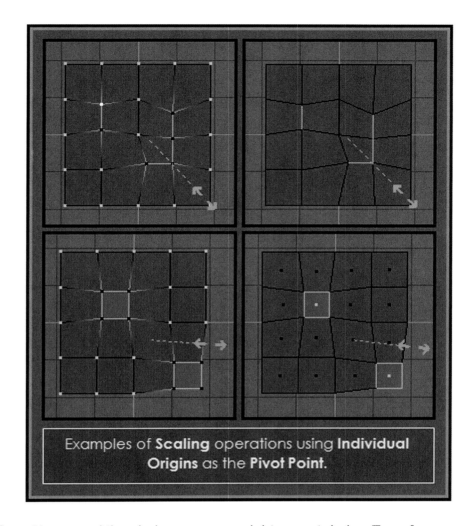

Examples of **Scaling** operations using **Individual Origins** as the **Pivot Point.**

Faces can form *Ngons* and they behave as you might expect during *Transform* operations.

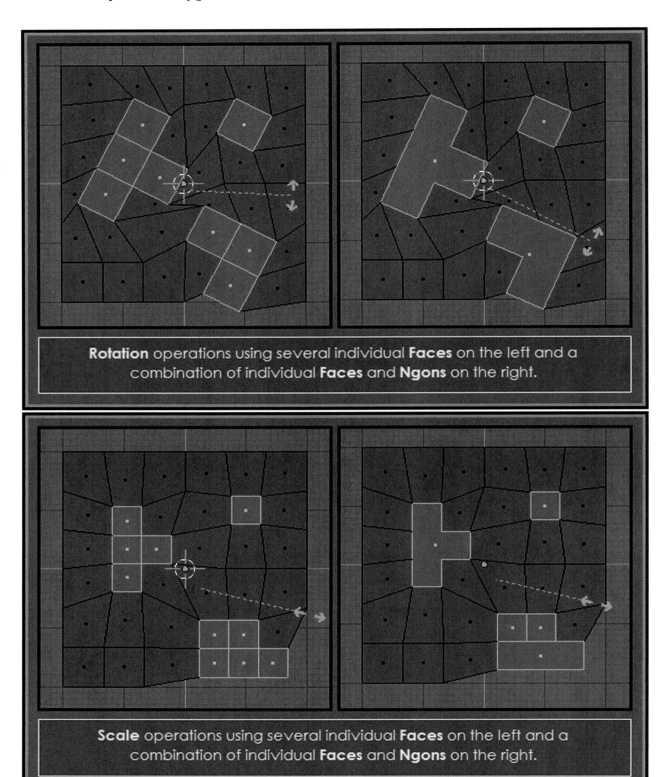

Rotation operations using several individual **Faces** on the left and a combination of individual **Faces** and **Ngons** on the right.

Scale operations using several individual **Faces** on the left and a combination of individual **Faces** and **Ngons** on the right.

3D Cursor

Using the *3D Cursor* as a *Pivot Point* offers the most flexibility of any of the *Pivot Point* types. The reason for this is you have 100% control when it comes to *3D Cursor* placement. Using the

3D Cursor in conjunction with *Snapping* allows you to pretty much make any *Location* in your *3D Space* act as a *Pivot Point*.

Snapping is essential when you want to place the *3D Cursor* with precision. This section of the book will talk about the behavior when rotating around the *3D Cursor* but not the specifics of placing the *3D Cursor* using the *Snap Menu* which is covered in **Chapter 7 – Snap Menu**.

You can place the *3D Cursor* manually using the LMB. To place the *3D Cursor*, simply click anywhere in the *3D View*. You need to be careful when using this method as the *3D Cursor* may not end up where you expected it. The best way to place the *3D Cursor* is to switch to one of the *Perpendicular 3D Views* (i.e. *Front*, *Side* or *Back View*) and place your *3D Cursor*. Note: Ensure you are in *Orthographic View Mode* when switching *3D View*. You can then switch to a different *3D View* to ensure the *3D Cursor* is where you want it.

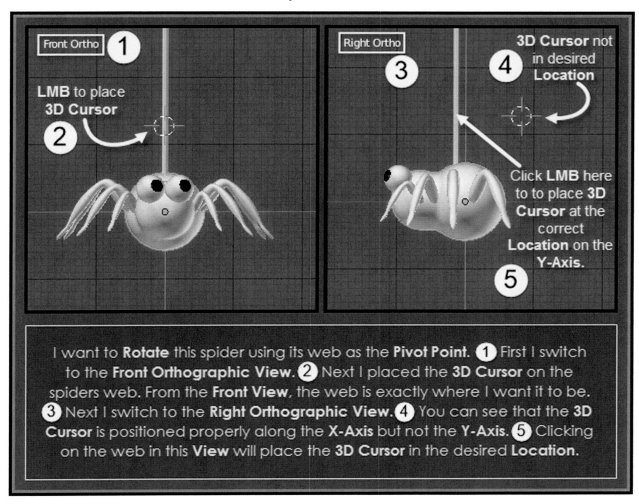

I want to **Rotate** this spider using its web as the **Pivot Point**. ❶ First I switch to the **Front Orthographic View**. ❷ Next I placed the **3D Cursor** on the spiders web. From the **Front View**, the web is exactly where I want it to be. ❸ Next I switch to the **Right Orthographic View**. ❹ You can see that the **3D Cursor** is positioned properly along the **X-Axis** but not the **Y-Axis**. ❺ Clicking on the web in this **View** will place the **3D Cursor** in the desired **Location**.

The above illustration shows that placing the *3D Cursor* in 1 View does not ensure it's exactly where you want it to be in the *3D Space*. In *Front View* I was able to place the *3D Cursor* at the desired *Location* along the *X* and *Z-Axis* but I needed to switch to the *Right View* to ensure the *3D Cursor* is at the desired *Location* along the *Y-Axis*. As you can see, manually placing the *3D Cursor* lacks precision and should be used sparingly.

Once placed, the *3D Cursor* can then be used as the *Pivot Point* for *Transform Operations*.

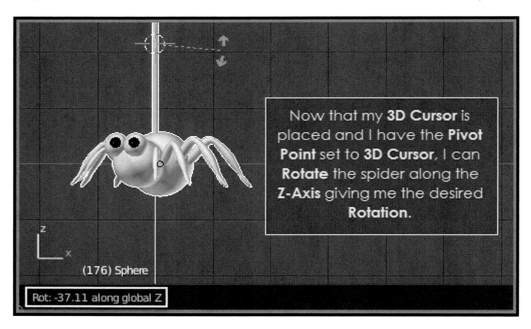

Note: I talk about constraining *Transform* operations along a specific *Axis* later in the chapter.

It should also be noted that you can also place the *3D Cursor* using the *3D Cursor Panel* located on the *Properties Shelf*.

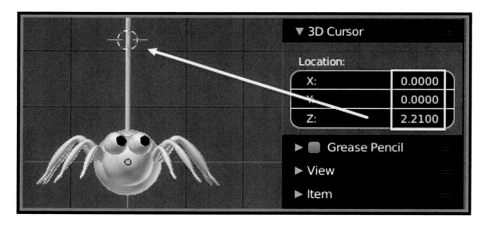

Using the *Snap Menu* allows you to place the *3D Cursor* more precisely. In the above example, I could have simply *Snapped* the *3D Cursor* to a *Mesh Element* (in this case the spider web) to get precisely the placement I wanted.

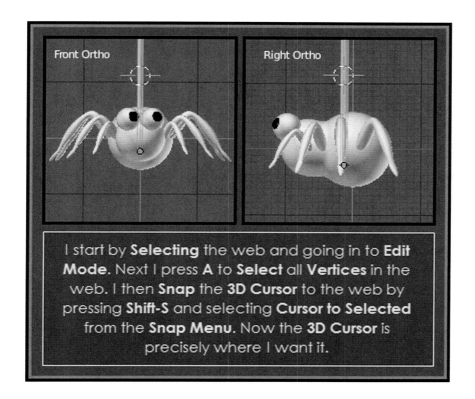

I start by **Selecting** the web and going in to **Edit Mode**. Next I press **A** to **Select** all **Vertices** in the web. I then **Snap** the **3D Cursor** to the web by pressing **Shift-S** and selecting **Cursor to Selected** from the **Snap Menu**. Now the **3D Cursor** is precisely where I want it.

As you can see from the above illustration, I was able to place the *3D Cursor* with precision by using the *Snap Menu*. Again, see **Chapter 7 – Snap Menu** to get an idea of how much control you can have when placing the *3D Cursor*. This control allows you to perform *Transform* operations around just about any *Location* in the *3D View*.

Here are some examples of *Transform* operations using the *3D Cursor*.

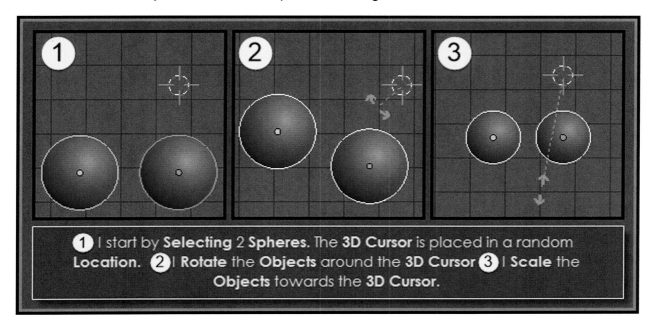

1 I start by **Selecting** 2 **Spheres**. The **3D Cursor** is placed in a random **Location**. **2** I **Rotate** the **Objects** around the **3D Cursor** **3** I **Scale** the **Objects** towards the **3D Cursor**.

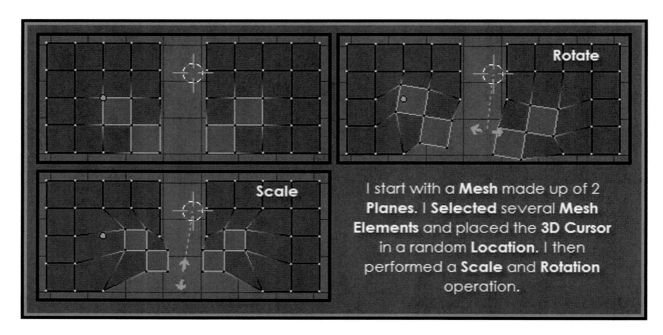

I start with a **Mesh** made up of 2 **Planes**. I **Selected** several **Mesh Elements** and placed the **3D Cursor** in a random **Location**. I then performed a **Scale** and **Rotation** operation.

Bounding Box Center

To understand the *Bounding Box Center Pivot Point*, think of being asked to put your *Object Origins* or *Mesh Element*(s) in a box. The *Box* is the exact size needed to fit your *Object Origins* or *Mesh Elements*. The *Pivot Point* for this *Box* (a.k.a. *Bounding Box*) is the center of the *Box*.

In *Object Mode* the *Pivot Point* is the center of the *Object Origins* of all *Selected Objects*. If there is only 1 *Object Selected*, the *Origin Point* of that *Object* then becomes the *Pivot Point*. It's identical to using the *Median Point Pivot* option. With multiple *Objects*, the *Bounding Box* is the exact size needed to fit the *Origin Points* of all *Selected Objects*.

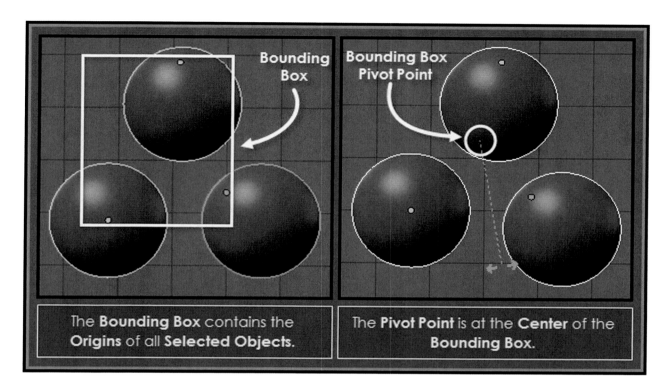

You can see in the above illustration how the *Object Origins* and not the *Object Geometry* determines the boundary of the *Bounding Box*.

In *Edit Mode*, the boundary of the *Bounding Box* is dictated by the selected *Vertices*. The *Object Origins* play no role in determining the *Bounding Box*.

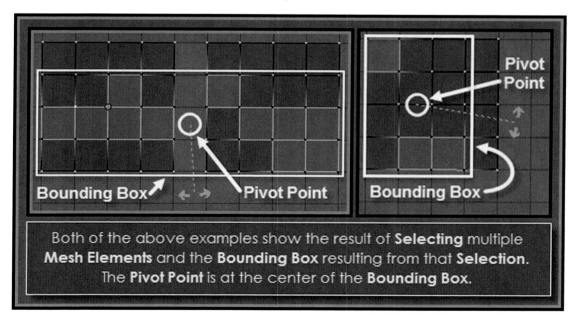

I personally use the *3D Cursor* and *Bounding Box* the majority of the time when *Modeling*. The results are always predictable and I have grown used to using those 2 *Pivot Point* modes. The

Rotate Around Individual Origins option also comes in handy on occasion and consequently it's a distant 3rd on my list.

Constraining Transform Operations

Transform operations can be constrained along the *X, Y* or *Z-Axis*. This is particularly useful when *Hard Surface Modeling.* **You can** *Transform* along an *Axis* by pressing X, Y or Z after activating a *Transform Tool.* **For example,** G followed by X will constrain the *Grab* operation along the *X-Axis* or more specifically, along the *Global X-Axis* (I talk about the *Global Transform Orientation* in the next section). You can also constrain along any *Axis* by selecting the appropriate check box on the *Operator Panel* after you confirm the *Transform* operation (see **The Basics** in this chapter for more info on the *Operator Panels* for each of the *Transform Tools*).

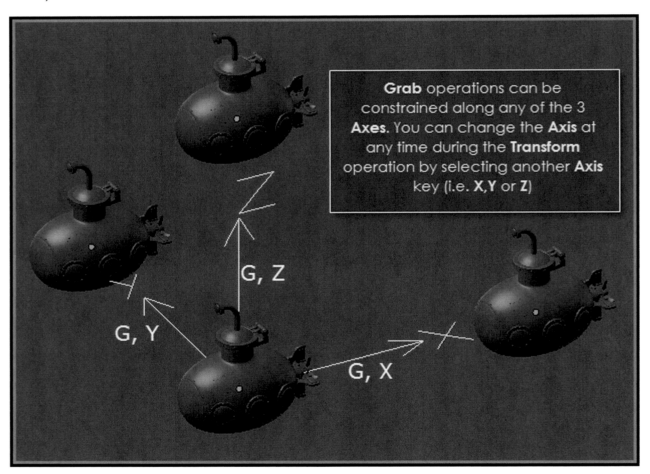

The end result of *Transforming* while constraining along an *Axis* differs between *Transform Tools.* Remember, G by itself will initiate a *Grab* operation in *Free Form Mode* which is to say the operation is not constrained in any way. I will have a lot more to say about the behavior for each of the *Transform Tools* in their respective sections later in the chapter including how to make more precise *Transformations.* First I need to get some of the basics out of the way which I will detail using the *Grab Transform* operation.

Transform Orientation Menu

There are other options in *Blender* that allow for more control over *Transform* operations. The *Transform Orientation Menu*, as you might expect, affects the behavior of the *Transformation Tools* (*Grab*, *Rotate* and *Scale*). You can find the *Transform Orientation Menu* in the header of the *3D Window* or by using the keyboard shortcut Alt + Space. Your currently selected *Transform Orientation* will directly affect transform operations along a constrained or locked *Axis* i.e. when you constrain a *Transform* operation along a particular *Axis*.

It's important to remember that the currently selected *Transform Orientation* is available by clicking X, Y or Z twice after hitting a *Transform Operation* keyboard shortcut. To clarify, if you want to initiate a *Grab* operation along the *X-Axis* you would use the keyboard shortcut G, X. The *Grab* operation in this case will be constrained to the *Global X-Axis*. If you want to use the currently selected *Transform Orientation* you need to hit X again. So if you have *Local* selected you would hit G, X to constrain along the *Global X-Axis* or G, X, X to constrain along the *Local X-Axis*. The *Global Transform Orientation* is always the default when you hit one of the *Axis Selection* keys (X, Y or Z). To use the selected *Transform Orientation*, you need to hit the *Axis* selection keys twice.

So you may be wondering, how do I know what *Transform Orientation* is currently being used. *Blender* provides information about the current *Transform* operation in a bar at the bottom of the *3D View*.

The information related to the current *Transform Operation* differs depending on the *Transform Tool* and wether or not the operation is constrained.

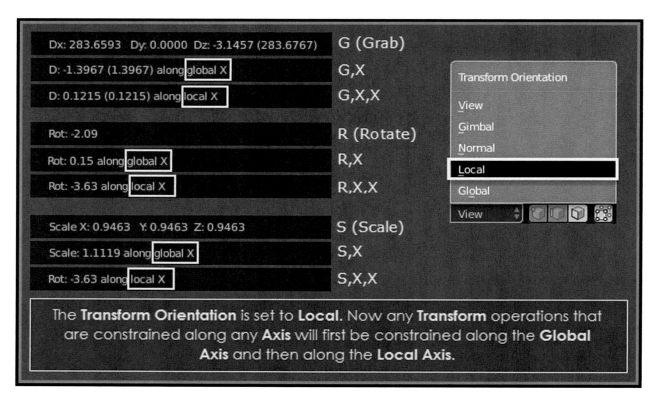

The above illustration shows all 3 *Transform* operations and the result of constraining those *Transform Operations* along an *Axis* (in this example, the *X-Axis*). Pressing *X* once after initiating a *Transform* operation will constrain the *Transform* along the *Global X-Axis*. Pressing *X* twice after initiating a *Transform* operation will constrain the *Transform* along the currently selected *Transform Orientation*.

Global Transform Orientation

You can think of the *Global Orientation* as *Blender's* representation of the *X, Y* and *Z-Axis* as it relates to the *3D World*. The orientation of many *Objects* in your project may change but the *Global X, Y* and *Z* will never change.

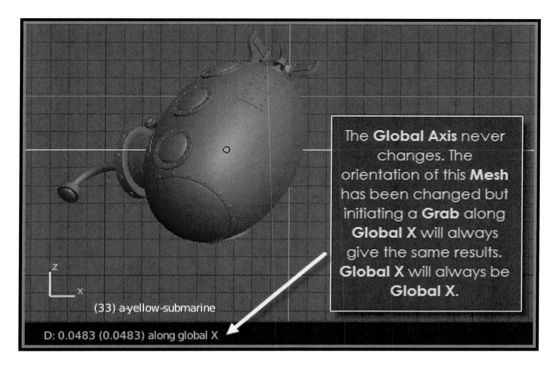

The **Global Axis** never changes. The orientation of this **Mesh** has been changed but initiating a **Grab** along **Global X** will always give the same results. **Global X** will always be **Global X**.

(33) a-yellow-submarine

D: 0.0483 (0.0483) along global X

Local Transform Orientation

The *Local Orientation* represents the *Axis* of the currently selected *Object*. The *Global Orientation* never changes but the *Local Orientation* can be different from *Object* to *Object* after performing certain types of *Transform* operations. The *Rotate Transform Operation* has the biggest effect on an *Objects Local Orientation*. Specifically, a *Rotate Transform* operation done in *Edit Mode* will change how *Blender* interprets the *Local X, Y* and *Z-Axis* of an *Object*.

If you are ever wondering about the current *Global* and *Local X, Y* and *Z-Axis* as it relates to an *Object* you can use *Blender's 3D Manipulators* in conjunction with the *Transform Orientation Menu* to quickly determine that information.

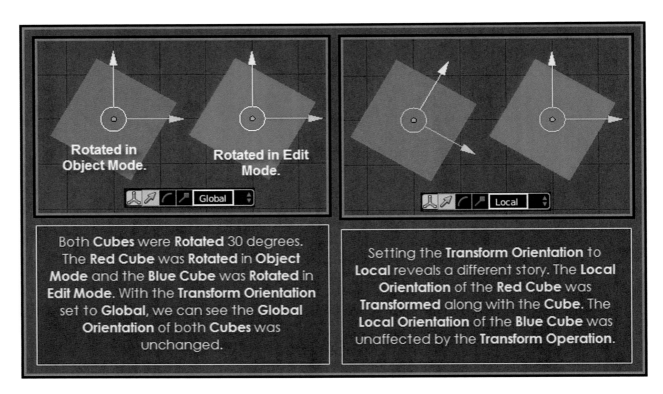

As we can see in the above illustration, *Transform Operations* in *Edit Mode* have a different effect on the *Orientation* of the *Local X, Y* and *Z-Axis* than those done in *Object Mode*. Any *Rotation* done in *Object Mode* will affect the *Local Orientation*.

There are no hard and fast rules around doing *Transform* operations in *Object* vs. *Edit Mode*. For me personally, I tend to do initial *Rotation* operations in *Object Mode* to preserve the *Local X, Y* and *Z-Axis* which can be advantageous in some situations. As you will soon find out, there are several other options when it comes to setting the *Transform* orientation. There is even an option of set a *Custom Transform Orientation*. You can also have a look at **Chapter 7 – Objects and Mesh Data** for a technique that allows share the *Mesh Data* between 2 *Mesh Objects*. You can then work on one *Object* using *Global X, Y,* and *Z-Axis* with the result being mirrored on the other *Object*.

Normal Transform Orientation

The *Normal Orientation* allows you to perform *Transform Operations* along the *Normal* of 1 or more *Mesh Elements*. Specifically, selecting any *Face* will cause the *Z-Axis* to be aligned with the *Normal* on that *Face*. In other words, selecting any *Face* and performing a *Transform* operation that is constrained along the *Z-Axis* will constrain the angle of the *Transform* to the angle of the *Normal* for that *Face*. If you select multiple *Faces*, the *Transform Operation* is done at an angle calculated by *Blender* (it appears to be an angle that is an average angle between all of the selected *Face Normals*). You will quickly become very familiar with the behavior of *Transforming* along the *Normal* as the *Normal Transform Orientation* is the default when extruding a *Face*. To demonstrate I will use the following *Mesh*.

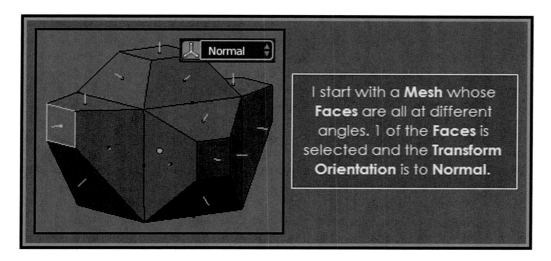

I start with a **Mesh** whose **Faces** are all at different angles. 1 of the **Faces** is selected and the **Transform Orientation** is to **Normal.**

Now I will *Transform* the *Selected Face* using a *Grab* operation.

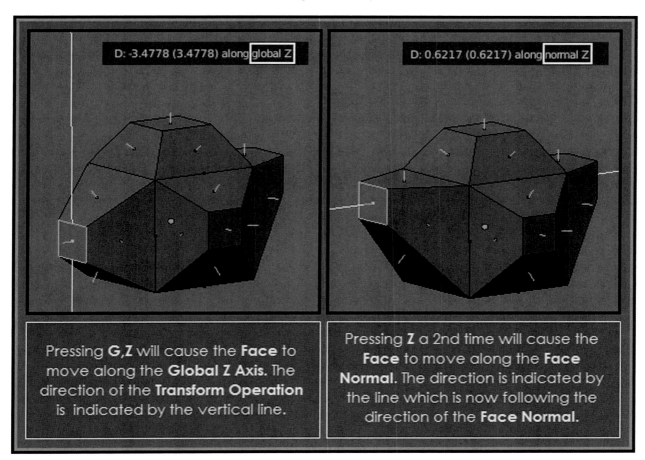

Pressing **G,Z** will cause the **Face** to move along the **Global Z Axis**. The direction of the **Transform Operation** is indicated by the vertical line.

Pressing **Z** a 2nd time will cause the **Face** to move along the **Face Normal**. The direction is indicated by the line which is now following the direction of the **Face Normal.**

You could initiate a *Transform* operation on any of the *Faces* in the above illustration and have it constrained along the direction indicated by the *Normal*.

Transforming along the *Normal* works on multiple *Faces* as well. The result of the *Transform* operation depends on whether or not the *Faces* are connected. To demonstrate I will use the following *Mesh*.

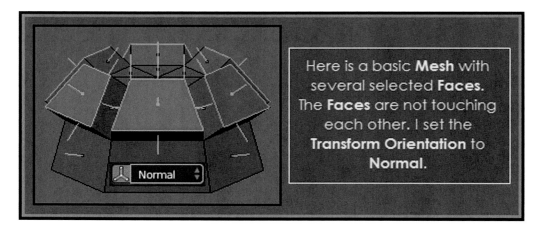

Now I will *Transform* the *Selected Faces* using a *Grab* operation.

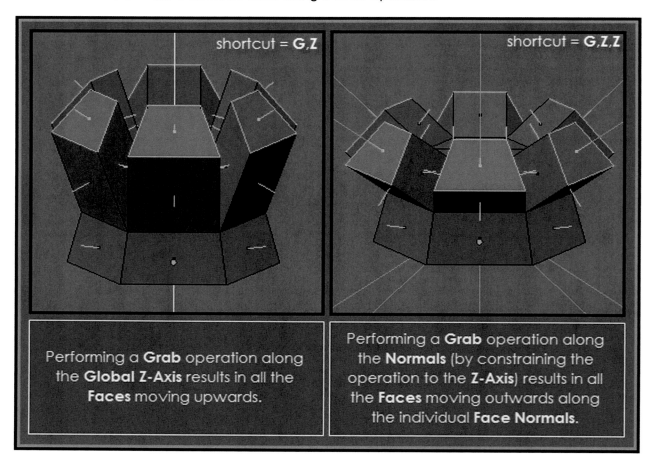

Performing a *Grab* operation along the individual *Normal* for each *Face* looks a little more natural, at least in my opinion. Now for an example where I *Extrude* 2 connected *Faces*.

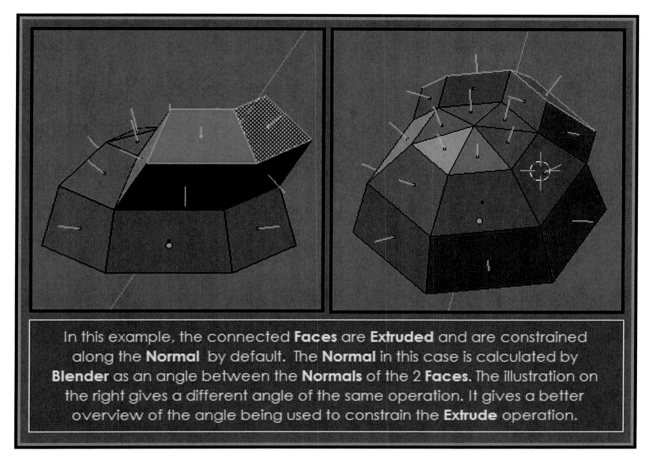

In this example, the connected **Faces** are **Extruded** and are constrained along the **Normal** by default. The **Normal** in this case is calculated by **Blender** as an angle between the **Normals** of the 2 **Faces**. The illustration on the right gives a different angle of the same operation. It gives a better overview of the angle being used to constrain the **Extrude** operation.

As you can see, the *Normal Transform Orientation* is very versatile. The fact that it's the default for *Extrusion* operations speaks to its usefulness in my opinion.

Gimbal Transform Orientation

I don't have much to say about the *Gimbal Transform Orientation*. I have never seen it used in a *Modeling* tutorial. From what I can gather, it can be important when creating animations which are not the focus of this book. There is information on the net about gimbals in general if you are interested. The topic can be quite complicated and is outside the scope of this book.

View Transform Orientation

The *View Transform Orientation* will constrain *Transform* operations to the current *3D View*. Your position in the *3D World* has no effect here. You can think of it as the *Up, Down, Left, Right, Forward, Back* of your current screen. As an example, performing a *Transform* operation along the *X-Axis* when your *Transform Orientation* is set to *View* will always result in the *Transform Operation* being constrained from *left* to *right* or *right* to *left* on your screen. Although I don't use often I have found it especially useful when setting up screen shots for this book.

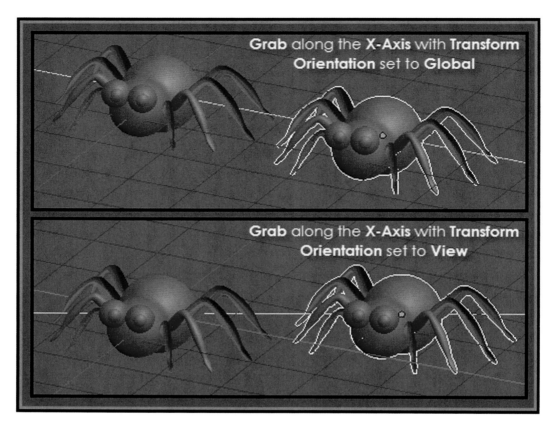

Custom Orientation

Blender offers many options for constraining a *Transform* operation but if you want the ultimate in flexibility you can define your own *Custom Orientation*. *Custom Orientations* can be defined from *Objects* or selected *Mesh* elements such as *Faces*, *Edges* and *Vertices*.

You can manage custom *Transform Orientations* using the *Transform Orientations Panel* which can be found on the *Properties Shelf*.

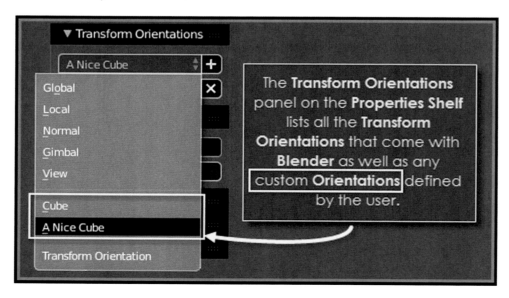

The first thing you may be wondering is why my new *Custom Transform Orientation* is named "*A Nice Cube*". The name was assigned by *Blender* when the *Custom Orientation* was created. The default name depends on what you currently have selected when defining the new *Custom Orientation*. For example, if you currently have an *Object* named "*MyObject*" selected and you create a new *Custom Orientation*, the name of the *Custom Orientation* will be "*MyObject*". As you have probably guessed by now, I used a *Cube* named "*A Nice Cube*" in the above example.

When in *Edit Mode*, the name given to the *Custom Transform Orientation* will be whatever *Mesh Element* you have selected. If you have a *Face* selected, the *Custom Orientation* will be named *Face*. Fortunately, you can rename the *Custom Orientation* to anything you like by clicking on the *Name* field and entering a new name.

Using *Objects* to define a *Custom Orientation* will result in the *Objects Local Orientation* defining the new *Orientation*. Remember, you can quickly view an *Objects Local Orientation* using the *3D Manipulators* in conjunction with the *Transform Orientation Menu*.

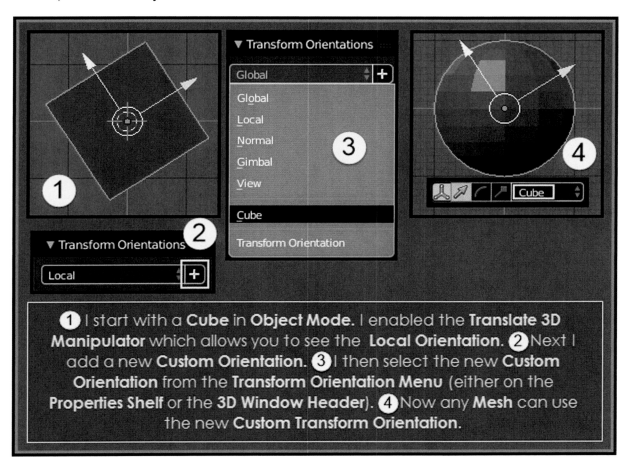

1 I start with a **Cube** in **Object Mode**. I enabled the **Translate 3D Manipulator** which allows you to see the **Local Orientation**. **2** Next I add a new **Custom Orientation**. **3** I then select the new **Custom Orientation** from the **Transform Orientation Menu** (either on the **Properties Shelf** or the **3D Window Header**). **4** Now any **Mesh** can use the new **Custom Transform Orientation**.

The *Sphere* in the above illustration is now able to perform *Transform* operations constrained along the *Custom Orientation* we created using the *Local Orientation* of the *Cube*.

As previously mentioned, any mesh element can be used to define a new *Custom Orientation*. A *Mesh Face* is the *Mesh Element* I use most frequently when defining a new *Custom Orientation*.

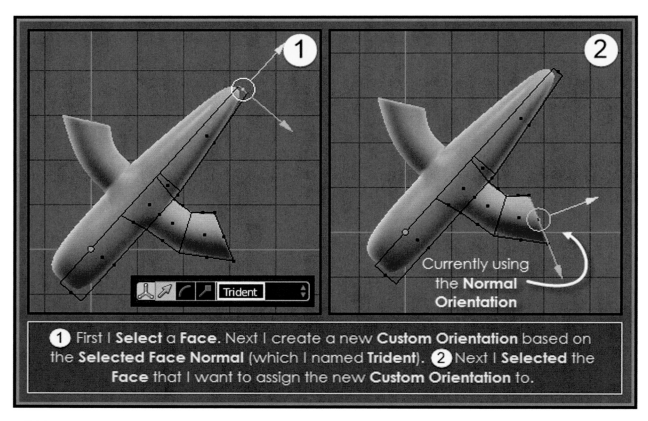

1 First I **Select** a **Face**. Next I create a new **Custom Orientation** based on the **Selected Face Normal** (which I named **Trident**). 2 Next I **Selected** the **Face** that I want to assign the new **Custom Orientation** to.

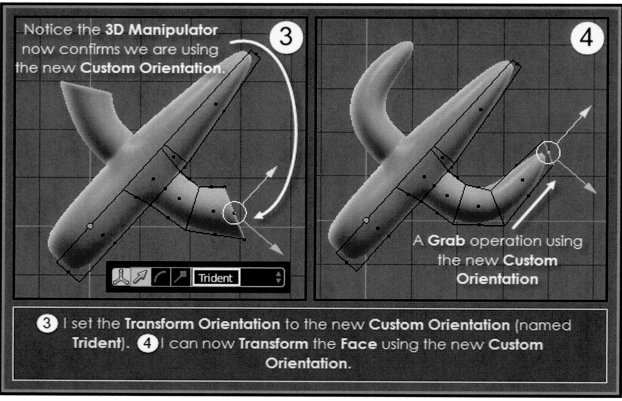

3 I set the **Transform Orientation** to the new **Custom Orientation** (named **Trident**). 4 I can now **Transform** the **Face** using the new **Custom Orientation**.

As you can see, the possibilities are endless when it comes to creating *Custom Orientations*. If offers the ultimate in flexibility and once you start using it you will find that it quickly becomes an important tool in your *Modeling* arsenal.

Plane Locking

Up to this point all the *Transform* operation examples have been constrained along 1 *Axis*. In other words, I have only ever *Transformed* along the *X*, *Y* or *Z-Axis*. *Blender* also allows you to constrain *Transform* operations along 2 *Axis*. In other words, you are <u>preventing</u> *Transformations* along 1 *Axis*. This type of *Axis Locking* is referred to as *Plane Locking* and is only valid for *Grab* and *Scale* operations. To constrain a *Transform* operation along 2 different *Axes* simply prefix the shortcut with the Shift key. For example, if you want to be able to move an object along the *X* and *Y-Axis* but not the *Z-Axis*, you would press G followed by Shift + Z.

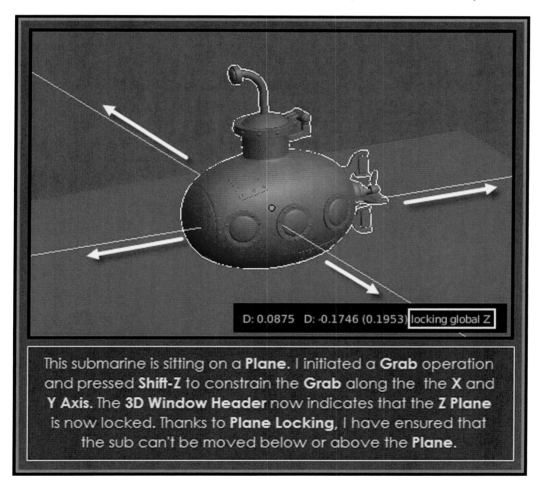

D: 0.0875   D: -0.1746 (0.1953) locking global Z

This submarine is sitting on a **Plane.** I initiated a **Grab** operation and pressed **Shift-Z** to constrain the **Grab** along the the **X** and **Y Axis.** The **3D Window Header** now indicates that the **Z Plane** is now locked. Thanks to **Plane Locking,** I have ensured that the sub can't be moved below or above the **Plane.**

I find *Plane Locking* especially useful when *Resizing* as it allows me to preserve 1 *Axis* while *Transforming* the other 2. For example, when performing *Mesh* operations like *Resizing* a *Tube* I often want to *Scale* down the circumference of a *Tube* without affecting its length.

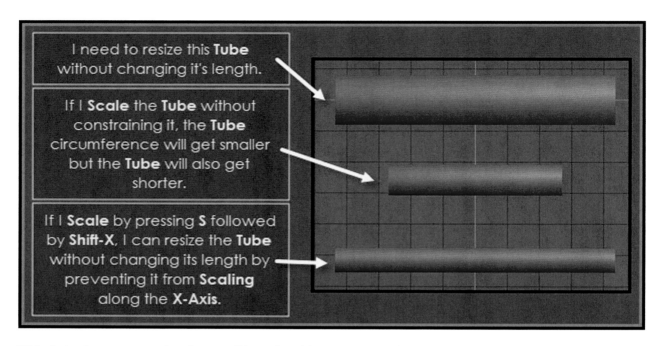

This is just one example of were *Plane Locking* can come in handy. I find it can sometimes produce undesired results but when it works as expected it can also be a great time saver.

The Transform Properties Panel

There are several shortcuts for doing *Transform* operations but you can also perform *Transform* operations via the *Transform Panel* on the *Properties Shelf*. The *Transform Panel* gives you information about the currently selected *Objects Location*, *Rotation* and *Scale*.

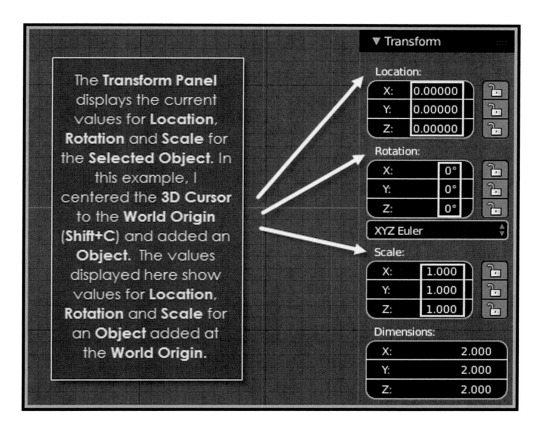

The **Transform Panel** displays the current values for **Location**, **Rotation** and **Scale** for the **Selected Object**. In this example, I centered the **3D Cursor** to the **World Origin** (**Shift+C**) and added an **Object**. The values displayed here show values for **Location**, **Rotation** and **Scale** for an **Object** added at the **World Origin**.

In the above illustration I centered the cursor before adding the *Sphere* (using Shift + C which centers the *3D Cursor* to the *3D World Origin* located at coordinates *0,0,0*). If I hadn't centered the *3D Cursor* the value for the *Objects Location* would not have been *0.000* for all 3 *Axis*.

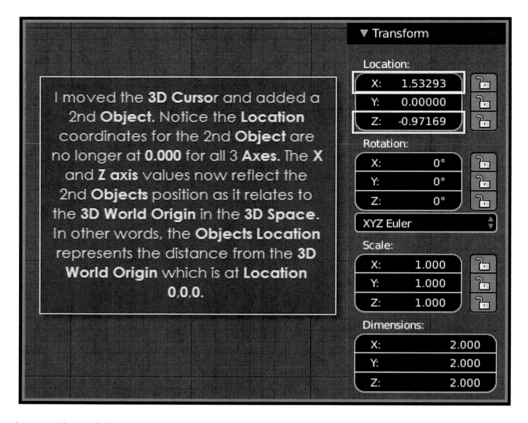

I previously mentioned the term *3D World Origin*. In *Blender*, the *3D World Origin* is a fixed point in the *3D Space* whose *Global Location* is *0,0,0*. If you snap your *3D Cursor* to the *3D World Origin* (Shift + C) and add an *Object*, your new *Object* will have the value *0.000* for all 3 *Location Axis*. The reason for this is that *Object* was added at the *Location* of the *3D Cursor* and the *3D Cursor* is located at the *3D World Origin*.

The *Transform Properties Panel* has a different set of options when in *Edit Mode*.

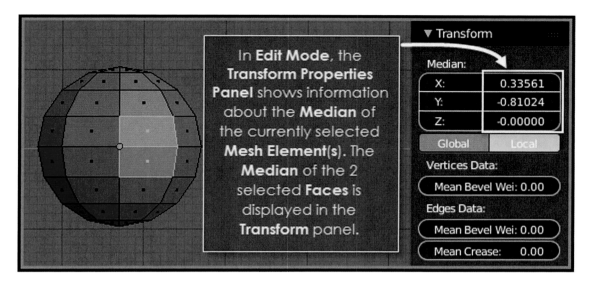

As indicated in the above illustration, the *Median* displays the coordinates of the selected *Mesh Elements* and not the entire *Object*. Notice there are also buttons to toggle displaying the *Local* or *Global Median* for selected *Mesh Elements*.

As you might have guessed by now, the *Transform Panel* can be used to *Transform* an *Object* or *Mesh Element* by changing the values in the related fields for each of the *Transform* operations. This allows a user to manually enter precise coordinates for an *Object* or *Mesh Element*. You can also change the coordinates using the mouse by clicking and dragging in one or more of the coordinate fields. I don't use the *Transform Panel* to do *Transform* operations very often but I do use it to get the current coordinates of an *Object*, especially *Scale* and *Rotation* coordinates as they can affect other operations in *Blender*.

Beside each of the coordinate fields is a little lock icon. This icon can be used to lock an *Axis* preventing a user from *Transforming* along that *Axis*.

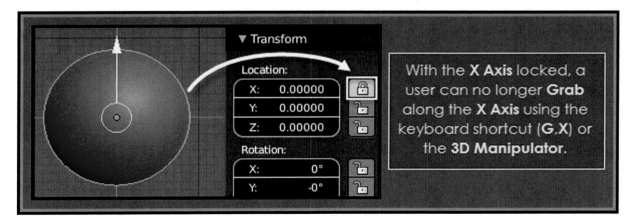

You can still use the *Transform Panel* to perform a *Transform* operation even if it's locked. Locking only applies to *Transform* operations done via the keyboard shortcuts or the *3D Manipulators*.

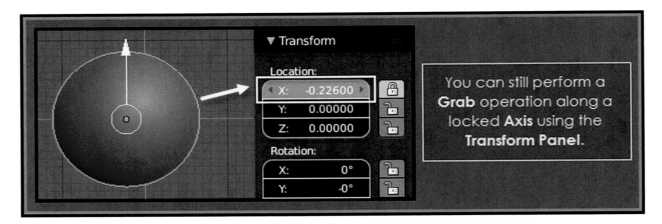

The *3D Manipulators* also give you a quick visualization of which *Axis* are locked for each of the *Transform* types.

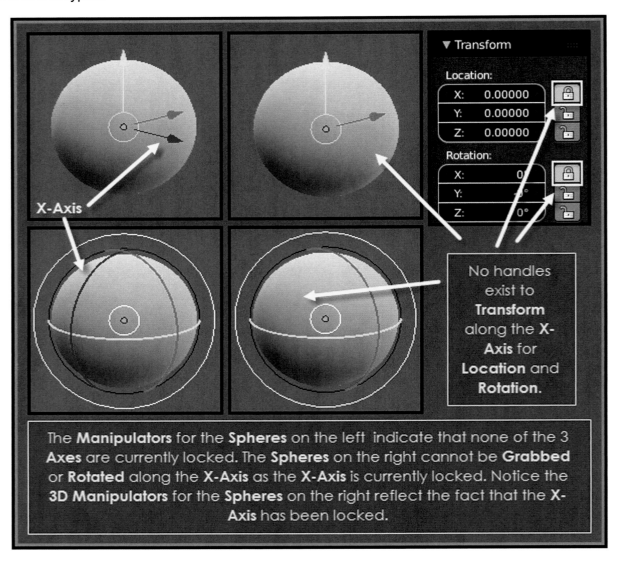

Applying and Clearing Object Transformations

Any *Transformation* done in *Object Mode* can be *Cleared* or *Applied*. *Clearing* and *Applying* *Transformations* is important when working with some *Modifiers* or *Constraints*.

Clearing Object Transformations

To clear a *Transform* simply press Alt plus the shortcut you would use to do the *Transform* that you are trying to clear. In other words, if you are trying to clear the *Rotation* for an *Object*, you would press Alt + R. You can clear the *Location* with Alt + G, *Scale* with Alt + S, *Rotation* with Alt + R and *Origin* with Alt + O. You can also clear *Object Transformations* via the *Object Menu*.

Clearing the *Location* will move the selected *Object* back to the coordinates *0,0,0* which is also known as the *3D World Origin*. It doesn't matter where you added the *Object*, it will always be returned to the coordinates of the *Origin* and not the *Location* where it was added. More specifically, the <u>*Origin*</u> of the selected *Object* will be moved to the *Origin* of the *3D World*.

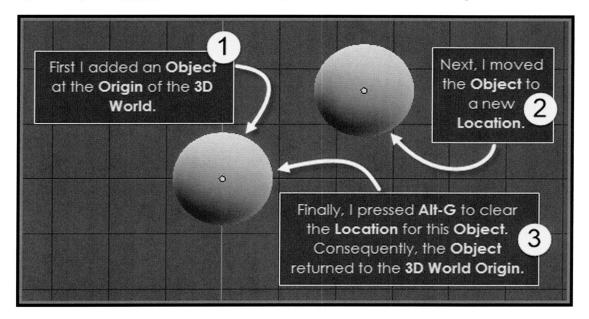

As previously mentioned, the *Location* where the *Object* was added doesn't affect the destination when you clear the *Location*. It will always be moved to coordinates *0,0,0*.

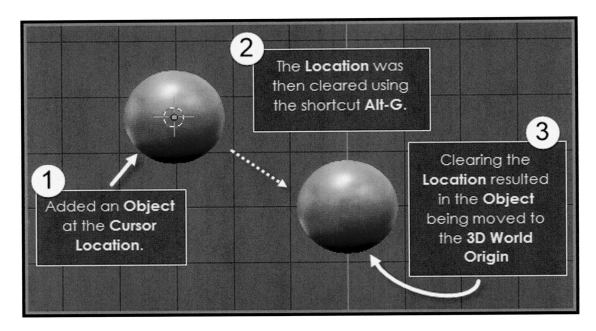

Clearing the Rotation will reset the Rotation of each Axis to 0.

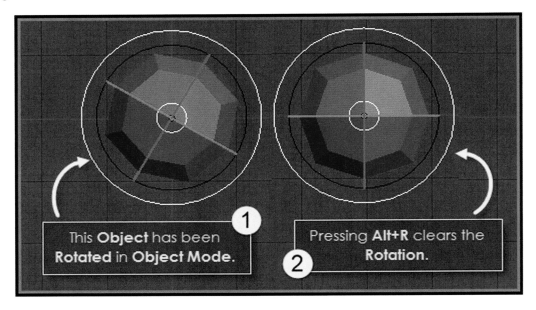

One example of where I might want to Clear the Rotation (or Location, Scale) for an Object is if I am using the Object as an Object Offset for an Array Modifier (see **Chapter 9 – The Array Modifier**). Transforming the Object being used as the Object Offset will affect various attributes of the Array of Objects. Clearing the Offset Objects Transforrn data can quickly get you out of Trouble if you perform a Transform operation that yields undesired results.

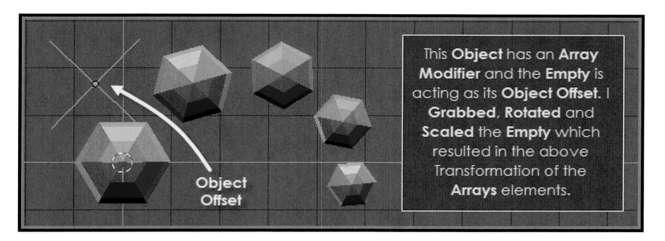

Now I will go ahead and *Clear* the *Location*, *Rotation* and *Scale* of the *Empty*.

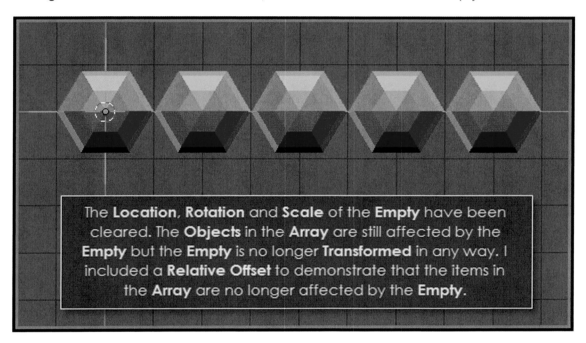

So to be clear, by clearing the *Size*, *Scale* and *Location* of the *Empty*, the effect it had on the *Array Elements* is also cleared.

Clearing the *Scale* will resize the *Object* back to its original size at the time the *Object* was created.

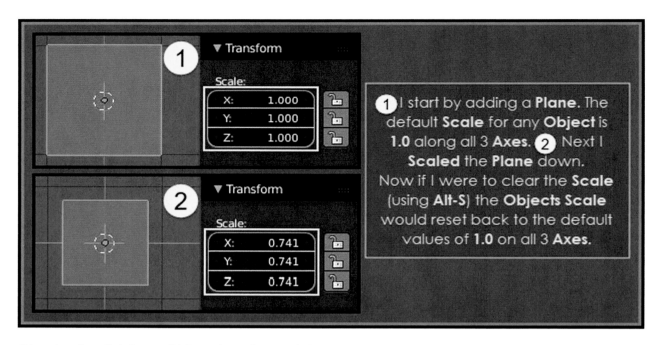

1 I start by adding a **Plane**. The default **Scale** for any **Object** is 1.0 along all 3 **Axes**. **2** Next I **Scaled** the **Plane** down. Now if I were to clear the **Scale** (using **Alt-S**) the **Objects Scale** would reset back to the default values of **1.0** on all 3 **Axes**.

Clearing the *Origin* on *Objects* in a *Parent / Child* relationship allows you to set the *Location* of the *Child Objects* to the *Origin* of the *Parent Object*. (see **Chapter 7 – Parenting**).

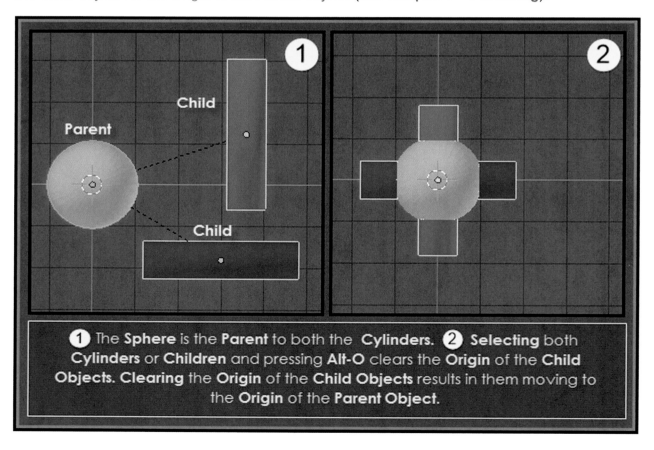

1 The **Sphere** is the **Parent** to both the **Cylinders**. **2** **Selecting** both **Cylinders** or **Children** and pressing **Alt-O** clears the **Origin** of the **Child Objects**. **Clearing** the **Origin** of the **Child Objects** results in them moving to the **Origin** of the **Parent Object**.

Keep in mind that *Clearing* the *Origin* moves the *Children* to the *Origin* of their *Parent*. If the *Origin* of the *Parent* is outside the boundaries of the *Mesh* then the *Child Objects* may end up in an undesired *Location*.

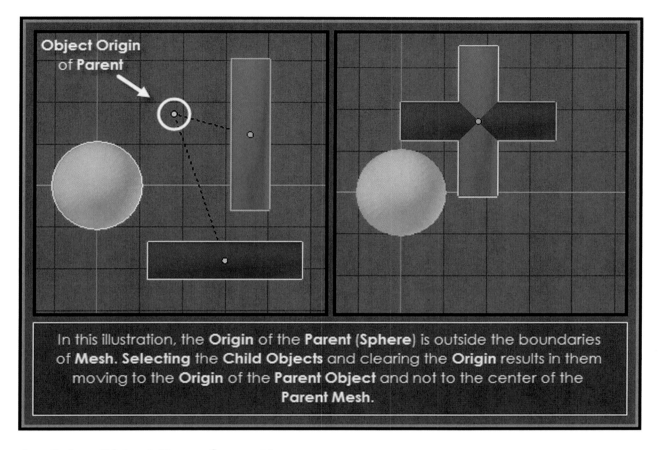

In this illustration, the **Origin** of the **Parent (Sphere)** is outside the boundaries of **Mesh. Selecting** the **Child Objects** and clearing the **Origin** results in them moving to the **Origin** of the **Parent Object** and not to the center of the **Parent Mesh.**

Applying Object Transformations

Before describing how to *Apply* an *Object Transformation* I thought I would talk about why you might want to do it.

When you add a new *Mesh Primitive* (mesh shapes that come with *Blender* such as *Cube*, *Sphere* etc.) the *Scale* will always be set to *1.0* on all 3 *Axes* and the *Rotation* will always be set to *0* on all 3 *Axes*. The *Objects Location* will depend on where you added the *Object*. The coordinates for the *Location* are based on the distance from the *Origin Point* of the *3D World*. After *Transforming* your new *Object* by *Rotating* and / or *Scaling* it you may want to tell *Blender* that no matter how your *Object* got there, you want *Blender* to treat the *Object* as if you had just added it. In other words, set the *Scale* back to *1.0* on all 3 *Axes* and *Rotation* back to *0* on all 3 *Axes*.

Notice I left *Location* out as *Applying* the *Location* isn't done as often as *Applying Rotation* and *Scale*. I will touch on *Applying Location* later in the chapter. Again, by *Applying* the *Transformation* you are telling *Blender*, it doesn't matter how this *Object* got here, I want to reset its coordinates to the values of a newly added *Object*.

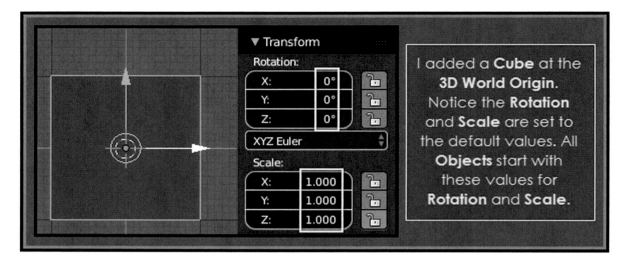

Next I will *Transform* the newly added *Cube*.

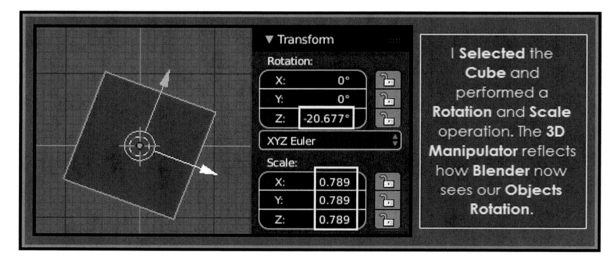

Notice the new values for the *Rotation* and *Scale* are now reflected in the *Transform Panel*. Now I can *Apply* the *Rotation* and *Scale* to set them back to default values.

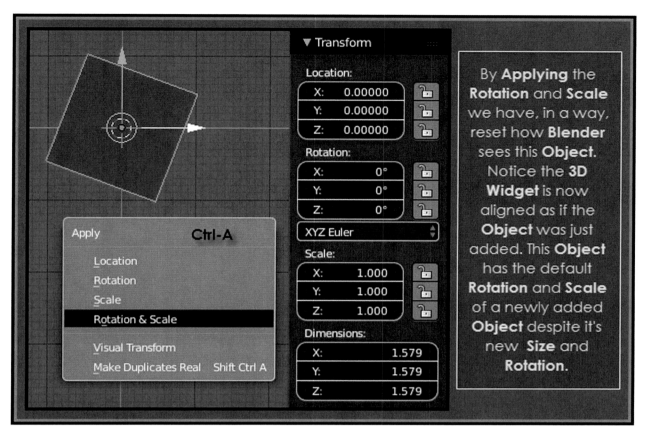

As we can see in the above illustration, *Applying* a *Transform* can be done via the *Apply Menu* which can be accessed using the keyboard shortcut Ctrl + A. It's also available through the *Object->Apply Menu*. By *Applying Rotation* we reset the *Rotation* to *0* degrees for all 3 *Axes* on the currently selected *Object*. By *Applying Scale* we reset the size of the *Object* to *1.0* on all 3 *Axes*. You may have noticed that you can *Apply* both *Rotation* and *Scale* at the same time via the *Apply Menu*. I assume modelers *Apply Rotation* and *Scale* often enough that the creators of *Blender* decided to make performing both operations as easy as 1 menu click away.

When you *Apply Location* on an *Object,* you effectively reset the *Object Center* or *Origin* to the *3D World Origin*. The *Object* itself won't move, just its *Origin*. The *Origin* will be moved to *Location 0,0,0*.

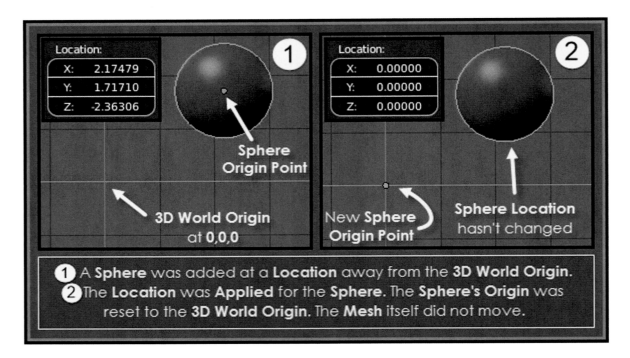

① A **Sphere** was added at a **Location** away from the **3D World Origin**.
② The **Location** was **Applied** for the **Sphere**. The **Sphere's Origin** was reset to the **3D World Origin**. The **Mesh** itself did not move.

It can be clearly seen in the above illustration that *Applying* the Location (Ctrl + A) only changes the *Origin* of the *Object*.

So why *Apply* a *Transformation*? Well, there are lots of reasons, some of which you may never see and consequently may never affect your day to day *Modeling* projects. When it comes to *Mesh Modeling,* having *Objects* whose *Transformations* aren't applied could cause issues with some *Modifiers*, *Constraints* and even some *Tools*. It's particularly important to not *Scale* your *Object* to negative values.

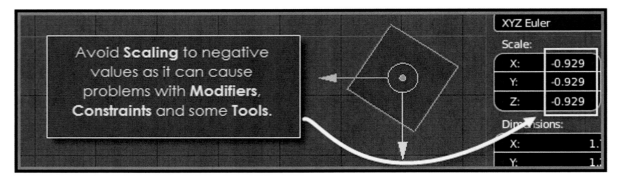

At the end of the day, the best way to avoid possible issues is to *Apply Rotation* and *Scale* on your *Objects* unless you have a good reason not to. In many of the tutorials I have watched or read the person doing the tutorial will *Apply Rotation* and *Scale* on a regular basis. It usually won't matter and everything should work as expected after *Rotating* and *Scaling* an *Object*. I personally *Apply Scale* and *Rotation* often and see it as a preventative measure. Although you may never see it, it will occasionally save you some grief.

Precise Transformations

Blender has several options that allow for more precise *Transform* operations. This is invaluable when you need accuracy during the *Modeling* process.

Numeric Input

You can use numeric values to precisely *Move*, *Rotate* or *Scale* an *Object* or *Mesh*. For *Grab* operations, you simply enter the number of *Blender Units* (assuming *Units* are set to *None*) you want to move after initiating the *Grab* operation (see **Chapter 5 – Units in Blender**). For *Rotation* operations you enter the number of degrees you want to *Rotate*. For *Scale* operations you enter a number to indicate how much you want to *Scale* the *Object* or *Mesh* element.

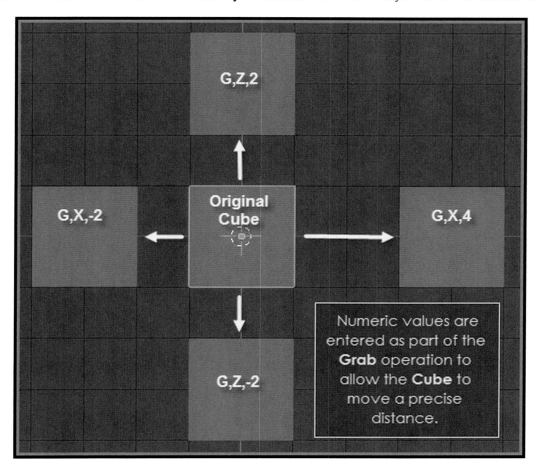

The above illustration demonstrates the result of performing *Grab* operations in *Front View* along an *Axis* and to a precise distance. Notice we enter either positive or negative numbers depending on the desired direction of the *Grab* operation. You don't actually have to constrain the *Grab* operation (or any *Transform* operations for that matter) along an *Axis*. In other words, using *G*, 4 will also work, just maybe not as expected. In *Front View* it appears to default to the positive *X-Axis*.

As mentioned above, *Transformation* using numeric values can be done in *Edit Mode* as well as *Object Mode*. In *Edit Mode*, you select the *Mesh Element* you want to *Transform* and perform the *Transform* operation using numeric values to move the *Mesh Elements* precisely. You aren't restricted to whole numbers; you can enter fractions as well.

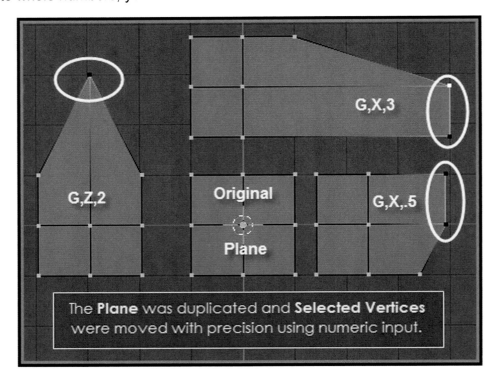

The **Plane** was duplicated and **Selected Vertices** were moved with precision using numeric input.

Some of the *Vertices* in the above illustration were moved a distance of .5. You can get as precise as you want when it comes to the numeric value you enter. Using G, X, .0003 is valid even though you probably won't be able to see that the *Object / Mesh* moved at all. The result that appears on the *Transform Panel* should reflect the precise result of the *Grab* operation if it was performed in *Object Mode*.

When it comes to *Rotation* operations, the value you enter will determine how many degrees to *Rotate*. Entering R, X, 25 will rotate the *Object / Mesh* element 25 degrees on the *X-Axis*.

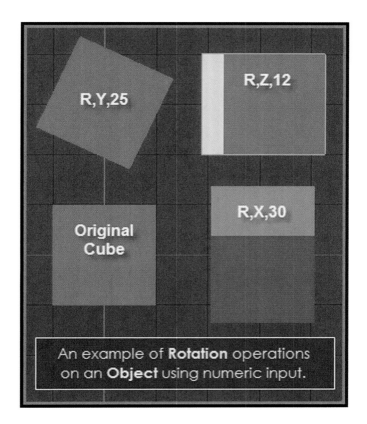

Here is an example on *Selected Mesh Elements*.

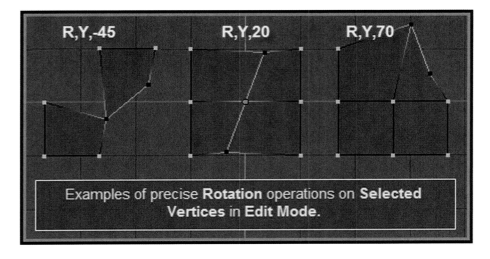

Numeric input during *Scale* operations behaves as you might expect.

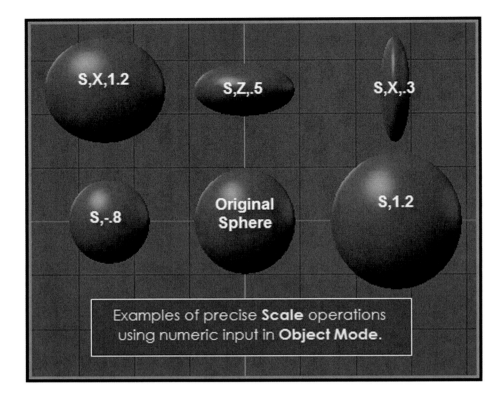

Examples of precise **Scale** operations using numeric input in **Object Mode**.

Here is an example on *Selected Mesh Elements*.

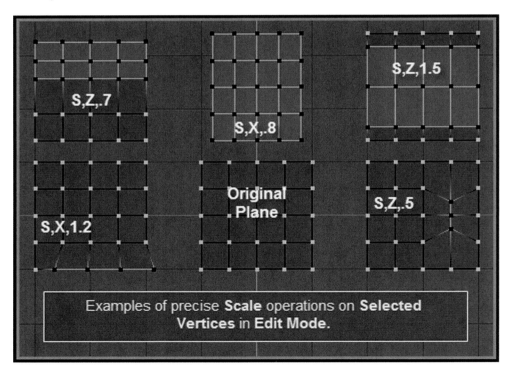

Examples of precise **Scale** operations on **Selected Vertices** in **Edit Mode**.

As you can see numeric input offers the ability to make extremely precise *Transformations*. Remember you can copy and paste from most fields in *Blender* so you can copy the exact *Transformation* value from one *Object* / *Mesh* element and *Paste* it to another. A couple of places where I find this handy are for *Edge Slide* operations (which I talk about later) or to create precise *Spacing*.

Using numeric input is an excellent way to align or flatten a set of *Mesh Elements* along a particular *Axis*. This can be done quickly by performing a *Scale* operation with *Numeric Input* whose value is 0. In other words, if I wanted to align all *Selected Vertices* to the same point along the *Z-Axis* I could press S, Z, 0 on the keyboard to obtain the desired result. The currently selected *Pivot Point* determines where on the *Z-Axis* the *Vertices* will be *Aligned*.

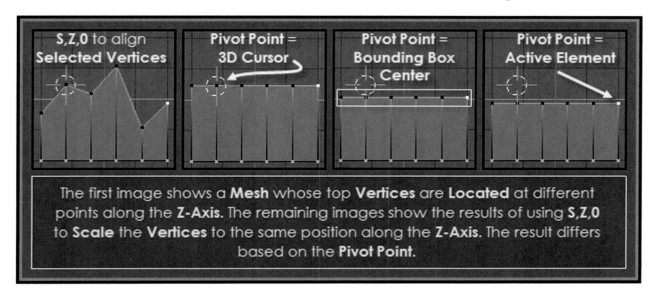

The first image shows a **Mesh** whose top **Vertices** are **Located** at different points along the **Z-Axis**. The remaining images show the results of using S,Z,0 to **Scale** the **Vertices** to the same position along the **Z-Axis**. The result differs based on the **Pivot Point**.

Shift Key

Holding the Shift key while transforming will slow down the *Transform* operation allowing for very fine control. Keep in mind that the *Transform* operation is not being done at any fixed increments so although you gain control, you don't gain precision. You can also use Shift in conjunction with the *3D Manipulators*. You can press Shift anytime during the *Transform* operation. That way you could perform a *Grab* operation moving the *Object* / *Mesh* element quickly and pressing Shift as you get close to the final destination to get the fine control.

Ctrl Key

Using the Ctrl key during *Transform* operations allows you to *Incrementally Transform* an *Object*. This is effectively a *Snapping Mode* option which I discuss further in **Chapter 8 – The Snap To Mesh Tool**. The only thing to remember at this point is that you must have *Increment* selected in the *Snap Menu* for this type of *Transform* operation to behave as expected.

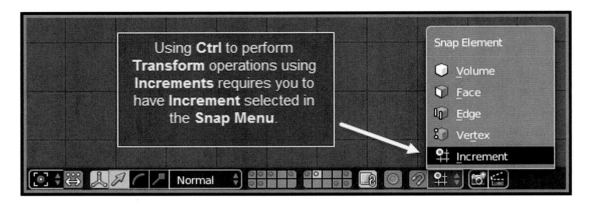

Using Ctrl in conjunction with a *Grab* operation will allow you to move an *Object / Mesh Element* in increments of 1 *Blender Unit*.

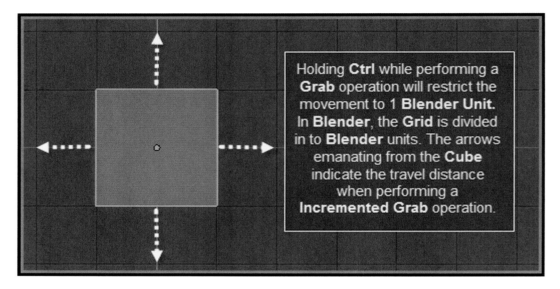

The same results can be seen in *Edit Mode*.

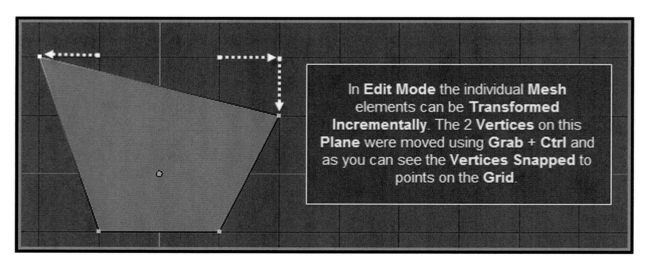

The *Zoom* level also plays a part in how far a *Grab* operation will travel. The *Grid* changes depending on your current *Zoom* level and this affects *Grab* operations. When you *Zoom* in, the *Grid* will be subdivided based on your *Grid* settings. At the default *Zoom* level, 1 *Increment* equals 1 *Blender Unit*. *Zooming* in will cause the *Grid* to be subdivided further and 1 *Increment* will now be equal to 1/10th of a *Blender Unit* and so on.

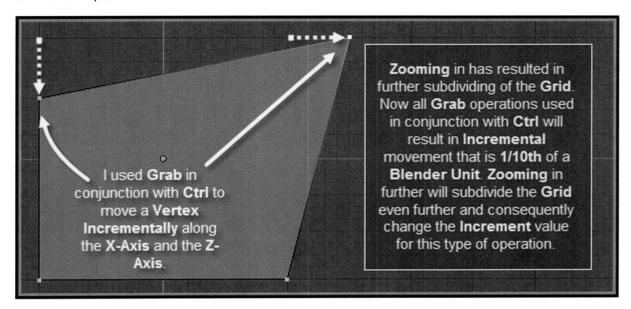

I used **Grab** in conjunction with **Ctrl** to move a **Vertex Incrementally** along the **X-Axis** and the **Z-Axis**.

Zooming in has resulted in further subdividing of the **Grid**. Now all **Grab** operations used in conjunction with **Ctrl** will result in **Incremental** movement that is **1/10th** of a **Blender Unit**. **Zooming** in further will subdivide the **Grid** even further and consequently change the **Increment** value for this type of operation.

Holding down *Ctrl* during *Rotation* operations will allow you to *Rotate* in 5 degree *Increments*.

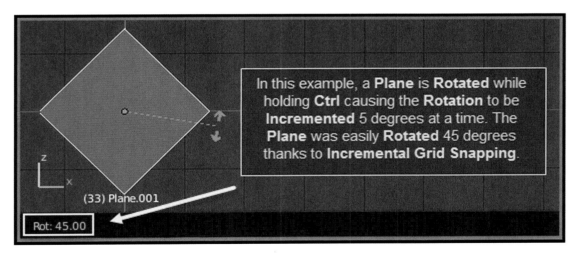

In this example, a **Plane** is **Rotated** while holding **Ctrl** causing the **Rotation** to be **Incremented** 5 degrees at a time. The **Plane** was easily **Rotated** 45 degrees thanks to **Incremental Grid Snapping**.

(33) Plane.001

Rot: 45.00

This can be very handy when you create duplicates of an *Object* and you want to *Rotate* them an equal number of degrees. In the next illustration, I will create a simple flower pattern using *Incremented Rotation*.

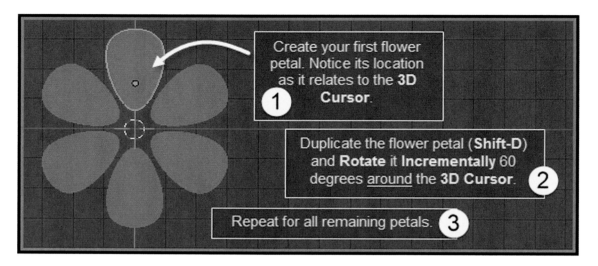

Rotation operations behave the same way in *Edit Mode*. You can *Rotate* any selected *Mesh* elements *Incrementally* using the C̄t̄r̄l̄ key.

When it comes to *Scaling Objects / Mesh Elements*, holding C̄t̄r̄l̄ while *Scaling* will allow you to *Scale* the *Object / Mesh Elements Incrementally* by 0.1 *Blender Unit*. The *Grid Zoom Level* has no effect on the distance of each *Increment* during *Scale* operations as it does with *Grab* operations.

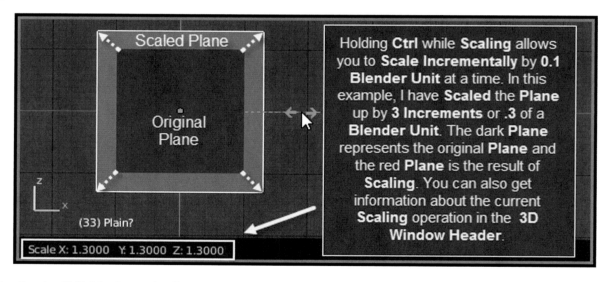

Scaling in *Edit Mode* works the same way as in *Object Mode*.

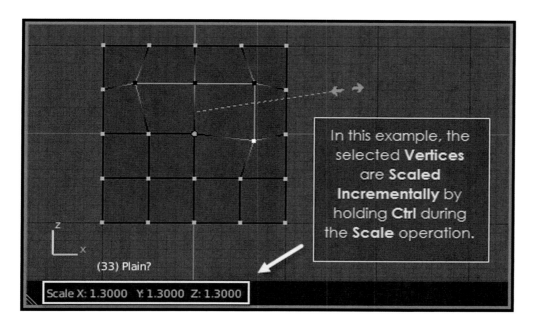

In this example, the selected **Vertices** are **Scaled Incrementally** by holding **Ctrl** during the **Scale** operation.

(33) Plain?

Scale X: 1.3000 Y: 1.3000 Z: 1.3000

Using Ctrl for *Incremental Transform* operation also works with the *3D Manipulators*. Simply hold Ctrl while performing *Transform* operations using the *3D Manipulator* handles to perform *Incremental Transform* operations. You can of course use Ctrl when constraining *Transform* operations along a particular *Axis*. For example, to *Scale Incrementally* along the *X-Axis*, you would press S, X and then hold Ctrl. I find using numeric input more flexible but there are certainly situations where using the Ctrl key can be a time saver.

Ctrl + Shift

Holding Ctrl + Shift during *Transform* operations allows for even finer control over the values used for *Incrimination*.

For *Grab* operations, holding Ctrl + Shift will allow for Incremental movement that is 1/10th of the *Increment* value seen when holding Ctrl. For example, at the default *Zoom* level, holding Ctrl results in *Incremental* movement of 1 *Blender Unit* while holding Ctrl + Shift will result in *Incremental* movement of 1/10th of a *Blender Unit*. The same behavior can be seen at any *Zoom* level. In other words, the value of 1 *Increment* when using Shift + Ctrl is 1/10th the value of 1 *Increment* when using just Ctrl.

For *Rotation* operations, holding Ctrl + Shift will allow you to *Incrementally Rotate* 1 degree at a time. For *Scale* operations, holding Ctrl + Shift will allow you to *Scale* in *Increments* of 0.01 *Blender Unit*. The *Zoom* level plays no role in Ctrl + Shift *Scale* operations.

Operator Panels

Precise values can be entered on the *Operator Panels* for each of the *Transform Tools*. See **Chapter 5 – Transform Tools Operator Panels** for more info on the *Operator Panels* for each *Transform Tool*.

As you can see, *Blender* offers plenty of choices for doing precise operations. Knowing of their existence and how to use them will expand your modelling toolbox immensely. If you haven't done so already, I encourage you to try each of the examples in this portion of the chapter.

3D Transform Manipulators

The *3D Transform Manipulators* are a set of *Widgets* used to perform *Transform Operations*. The added benefit of using the *Manipulators* is that they are automatically constrained along one of 3 *Axes*. There are 3 *Widgets* that allow for *Grab*, *Rotate* and *Scale* operations.

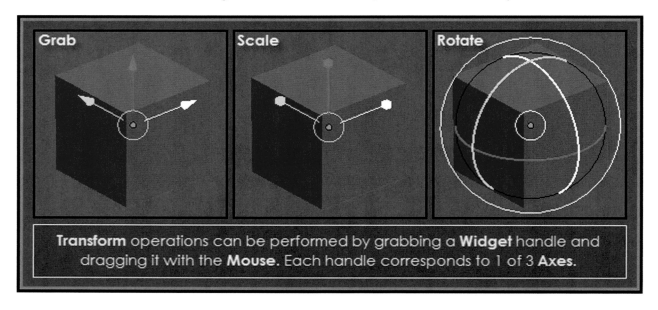

Transform operations can be performed by grabbing a **Widget** handle and dragging it with the **Mouse.** Each handle corresponds to 1 of 3 **Axes.**

As with other *Transform Operations*, you can press the Ctrl and Shift key to get more precision during *Transform* operations using the *Widgets*. You can also get very fine precision using numeric input. Just remember to keep the *Mouse Button* held down when entering any numeric values.

The *Transform Widgets* also works in *Edit Mode*. Select one or more *Mesh Elements* and the *Widget* will *Snap* to a *Location* based on you current *Pivot Point*. Here is an example using 3 different *Pivot Points*.

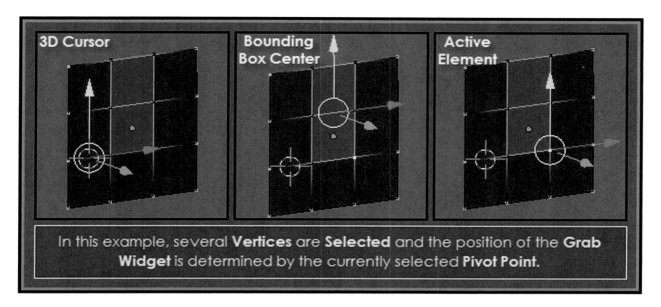

In this example, several **Vertices** are **Selected** and the position of the **Grab Widget** is determined by the currently selected **Pivot Point**.

Here is another example in *Object Mode*.

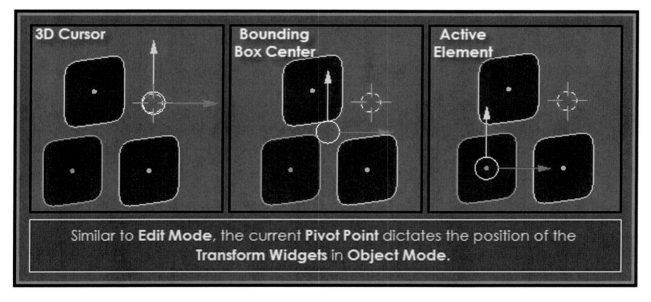

Similar to **Edit Mode**, the current **Pivot Point** dictates the position of the **Transform Widgets** in **Object Mode**.

As I mentioned earlier in this chapter, the *Transform Orientation* also plays a role in how *Blender* positions the *Transform Widgets*.

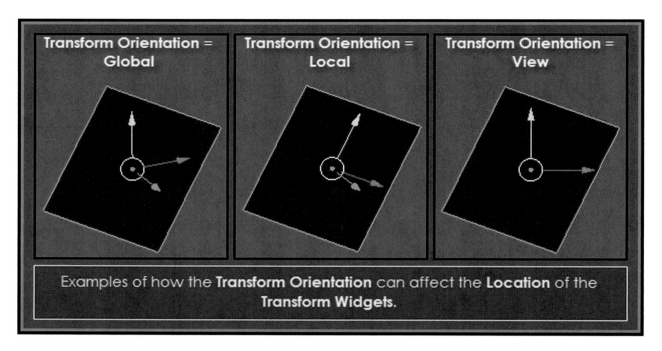

Examples of how the **Transform Orientation** can affect the **Location** of the Transform Widgets.

Between the *Pivot Point* and the *Transform Orientation* you have several options when it comes to the *Location* of the *Transform Widgets*.

I personally don't use the *Transform Widgets* very often. Part of the reason is that I started using *Blender* at a time when the *Transform Widgets* didn't exist. I am used to using the keyboard to do my *Transform Operations*. I also find they can get in the way of what I'm doing. On a side note, I rarely see them used in tutorials. Having said that, they can be very powerful and handy and I encourage you to at least try them to see if they are something you want to incorporate into your workflow.

Aligning Objects

There is functionality in *Blender* that allows you to *Align Objects* along a particular *Axis*. Simply select 2 or more *Objects* and choose *Align Objects* in the *Object->Transform Menu*. You choose which *Axis* to *Align* with in the *Operator Panel* on the *Tools Shelf* or you can open the same panel using F6 immediately after initiating the *Align* operation.

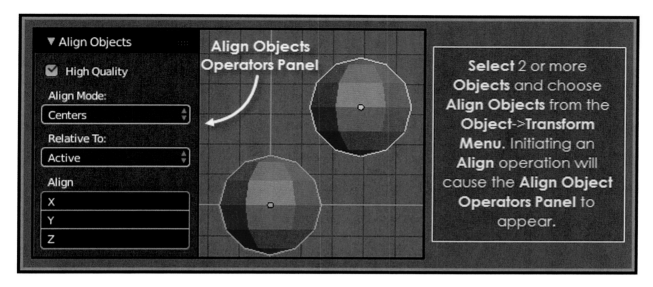

I can now use the *Align Objects Operator Panel* to define which *Axis* to align to as well as choosing how to do the *Alignment* via the *Relative To: Menu*.

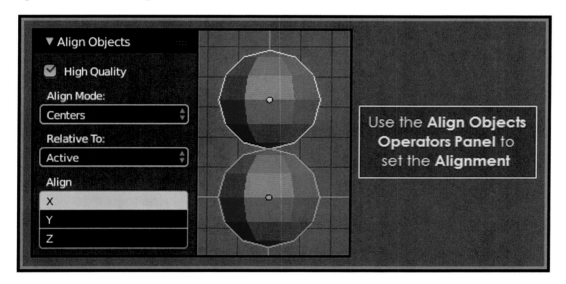

The options are *Align Relative To: Active*, *Selection*, *3D Cursor* and *Scene Origin* (all of which you should be familiar with by now if you read this chapter from the beginning).

Most of the time you can accomplish alignment operations in *Edit Mode* but I have found the ability to *Align Objects* useful in specific situations.

Edge Slide

The *Edge Slide* functionality allows you to *Slide* one or more *Edges* in such a way that they follow the contours of your model. The behavior of the *Edge Slide* is determined by the position of *Faces* that are neighbors of the currently *Selected Edges*. This allows the *Selected Edge Loop* to follow the contours of a *Mesh* without affecting its shape. If I *Select* an *Edge Loop* and perform a regular *Grab* operation, the result will often distort the shape of the mesh. *Edge Loops* are discussed later in the book (see **Chapter 8 – The Loop Cut Tool**) but it's essentially a *Loop* or ring of *Connected Edges*.

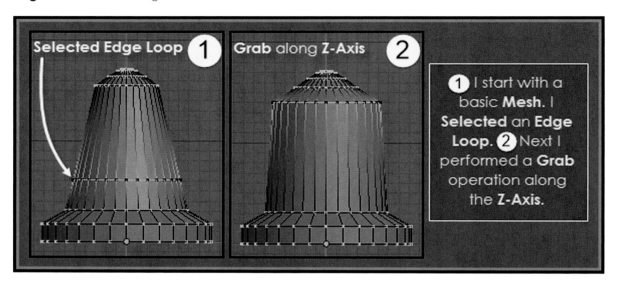

As you can see in the above illustration, performing a *Grab* operation along the *Z-Axis* results in a change to the shape of the *Mesh*. If I wanted to move the *Edge Loop* in such a way that it followed the contours of the *Mesh*, I could perform a *Grab* operation and then use *Scale* to try and keep the shape of the *Mesh* intact. A better solution is to perform an *Edge Slide* operation. To initiate an *Edge Slide* operation you simply use the keyboard shortcut G, G.

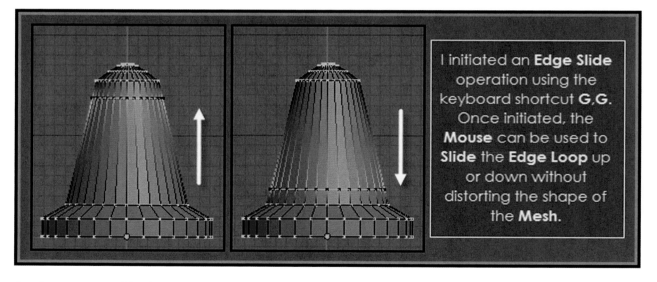

As demonstrated in the above illustration, performing an *Edge Slide* operation allows a user to move the *Edge Loop* without affecting the shape of the *Mesh*. Once the *Edge Loop* is in the desired *Location*, you can press LMB to complete the *Edge Slide* operation. You can also press RMB at any time to cancel the *Edge Slide* operation. You can use Shift for higher precision and Ctrl to enable *Snapping* (see **Chapter 5 – Precise Transformations**).

Edge Slide operations are not restricted to *Edge Loops* and they can be performed on any *Selected Edges*. They can also be performed in both *Vertex* and *Face Mesh Select Mode*.

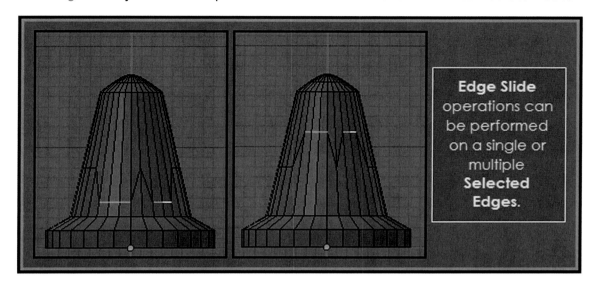

Once an *Edge Slide* is initiated the *3D Window Header* will display information about the *Edge Slide* operation.

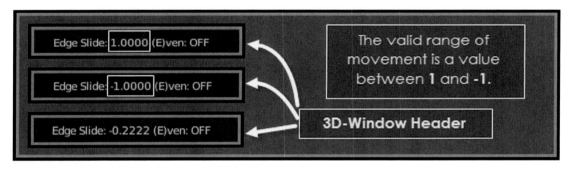

As you can see in the above illustration, the minimum value for an *Edge Slide* is *-1* and the maximum is *1*. You can perform *Precise Edge Slide* operations by entering a numeric value between *-1* and *1* <u>after</u> initiating an *Edge Slide*. (e.g. *.35, -.40* etc.).

By default, *Blender* moves the *Edges* a percentage of distance based on their original position. The result can often be uneven. You may have noticed in the above illustration next to the numeric value is the text *(E)ven: OFF*. As you might have guessed, pressing E during an *Edge Slide* operation turns on the *Even* option which will affect how *Blender* calculates the movement on an *Edge Slide* operation.

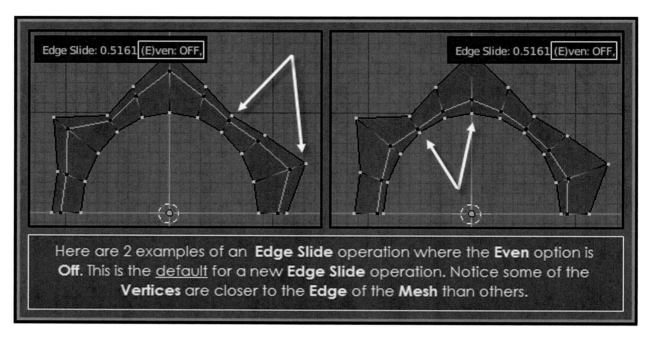

Here are 2 examples of an **Edge Slide** operation where the **Even** option is **Off**. This is the <u>default</u> for a new **Edge Slide** operation. Notice some of the **Vertices** are closer to the **Edge** of the **Mesh** than others.

Is the above illustration we can see during the *Edge Slide* operation that the *Edge Loop* doesn't follow the contour of the neighboring *Edge Loop*. Wouldn't it be nice if there was an option to make the *Edge Slide* more *Evenly* distributed. In case you missed my subtle attempt at humor, the *Even* option can help. Enabling the *Even* option will result in the *Edge Loop* matching the shape of 1 of the neighboring *Edge Loops*. To enable the *Even* option, press E after initiating an *Edge Slide* operation.

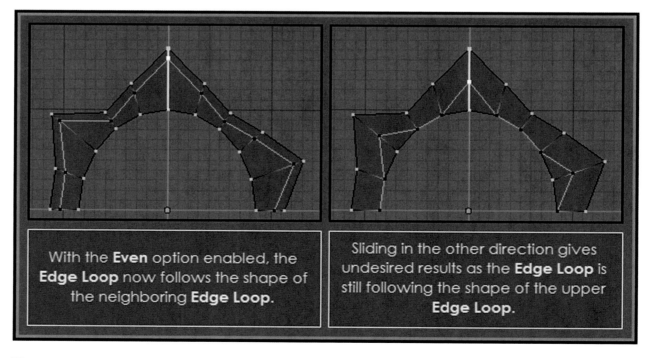

With the **Even** option enabled, the **Edge Loop** now follows the shape of the neighboring **Edge Loop**.

Sliding in the other direction gives undesired results as the **Edge Loop** is still following the shape of the upper **Edge Loop**.

The above illustration is a good example of how using the *Even* option can produce undesired results depending on which neighboring *Edge Loop* is influencing the shape of the *Selected*

Edge Loop. Fortunately, you can indicate which *Edge Loop* should be used to influence the *Edge Slide* result. If you perform an *Edge Slide* operation using the *Even* option and you aren't getting the result you are expecting, you can press F to turn on the *Flipped* option.

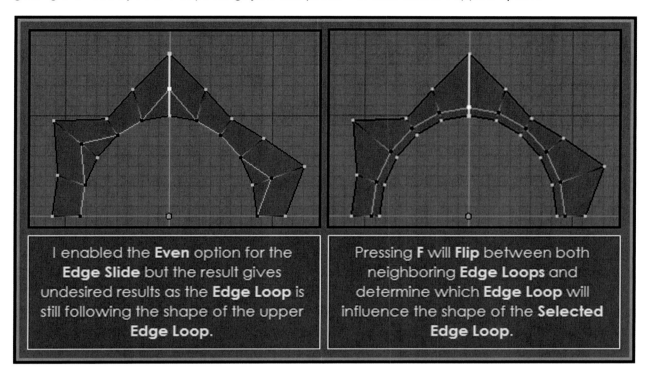

| I enabled the **Even** option for the **Edge Slide** but the result gives undesired results as the **Edge Loop** is still following the shape of the upper **Edge Loop**. | Pressing **F** will **Flip** between both neighboring **Edge Loops** and determine which **Edge Loop** will influence the shape of the **Selected Edge Loop**. |

Just remember that if you are performing an *Edge Slide* operation with the *Even* option on, it's a good idea to toggle F to ensure you are getting the desired result. If both neighboring *Edge Loops* are fairly close in terms of their shape, you may not notice much of a difference but it's still a good habit to get in to in my opinion.

You may have noticed that one of the *Edges* is yellow (the color of the *Edge* may be different depending on your current *Theme*). The yellow *Edge* is the *Edge* that is used to calculate the proportion of the *Edge Slide* in *Even Mode*. It influences how far an *Edge Slide* operation can move when the *Edge Slide* is moving <u>away</u> from the *Edge Loop* that is influencing the currently *Selected Edge Loop*. That's a mouth full. An illustration help clarify things. I will refer to the *Yellow Edge* as the *Selected Edge*.

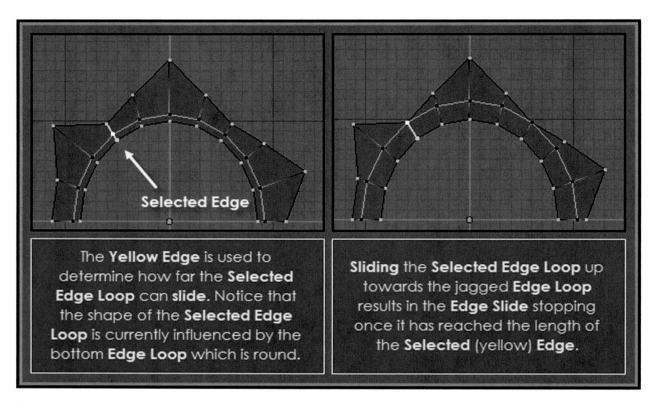

The **Yellow Edge** is used to determine how far the **Selected Edge Loop** can **slide**. Notice that the shape of the **Selected Edge Loop** is currently influenced by the bottom **Edge Loop** which is round.

Sliding the **Selected Edge Loop** up towards the jagged **Edge Loop** results in the **Edge Slide** stopping once it has reached the length of the **Selected** (yellow) **Edge.**

The *Selected Edge Loop* in the above illustration has the *Even* option enabled and its shape is currently influenced by the bottom neighboring *Edge Loop* (that is circular in shape). If you decided to *Slide* the *Edge Loop* toward the bottom *Edge Loop*, the *Selected* (yellow) *Edge* would not significantly affect the *Edge Slide* operation. Sliding it toward the upper *Edge Loop* shows a different result. The *Edge Loop* can only be *Slid* the distance of the *Selected* (yellow) *Edge* and no further. So what happens if a different (yellow) *Edge* is *Selected*? Here is the same *Mesh* with a different *Selected* (yellow) *Edge* is *Selected*.

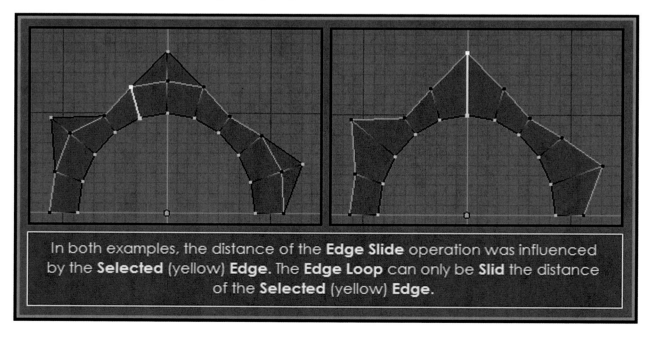

In both examples, the distance of the **Edge Slide** operation was influenced by the **Selected** (yellow) **Edge.** The **Edge Loop** can only be **Slid** the distance of the **Selected** (yellow) **Edge.**

As you can see, if the *Selected* (yellow) *Edge* is the longest available *Edge* the *Selected Edge Loop* can be slid the maximum allowable distance.

Here is an example where the top (jagged) *Edge Loop* is influencing the *Selected Edge Loop* and the *Selected Edge Loop* is moved towards the bottom (circular) *Edge Loop*.

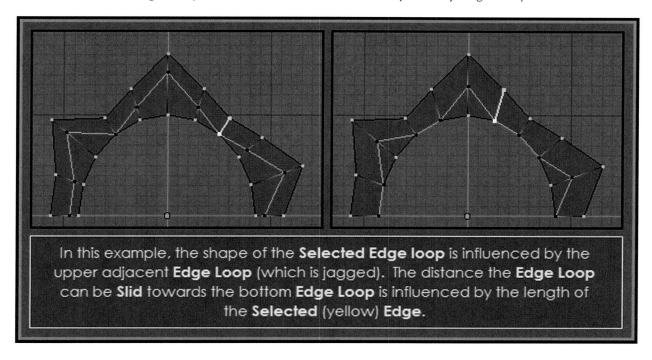

In this example, the shape of the **Selected Edge loop** is influenced by the upper adjacent **Edge Loop** (which is jagged). The distance the **Edge Loop** can be **Slid** towards the bottom **Edge Loop** is influenced by the length of the **Selected** (yellow) **Edge**.

You define which *Edge* becomes the *Selected* (yellow) *Edge* by hovering your mouse cursor over the desired *Edge* <u>before</u> switching to *Even Mode*. I have read that you can change the *Selected Edge* during the *Edge Slide* operation but I was unable to get it working in *Blender 2.74*. To change the *Selected Edge*, I was forced to cancel the *Edge Slide*, hover the mouse cursor over the *Edge* I want to *Select* and initiate a new *Edge Slide* operation.

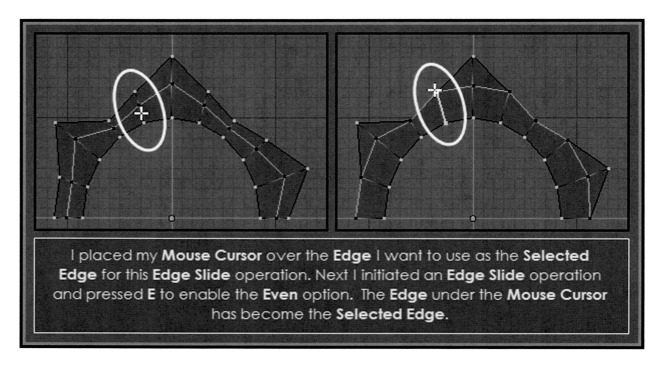

I placed my **Mouse Cursor** over the **Edge** I want to use as the **Selected Edge** for this **Edge Slide** operation. Next I initiated an **Edge Slide** operation and pressed **E** to enable the **Even** option. The **Edge** under the **Mouse Cursor** has become the **Selected Edge.**

Despite what seems like a myriad of options, using *Edge Slide* is pretty easy to use overall. I usually look at the result of a default *Edge Slide*, I then press E and see if it's closer to what I want. It will become second nature it no time.

Vertex Slide

The *Vertex Slide* functionality allows you to *Slide* a *Vertex* along one if it's neighboring *Edges*. To initiate a *Vertex Slide*, select a *Vertex* and press G, G. Once initiated, you can use your mouse to choose which *Edge* to align to.

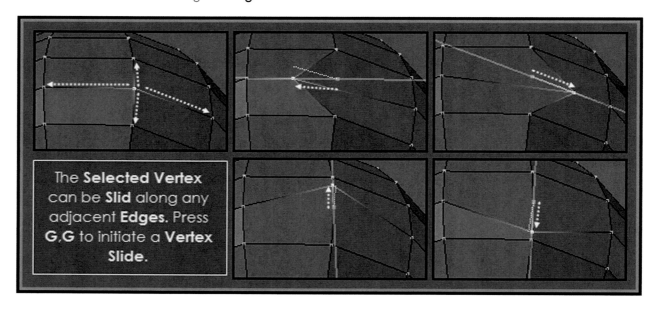

The **Selected Vertex** can be **Slid** along any adjacent **Edges.** Press **G,G** to initiate a **Vertex Slide.**

After initiating a *Vertex Slide*, move the *Mouse* cursor towards any *Edge* to have the *Vertex* align with that *Edge*. Press LMB to complete the *Vertex Slide* operation. During *Vertex Slide* operations, you can use Shift to get higher *Precision* and Ctrl to allow *Snapping*.

Similar to *Edge Sliding*, the details for a *Vertex Slide* can be seen in the *3D Window Header*.

Vert Slide: 0.5949 (E)ven: OFF, Alt or (C)lamp: ON

The valid range for a *Vertex Slide* is between *0* and *1*. You can enter a numeric value for precise *Vertex Slide* operations. The numeric value applies to the *Edge* that the *Vertex* is currently aligned with. *Vertex Slide* has 2 options that are available after initiating a new *Vertex Slide* operation. The first is the *Even* option which, once initiated, also has a *Flip* option. I was unable to find any information about the effect of enabling the *Even* option and I personally couldn't see any difference when I tried it. I will update the book if I get more information. There is also a *Clamp* option which I talk about next.

You can press C or hold Alt during a *Vertex Slide* to toggle *Clamping* mode. When *Clamping* is disabled, the *Vertex* will follow the path of the *Edge* your *Vertex* is currently aligned with. The *Vertex* can even be moved beyond the boundary of the *Edge*. *Clamping* is on by default.

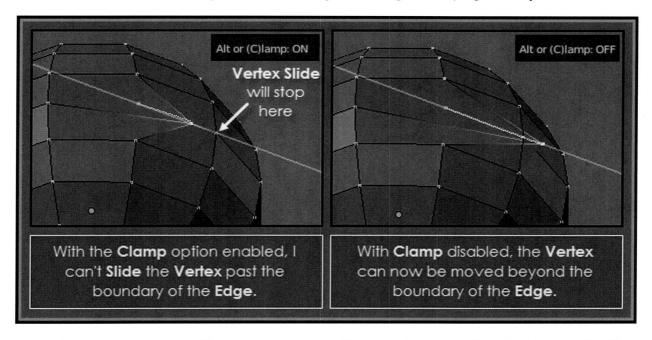

As can be seen in the above illustration, once the *Clamp* option is disabled the *Vertex* will slide beyond the boundary of the *Edge* it's currently aligned to instead of stopping at the boundary of the *Edge*. Keep in mind that it will not follow the shape of the *Mesh* and consequently may not result in a smooth outcome.

I find *Vertex Sliding* useful when fine tuning an *Edge Slide* operation. If, after an *Edge Slide* operation, one or more single *Vertices* aren't quite where I want them I can use *Vertex Slide* to make adjustments 1 *Vertex* at a time.

Chapter 6 - Selection Tools

It's safe to say a large portion of *Modeling* involves *Selecting* and *Transforming* parts of your *Mesh*. *Blender* has several options for *Selecting* and *Transforming Object*(s) / *Mesh Element*(s).

Mesh Select Mode

Before *Selecting* any *Mesh Element* in *Blender* you have to tell *Blender* whether you want to *Select Vertices*, *Edges* or *Faces*. To do this you need to select a *Mesh Select Mode*. The *Mesh Select Mode* can be set by pressing Ctrl+Tab to access the *Mesh Select Mode Menu* while in the *3D View*. There are also icons on the *3D Window Header* that allow you to set the *Mesh Select Mode*.

As you can see in the above illustration, there are 3 options when setting the *Mesh Select Mode*. Actually, there are more than 3 options which I will elaborate on later in this section. You can choose between *Vertex Select Mode*, *Edge Select Mode* and *Face Select Mode*.

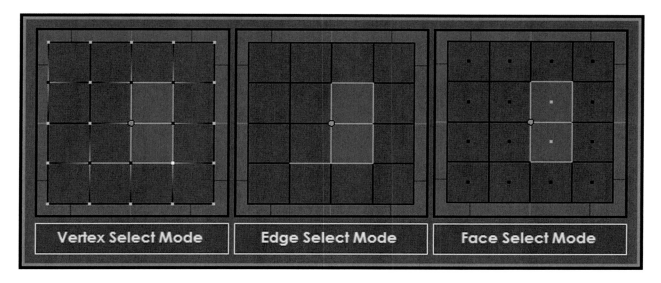

You can also enable multiple *Select Modes* at the same time by holding Shift while selecting a mode either via the *Mesh Select Mode Menu* or the *3D Window Header*. For the menu, you must first press Ctrl + Tab to access the *Mesh Select Mode Menu*, then hold Shift before making your selection.

I will refer to the *Mesh Select Mode* throughout the book. The behavior of many tools and operations are affected by the *Mesh Select Mode* so it helps to be aware of your current *Mesh Select Mode* during the course of *3D Modeling*.

Adding and Removing from a Selection

To select individual *Object(s) / Element(s)* you simply click on an *Object / Mesh Element* with the RMB. Clicking on an *Object / Mesh Element* will make it the currently *Selected* item (and any previously *Selected* items will no longer be *Selected*).

Hold Shift and continue to click to add / remove from the current *Selection*. To be clear, if an item is not part of a *Selection* it will be added to the *Selection*, and if it's already part of a *Selection* it will be removed from the *Selection*.

Active Objects and Elements

As you start adding *Object(s) / Mesh Element(s)* to a *Selection* you will notice that the last item you added has a different color than all other items in the *Selection*. This item is referred to as the *Active Object* in *Object Mode* and *Active Element* in *Edit Mode*. The *Active Object / Element* is very important when using certain tools or performing certain operations. I talk more about the *Active Object / Element* at various times in the book where applicable.

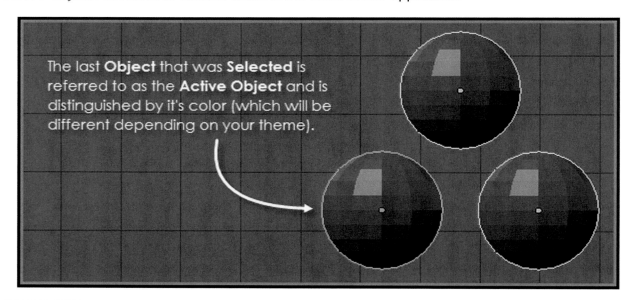

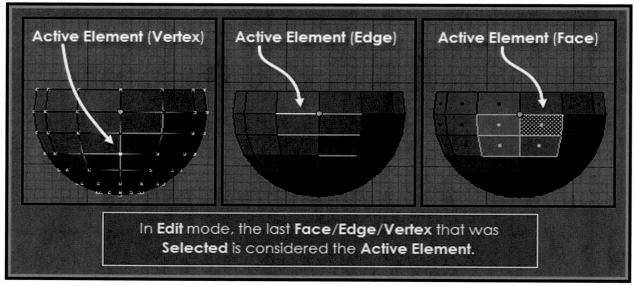

Select All

You can toggle the *Selection / Deselection* of all elements on the screen in *Object Mode* or *Mesh Elements* in *Edit Mode* using the keyboard shortcut A. In *Object Mode*, all elements including *Lamps, Cameras* etc. will be *Selected / Deselected*. In *Edit Mode* all *Elements* of the active *Mesh* will be *Selected / Deselected*.

I often use *Select All* in *Object Mode* when I want to save one or more *Objects* to a *.blend* file. I will put the *Object*(s) I want to save on their own *Layer*. I then select all *Layers* except the *Layer* that contains the *Object*(s) I want to save. I then use the shortcut A to select all *Objects* and then delete all the *Selected Objects*. Now everything except the *Objects* I put in their own *Layer* have been *Deleted*. I can then save the *Objects*(s) to a new *.blend* file.

Select Inverse

The *Select Inverse Selection Tool*, as you would expect, inverts the current selection. The keyboard shortcut for *Select Inverse* is Ctrl + I. It's also available in the *Select Menu*. Once activated, all *Selected Elements* will be *Deselected* and all *Deselected Elements* will be *Selected*. This tool is available in both *Edit* and *Object* mode.

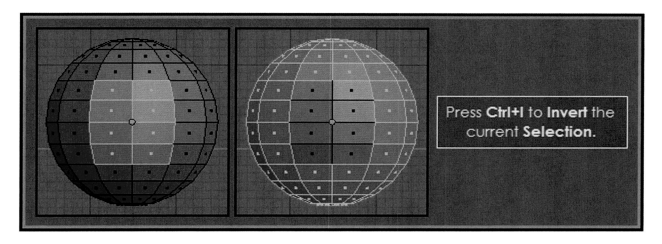

Region Selection Tools

Region Selection Tools allow you to *Select* one or more *Objects / Mesh Elements* in the current *3D View*. *Blender* has a few *Region Selection Tools* but first I need to touch on a setting that affects the result of using the *Region Selection Tools*.

Limit Selection to Visible

The *Limit Selection to Visible* setting determines how much of a *Mesh* is *Selected* by the *Selection Tools*. You can toggle between *Selecting* the *Mesh Elements* that can be seen in the current *View* or all *Mesh Elements*. In other words, *Selecting Mesh Elements* with *Limit Selection to Visible* enabled will result in only the front facing *Mesh Elements* being *Selected*. By front facing I mean *Mesh Elements* that are visible in the current *3D View*. With *Limit Selection to Visible* disabled, any *Mesh Elements* that are within the *Selection Box* will be *Selected* whether they are front facing or not.

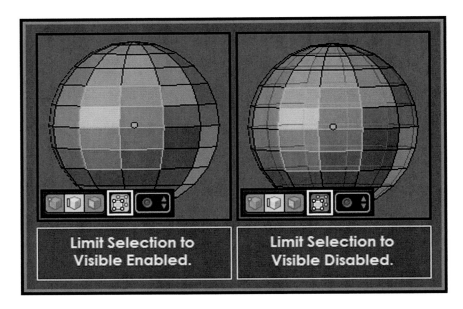

As you can see in the above illustration, when *Limit Selection to Visible* is disabled, the *Selection Tool* will add *Faces* from both the front and back of the *Mesh* to the *Selection*.

You need to keep an eye on this setting as often you don't realized the setting is disabled and you end up inadvertently *Selecting* and *Transforming Mesh Elements* you hadn't intended.

Border Region Select

Border Select allows you to draw a box around one or more *Objects* or *Mesh Elements*. Any items that touch or lie within the box become part of the *Selection*. Press B and then press and hold the LMB and drag to create a *Selection Box*. Hold Shift before dragging to deselect *Object(s)* / *Mesh Element(s)*.

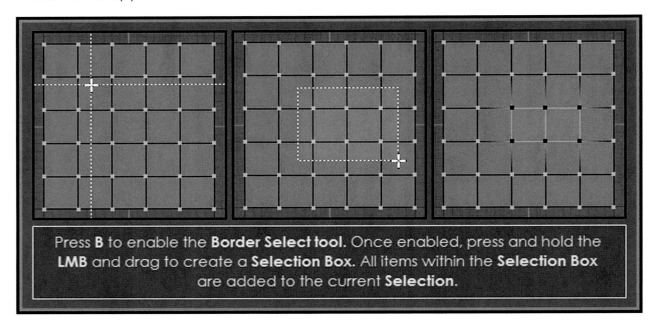

Press **B** to enable the **Border Select tool**. Once enabled, press and hold the **LMB** and drag to create a **Selection Box**. All items within the **Selection Box** are added to the current **Selection**.

You could of course press B again to add or remove *Vertices* from the current *Selection*. You can use any of the *Region Selection Tools* to add or remove *Objects* or *Mesh Elements* at any time.

In *Object Mode*, any *Objects* within the *Selection Box* will be added to the current *Selection*. Even if only a portion of the *Object* is in the *Selection Box*, it will still be added to the current *Selection*. The *Object Origin* plays no role with this *Selection Tool*.

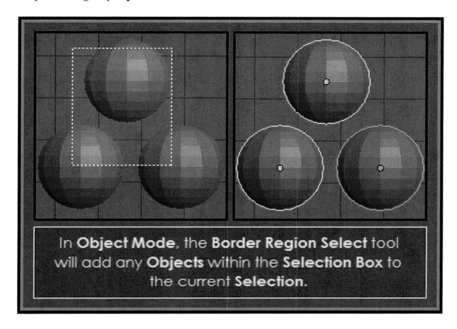

In **Object Mode**, the **Border Region Select** tool will add any **Objects** within the **Selection Box** to the current **Selection**.

Circle Region Select

Pressing C will activate the *Circle Select Tool* and results in a circle with a small cross in the center. Place the circle over the *Object(s) / Mesh Element(s)* you want to *Select* and press and hold the LMB to begin *Selecting*. You can modify the size of the *Selection Circle* using the *Mouse Wheel* or NumPad + / NumPad -. Hold Shift before pressing LMB to deselect *Object(s) / Mesh Element(s)*.

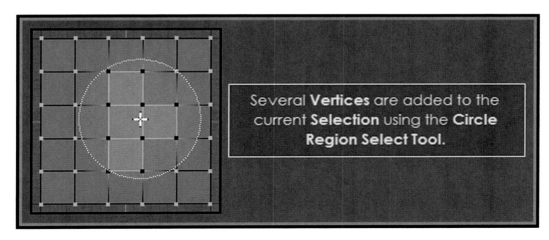

Several **Vertices** are added to the current **Selection** using the **Circle Region Select Tool**.

Using the *Circle Select Tool* in *Object Mode* behaves slightly differently than the *Border Select Tool*. With the *Border Select Tool* any *Objects* within the *Selection* region will be added to the current *Selection*. The *Circle Select Tool* will only include *Object's* whose *Origin* falls within the *Circular Selection Region*.

Lasso Region Select

The *Lasso Selection Tool* allows you to *Select* a *Region* by drawing the *Selection Region* using Ctrl+LMB. Any *Object(s)* / *Mesh Element(s)* within the *Region* will be added to the current *Selection*. You can *Deselect Object(s)* / *Mesh Element(s)* using Ctrl+Shit+LMB and dragging to create a *Selection Region*.

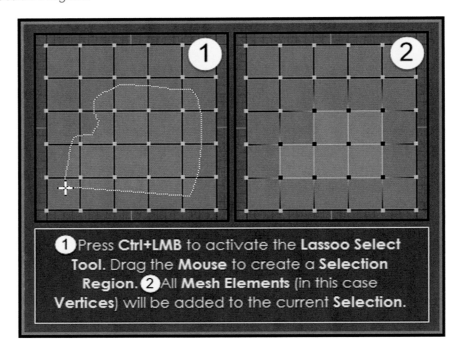

❶Press **Ctrl+LMB** to activate the **Lassoo Select Tool.** Drag the **Mouse** to create a **Selection Region.** ❷All **Mesh Elements** (in this case **Vertices**) will be added to the current **Selection.**

Using the *Lasso Select Tool* in *Object Mode* behaves similarly to the results you get from the *Circle Select Tool*. The *Lasso Select Tool* will only include *Objects* whose *Origins* falls within the *Selection Region*.

Select Linked

The *Select Linked Selection Tool* allows you to *Select* all *Vertices* / *Edges* / *Faces* connected to the currently selected *Mesh Element*. This tool is especially helpful when you have a complex *Mesh* with several groups of disconnected *Vertices*. You can use the *Select Linked Tool* to select all *Vertices* from one section of your *Mesh*. You can then isolate the *Selected Mesh Elements* making it easier to work on them.

There are 2 ways to select *Linked Mesh Elements*. The first is to *Select* an *Element* and then press Ctrl+L to *Select* all *Mesh Elements* connected to that *Element*.

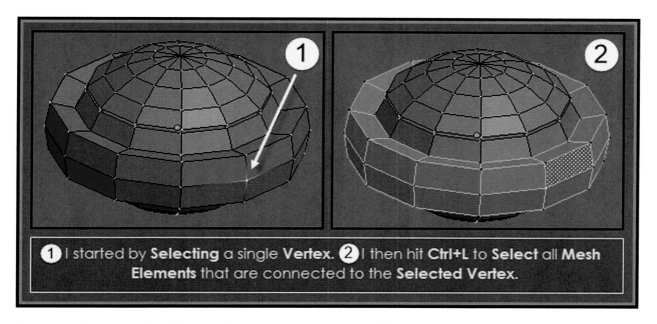

I started by **Selecting** a single **Vertex.** ② I then hit **Ctrl+L** to **Select** all **Mesh Elements** that are connected to the **Selected Vertex.**

You can also hover the *Mouse Cursor* over any *Vertex / Edge / Face* of a *Mesh* and use the shortcut L and *Blender* will attempt to identify the *Mesh Element* under your cursor and *Select* all connected *Elements*. This method is slightly prone to error (almost always human) but I have found it works as you would expect most of the time and you will start to understand the nuances of the tool with experience.

You can also remove *Linked* mesh elements from your current *Selection* by hovering your mouse cursor over any *Vertex / Edge / Face* and using the Shift + L shortcut.

Select Less / More

Blender allows you to increase or decrease your current *Selection* by selecting the immediate neighbors of the currently *Selected Mesh Elements*. In other words, you can expand or collapse your *Selection* based on the outer boundaries of the current *Selection*. This works in all 3 selection modes. The shortcut to *Select Less / More* is Ctrl + [Numpad +] / Ctrl + [Numpad -] i.e. The Ctrl key plus the + or - key on the number pad. I put the Numpad portion of the shortcut in brackets so that there is no confusion around the + and -.

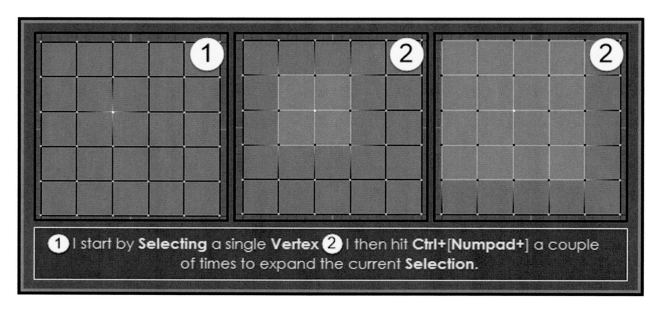

1 I start by **Selecting** a single **Vertex** 2 I then hit **Ctrl+[Numpad+]** a couple of times to expand the current **Selection**.

The result of a *Select Less* operation may be a little unexpected depending on what *Mesh Elements* you have *Selected*. I find the result shrinking the *Selection* hard to predict.

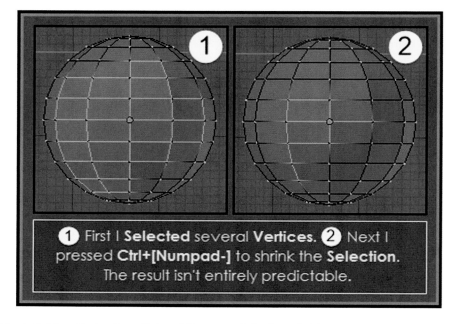

1 First I **Selected** several **Vertices**. 2 Next I pressed **Ctrl+[Numpad-]** to shrink the **Selection**. The result isn't entirely predictable.

I find this tool helpful for *Selecting Edge Rings* and their neighbors.

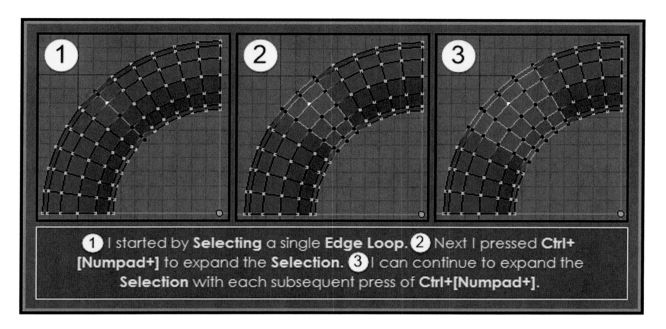

1 I started by **Selecting** a single **Edge Loop**. **2** Next I pressed **Ctrl+[Numpad+]** to expand the **Selection**. **3** I can continue to expand the **Selection** with each subsequent press of **Ctrl+[Numpad+]**.

As you can see in the above illustration, *Selecting Mesh Elements* using Ctrl + Numpad + or - gives a nice clean result.

I often use the *Select More Tool* to help me isolate a portion of the *Mesh* I want to work on. I will *Select* the *Mesh Elements* I want to work on, use *Select More* to expand the *Selection*, and then hide any *Non-Selected Mesh Element* (Shift + H). I can then work on a specific portion of the *Mesh* without having to deal with the surrounding *Mesh Elements* inhibiting my view. To demonstrate I will *Select* and expand several *Mesh Elements*.

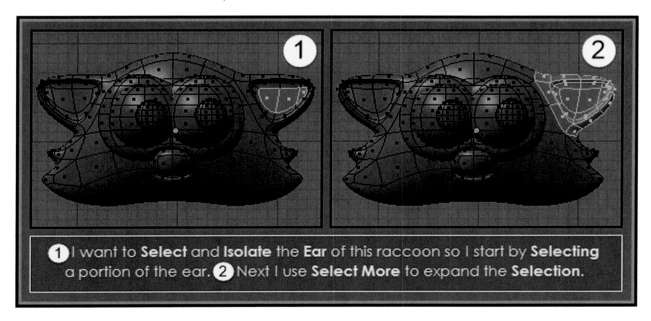

1 I want to **Select** and **Isolate** the **Ear** of this raccoon so I start by **Selecting** a portion of the ear. **2** Next I use **Select More** to expand the **Selection**.

Now I can *Hide Non-Selected Mesh Elements* allowing me to focus on the ear.

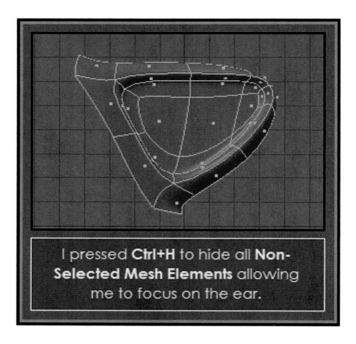

I pressed **Ctrl+H** to hide all **Non-Selected Mesh Elements** allowing me to focus on the ear.

Select Edge Loop

The *Select Edge Loop Tool* will allow you to select a ring or loop of *Edges* that are connected in a line end to end. You can select an *Edge Loop* by clicking Alt + RMB on an *Edge* or *Vertex* in *Edge Selection Mode*. More specifically, click on an *Edge* that is part of the *Edge Loop* you want to *Select*. You can *Select* multiple *Edge Loops* with Shift + Alt + RMB.

The result of a *Select Edge Loop* operation will depend on the topology of the *Loop*. If the *Loop* is closed, the entire *Loop* will be selected. If the *Loop* is open, the *Loop* will terminate at any point that is connected to more than 4 *Edges*.

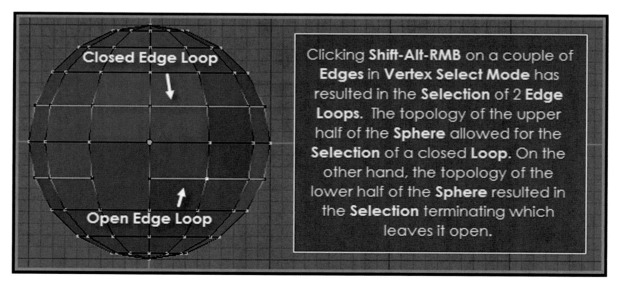

Clicking **Shift-Alt-RMB** on a couple of **Edges** in **Vertex Select Mode** has resulted in the **Selection** of 2 **Edge Loops**. The topology of the upper half of the **Sphere** allowed for the **Selection** of a closed **Loop**. On the other hand, the topology of the lower half of the **Sphere** resulted in the **Selection** terminating which leaves it open.

If you have done any *3D Modeling* in *Blender*, you know what an *Edge Loop* is because you have probably used them numerous times. *Edge Loops* are one of the primary tools you will use to add geometry and being able to select *Edge Loops* is a necessity as manually selecting an *Edge Loop* would be an exercise in frustration. I talk about more about creating *Edge Loops* in a later chapter – see **Chapter 8 – The Loop Cut Tool**.

Select Face Loop

The *Select Face Loop Tool* will allow you to *Select* a ring or *Loop* of *Faces* that are connected in a line end to end. You can select a *Face Loop* by using Alt + RMB to click on the *Edge* of a *Face* in *Face Select Mode*. The *Edge* you select will determine the direction of the *Face Loop*. You can continue to add *Face Loops* to the *Selection* using the Shift + Alt + RMB shortcut.

Many of the rules and properties of this tool are very similar to those of the *Select Edge Loop Tool*. The topology of the mesh will determine the results of the *Select Face Loop Tool*. If the *Loop* is closed, the entire *Loop* will be selected. If the *Loop* is open, the *Loop* will terminate at the point where the *Face Loop* can no longer continue based on the algorithm used to calculate a *Face Loop*. On a side note, I have no understanding of such algorithms as I got a **B-** in Math.

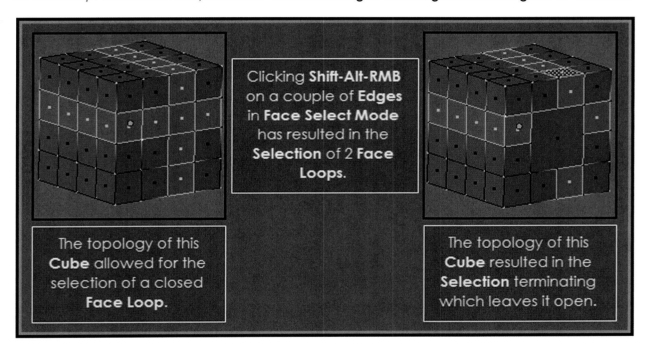

Clicking **Shift-Alt-RMB** on a couple of **Edges** in **Face Select Mode** has resulted in the **Selection** of 2 **Face Loops.**

The topology of this **Cube** allowed for the selection of a closed **Face Loop.**

The topology of this **Cube** resulted in the **Selection** terminating which leaves it open.

Select Boundary Loop

The *Select Boundary Loop Tool* will *Select* the outer edges of any selected *Faces* or group of *Faces*. To use *Select Boundary Loop*, open the *Edges Menu* (using Ctrl + E) and choose *Select Boundary Loop* from the *Menu*. Invoking *Select Boundary Loop* will switch you to *Edge Select Mode* and all *Edges* that represent the *Selection* boundary will be highlighted.

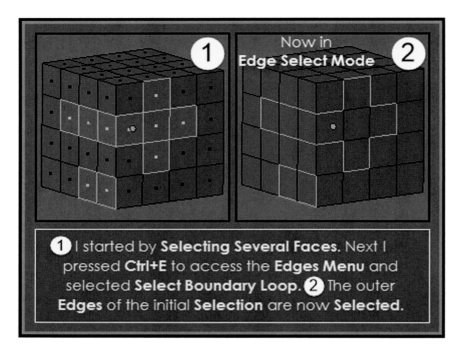

Select Loop Inner Region

The *Select Loop Inner Region Tool* will select all *Mesh Elements* that are enclosed in a *Selection* comprised of *Edges*. In other words, if you *Select Mesh Elements* in *Edge Select Mode* and those *Elements* form a closed *Loop*, *Select Loop Inner Region* will select all *Edges* within that *Loop*.

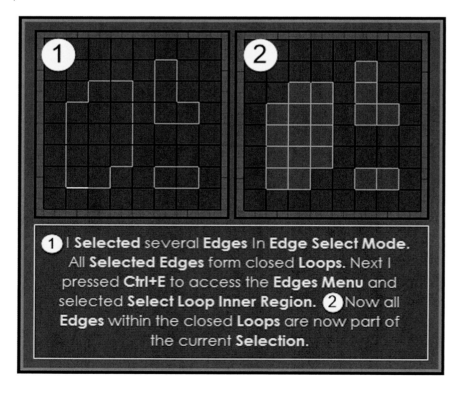

Select Loop Inner Region will often yield unexpected results and should probably be avoided. If none of the *Selected Mesh Elements* form a closed *Loop* the results will include all connected *Edges* which usually results in *Selecting* the entire *Mesh*. Having some *Selected Mesh Elements* form a closed *Loop* and some not could also yield unexpected results.

Select Edge Ring

The *Select Edge Ring Tool* allows you to select a row of *Edges* that are parallel to the *Edge* or *Edges* you currently have selected. The *Edges* that are added to the *Selection* run along the *Face Loop* for the selected *Edge*. This tool is easier to demonstrate than it is to explain. First I will select an *Edge Ring* using the *Edges Menu*.

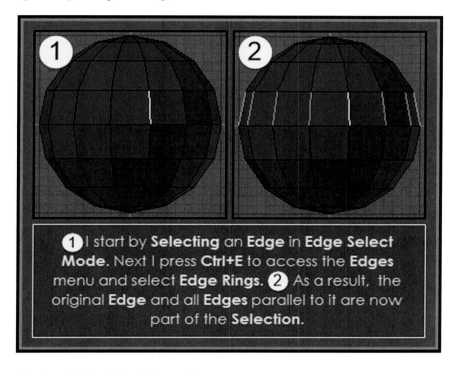

① I start by **Selecting** an **Edge** in **Edge Select Mode**. Next I press **Ctrl+E** to access the **Edges** menu and select **Edge Rings**. **②** As a result, the original **Edge** and all **Edges** parallel to it are now part of the **Selection**.

You can also select multiple *Edge Rings* at once.

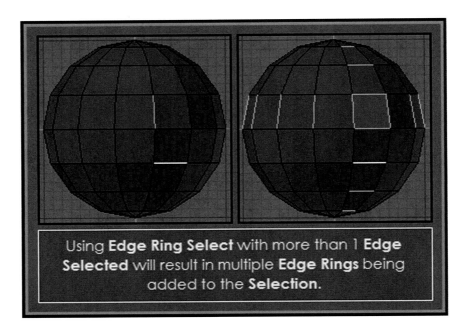

Using **Edge Ring Select** with more than 1 **Edge Selected** will result in multiple **Edge Rings** being added to the **Selection.**

You can also select an *Edge Ring* directly using the mouse by pressing and holding Ctrl + Alt before selecting an *Edge* with the RMB. Holding Ctrl + Alt + Shift before selecting an *Edge* will add an *Edge Ring* to the current *Selection*.

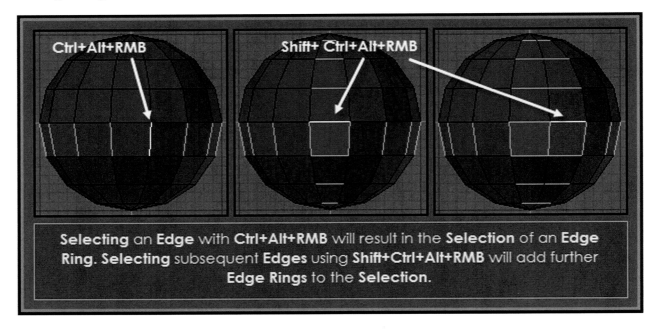

Selecting an **Edge** with **Ctrl+Alt+RMB** will result in the **Selection** of an **Edge Ring. Selecting** subsequent **Edges** using **Shift+Ctrl+Alt+RMB** will add further **Edge Rings** to the **Selection.**

Select Mirror

The *Select Mirror Selection Tool* allows you to *Select* one or more *Vertices / Edges / Faces* at the *Mirrored Location* along the *X-Axis* of the currently *Selected Mesh Element*. If no *Mesh Element* exists in what *Blender* considers the *Mirrored Location*, no *Mesh Element* will be *Selected*. This operation causes the original *Mesh Element* to be *De-Selected*. The *Pivot Point* of the *Mesh* you are attempting the *Select Mirror* operation on plays a role in getting results.

Select Mirror appears to calculate whether a *Mesh Element* has a valid *Mirror* result based on the position of the *Pivot Point*.

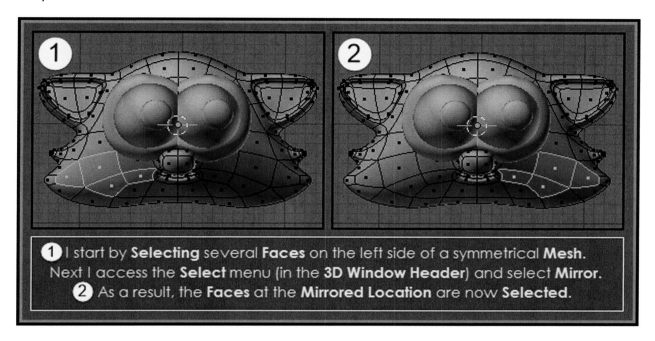

1 I start by **Selecting** several **Faces** on the left side of a symmetrical **Mesh**. Next I access the **Select** menu (in the **3D Window Header**) and select **Mirror**. **2** As a result, the **Faces** at the **Mirrored Location** are now **Selected**.

Checker Deselect

The *Checker Deselect Selection Tool* will *De-Select* alternating *Faces* based on the current *Selection*. The result is a *Selection* that resembles a checker pattern.

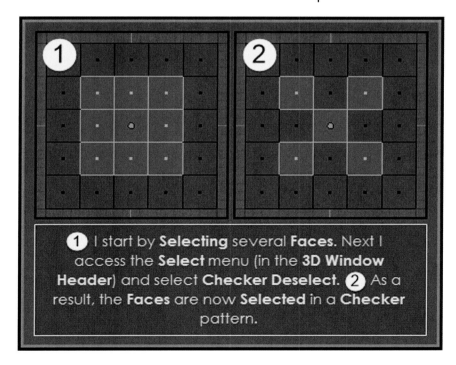

1 I start by **Selecting** several **Faces**. Next I access the **Select** menu (in the **3D Window Header**) and select **Checker Deselect**. **2** As a result, the **Faces** are now **Selected** in a **Checker** pattern.

I recently used *Checker Deselect* to help me model a very basic castle.

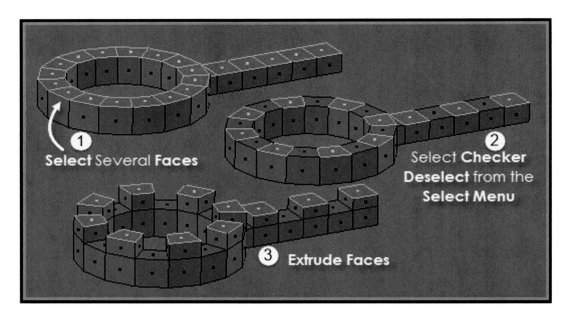

As you can see in the above illustration I was able to create the beginnings of a castle wall and turret with very little effort.

Select Menu

There are times when you might want to *Select* an *Object* that might be behind 1 or more *Objects*. In *Blender* you can bring up a *Select Menu* in *Object Mode* that allows you to *Select* an *Object* among a group of overlapping *Objects*. The *Objects* don't need to touch one another as long as they overlap in your current *3D View*.

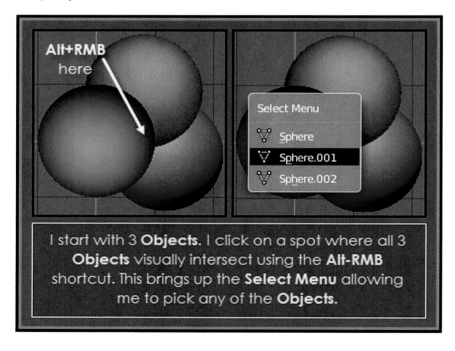

Hiding Objects and Elements

Blender allows you to *Hide* and *Unhide Elements* of your *Scene* in both *Edit* and *Object Mode*. The most obvious use for *Hiding* is to reduce clutter allowing you to focus on 1 *Element* of the *Scene*.

- H = *Hide Selected* - *Hide Selected Objects* or *Selected Elements* of a *Mesh*
- Shift + H = *Hide Un-Selected* - Hide any *Objects* or *Mesh Elements* that aren't currently *Selected*
- Alt + H = *Show* or *Reveal Hidden* - all *Hidden Objects* or *Mesh Elements* are *Unhidden*.

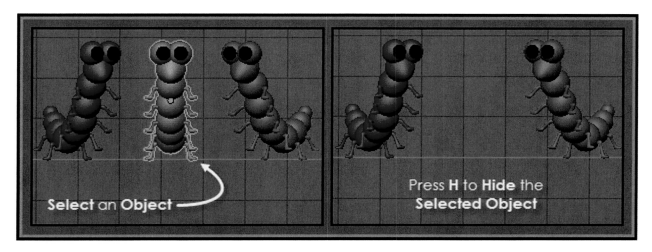

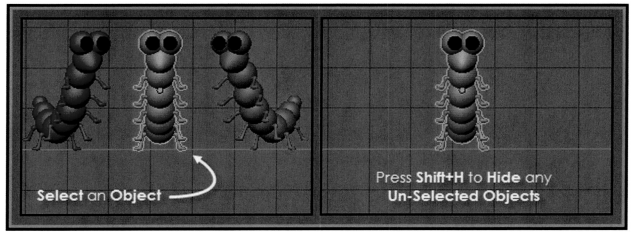

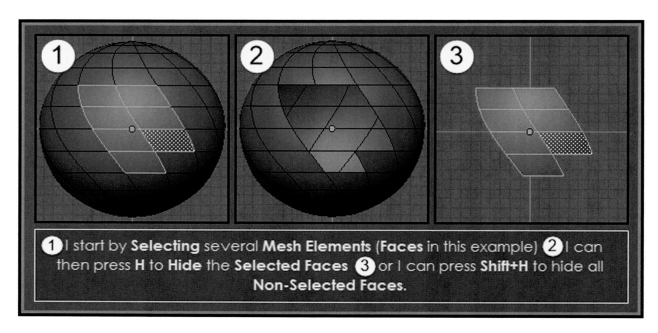

① I start by **Selecting** several **Mesh Elements (Faces** in this example) ② I can then press **H** to **Hide** the **Selected Faces** ③ or I can press **Shift+H** to hide all **Non-Selected Faces.**

One thing to keep in mind is that any *Elements* of a *Mesh* that are *Hidden* will not be affected by use of certain tools like the *Proportional Editing Tool* or when creating *Loop Cuts*. This can both and advantage and disadvantage depending on what you are trying to accomplish.

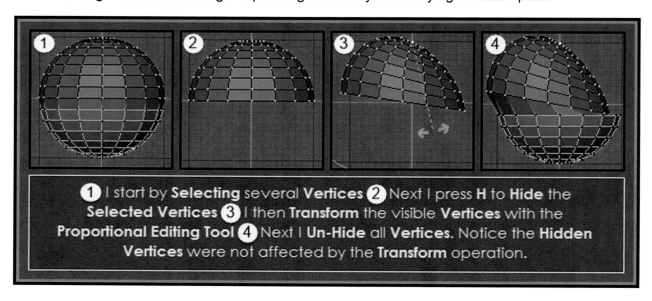

① I start by **Selecting** several **Vertices** ② Next I press **H** to **Hide** the **Selected Vertices** ③ I then **Transform** the visible **Vertices** with the **Proportional Editing Tool** ④ Next I **Un-Hide** all **Vertices**. Notice the **Hidden Vertices** were not affected by the **Transform** operation.

The above diagram shows the result of *Editing* a *Sphere* that has *Hidden Vertices*. There may be times when only affecting part of a *Mesh* is desirable. Another example is when *Smoothing* out a portion of a *Mesh*. You can hide *Vertices* to ensure the *Smoothing* operation is confined to the desired area. Just remember that *Hidden Vertices* are not affected by *Mesh Editing* operations.

You need to be careful when working with *Hidden Vertices* as it's easy to add undesirable geometry to you *Mesh* when a portion of it is hidden. Here is an example using a *Loop Cut* operation (for more on *Loop Cuts* see **Chapter 8 – The Loop Cut Tool).**

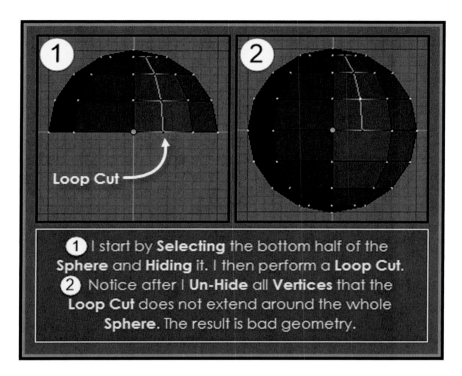

1 I start by **Selecting** the bottom half of the **Sphere** and **Hiding** it. I then perform a **Loop Cut**.
2 Notice after I **Un-Hide** all **Vertices** that the **Loop Cut** does not extend around the whole **Sphere**. The result is bad geometry.

I often use the *Isolate* and *Hiding* functionality in conjunction with each other. If I need to *Hide* all *Objects* except the currently *Selected Object*, I will just *Select* and *Isolate* the *Object* (Numpad/) which will produce the same result as using Shift + H. I can then go into *Edit Mode* and use the *Hide* functionality to *Hide Mesh Elements* as needed.

There are times when you are working on a *Mesh* and the back portion of the *Mesh* is visible either through a hole in the front of the *Mesh* or because *Elements* at the front of the *Mesh* are *Hidden*. I often use the *Hide* functionality to *Hide* the back of a *Mesh* so I can work on the front without risking *Selecting* a back *Element*. I also find it less cluttered.

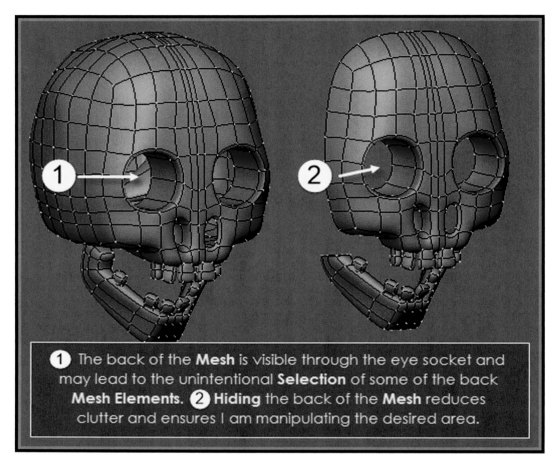

① The back of the **Mesh** is visible through the eye socket and may lead to the unintentional **Selection** of some of the back **Mesh Elements.** ② **Hiding** the back of the **Mesh** reduces clutter and ensures I am manipulating the desired area.

You can *Hide* / *Unhide* items in the *Outliner*. When you hide an *Object* using the H key, the *Object* will also appear as *Hidden* in the *Outliner* (see **Chapter 2 – Outliner**).

The Clipping Border Tool

The *Clipping Border Tool* is another interesting tool that allows you to *Hide* a portion of the viewing area. Alt + B will activate the tool and allow you to draw a box using the LMB. The result is like cutting a box into the *Scene*. The interior of a *Mesh* is visible and although I don't use this shortcut often I find the result both interesting and mildly disturbing ☺. Pressing Alt + B will cancel the *Clipping*.

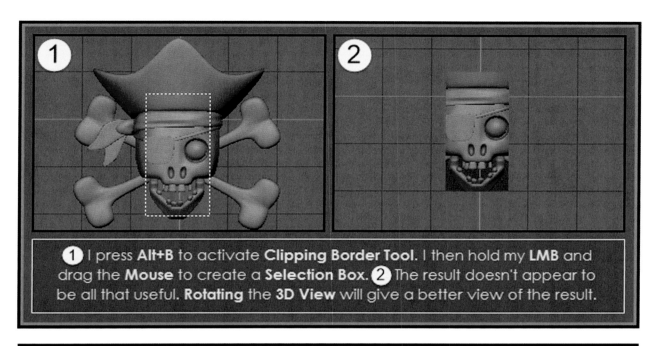

1 I press **Alt+B** to activate **Clipping Border Tool.** I then hold my **LMB** and drag the **Mouse** to create a **Selection Box.** 2 The result doesn't appear to be all that useful. **Rotating** the **3D View** will give a better view of the result.

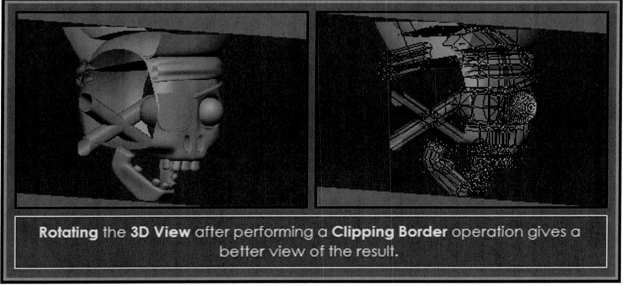

Rotating the **3D View** after performing a **Clipping Border** operation gives a better view of the result.

As you can see, the *Clipping Border Tool* acts like a virtual scalpel. If you need to perform an autopsy on your *Mesh*, accept no substitutes.

Chapter 7 - Tools and Editing

The Mirror Tool

Blender has a *Mirror Modifier* and it will be what you use most of the time for *Mirroring* a *Mesh* but there are times when you simply want to *Mirror* one half of the *Mesh* without using the *Mirror Modifier* (see **Chapter 9 – The Mirror Tool**). The big difference is the *Mirror Modifier* allows you to continue *Modeling* were as using the *Mirror Tool* is a onetime operation. You might want to do a *Mirror* operation when you are done *Modeling* one side of a *Mesh* and you want to *Mirror* those changes to the other side of the *Mesh*. This all assumes a symmetric *Mesh* of course. You can perform a *Mirror* operation using the Ctrl+M shortcut.

Here is an end to end example. I omitted a few steps which I will talk about later in the section.

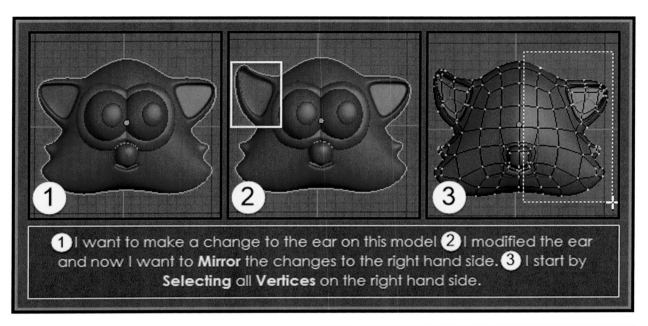

1 I want to make a change to the ear on this model **2** I modified the ear and now I want to **Mirror** the changes to the right hand side. **3** I start by **Selecting** all **Vertices** on the right hand side.

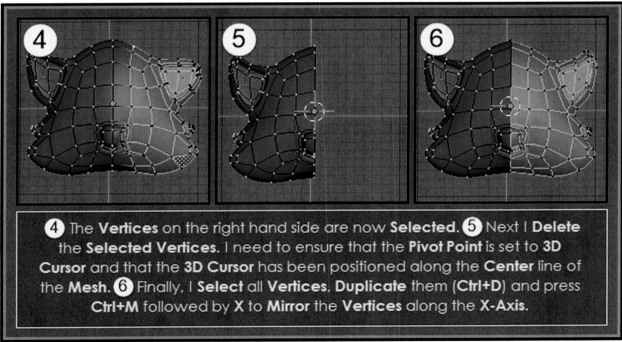

4 The **Vertices** on the right hand side are now **Selected.** **5** Next I **Delete** the **Selected Vertices.** I need to ensure that the **Pivot Point** is set to **3D Cursor** and that the **3D Cursor** has been positioned along the **Center** line of the **Mesh.** **6** Finally, I **Select** all **Vertices, Duplicate** them **(Ctrl+D)** and press **Ctrl+M** followed by X to **Mirror** the **Vertices** along the **X-Axis.**

As I indicate in the above illustrations, the *Pivot Point* plays a role during *Mirror* operations. I recommend you change the *Pivot Point* to *3D Cursor* and place the *3D Cursor* before performing the *Mirror* operation. The *3D Cursor* should be placed at a *Location* that will be the *Center* of the *Mesh* once the *Mirror* operation is finished. The easiest way to do this is to *Select* 1 or more *Vertices* at the *Center* of the *Mesh* and *Snap* the *3D Cursor* to the *Selected Vertices* (Press Shift + S and select *Cursor to Selected*). Remember that *Mirror* operations are only useful on *Meshes* that are *Symmetric* so a ring of *Vertices* should exist at the *Center* of the *Mesh*. If that isn't the case, your *Mesh* is not *Symmetric* and *Mirror* operations will produce undesired results. If the *Object Origin* is at the *Center* of the *Mesh* you can *Snap* the *3D Cursor* to that as well.

There is one final step you need to do to complete the *Mirror* operation. The *Mirror* operation has left duplicate *Vertices* along the center of the *Mesh*.

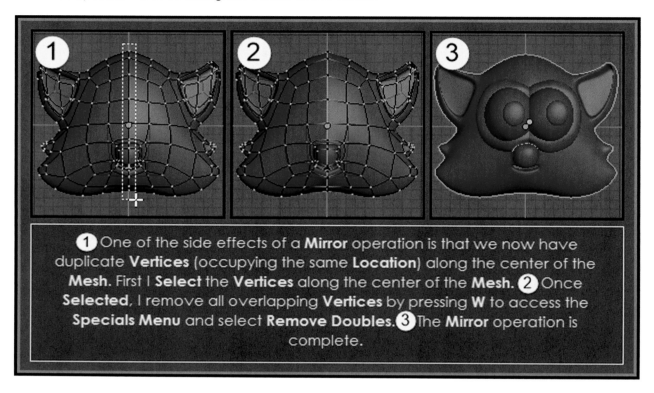

① One of the side effects of a **Mirror** operation is that we now have duplicate **Vertices** (occupying the same **Location**) along the center of the **Mesh**. First I **Select** the **Vertices** along the center of the **Mesh**. **②** Once **Selected**, I remove all overlapping **Vertices** by pressing **W** to access the **Specials Menu** and select **Remove Doubles**. **③** The **Mirror** operation is complete.

As described above, one of the final steps in a *Mirror* operation is to *Select* all *Vertices* along the *Center* of the *Mesh* and perform a *Remove Doubles* operation (see **Chapter 8 – Remove Doubles**). This will result in all duplicate *Vertices* in the same *Location* being removed and the *Mesh* will now be connected at the *Middle*. Ensure *Limit Selection to Visible* is disabled to ensure all *Vertices* are *Selected* before performing the *Remove Doubles* operation (see **Chapter 6 – Limit Selection to Visible**). You many also have to *Recalculate* the *Normals* after completing the *Mirror* operation (by pressing Ctrl + N).

As I mentioned above, you can also perform a *Mirror* operation by performing a *Scale* operation. Instead of pressing Ctrl + M followed by X after *Duplicating* the *Vertices* in your *Mesh*, you would press S, X, -1. That translates to a *Scale* operation constrained along the *X-Axis*. The value -1 results in the *Mirror* operation. An alternative method is to press Ctrl + M and then press the Middle Mouse Button and drag the mouse to choose an *Axis*.

Objects and Mesh Data

Blender allows you to have multiple *Objects* share the same *Mesh Data*. This allows you to have 2 identical *Objects* and work done on one is reflected on the other. Here is how it works.

1. Add a *Cube* and duplicate it.

2. Go to the *Data Properties Context Window* and make a note of the *Name* of the first *Cube*.
3. Select the 2nd *Cube* and give it the same *Name* as the first via the *Menu*. By selecting a different *Name* in the pull-down menu, we are assigning the *Mesh Data* of another *Object* to the current *Object*.
4. Now any work done on one *Cube* is reflected on the other.

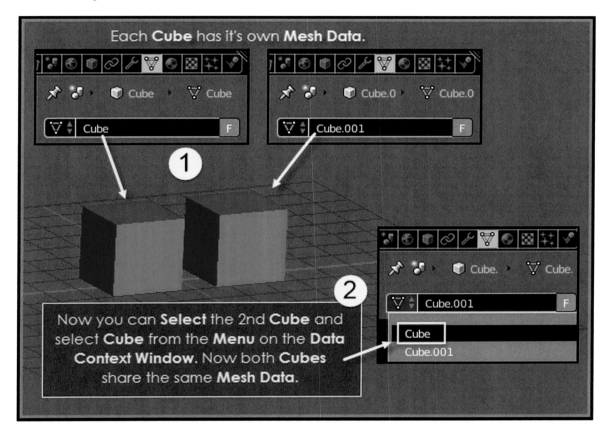

Once you assign the same *Mesh Data* to the both *Objects*, you can verify that the *Cube Mesh Data* is now shared by 2 *Objects* in the *Data Context Window*.

Ok, so now what did that give us? The answer to that question can be easily seen once you start *Transforming* one of the *Cubes* in *Edit Mode*.

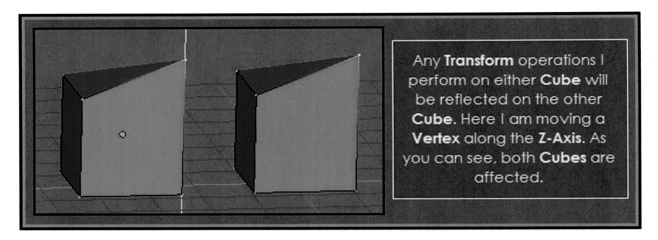

Any **Transform** operations I perform on either **Cube** will be reflected on the other **Cube**. Here I am moving a **Vertex** along the **Z-Axis**. As you can see, both **Cubes** are affected.

Now I will *Transform* 1 of the *Cubes* in *Object Mode*.

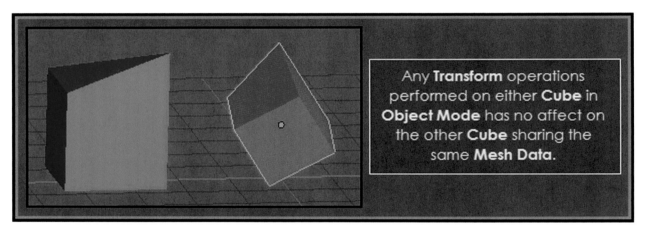

Any **Transform** operations performed on either **Cube** in **Object Mode** has no affect on the other **Cube** sharing the same **Mesh Data**.

I will switch back to *Edit Mode* to perform another *Transform* operation.

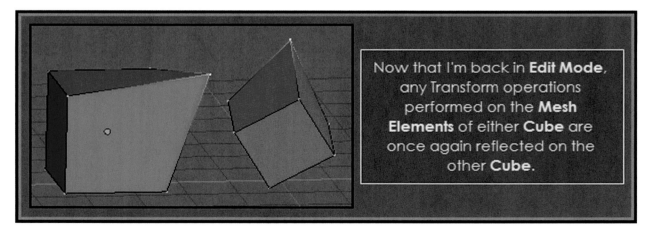

Now that I'm back in **Edit Mode**, any Transform operations performed on the **Mesh Elements** of either **Cube** are once again reflected on the other **Cube**.

Transforming the *Cube* (or any *Mesh* that shares *Mesh Data*) in *Edit Mode* allows you to do some interesting and useful things while *Modeling*.

There is actually an easier way to link the *Data* between 2 *Objects*. You can *Select* an *Object* and press Alt + D. I know what you're thinking, why go through all the trouble of showing me how to do it the hard way? I thought it important to explain a little about how it works instead of just talking about the shortcut. Now if something goes wrong you know where to go to fix it.

Let's talk about a practical example. Imagine you are *Modeling* a motorcycle and you are starting work on the exhaust. The final *Location* of the exhaust will be at an angle. You could start *Modeling* the exhaust and change its angle to match what you want in the final result but it's easier to model the exhaust in *Front View* without having to worry about angles when extruding etc. Well with the above technique you can have the best of both worlds.

Start *Modeling* your exhaust using the *Global X*, *Y* and *Z-Axis*. Now *Duplicate* the *Mesh* and assign it the same *Name* as the original (as explained above) - or just use Alt + D to *Duplicate* the *Object*. Now take the *Duplicate* and *Rotate* it in *Object* mode to the desired angle. You can now continue to manipulate the original *Mesh* while simultaneously seeing the result on the duplicate *Mesh*.

Here is an example of *Modeling* a dirt bike muffler after having moving it to its final *Location* (I threw together a basic dirt bike so forgive the lack of detail).

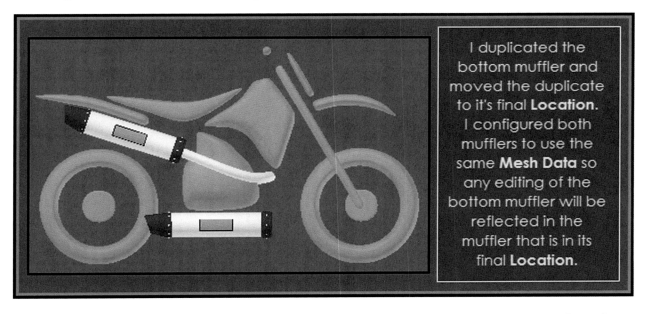

I duplicated the bottom muffler and moved the duplicate to it's final **Location**. I configured both mufflers to use the same **Mesh Data** so any editing of the bottom muffler will be reflected in the muffler that is in its final **Location**.

This technique is useful in *Hard Surface Modeling* and once you start using it you will find all kinds of situations where it comes in handy. Have a duplicate of your mesh that hasn't been *Rotated* makes it easy to go back and quickly modify the mesh using the *Global X, Y, Z-Axis.* You won't have to worry about ensuring you are at the proper angles when *Extruding / Sliding* etc.

Other places you might use this technique:

- Wheels on a motorcycle. If both wheels are the same, you can save time by having them share the same *Mesh Data* and just working on one of them.
- Front forks on a bicycle or motorcycle. You can *Duplicate* them and put them in place while you continue to *Model* them in *Front View*.

- Modeling a musical instrument such as a guitar. More often than not you are going to want to have your guitar at various angles when doing the final render. Using a duplicate to position your guitar will allow you maximum flexibility while still allowing you to go back and easily modify the guitar as needed.

When you are done *Modeling* you can move the *Mesh* you are *Modeling* to another *Layer* in case you need it again. Alternatively, you can press U to bring up the *Make Single User Menu* and select *Object & Data*. Both *Objects* should now have separate *Mesh Data*.

Snap Menu

The *Snap Menu* allows you to place or *Snap* the *Current Selection* or *3D Cursor* to a specific point. *Snapping* is powerful and very useful as it has a variety of uses.

The *Snap Menu* itself can be accessed using the keyboard shortcut Shift + S.

As you can see, there are 3 options for *Snapping* the *Current Selection* to a *Location* and 4 options for *Snapping* the *3D Cursor* to a *Location*.

Snap Selection to Grid

Snap Selection to Grid as the name implies will move an *Object* / *Mesh Element* to the nearest intersection of 2 *Grid Lines*.

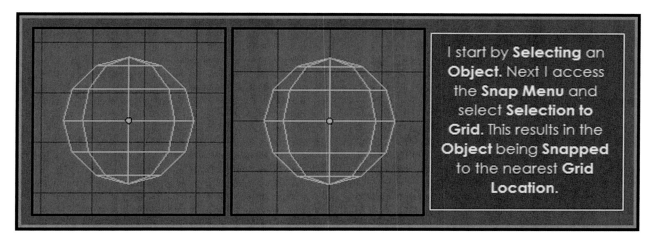

I start by **Selecting** an **Object**. Next I access the **Snap Menu** and select **Selection to Grid**. This results in the **Object** being **Snapped** to the nearest **Grid Location**.

Snapping multiple *Objects* results in each individual *Object* being *Snapped* to the closest *Grid Location* for that *Object*.

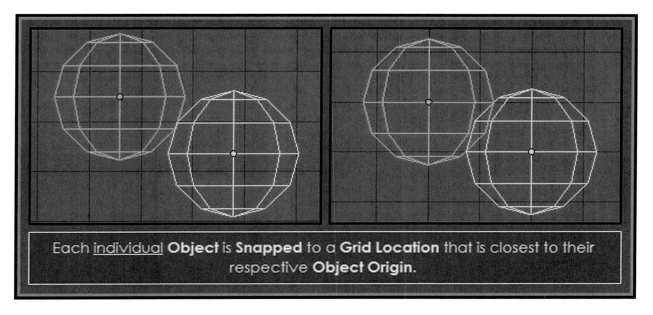

Each individual **Object** is **Snapped** to a **Grid Location** that is closest to their respective **Object Origin**.

As we can see above by *Object* we mean *Object Origin* (see **Chapter 7 – Object Origins**). Keep an eye on the *Location* of your *Object Origin* to ensure you get the desired results when *Snapping* to *Grid*.

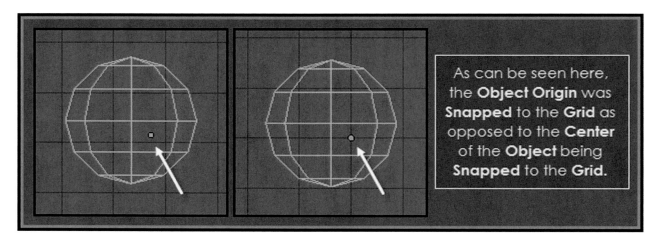

As can be seen here, the **Object Origin** was **Snapped** to the **Grid** as opposed to the **Center** of the **Object** being **Snapped** to the **Grid**.

The *Snap Selection* to *Grid Snaps* to the nearest *Grid* intersection so the *Zoom Level* has an effect on this type of *Snap* operation. *Zooming* in on the *3D View* causes the *Grid* to subdivide which as you might expect will affect the result of *Snapping* a *Selection* to *Grid*.

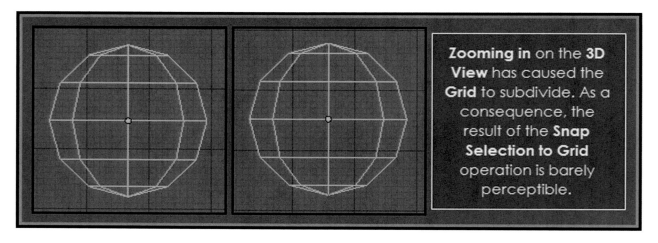

Zooming in on the **3D View** has caused the **Grid** to subdivide. As a consequence, the result of the **Snap Selection to Grid** operation is barely perceptible.

Snap Selection to *Grid* also works in *Edit Mode*. **Any** *Selected Mesh Elements* will *Snap* to the nearest *Grid* Intersection for each individually *Selected Mesh Element*.

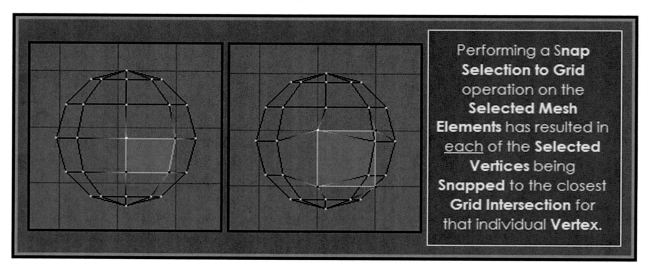

Performing a **Snap Selection to Grid** operation on the **Selected Mesh Elements** has resulted in <u>each</u> of the **Selected Vertices** being **Snapped** to the closest **Grid Intersection** for that individual **Vertex**.

As can be seen in the above illustration, *Snapping* individual *Mesh Elements* to the *Grid* leads to a result that deforms the *Geometry*. I have never seen anyone do this type of operation in a tutorial and I personally have never used it. I imagine if you are modelling a building or something similar it may come in handy.

Snap Selection to Cursor

The *Snap Selection to Cursor* option will *Snap* the currently *Selected Object / Mesh Element* to the *3D Cursor*.

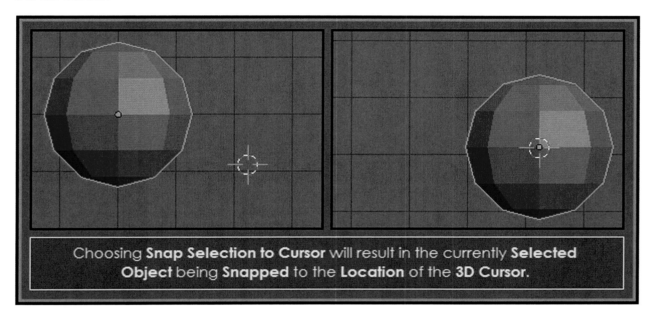

Choosing **Snap Selection to Cursor** will result in the currently **Selected Object** being **Snapped** to the **Location** of the **3D Cursor**.

To be clear, choosing *Snap Selection to Cursor* will *Snap* the *Origin* of the currently *Selected Object* to the *3D Cursor*. If the *Object Origin* is outside the boundary of the *Mesh*, you may get an undesired result.

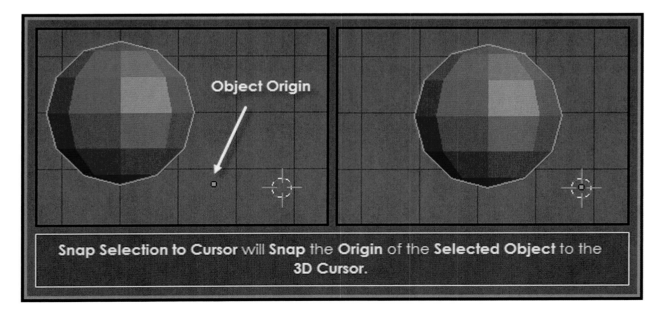

Snap Selection to Cursor will **Snap** the **Origin** of the **Selected Object** to the **3D Cursor**.

Performing a *Snap Selection to Cursor* when multiple *Objects* are *Selected* will result in each individual *Object* being Snapped to the *3D Cursor*.

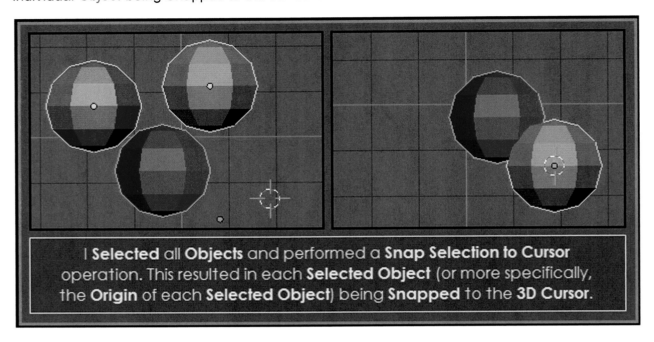

I Selected all Objects and performed a Snap Selection to Cursor operation. This resulted in each Selected Object (or more specifically, the Origin of each Selected Object) being Snapped to the 3D Cursor.

As I mentioned above, you can also *Snap Selected Mesh Elements* to the *3D Cursor*. This will result in each individually *Selected Mesh Element* being *Snapped* to the *3D Cursor*.

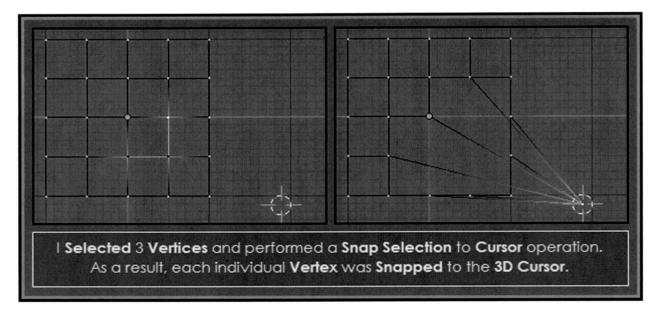

I Selected 3 Vertices and performed a Snap Selection to Cursor operation. As a result, each individual Vertex was Snapped to the 3D Cursor.

So you are probably thinking, how could this possible be useful? I can tell you that I use *Snap Selection to 3D Cursor* in conjunction with *Snap 3D Cursor to Selected* all the time. They are best friends and are very useful together. I will give some examples of where I use the *Snap Menu* after I am done covering the *Snap Menu* itself.

Snap Selection to 3D Cursor (Offset)

Snap Selection to 3D Cursor with Offset is similar to *Snap Selection to 3D Cursor* except that the *Selected Mesh Elements* maintain their shape. In other words, instead of each *Mesh Element* being *Snapped* to the *3D Cursor*, the *Mesh Elements* are *Snapped* as a whole and the *Center* or *Median Point* of the *Selected Elements* are *Snapped* to the *3D Cursor*.

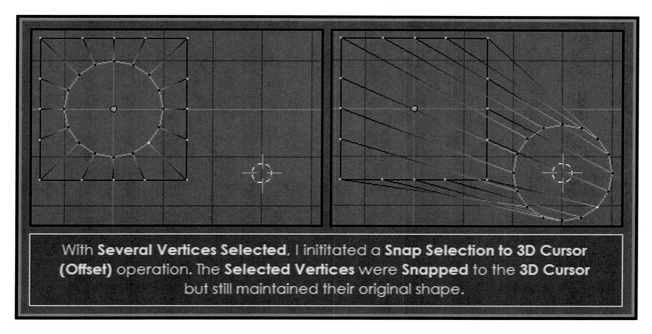

With **Several Vertices Selected**, I inititated a **Snap Selection to 3D Cursor (Offset)** operation. The **Selected Vertices** were **Snapped** to the **3D Cursor** but still maintained their original shape.

You can toggle the *Offset* option on and off via the *Operator Panel* which is visible on the *Tools Shelf* or by pressing F6 on the keyboard after initiating a *Snap Selection to Cursor (Offset)* operation. The option to toggle *Offset* is also available when you perform a *Snap Selection to 3D Cursor* operation (without the *Offset* option). In the end it doesn't matter which variation of the *Snap Selection to 3D Cursor* operation you choose from the *Snap Menu* as both have the option to toggle the *Offset* option.

Snap Cursor to Selected

The *Snap Cursor to Selected* functionality will *Snap* the *3D Cursor* to the *Selected Object / Mesh Element*. In *Object Mode*, the *3D Cursor* will *Snap* to the *Object Origin*.

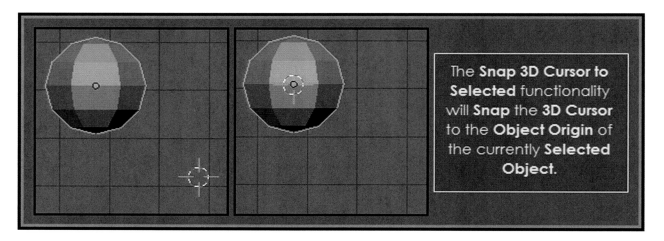

When multiple *Objects* are *Selected*, the *3D Cursor* will *Snap* to the mid-point of all *Selected Objects*.

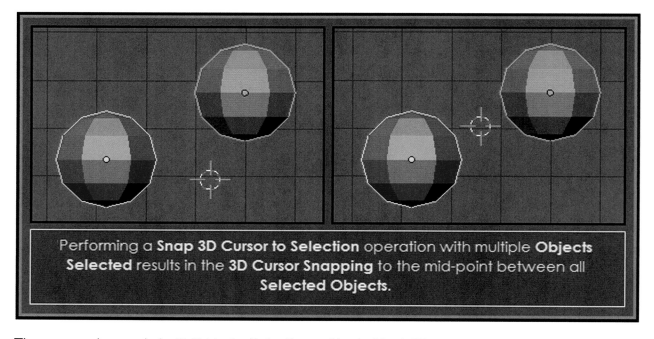

The same rules apply in *Edit Mode*. Selecting a *Single Mesh Element* will result in the *3D Cursor* being *Snapped* to that *Element*. Selecting *Multiple Mesh Elements* will result in the *3D Cursor Snapping* to the mid-point of all *Selected Elements*.

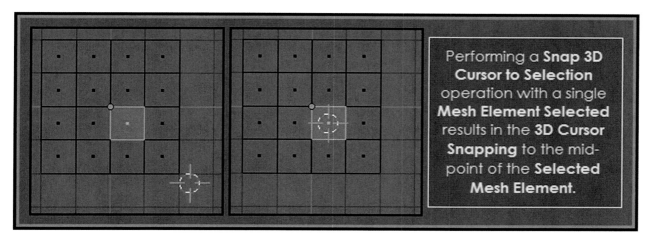

Performing a **Snap 3D Cursor to Selection** operation with a single **Mesh Element Selected** results in the **3D Cursor Snapping** to the mid-point of the **Selected Mesh Element**.

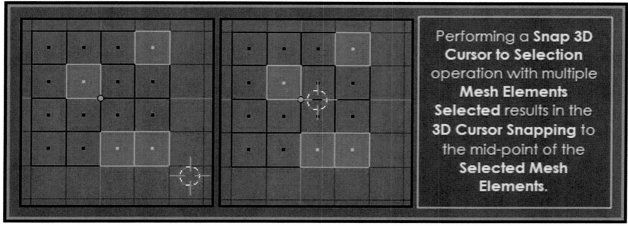

Performing a **Snap 3D Cursor to Selection** operation with multiple **Mesh Elements Selected** results in the **3D Cursor Snapping** to the mid-point of the **Selected Mesh Elements**.

Snap Cursor to Center

Performing a *Snap Cursor to Center* operation results in the *3D Cursor* being *Snapped* to the *3D World Origin* (*Location* 0,0,0).

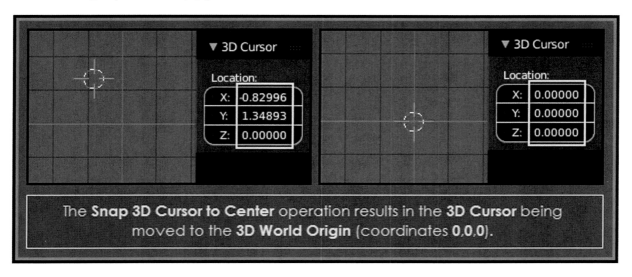

The **Snap 3D Cursor to Center** operation results in the **3D Cursor** being moved to the **3D World Origin** (coordinates **0,0,0**).

Snap Cursor to Grid

Performing a *Snap Cursor to Grid* operation will result in the *3D Cursor* being *Snapped* to the nearest *Grid* intersection.

Snap Cursor to Active

Performing a *Snap Cursor to Active* operation will result in the *3D Cursor* being *Snapped* to the *Active Object* / *Mesh Element*. Remember that the last *Object* / *Mesh Element* you *Selected* is the *Active Object* / *Mesh Element*. If only 1 *Object* / *Mesh Element* is *Selected* it then becomes the *Active Object* / *Mesh Element*.

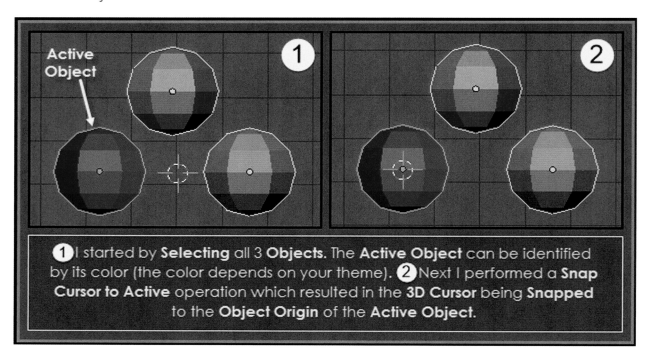

Like many of the other *Snap Menu* options, *Snapping* to an *Object* will result in the *3D Cursor* *Snapping* to the *Object Origin*.

Here is an example using a *Mesh* in *Face Select Mode*.

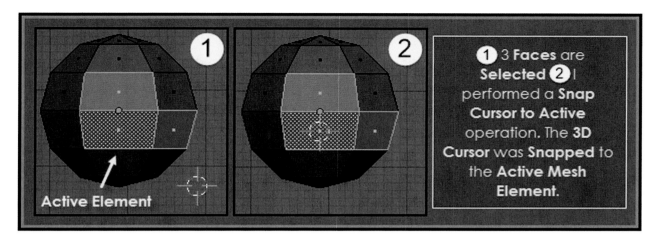

Using Snap

Now that the basics of the *Snap Menu* are covered we can move on to practical examples of using the *Snap Functionality*.

Setting the *Pivot Point to 3D Cursor* and using the *Snap* functionality allows you to perform *Transform Operations* at just about any *Location*.

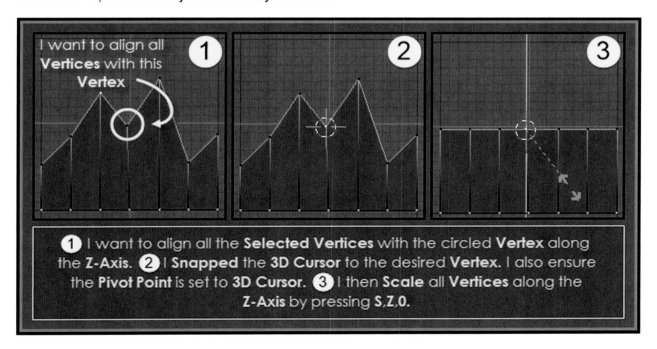

During the course of *Modeling* the *Object Origin* will often end up in a *Location* that is outside the boundaries of the *Mesh*. You can use *Snapping* to help re-center the *Object Origin* or to place the *Object Origin* at any *Location*.

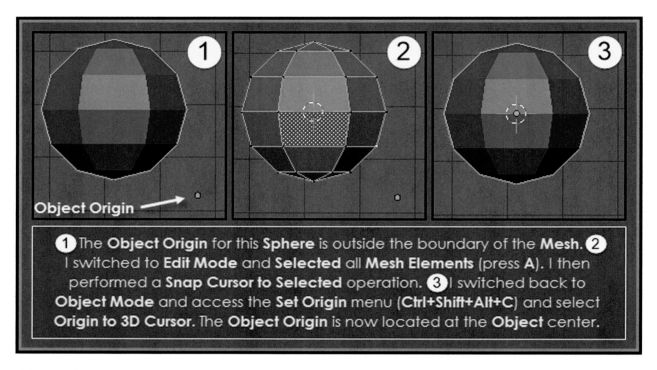

1 The **Object Origin** for this **Sphere** is outside the boundary of the **Mesh**. 2 I switched to **Edit Mode** and **Selected** all **Mesh Elements** (press A). I then performed a **Snap Cursor to Selected** operation. 3 I switched back to **Object Mode** and access the **Set Origin** menu (**Ctrl+Shift+Alt+C**) and select **Origin to 3D Cursor**. The **Object Origin** is now located at the **Object** center.

You might also want to move the *Object Origin* to allow for *Rotation* at a specific *Location* as it relates to the *Mesh*. As an example, consider the following *Mesh*.

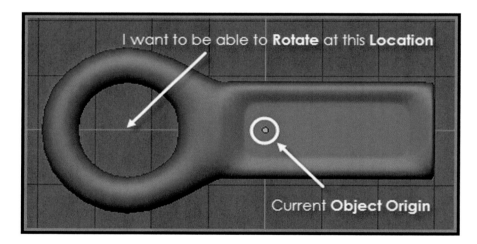

To move the *Object Origin* (with precision), start by going into *Edit Mode*. Next, *Select* the inner *Face Loop* and *Snap* the *3D Cursor* to the *Selection*.

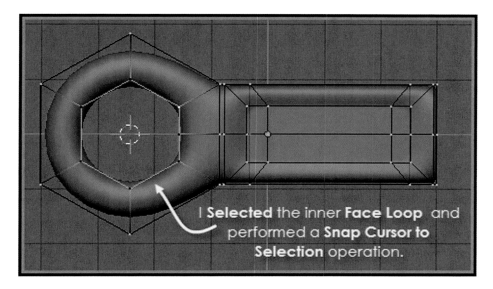

I **Selected** the inner **Face Loop** and performed a **Snap Cursor to Selection** operation.

Here is a different angle to better demonstrate the current *Selection*.

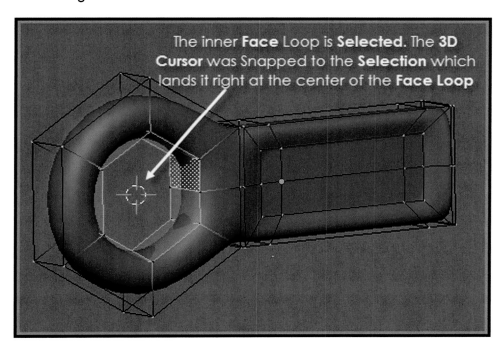

The inner **Face** Loop is **Selected**. The **3D Cursor** was Snapped to the **Selection** which lands it right at the center of the **Face Loop**

Now the *Origin Point* can be moved to the *Location* of the *3D Cursor*.

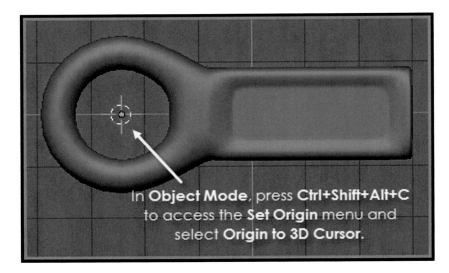

Rotating the *Object* can now be done around the *Center* of the ring portion of the *Mesh*.

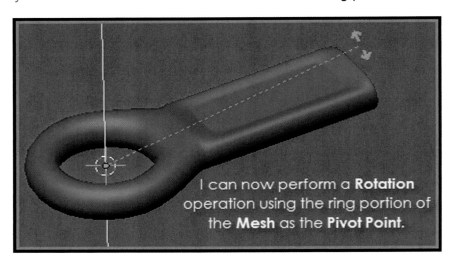

I have only scratched the surface in terms of what can be done using the *Snap Menu*. If you aren't using it on a regular basis you are probably spending more time accomplishing various *Modeling* tasks than you need to. You have the added bonus of being able to perform operations with precision.

In the next chapter I cover **The Snap Mesh Tool**. You can *Snap Mesh Elements* to each other with the *Snap To Mesh Tool* and it expands on the *Snapping* functionality to greatly increase its versatility.

Empties

There is a type of *Object* in *Blender* known as an *Empty Object* or just *Empty* that has the following characteristics

- *Empties* have no properties other than values for *Location*, *Rotation* and *Scale*.

- An *Empty* can be placed anywhere in the *3D View* and can be *Transformed* like any other *Object*.
- Although visible in the *3D View*, an *Empty* does not appear in the final *Render*.

Empties in *Blender* have several uses but my discussion will be limited to what they are and how they can help you with your *3D Modeling*.

There are several options when adding an *Empty* in terms of its appearance. To add an *Empty* simply press Shift + A to access the *Add Menu*, select *Empty* and choose a display style.

Here is a look at the different display styles in *Front View*.

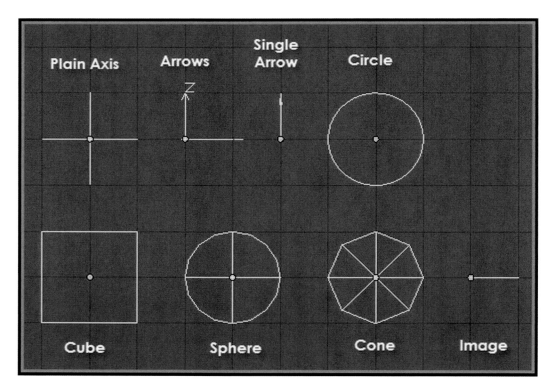

Here is a different angle which gives you a better idea of each display style.

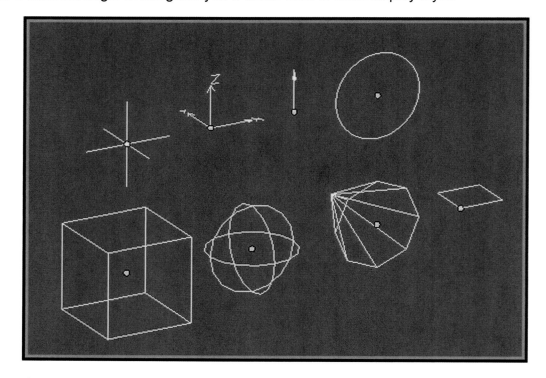

You can change the size and display style of your *Empty* at any time on the *Data Context Panel*.

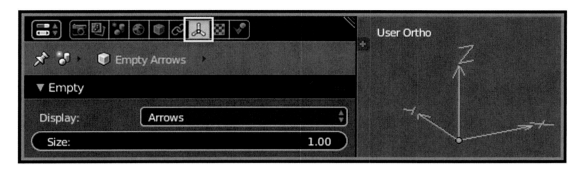

You should always use the *Data Context Panel* to resize your *Empty*. If you resize the *Empty* by *Scaling* it you will get undesired results when you use it in a *Parenting* (which I talk about in the next section) operation or as part of an *Array Modifier* operation (see **Chapter 9 – The Array Modifier**). The reason for this is the *Transform Data* for an *Empty* will affect the *Children* / *Array Elements* when using the *Empty* in either of those operations.

An *Empty* with the *Display Style* set to *Image* is a handy way to set up background images. I talk about it more in the **Background Image** section of this chapter.

I always encourage giving your *Empties* a good *Name* and enabling the *Name* option on the *Display Panel* of the *Object Context Window*. See **Chapter 3 – Object Display Sub-Panel** for more info.

As I mentioned previously, any *Empties* in your *3D View* will not be seen in the final *Render*. Here is an example *Scene* set to *Camera View* with an *Object* and several *Empties*.

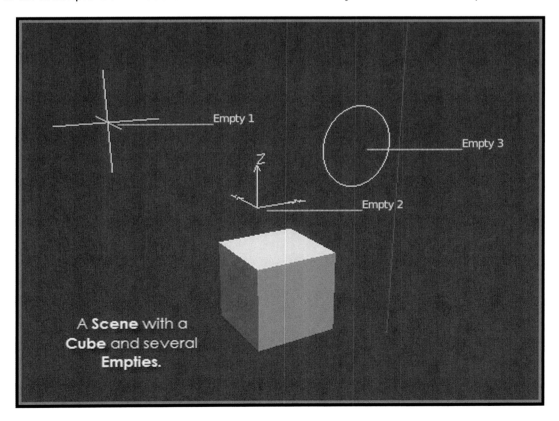

Here is a *Render* of the same *Scene*.

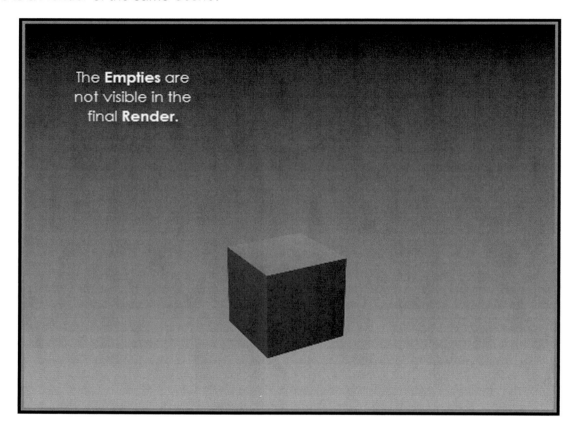

I cover some of the ways to use *Empties* as part of the *Modeling* process in other sections of this book.

Parenting

Blender allows you to make 1 *Object* the *Parent* of 1 or more other *Objects*. Once an *Object* becomes a *Parent*, any *Transform Operations* on the *Parent Object* will be reflected on the *Child Objects*. To make an *Object* a *Parent*, select 2 or more *Objects* and press Ctrl + P. The *Active Object* in your *Selection* will become the *Parent Object*.

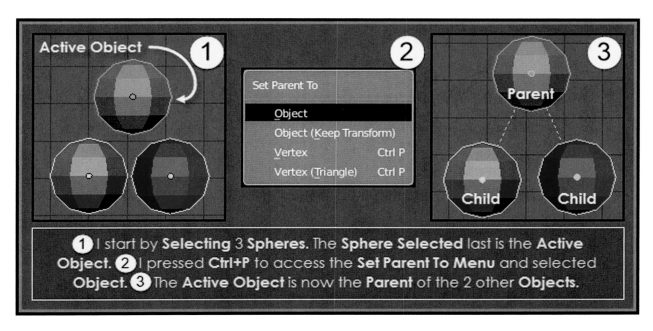

① I start by **Selecting** 3 **Spheres**. The **Sphere Selected** last is the **Active Object**. ② I pressed **Ctrl+P** to access the **Set Parent To Menu** and selected **Object**. ③ The **Active Object** is now the **Parent** of the 2 other **Objects**.

Now any *Transform* operations performed on the *Parent* will affect any *Child Objects*. If you move a *Parent*, the *Children* come with it. If you *Scale* the *Parent*, the *Child Objects* will *Scale* as well. *Rotating* the *Parent* will *Rotate* all *Child Objects* around the *Parent*.

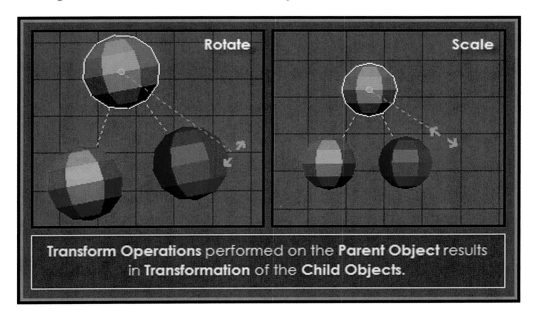

Transform Operations performed on the **Parent Object** results in **Transformation** of the **Child Objects**.

You may have noticed that when you define a *Parent* that there are lines that connect the *Parent* to each of its *Children*. Those lines are drawn from the *Object Origin* of the *Parents* to the *Object Origin* of the *Child Objects*.

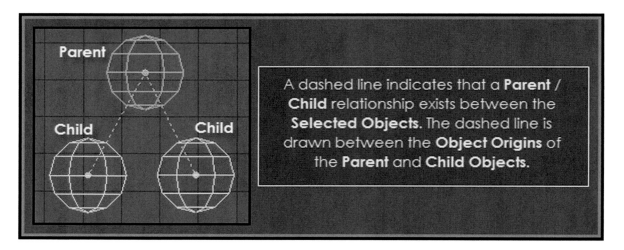

If you move the *Object Origin* of the *Parent* outside the boundaries of the *Mesh*, the line connecting the *Parent* and *Child* will appear odd as it appears the *Child Object* isn't pointing to any *Parent*.

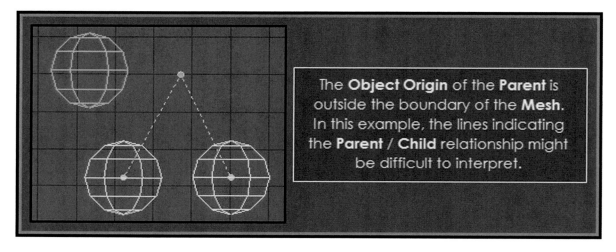

Although *Transforming* the *Parent Object* will affect any *Child Objects*, *Transforming* the *Child Objects* will not affect the *Parent*. You can *Transform* the *Child Objects* in *Object* or *Edit Mode* without affecting the *Parent Object*.

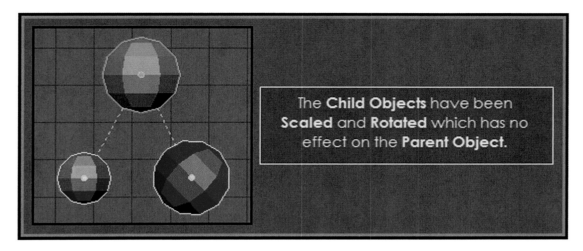

You can clear the *Parent / Child* relationship by *Selecting* the *Parent Object* and at least 1 *Child Object* and pressing Alt + P. If you *Select* only 1 *Child*, the *Clear Parent* operation will only affect that 1 *Child Object*. All other *Child Objects* will still have a *Parent*.

You will notice when you access the *Clear Parent Menu* (using Alt + P) that there are several options.

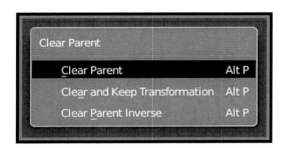

Selecting *Clear Parent* will not only clear the *Parent / Child* relationship between all *Selected Objects*, it will also cause all *Child Objects* to revert to their original state in terms of *Scale, Rotation* and *Location*. In other words, any *Transform* operations done on the *Parent Object* that affected the *Child Objects* will be reverted. I can tell you from experience that I have on more than one occasion performed a *Clear Parent* operation only to see the *Child Objects* disappear from my *3D View* as their *Location* coordinates were reverted to their original value. By original value I mean the *Location* coordinates of the *Child Object* at the time of the *Parent* operation.

To demonstrate the first option, I start with 3 *Spheres* in a *Parent / Child* relationship. All 3 *Spheres* are at the *Location* where I performed the *Parent* operation.

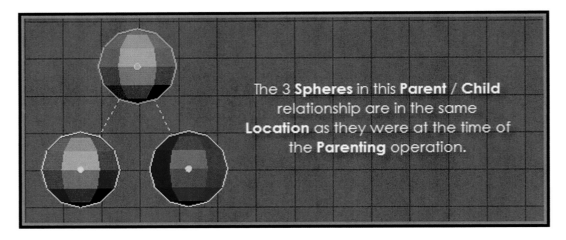

The 3 **Spheres** in this **Parent / Child** relationship are in the same **Location** as they were at the time of the **Parenting** operation.

Next I *Grab* the *Parent Object* and move it to a new *Location*.

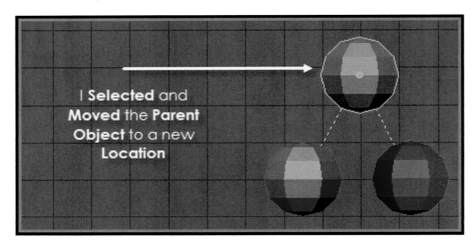

I **Selected** and **Moved** the **Parent Object** to a new **Location**

Now I perform a *Clear Parent* operation (with all 3 *Objects Selected*) by accessing the *Clear Parent Menu* and selecting *Clear Parent*.

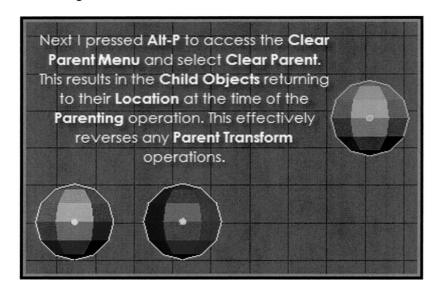

Next I pressed **Alt-P** to access the **Clear Parent Menu** and select **Clear Parent**. This results in the **Child Objects** returning to their **Location** at the time of the **Parenting** operation. This effectively reverses any **Parent Transform** operations.

As you've probably guessed by now, the *Clear and Keep Transformation* option in the *Clear Parent Menu* allows the *Child Objects* to keep any *Transform* operations done to the *Parent Object*. To demonstrate, I will start with the same *Parent / Child* setup as I used in the last example.

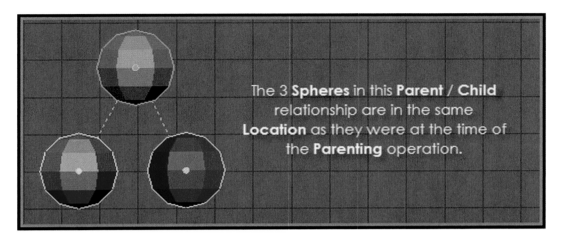

The 3 **Spheres** in this **Parent / Child** relationship are in the same **Location** as they were at the time of the **Parenting** operation.

Next I *Grab* the *Parent* and move it to a new *Location*. I also *Scaled* and *Rotated* one of the *Child Objects*.

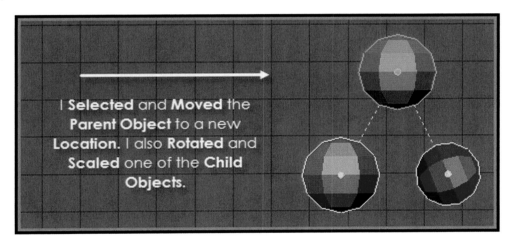

I **Selected** and **Moved** the **Parent Object** to a new **Location**. I also **Rotated** and **Scaled** one of the **Child Objects**.

Now I perform a *Clear Parent* operation (with all 3 *Objects Selected*) by accessing the *Clear Parent Menu* and selecting *Clear and Keep Transformation*. This option allows all *Objects* to keep any *Transformations* performed during the *Parent / Child* relationship.

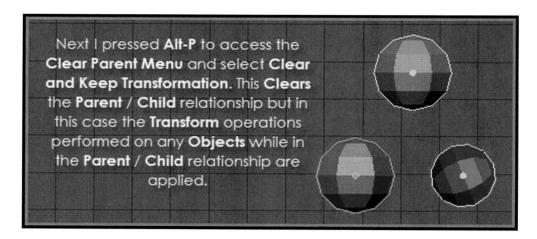

Parenting has many more uses outside the scope of *3D Modeling* which I won't cover in this book. In terms of *3D Modeling* I used to use *Parenting* to help group and organize my *Objects*. I have switched to using the *Outliner* (see **Chapter 2 – Outliner**) to group my *Objects* as it allows me to see all my *Groups* of *Objects* in 1 place and I can also quickly *Select* , *Lock* and *Hide* any *Group* of *Objects*. Another advantage (or disadvantage depending on your point of view) is that using *Grouping* does not maintain any *Transform* relationships between the *Objects*.

Grouping Objects

Blender allows you to *Group* several *Objects* together which can be indispensable when trying to keep your *Objects* organized. To create a *Group* simply *Select* 2 or more *Objects* and press Ctrl + G. You can also create a *Group* by *Selecting* several *Objects* and then pressing the *Add to Group* button in the *Groups Panel* on the *Object Context Window*. You can then rename the *Group* on the same panel.

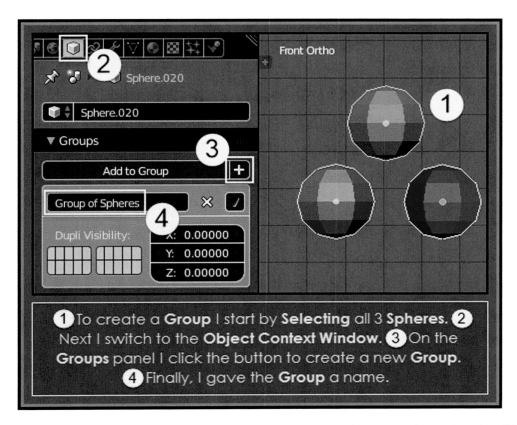

① To create a **Group** I start by **Selecting** all 3 **Spheres.** ② Next I switch to the **Object Context Window.** ③ On the **Groups** panel I click the button to create a new **Group.** ④ Finally, I gave the **Group** a name.

As I mentioned above, I could have just as easily created the *Group* by *Selecting* the *Objects* and pressing Ctrl + G.

Now that I have a *Group* of *Objects*, I can use the *Outliner* (see **Chapter 2 – Outliner**) to take full advantage of the benefits that come with using *Groups.*

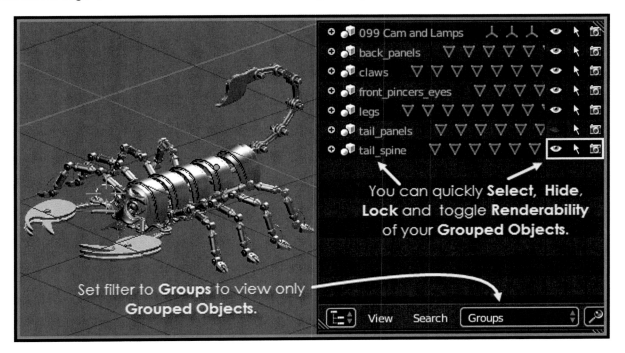

You can quickly **Select, Hide, Lock** and toggle **Renderability** of your **Grouped Objects.**

Set filter to **Groups** to view only **Grouped Objects.**

As you can see in the above illustration, keeping your *Objects* in *Groups* comes with plenty of benefits aside from just keeping things organized. Using the *Outliner,* you can quickly *Select* a *Group* by clicking on the *Group Name.* You can *Hide* a *Group* of *Objects* by clicking on the little *Eye Icon.* You can *Lock* a *Group* of *Objects* (which means they can't be *Selected*) by clicking on the little *Arrow Icon.* You can also toggle whether or not a *Group* of *Objects* is *Rendered* with the little *Camera Icon.* Not only can you *Select* a group of *Objects* but you can also *Select* each individual *Object* in a *Group.*

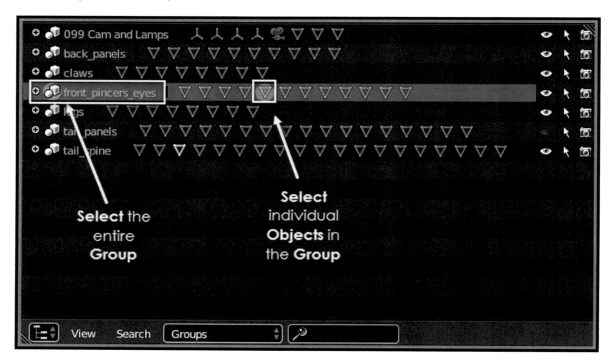

You can expand any *Group* in the *Outliner* to get more details about the *Group.*

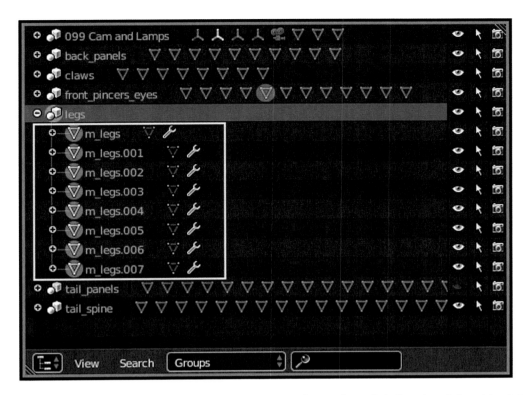

You can expand each *Mesh Element* even further to view other details about the *Mesh* including any *Materials* or *Modifiers* that are assigned to the *Mesh*.

You can add an *Object* to an existing *Group* by *Selecting* the *Object* you want to add and then *Selecting* any *Object* in the *Group* you want to add the *Object* to. Press Ctrl + Shift + G and select the *Group* you want to add the *Object* to from the *Menu* that appears.

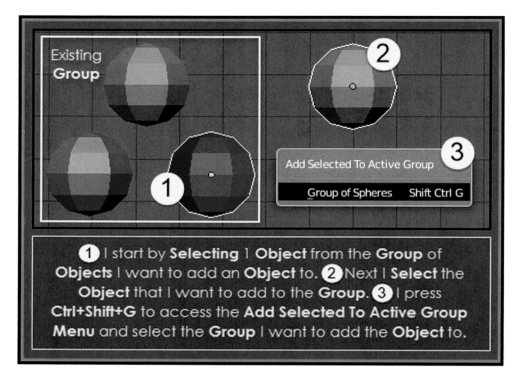

An *Object* can be part of more than 1 *Group* which allows you to organize your *Objects* even further.

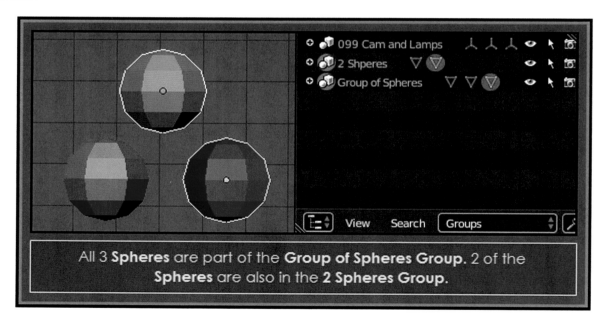

You can remove one or more *Objects* from any *Groups* that the *Object* belongs to. To remove one or more *Objects* from a *Group*, *Select* the *Object(s)* you want to remove and press Shift + Alt + G to access the *Remove Selected From Active Group Menu*. You can choose to remove the *Object(s)* from *All Groups* that the *Object(s)* belongs to or from any individual *Group* that the *Object(s)* belongs to.

If you are wondering about why each *Group* has 1 *Object* with a small circle around it, that *Object* is the *Active Object*.

If you want to *Un-Group* a *Group* of *Objects* simply Right-Click on the *Group* in the *Outliner* and select *Unlink Group*.

I personally think *Grouping Objects* used in conjunction with the *Outliner* is the best way to keep *Objects* organized. Being able to quickly *Select*, *Hide* and *Lock* the *Groups* is just icing on the cake. I mention earlier in the book that I always have an *Outliner Window* filtered by *Groups* open at all times. If you don't already use *Groups* I encourage you to give *Grouping* a try. I believe it won't take too long before they are a permanent part of your *Modeling* workflow.

Joining Objects

You can *Join* 2 or more *Objects* into 1 *Object* by *Selecting* the *Objects* you want to *Join* and pressing Ctrl + J.

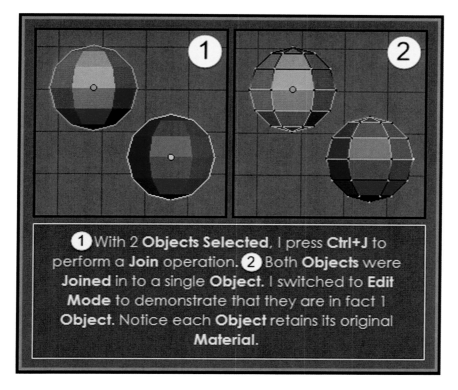

One thing to keep in mind is if any of the *Objects* you are *Joining* have *Modifiers* the *Active Object* will determine what *Modifiers* are added to the new *Object*.

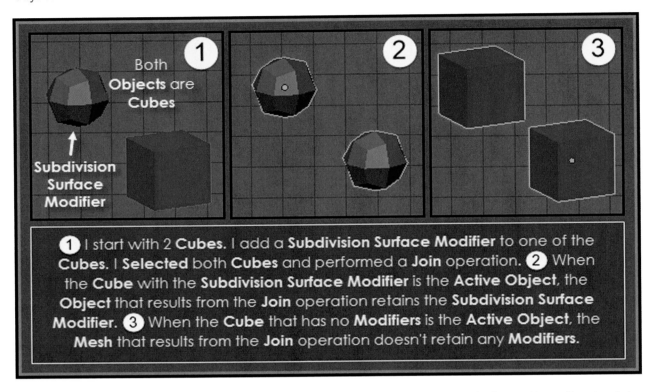

① I start with 2 **Cubes**. I add a **Subdivision Surface Modifier** to one of the **Cubes**. I **Selected** both **Cubes** and performed a **Join** operation. **②** When the **Cube** with the **Subdivision Surface Modifier** is the **Active Object**, the **Object** that results from the **Join** operation retains the **Subdivision Surface Modifier**. **③** When the **Cube** that has no **Modifiers** is the **Active Object**, the **Mesh** that results from the **Join** operation doesn't retain any **Modifiers**.

It's important to know what *Modifiers* are added to any of your *Objects* before attempting to *Join* them with other *Objects* as the result could be very much unexpected.

Separating a Mesh into Objects

As a *Mesh* gets bigger and consequently more unwieldy it's often desirable to break the *Mesh Elements* apart into separate *Objects*. You can break a *Mesh* apart by *Selecting* a portion of the *Mesh* and pressing P on the keyboard to access the *Separate Menu*. Choose the *Selection* option to separate the *Selected Mesh Elements* into their separate *Objects*.

Here is a raccoon head that I want to perform a *Separate* operation on.

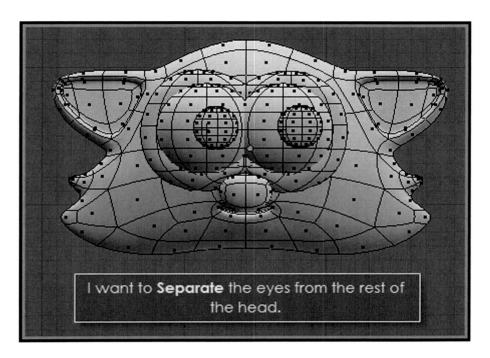

I want to **Separate** the eyes from the rest of the head.

First I need to *Select* the portion of the *Mesh* I want to *Separate*. In this example I want to *Separate* the eyes from the rest of the head.

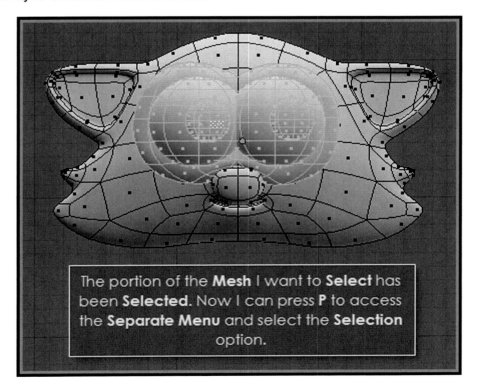

The portion of the **Mesh** I want to **Select** has been **Selected**. Now I can press **P** to access the **Separate Menu** and select the **Selection** option.

The eyes and head are now 2 separate *Objects*.

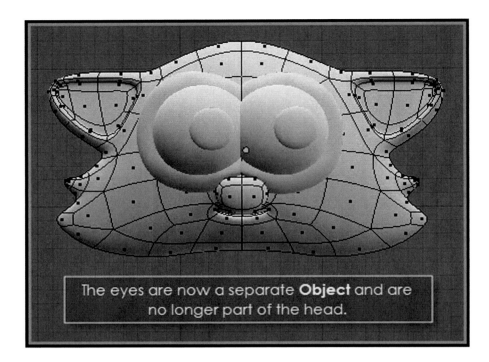

The eyes are now a separate **Object** and are no longer part of the head.

There are a couple of other options in the *Separate Menu*. The first is *Separate by Material*. This, as the name sounds, will break all *Mesh Elements* that have the same *Material* into their own *Objects*. I don't believe I have ever used this option but it's there if you find a need for it.

The next option is to *Separate By Loose Parts*. Selecting this option will *Separate* all *Mesh Elements* that aren't connected with each other into *Separate Objects*. Let's have another look at the raccoon head.

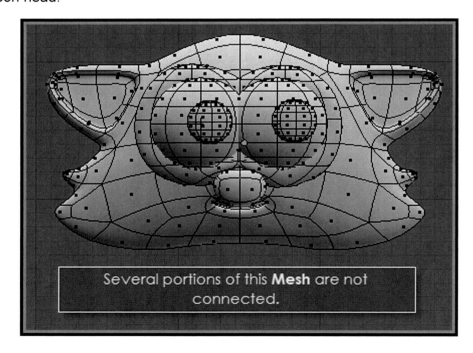

Several portions of this **Mesh** are not connected.

After *Selecting* all *Mesh Elements*, I press P to access the *Separate Menu* and select *By Loose Parts* to *Separate* the *Mesh Elements* that aren't connected into multiple *Objects*. Here is the result (I moved the *Objects* away from each to better demonstrate the result of the *Separate* operation).

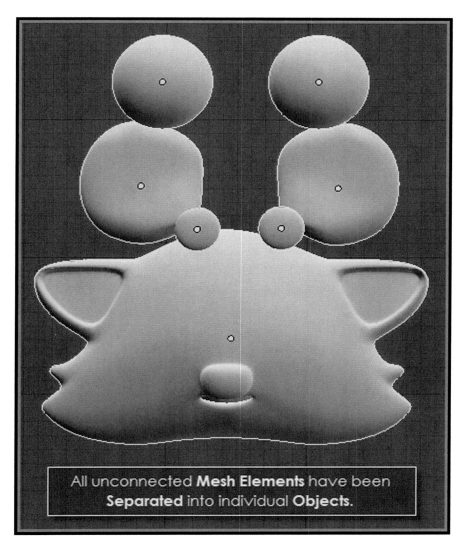

Vertex Groups

You can organize *Mesh Elements* (specifically *Vertices* in this case) by assigning them to *Vertex Groups*. A *Vertex Group* can be created by *Selecting* several *Vertices* in *Edit Mode*, pressing Ctrl + G to access the *Vertex Groups Menu* and selecting *Assign to New Group*. The resulting *Group* will have the name *Group* (don't worry, it can be renamed).

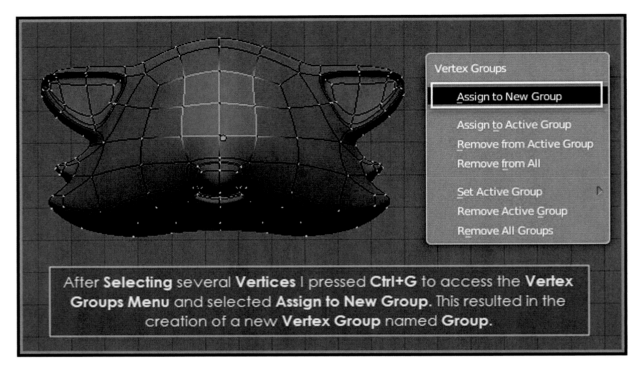

After **Selecting** several **Vertices** I pressed **Ctrl+G** to access the **Vertex Groups Menu** and selected **Assign to New Group**. This resulted in the creation of a new **Vertex Group** named **Group**.

Once created, you can go to the *Vertex Groups Panel* in the *Data Context Window* to access options and functionality related to the *Vertex Group*.

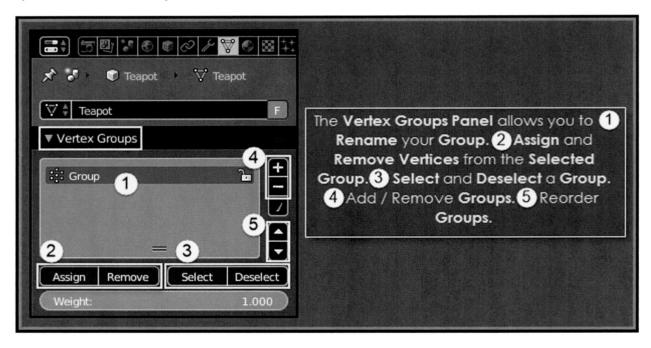

The **Vertex Groups Panel** allows you to ① **Rename** your **Group**. ② **Assign** and **Remove Vertices** from the **Selected Group**. ③ **Select** and **Deselect** a **Group**. ④ Add / Remove **Groups**. ⑤ Reorder **Groups**.

To rename a *Group* simply Double-Click the *Name* field and give it a new name.

The *Assign / Remove* buttons allow you to *Select* 1 or more *Vertices* and *Assign* or *Remove* them from the currently selected *Group* i.e. The *Group* you have selected in the *Vertex Groups*

Panel. Use the *Select / Deselect* buttons to ensure the *Assign / Remove* operation worked as expected.

The *Select / Deselect* buttons allow you to *Select* or *Deselect* all *Vertices* in a *Vertex Group.* It can be handy to *De-Select* all *Vertices* in the *3D View* and then *Select* a *Vertex Group* or, conversely, *Select* all *Vertices* in the *3D View* and *Deselect* a *Vertex Group.*

You can add a new *Vertex Group* with the plus button. This will create an *Empty Vertex Group.* It will then be up to you to *Select* and *Assign Vertices* to the new *Vertex Group.* The minus button will remove a *Vertex Group.*

Finally, the small up arrow / down arrow buttons allow you to reorder your *Groups.*

There is also a *Specials Menu* that has several options related to working with *Vertex Groups.*

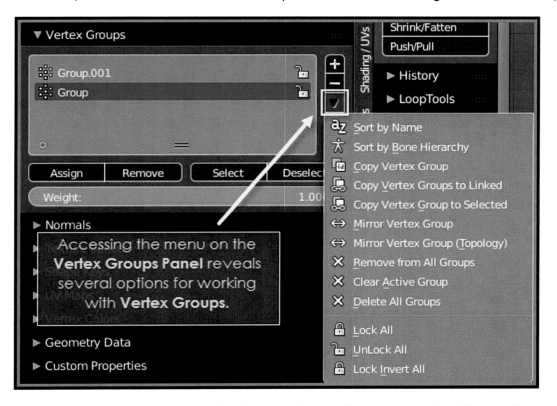

Accessing the menu on the **Vertex Groups Panel** reveals several options for working with **Vertex Groups.**

The *Weight* field will not be covered in this book as it isn't directly related to *3D Modeling.*

Now that you know how to create *Vertex Groups,* why would you use them? We learned in the last section that we can *Separate Mesh Elements* into separate *Objects.* Having separate *Objects* allows you to quickly *Select* and *Edit* any individual *Object.* With *Vertex Groups* you can accomplish the same thing without breaking the *Mesh* apart into separate *Objects.* Simply organize your *Vertices* into different *Groups.* You can then *Select* a *Vertex Group* and *Isolate* it so you can work on it without anything obstructing your *View.* You can also quickly *Select* 1 or more *Vertex Groups* and *Hide* them to reduce clutter. *Vertex Groups* give you many of the benefits of breaking a *Mesh* into separate *Objects. Vertex Groups* are also very useful if during the *Modeling* process you need to *Select* the same *Group* of *Vertices* over and over again. Repeatedly having to manually *Select* a *Group* of *Vertices* can be very tedious. A *Vertex* can be part of multiple *Groups* so you can *Group* the *Vertices* in any way you like allowing you multiple options when organizing your *Mesh*.

Let's go back to our Raccoon. I could create *Vertex Groups* that would allow me to quickly *Select* specific *Mesh Elements*.

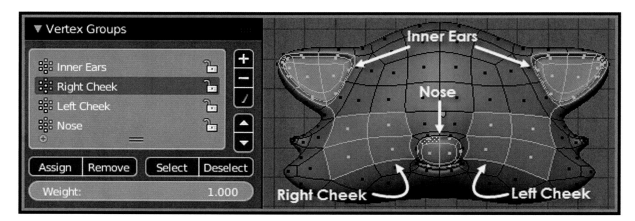

In the above illustration I created 4 *Vertex Groups*. I can now quickly *Select* and *Manipulate* the *Vertices* in any of the *Vertex Groups*. I could also *Select* the *Right Cheek* and *Left Cheek Vertex Groups* and create a new *Vertex Group* (which I might call *Both Cheeks*). I would then have the option of choosing the *Vertices* for each cheek or for both cheeks at once. All *Vertices* in both cheeks would then be part of 2 *Vertex Groups*.

 Vertex Groups are also used with the *Shrink Wrap Modifier* (see **Chapter 9 – The Shrinkwrap Modifier**).

Dupliverts

Dupliverts allow you to *Duplicate Objects* and the destination of the *Duplicates* are dictated by the position of the *Vertices* of a 2nd *Mesh* (sometimes referred to as the *Pattern Mesh*). In other words, you start with a *Base Object* (like a fence post or telephone pole) and a 2nd *Object* whose *Vertices* will be used to define the number and position of any *Duplicates*. Before I get in to how to create *Dupliverts* here is a basic example.

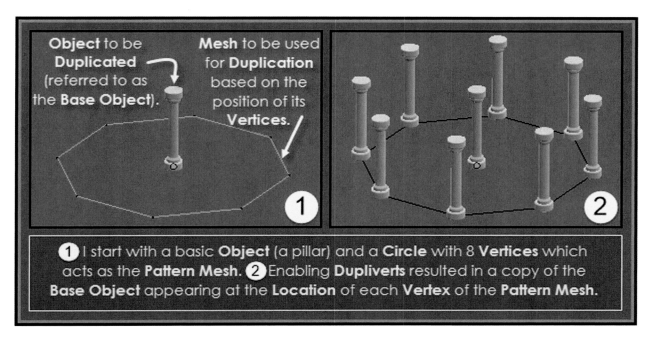

1 I start with a basic **Object** (a pillar) and a **Circle** with 8 **Vertices** which acts as the **Pattern Mesh**. **2** Enabling **Dupliverts** resulted in a copy of the **Base Object** appearing at the **Location** of each **Vertex** of the **Pattern Mesh**.

The *Base Object* appears in the *3D View* but will not appear in the final *Render*.

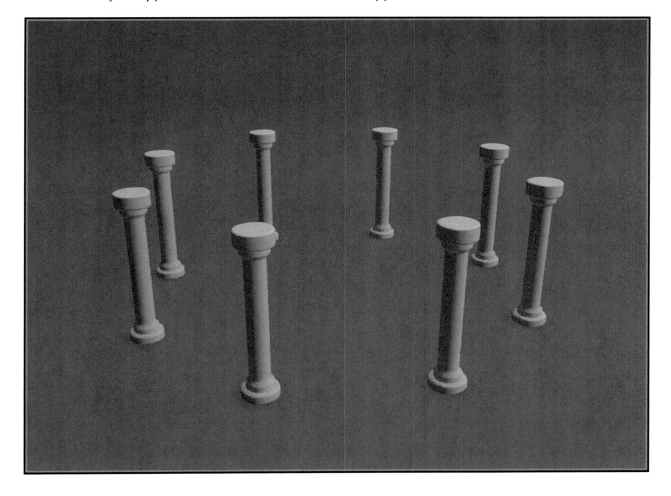

Setting up *Dupliverts* can be done as follows (I will use the above *Base Object* and *Pattern Mesh*).

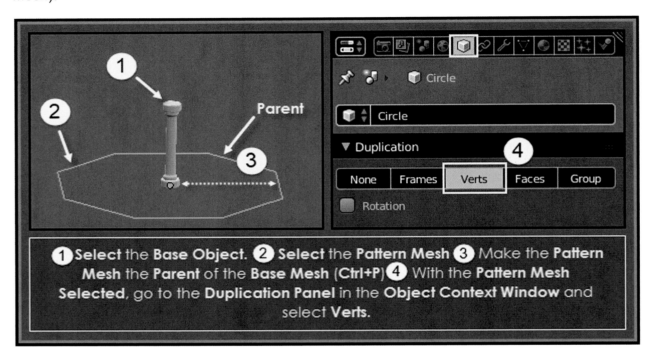

① Select the **Base Object**. ② Select the **Pattern Mesh** ③ Make the **Pattern Mesh** the **Parent** of the **Base Mesh (Ctrl+P)** ④ With the **Pattern Mesh** Selected, go to the **Duplication Panel** in the **Object Context Window** and select **Verts.**

Now any changes we make to the *Pattern Mesh* will change the result of the *Duplication* operation. I can *Move Vertices* in the *Pattern Mesh* allowing me to reposition each *Duplicate*. I can also add or remove *Vertices* from the *Pattern Mesh* to increase or decrease the number of *Duplicates* .

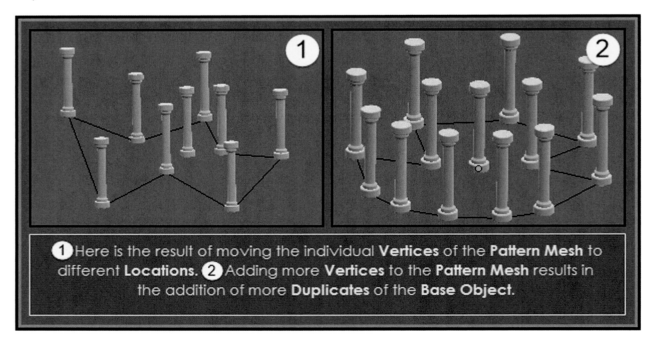

① Here is the result of moving the individual **Vertices** of the **Pattern Mesh** to different **Locations**. ② Adding more **Vertices** to the **Pattern Mesh** results in the addition of more **Duplicates** of the **Base Object.**

As you can see, you can arrange the *Pattern Mesh* any way you like. For example, if you are using *Dupliverts* to create several trees, you can change the *Location* of each tree individually by *Transforming* the individual *Vertices* of the *Pattern Mesh*.

I also demonstrate in the above illustration that it's very easy to add and remove *Duplicates* by simply adding / removing *Vertices*. The ability to *Transform* and add / remove *Duplicates* creates enormous flexibility when using *Dupliverts*.

As you might expect, any changes to the *Base Object* in *Object* or *Edit Mode* will be reflected on the *Duplicates*.

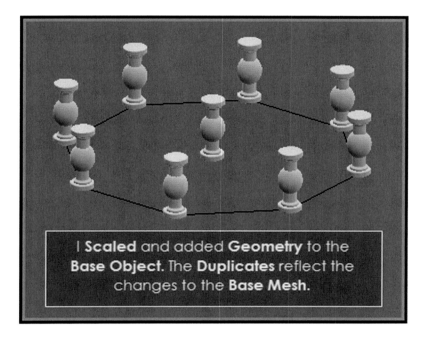

I **Scaled** and added **Geometry** to the **Base Object**. The **Duplicates** reflect the changes to the **Base Mesh**.

Let's see what happens when I enable *Dupliverts* using a *Sphere* as the *Pattern Mesh*.

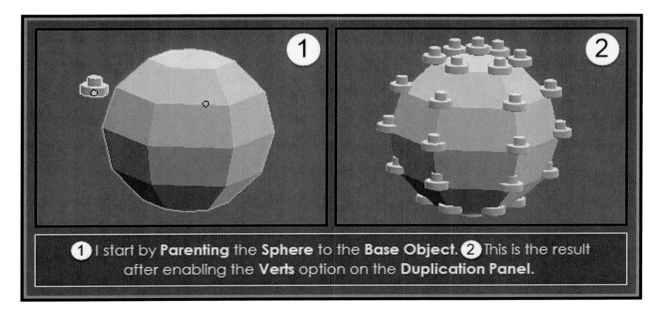

1 I start by **Parenting** the **Sphere** to the **Base Object**. **2** This is the result after enabling the **Verts** option on the **Duplication Panel**.

Well that's an interesting result. I would prefer if the *Duplicates* were pointing outwards. Fortunately, you can change the *Orientation* of the *Duplicated Objects*.

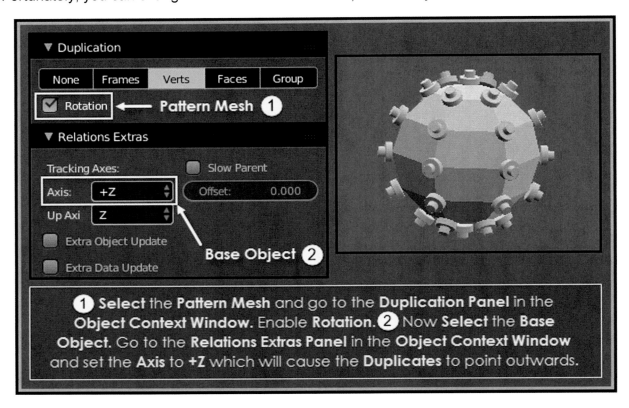

① **Select** the **Pattern Mesh** and go to the **Duplication Panel** in the **Object Context Window**. Enable **Rotation**. ② Now **Select** the **Base Object**. Go to the **Relations Extras Panel** in the **Object Context Window** and set the **Axis** to **+Z** which will cause the **Duplicates** to point outwards.

Now all I have to do is move the *Pattern Mesh* to another *Layer* and add a *Sphere* and you have something that looks like a World War 2 underwater sea mine.

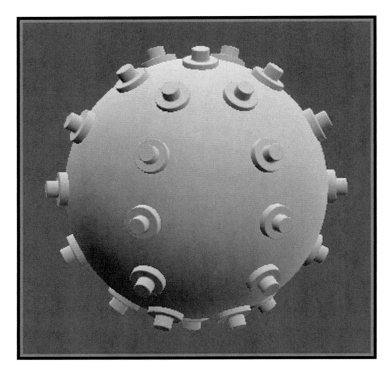

If your happy with the result and you want to turn all the *Duplicates* into individual *Objects* you can simply *Select* the *Pattern Mesh* and press Shift + Ctrl + A. The *Duplicates* should now be separate *Objects*. Also, the *Objects* (formerly *Duplicates*) are no longer affected by the *Pattern Mesh*.

The ability to have any changes to the *Base Mesh* be reflected on the *Duplicates* means you can go back and change the *Base Mesh* at any time. One example of where I found this handy was when I added rivets to my submarine *Model*. I created a rivet as a *Base Mesh* and used a *Circle* or *Plane* as the *Pattern Mesh*. After putting everything in place, I could quickly adjust the rivet size and count to get the result I was looking for.

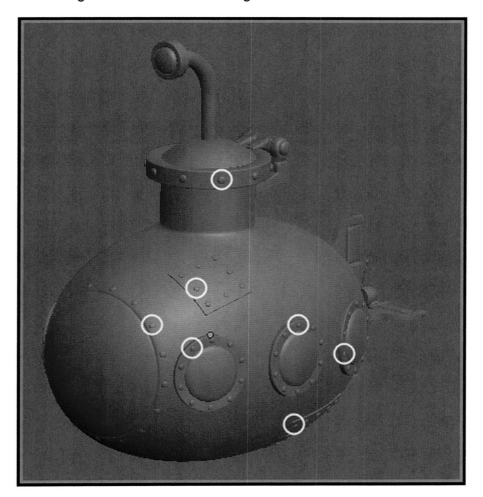

Each of the circled rivets in the above illustration is part of a group of *Objects* created using *Dupliverts*.

Background Image

One of the best ways to ensure your *Mesh* has accurate dimensions is to use a photo or blueprint to help guide the *Modeling* process. *Blender* allows you to load *Images* into the *Background* of the *3D View*. There are a few things to keep in mind.

- These *Images* only appear in the *3D View* and not in the final *Render*.
- *Background Images* can only be seen in *Orthographic View*.
- *Background Images* can only be seen in *Front*, *Back*, *Side*, *Top* and *Bottom View*. This makes sense as it's the only way to assure precise *Mesh Modeling*.

A *Background Image* can be a photo or drawing. You can also use a blueprint which will do the best job of ensuring accurate dimensions. You can find plenty of free blueprints online using a simple google search. I created my own basic blueprints for this book (to avoid copyright issues) but they are just to demonstrate the *Background* functionality. They aren't really blueprints to be honest but they should get the idea across. Most of what you find online will be of much higher quality. On a side note, I used *Blender* to generate my blueprints. What a versatile piece of software.

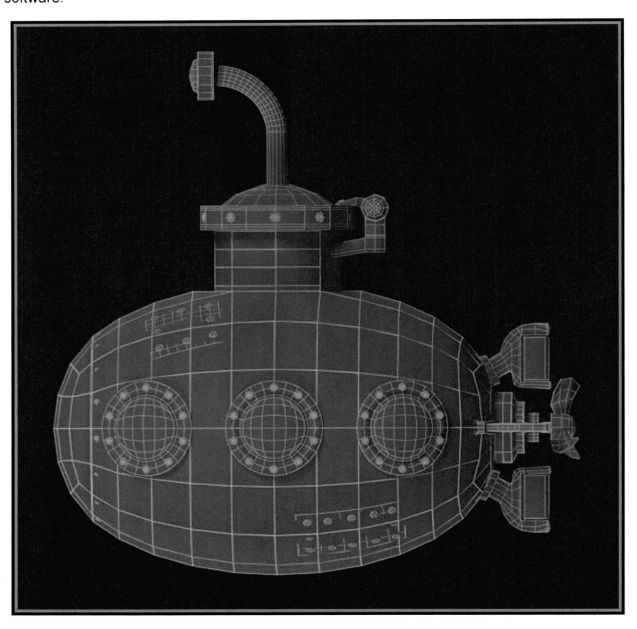

To add a *Background Image* open the *Properties Shelf* and enable the checkbox on the *Background Images Tab*. You could also press the *Add Image* button on the *Background Images Tab* which would also enable *Background Images*. Once enabled, if you haven't done so already, press *Add Image*. A dialog will pop up with a few buttons.

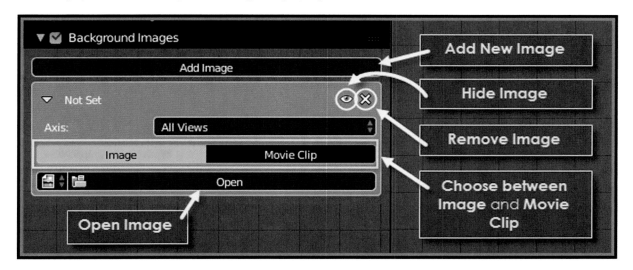

Each new *Image* you add will have its own dialog box. Press the *Add Image* button to continue adding new *Images*. The dialog has an icon (little eye) that allows you to toggle visibility of the *Image* in the *3D Space*. There is a little x icon that allows you to remove the *Image* dialog from the list of *Image* dialog boxes. There is an *Axis: Pulldown Menu* which I will talk about below. There are buttons to choose between using an *Image* or a *Movie Clip*. I will only cover using *Images* in this book. Finally, there is a button to open and select a *Background Image*. Once you open an *Image*, many more options become available in the dialog box. I should mention that you can simply drag an Image into the *3D View* to add it as a *Background Image*. The *Image* will appear in the *3D View* and a new dialog box will be created for the newly added *Image*.

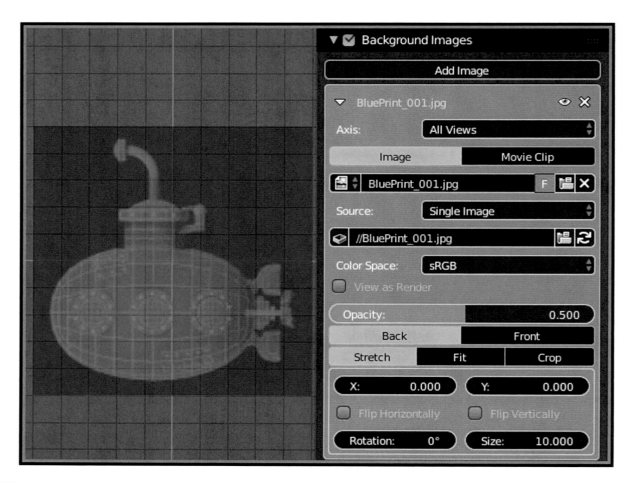

There are plenty of options available after adding an *Image* allowing you to tweak various *Image* properties. I talked about some of them earlier in the section and will cover some of the more important ones.

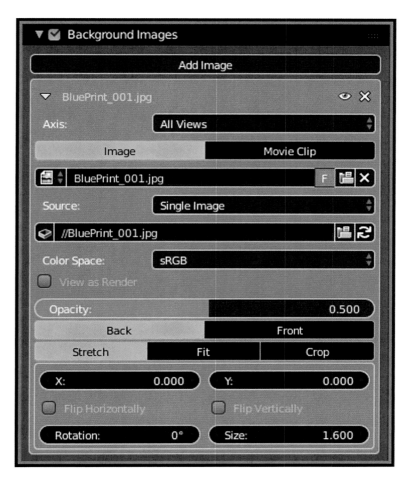

- The *Axis Menu* allows you to define which *View* an *Image* is visible in. I will expand on the *Axis Menu* a little later in this section.
- The *Opacity Slider* allows you to change the *Opacity* of the *Image*. I find myself changing this setting from time to time during the course of *Modeling*. There are times when I need to use the *Image* to do precise *Modeling* and other times when I just want it in the *Background* for general reference.
- The *Back* and *Front* buttons allow you to position the *Image* in front of all *Objects* or behind all *Objects*. If you keep it in front you will probably have to turn the *Opacity* down so you can have a pretty clear view of your *Mesh*.
- The *Stretch*, *Fit* and *Crop* buttons affect how the *Image* is displayed in *Camera View*. I don't usually like my *Background Images* displayed in *Camera View* but the option is there should you need it.
- The *X*, *Y* sliders allow you to re-position the *Image* in the *3D View*. You will almost certainly have to re-position an *Image* after adding it. *Blueprints* will often come with a *Front*, *Side* and *Top View*. You will usually have to re-position the *Images* so they line up correctly.
- The *Flip Horizontally* and *Flip Vertically* checkboxes allow you to *Flip* your *Image* in the *3D View*.
- The *Rotation Slider* allows you to *Rotate* the *Image* in the *3D View*

- The *Size Slider* allows you to re-size the *Image* in the *3D View*. Similar to the *X, Y Sliders,* you almost certainly will need to re-size an *Image* after adding it.

Often times when you get blueprints you may get separate *Images* for the *Front*, *Side* and *Top View* (or any combination of *Views*). In this case, you may want to only have a reference *Image* be visible in a specific *View*. With the *Axis Menu* you can configure an *Image* so that it's only visible in *Front View*. You can then load a 2nd *Image* and configure it so it's only visible in *Side View* and so on. You have the following options.

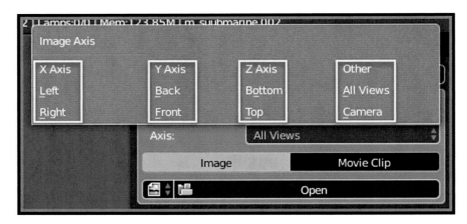

The default for a newly added Image is *All Views*. The available options are fairly straight forward.

Here is an example of 2 different *Images* both of which are set to be visible on a different *Axis*.

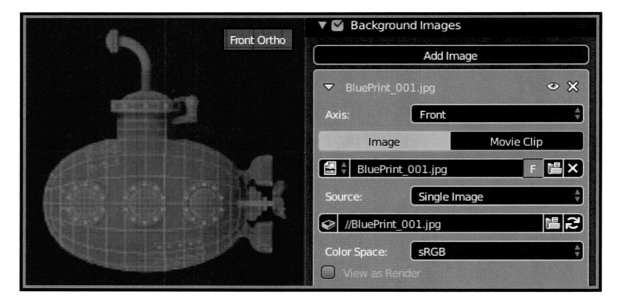

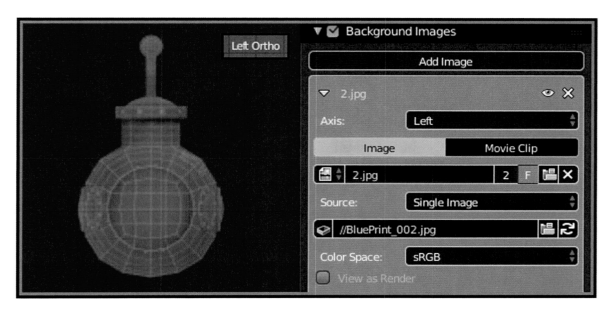

In the above illustrations I have 2 different *Images* loaded but because one image has an *Axis* setting of *Left* it will only be seen in the *Left View*. The other image has an *Axis* setting of *Front* and will only be seen in *Front View*. Switching to any other *View* will result in no *Images* being displayed.

You can disable the checkbox on the *Background Images* tab to temporarily hide all *Images*. You may want them out of the way during the course of *Modeling* and the checkbox is a quick and easy way to toggle the visibility of all *Images*. As I mentioned above, you can also toggle the visibility of each *Image* individually using the *Eye Icon* on the dialog box for that *Image*.

There is an alternative way to add reference *Images* to your *3D View* in *Blender*. As of *Blender* version 2.58, you can use an *Empty* to display an *Image* in the *3D View*. I find using an *Empty* is in many ways more versatile than a *Background Image* added via the *Properties Shelf*. (For more information on *Empties* see **Chapter 7 – Empties**).

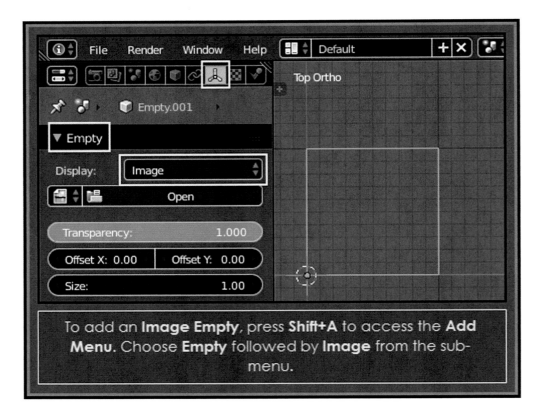

To add an **Image Empty**, press **Shift+A** to access the **Add Menu**. Choose **Empty** followed by **Image** from the sub-menu.

Notice in the above illustration that an *Image Empty* has controls that are very similar to the controls for adding a *Background Image* on the *Properties Shelf*. Once an *Image* is opened it will be visible in the *Empty*.

The **Image** is now visible in the **Empty**. Notice in the right hand **Empty** that the **Image** is visible in any **View**.

As I mentioned in the above illustration, you don't have to be in a specific *View* to see an *Image Empty*. You can *Rotate* the *3D View* and the *Image Empty* will always be visible.

You can use the controls on the *Empty* tab to change the *Size* and *Position* of the *Image* but you can also *Transform* the *Empty* to accomplish the same result. In fact, I find it quicker to just *Transform* the *Image Empty* like I would any other *Object* to get it positioned and sized correctly. I like the flexibility of *Image Empties* and use them exclusively when I need to use reference *Images*. I like being able to do the following.

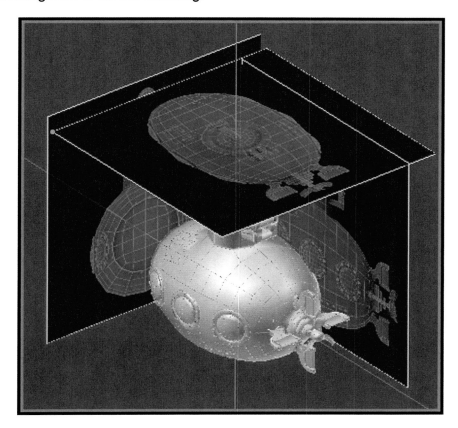

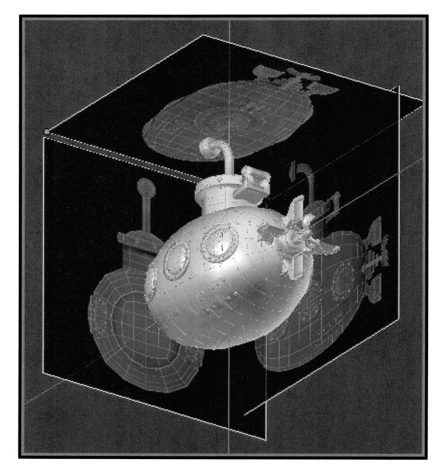

If you want to hide all of the *Images* simply put all the *Empties* on 1 *Layer* or in a *Group* and toggle the visibility of the *Layer* / *Group* as needed.

Aligning Objects

There are plenty of ways to *Align Objects* and *Mesh Elements* using *Snapping* and *The Snap To Mesh Tool* (which I cover later in this chapter) etc. *Blender* also provides functionality that allows you to *Align Objects* in the *3D View*. The *Align Objects* functionality is only available in *Object Mode*. To use the *Alignment* functionality *Select* 2 or more *Objects* and then select *Align Objects* from the *Object->Transform Menu*.

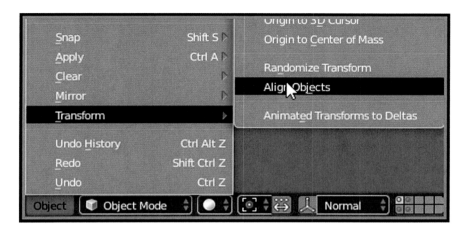

After initiating an *Align Objects* operation press F6 to access the *Operator Panel* to set the options. The *Operator Panel* also appears on the *Tools Shelf*.

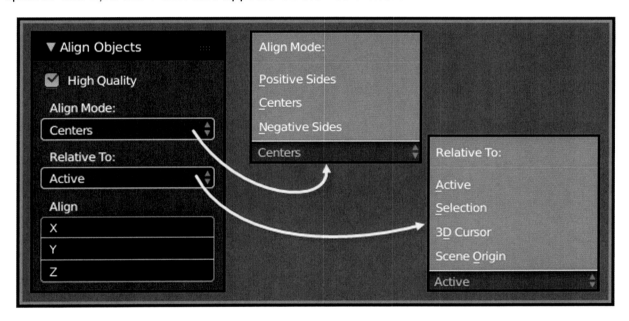

The first option is the *Align Mode Menu*. I can't say it any better than an illustration. I start with 3 *Cubes* of different sizes that are randomly positioned.

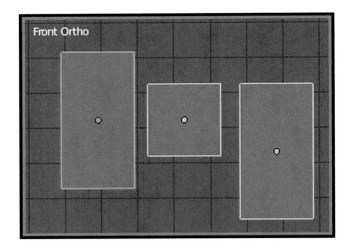

Now I will perform an *Align Objects* operation setting the *Align Mode* to *Positive Sides*.

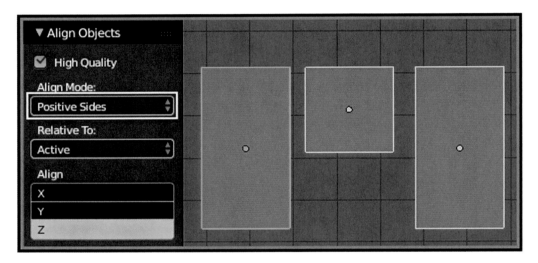

Notice the tops of the *Cubes* are now aligned along the *Z-Axis*. Let's switch to *Negative Sides*.

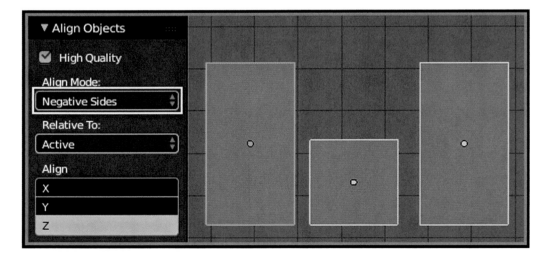

The result isn't surprising. The bottoms of the *Cubes* are now aligned along the *Z-Axis*. Finally I will set the *Align Mode* to *Centers*.

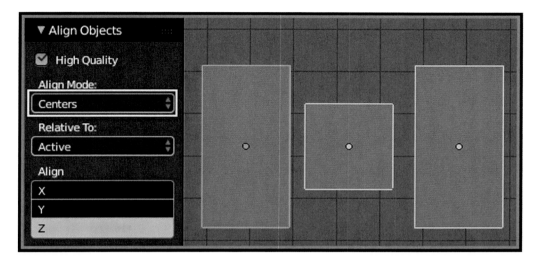

All *Objects* are now *Aligned* along the *Z-Axis* based on their *Centers*. *Centers* in this case refers to the *Center* of the *Mesh* and not the *Object Origin*.

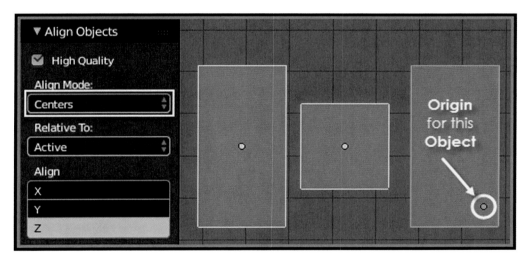

I moved the *Origin* for one of the *Cubes* and it had no effect on the *Alignment* operation.

Next we have the *Relative To: Menu*. You can set the *Alignment* to be *Relative* to the *Active Object*, the *Current Selection* , the *3D Cursor* or the *Scene Origin*.

The *Align* buttons allow you to indicate whether you want to align to the *X*, *Y* or *Z-Axis*. You can enable more than 1 *Align* button allowing you to *Align* with multiple *Axes* at once.

It's the combination of the *Align Mode Menu*, *Relative To Menu* and *Align* settings that offer plenty of options when *Aligning Objects*. With some experimentation you can usually get the result you're looking for.

Object Origins

Each *Mesh Object* in *Blender* has an *Origin Point*. When you add a new *Object* in *Blender*, the *Object Origin* will be at the *Center* of the *Objects* geometry and is represented by a round dot. As we have seen several times, the *Object Origin* can be moved which can have an effect on some *Blender* operations.

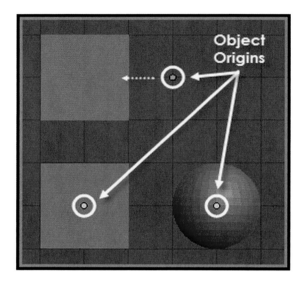

As you can see in the above illustration, the *Origin* for an *Object* can be *Located* outside the boundaries of the *Mesh*.

To help understand a little more about *Object Origins* start with an empty *Scene* and *Snap* the *Cursor* to the *3D World Origin* by pressing Shift + C. The *3D World Origin* is *Location 0,0,0* in the *3D World*.

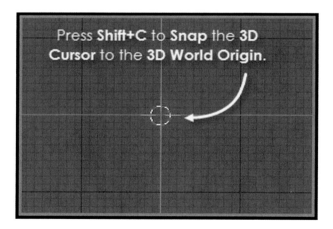

Now add a *Cube*. The *Cube* will be added at the *Location* of the *3D Cursor* and consequently will also be *Located* at the *3D World Origin*.

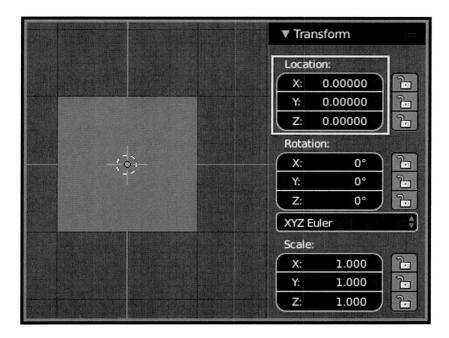

Now I will move the *Cube* in *Object Mode.*

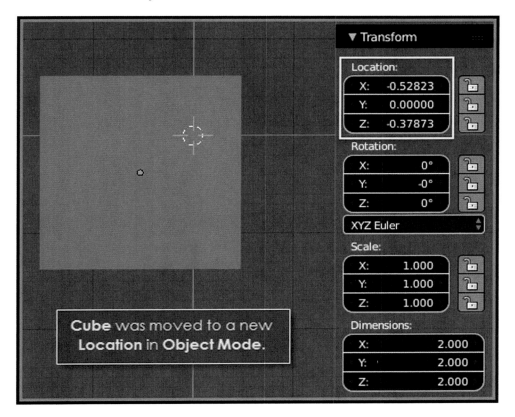

Notice that the *Location* coordinates have changed. The *Location* coordinates represent the position of the *Object Origin* of the *Cube* as it relates to the *3D World Origin*. That is the reason why when you apply the *Location* of an *Object*, it returns to the *3D World Location* (for more on

Applying Transformations see **Chapter 5 – Applying Object Transformations**). Now I will move the *Cube* back to the *3D World Origin* and move it to a new *Location* in *Edit Mode*.

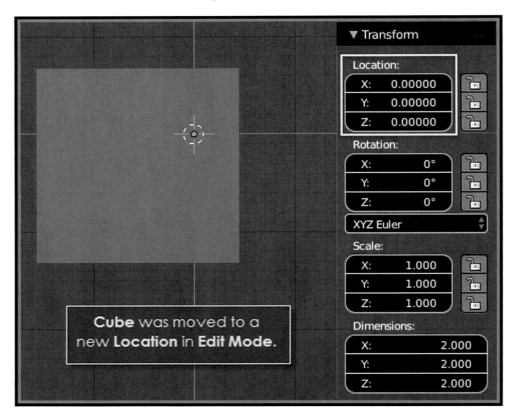

Moving the *Object* in *Edit Mode* did not result in any changes to the *Location* of the *Object Origin* (for more info on the results of performing *Transformations* in *Object Mode* vs *Edit mode* see **Chapter 5 – Local Transform Orientation**). As far as *Blender* is concerned, the *Cube* hasn't moved at all. The *Object Origin* of the *Cube* hasn't moved so to *Blender* the *Cube* hasn't moved.

Many operations in *Blender* involve using the *Object Origin* so it's always a good idea to ensure the *Object Origin* is where you expect it to be and hasn't accidentally taken a trip far and away from its corresponding *Mesh* (unless that was your intention).

You can at any time move the *Origin* of any *Object* to any *Location*. For example, let's say you want to move the *Object Origin* to the geometric center of a *Mesh*. Simply *Select* the *Object* and access the *Set Origin Menu* by pressing Shift + Ctrl + Alt + C. Select *Origin to Geometry* from the *Set Origin Menu* to move the *Object Origin* to the *Geometric Center* of the *Object*.

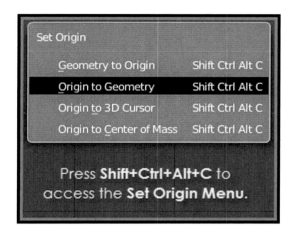

As you can see there is also an option to *Set* the *Geometry* to the current *Location* of the *Origin* for that *Object*. You can also set the *Origin* to the *3D Cursor*. This allows you to place the *Object Origin* just about anywhere which can be handy when performing *Transform* operations.

The *Object Origin* is more relevant in *Object Mode*. If you *Select* a *Mesh* in *Edit Mode* and *Snap* the *3D Cursor to Selection* the *3D Cursor* will move to the *Geometric Center* of the *Mesh*, regardless of the *Location* of the *Object Origin*. Performing the same *Snap* operation in *Object Mode* will result in the *3D Cursor* moving to the *Location* of the *Object Origin*, regardless of the *Mesh Location*.

Chapter 8 - Manipulating Geometry

In a book about *Modeling* in *Blender*, it's safe to say this chapter is the meat and potatoes of this book. *Modeling* involves adding, removing, extruding, transforming, cutting and ripping *Mesh Elements* (to name a few). Manipulating *Geometry* requires tools and fortunately *Blender* has a large selection of tools to help you transform and build your *Mesh*. A good set of tools helps expedite the *Modeling* process and allows you to focus more on inspiration and spend less time on tedious activities.

Mesh Primitives

When you begin a new *Model* you need a starting point. *Blender* comes with several basic *Mesh Objects* that can be used as the foundation for any new *Model*. These *Mesh Objects* are referred to as *Mesh Primitives*.

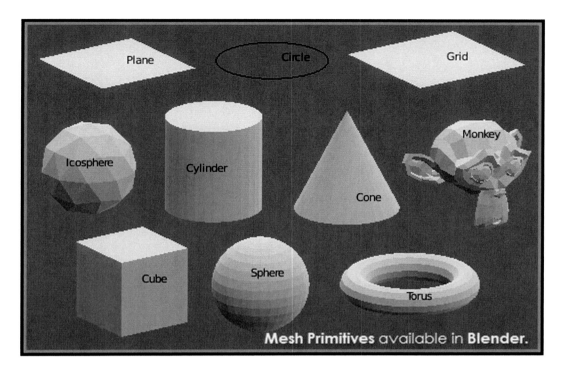

Mesh Primitives available in Blender.

You ca add a *Mesh Primitive* to your *Scene* by accessing the *Add Menu* (Shift + A).

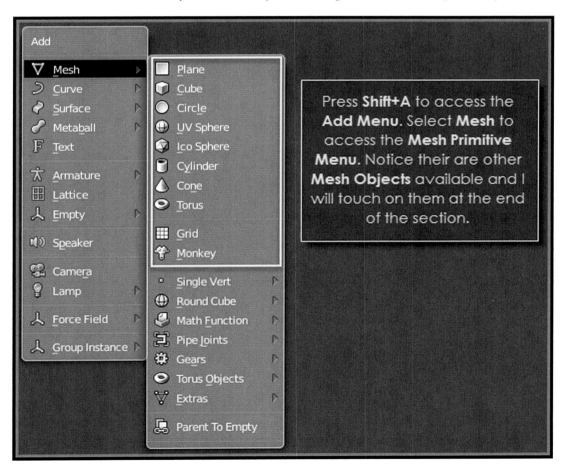

Press **Shift+A** to access the **Add Menu**. Select **Mesh** to access the **Mesh Primitive Menu**. Notice their are other **Mesh Objects** available and I will touch on them at the end of the section.

After you add a *Mesh Primitive*, you have access to the *Operator Panel* which allows you to modify the characteristics of the *Mesh* before you start using it. The *Operator Panel* is sometimes referred to as the *Context Panel*. To access the *Operator Panel* for each *Mesh Primitive*, press F6 after adding the *Mesh*. The *Operator Panel* also appears in the *Tools Shelf* if you have it open.

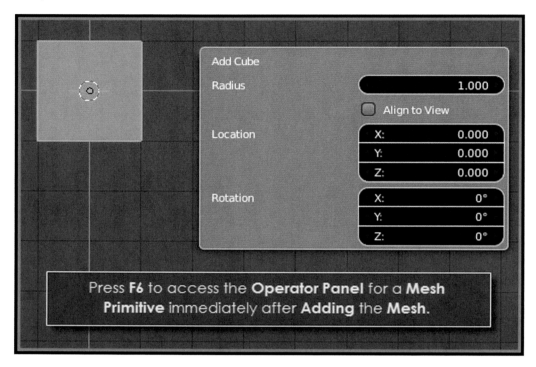

It's important to remember the *Operator Panel* is available until you perform a *Transform* operation or enter *Edit Mode*. Once the *Operator Panel* disappears you no longer have access to it. Pressing F6 at that point will give you access to a *Transform Panel* which contains some of the options available in the *Operator Panel* but not all.

Plane

The *Plane Mesh Primitive* is essentially a single *Face*. It's a flat *Mesh* containing 4 *Vertices*.

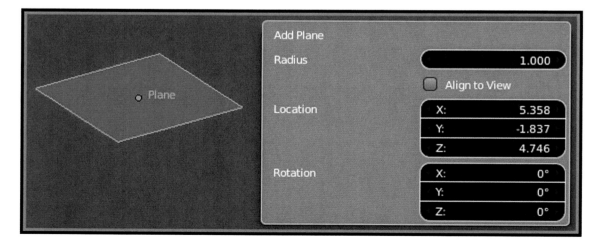

The options on the *Operator Panel* are as follows:

- *Radius* - change the *Plane* size.
- *Align to View* - Rotate the *Mesh* so that it's *Aligned* with the current *3D View*.
- *Location* and *Rotation* - perform *Transform* operations.

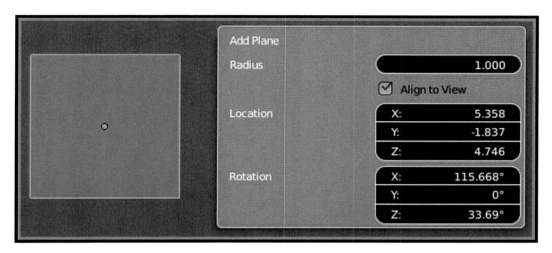

An example of when the *Align to View* option is handy is when you add a *Plane* in *Front View* and you want the *Plane* to be facing towards you and not the moon. Keep in mind this will affect the *Rotation* of the *Plane* and you may want to perform an *Apply Rotation* (see **Chapter 5 – Applying and Clearing Object Transformations**) operation before you start using the *Plane*.

Cube

The *Cube Mesh Primitive* is a simple 6 sided *Cube*.

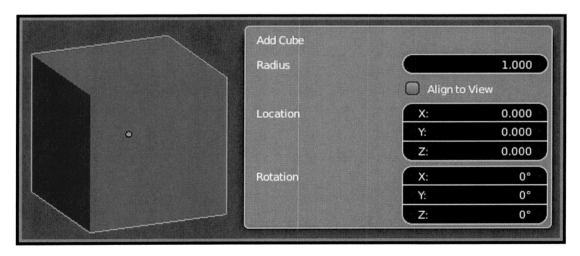

The options on the *Operator Panel* are as follows:

- *Radius* - change the *Cube* size.
- *Align to View* - Rotate the *Mesh* so that it's *Aligned* with the current *3D View*.
- *Location* and *Rotation* - perform *Transform* operations.

Circle

The *Circle Mesh Primitive* is a group of *Vertices* arranged in a perfect *Circle*.

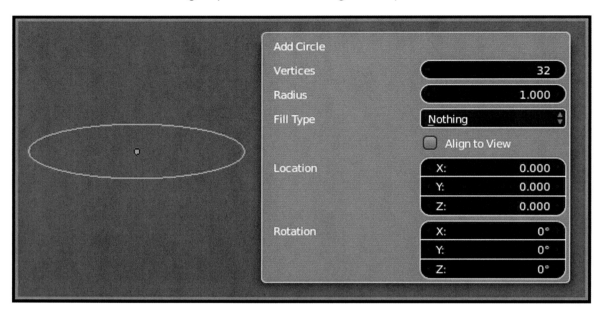

The options on the *Operator Panel* are as follows:

- *Vertices* - set the number of *Vertices* used to define the *Circle*.
- *Radius* - set the *Radius* or *Size* of the *Circle*.
- *Fill Type* - define how the *Circle* is filled - more below.
- *Align to View* - *Rotate* the *Mesh* so that it's *Aligned* with the current *3D View*.
- *Location* and *Rotation* - perform *Transform* operations.

The minimum number of *Vertices* needed for a *Circle* is 3. If you try to enter 2 or less in the *Operator Panel* it will just default to 3. A *Circle* with 3 *Vertices* is essentially a *Triangle* but because there are no hard rules on how many *Vertices* are required for a *Mesh* to be considered a *Circle*, it's technically also a *Circle*. You could probably argue that a *Plane* is a *Circle* with 4 *Vertices* and you would be right.

The *Operator Panel* also has a *Menu* labeled *Fill Type*. There are 3 options in the *Fill Type Menu*; they are *Triangle Fan*, *Ngon* and *Nothing*.

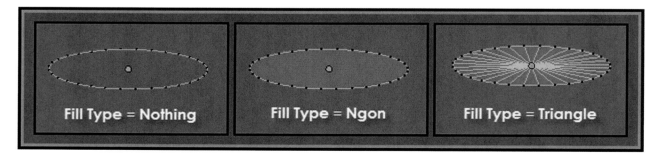

I personally always use a *Fill Type* of *Nothing*. If you have read through this book in order you know by now I am not a fan of *Triangles* or *Ngons* and I avoid using them as much as possible. I prefer this.

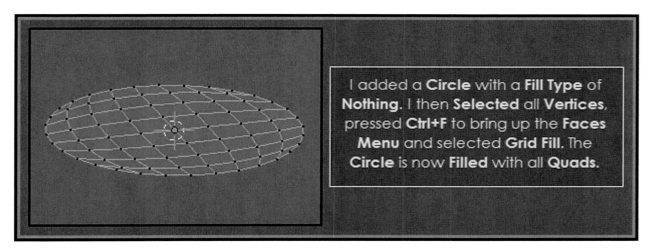

I added a **Circle** with a **Fill Type** of **Nothing**. I then **Selected** all **Vertices**, pressed **Ctrl+F** to bring up the **Faces Menu** and selected **Grid Fill**. The **Circle** is now **Filled** with all **Quads**.

UV Sphere

A *UV Sphere Primitive* is a *Sphere* made up of *Segments* and *Rings*. *Segments* are *Vertical* and run *North South* and *Rings* are *Horizontal* and run *East West*.

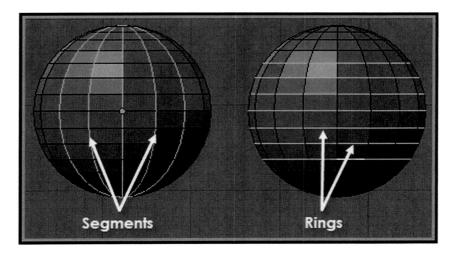

Segments   Rings

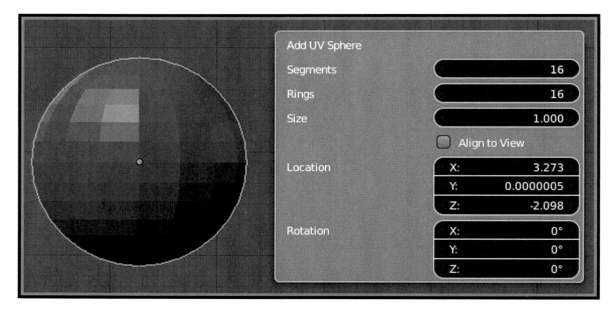

The options on the *Operator Panel* are as follows:

- *Segments*, *Rings* - set the number of *Segments* and *Rings* used to define the *UV Sphere*.
- *Size*, *Location* and *Rotation* - perform *Transform* operations.
- *Align to View* - Rotate the *Mesh* so that it's *Aligned* with the current *3D View*.

It should be noted that a *UV Sphere* contains *Triangles*. You can fix that easily with *Grid Fill* as detailed in the section on the *Circle Mesh Primitive*.

Ico Sphere

The *Ico Sphere Mesh Primitive* is a *Sphere* that is entirely made up of *Triangles*.

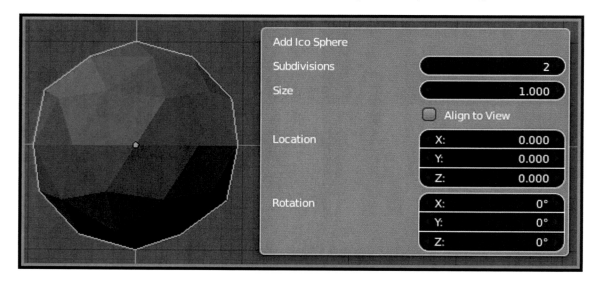

The options on the *Operator Panel* are as follows:

- *Subdivisions* - set the number of *Subdivisions* used to define the *IcoSphere*.
- *Size*, *Location* and *Rotation* - perform *Transform* operations.
- *Align to View* - Rotate the *Mesh* so that it's *Aligned* with the current *3D View*.

As a person who avoids *Triangles* during the *3D Modeling* process, you might think I would discourage the use of the *Ico Sphere* and on the whole you would be right. Still, there are situations where an *Ico Sphere* might be a better choice than a *UV Sphere*. For example, I have read that an *Ico Sphere* may yield better results when performing *UV Mapping* operations. UV Mapping is outside the scope of this book so I won't elaborate further. I would just consider when using an *Ico Sphere* that it comes with all the issues related to *Modeling* with *Triangles* (see **Chapter 4 – Quads, Triangles, Ngons**).

Cylinder

The *Cylinder Mesh Primitive* is a basic *Cylinder*.

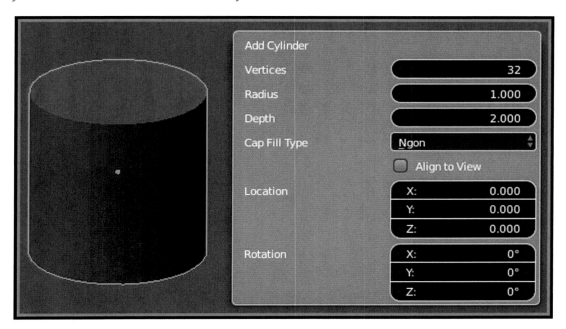

The options on the *Operator Panel* are as follows:

- *Vertices* - set the number of *Vertices* for both the top and bottom of the *Cylinder*.
- *Radius* - set the *Radius* or *Size* for both the top and bottom of the *Cylinder*.
- *Depth* - set the *Height* of the *Cylinder*.
- *Cap Fill Type* - allows you to set the *Fill Type* for the *Cylinder End Caps*. Like the *Circle Mesh*, the 3 available choices for the *Cylinder End Cap* are *Triangle Fan*, *Ngon* and *None*. As I mentioned previously in the *Circle Mesh Primitive* section, I prefer to set the *Fill Type* to *None* and if needed, I *Cap* the *Ends* with all *Quads*.
- *Align to View* - Rotate the *Mesh* so that it's *Aligned* with the current *3D View*.
- *Location* and *Rotation* - perform *Transform* operations.

Cone

The *Cone Mesh Primitive* is a basic *Cone* shaped *Mesh* that is in a lot of ways a variation of the *Cylinder*.

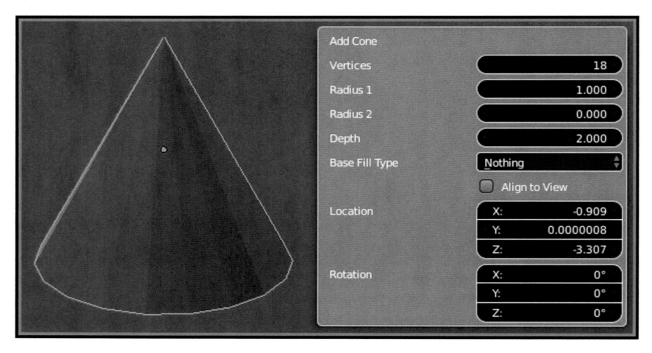

The options on the *Operator Panel* are as follows:

- *Vertices* - set the number of *Vertices* for both the top and bottom of the *Cone*.
- *Radius 1* and *Radius 2* - set the *Radius* or *Size* of the top and bottom of the *Cone*.
- *Depth* - set the *Height* of the *Cone*.
- *Base Fill Type* - set the *Fill Type* for the *Cone End Caps*. Like the *Circle Mesh*, the 3 available choices for the *Cone End Cap* are *Triangle Fan*, *Ngon* and *Nothing*.
- *Location* and *Rotation* - perform *Transform* operations.
- *Align to View* - *Rotate* the *Mesh* so that it's *Aligned* with the current *3D View*.

It should be noted that even though the top of the *Cone* is a sharp point, it's not a *Single Vertex*. As I mentioned above, a *Cone* is essentially a *Cylinder* with 1 of its *End Caps* sized down.

Torus

The *Torus Mesh Primitive* is a *Mesh* shaped like a tire or doughnut. You could achieve the same result by *Extruding* a *Circle Mesh* around an *Axis* but there are several options available when adding a *Torus* that make it a more versatile option.

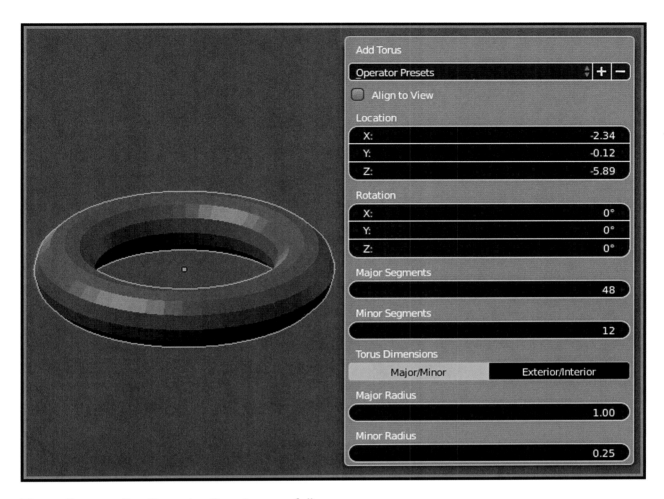

The options on the *Operator Panel* are as follows:

- *Operator Presets* - allows you to define custom presets for defining a *Torus*. After tweaking a *Torus* you can save the configuration to be used in a future *Modeling Project*. More on this below.
- *Align to View* - *Rotate* the *Mesh* so that it's *Aligned* with the current *3D View*.
- *Location* and *Rotation* - perform *Transform* operations.
- *Major Segments* - the number of *Segments* or *Circles* used to define the *Torus*.
- *Minor Segments* - the number of *Vertices* used to define the *Circles* that are used to define the *Torus*. In other words, the number of *Vertices* in each *Major Segment*.
- *Torus Dimensions* - I discuss *Torus Dimensions* in more detail below.

You can save your favorite *Torus* configurations in the *Operator Presets Menu*. Simply add a *Torus*, modify the *Torus* using the *Operator Panel* and then use the *Plus Button* next to the *Operators Presets Menu* to save the current *Torus* configuration for future use.

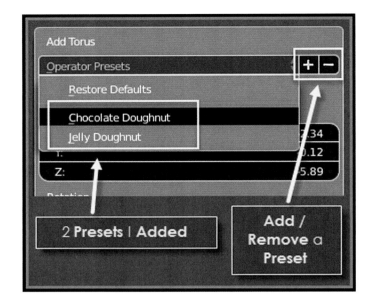

There is also a *Restore Defaults* option in the *Operator Presets Menu* to reset the *Operator Panel* setting back to default settings.

The *Torus Dimensions* section on the *Operator Panel* consists of 2 buttons labeled *Major / Minor* and *Exterior / Interior*. Below the *Torus Dimensions* section there are 2 *Sliders*. The label and functionality of those *Sliders* will change depending on which *Torus Dimensions* option you have selected.

Selecting *Major / Minor* in the *Torus Dimensions* section will change the *Slider Labels* to *Major Radius* and *Minor Radius*. The *Major Radius* changes the *Size* of the *Torus* without changing the *Size* of the *Circles* that define the *Torus*. The *Minor Radius* changes the *Size* of the *Circles* that define the *Torus*.

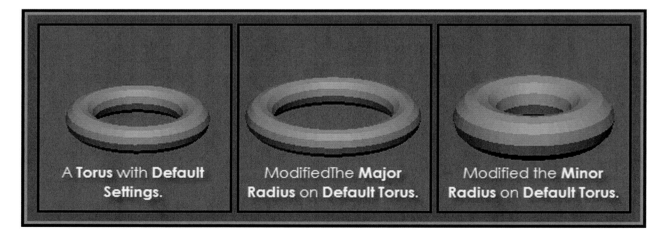

Selecting *Exterior / Interior* in the *Torus Dimensions* section will change the *Slider Labels* to *Exterior Radius* and *Interior Radius*. The *Exterior Radius* allows you to change the *Size* of the *Torus* including the *Circles* that define the *Torus*. The *Interior Radius* allows you to change the

Size of the *Center* (doughnut hole) of the *Torus* without affecting the outer radius of the *Torus*. The *Circles* that define the *Torus* also change with the *Interior Radius Slider*.

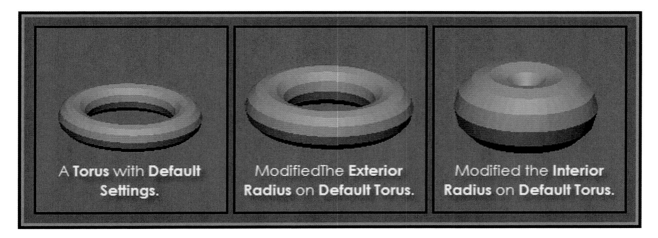

| A **Torus** with **Default** Settings. | Modified The **Exterior** **Radius** on **Default Torus**. | Modified the **Interior** **Radius** on **Default Torus**. |

As you can see there are plenty of options for changing the characteristics of a *Torus*. If you need a doughnut (or tire, or onion ring, or life preserver) and you want full control of its initial geometry, look no further.

Grid

The *Grid Mesh Primitive* is a simple *Grid*. It's essentially a *Subdivided Plane*.

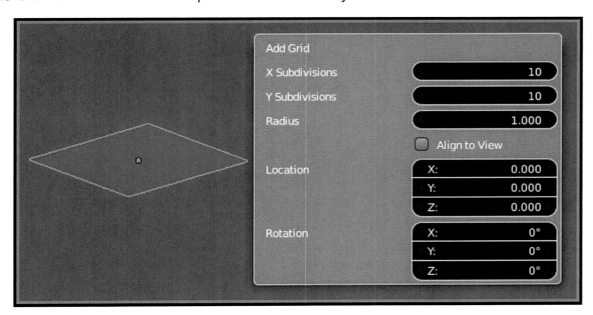

The options on the *Operator Panel* are as follows:

- *X* and *Y Subdivisions* - number of grid lines along the *X* and *Y-Axis* of the *Grid*. The minimum is 3.
- *Radius* - change the *Grid Size*.
- *Align to View* - *Rotate* the *Mesh* so that it's *Aligned* with the current *3D View*.

- *Location* and *Rotation* - perform *Transform* operations.

Monkey

A *Monkey*? Yes, one of the *Mesh Primitives* that comes with *Blender* is a *Monkey* (more specifically, the head of a *Monkey*). If you have any experience visiting *Blender* related web sites it's a very good bet you have seen the *Monkey*. The *Monkey* has been given the name *Suzanne* and has become a fixture in the world of *Blender*. So is *Suzanne* useful for anything? Think of *Suzanne* as a reference *Mesh* that you can use to quickly test a new *Lighting* setup or that *Material* you have been working on. You get a better idea of how something looks with *Suzanne* than you would with a *Plane* or *Cube*. When you need a quick test *Mesh* with a decent amount of detail, *Suzanne* is your *Mesh*.

Mesh Add-Ons

Wait, there's more. There are several *Add-Ons* included with *Blender* or available as *Add-Ons* that allow you to add a variety of *Mesh Objects* to your *Scene*. I won't go into detail about all of them as I am hoping to eventually finish writing the book. I will however talk briefly about some of my favorites.

Pipe Joints includes several *Mesh Primitives* that can be used as *Pipe Joints* among other things. This is a real time saver as creating a *Pipe Joint* with proper geometry can be time consuming and challenging. There are plenty of options on the *Operator Panel* to tweak the *Pipe Joint* to your liking.

The *Extras Add-On* provides several *Mesh Objects* that don't really fall in any category. Some of them make a good reference *Mesh* and others are a good base *Mesh* for specific situations. I also have to admit, some of them are pretty cool.

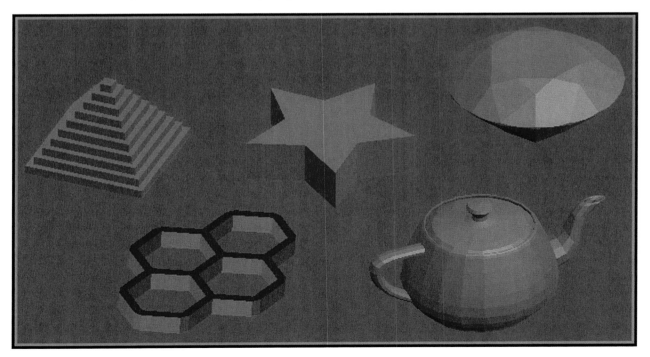

I encourage you to explore the *Add-Ons* as some of them can be real time savers. You can also search for and download *Add-Ons* from the internet.

Deleting Mesh Elements

Before I start talking about how to add *Geometry* to your *Mesh*, let me first talk about how to remove *Geometry* from your *Mesh*. You can remove *Mesh Elements* using the *Delete Menu* which is accessed by pressing X. The *Delete Menu* has options to *Delete Mesh Elements* in both a destructive and non-destructive way.

Vertices, Edges, Faces

The first 3 options in the *Delete Menu* are pretty self-explanatory. You can delete *Selected Vertices*, *Edges* or *Faces*. This type of *Delete* operation is destructive.

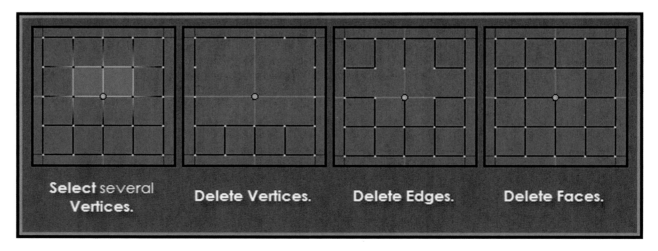

Select *several* **Vertices.**   **Delete Vertices.**   **Delete Edges.**   **Delete Faces.**

You can see the results of the *Delete* operations in the above illustration. *Deleting Vertices* was the most destructive as all connected *Edges* were also *Deleted*. Removing a *Vertex* also removes any *Edges* and *Faces* that are connected to that *Vertex*. When the *Edges* were *Deleted*, all *Selected Edges* and any *Faces* that were connected to those *Edges* were removed but the *Vertices* were not. *Deleting* the *Faces* resulted in the removal of both *Selected Faces* and any *Edges* that were shared by both *Faces*. The surrounding *Vertices* and *Edges* were not affected.

Here is another example with more *Mesh Elements Selected*.

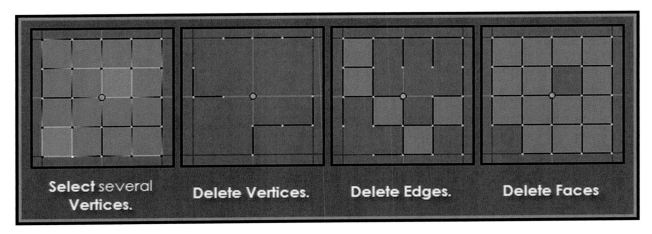

Only Edges and Faces, Only Faces

The *Only Faces* and *Only Edges and Faces* options are a little less destructive than the regular *Delete* options. Selecting *Only Edges and Faces* will remove any *Selected Edges* and *Faces* but not the *Vertices* that define the *Selected Edges / Faces*. Selecting *Only Faces* will delete the *Selected Faces* and not the *Edges* or *Vertices* that define the *Selected Faces*.

At first glance it appears using *Only Edges and Faces* and *Only Faces* produces the same results as *Deleting Vertices*, *Edges* and *Faces*. The results can often be identical based on your

Selection. In the above illustration, you can see that the *Vertex* at the bottom left was not removed as part of the *Delete* operation. That was not the case when performing a *Delete* operation by selecting *Vertices*, *Edges* or *Faces* from the *Delete Menu*.

Dissolve

The *Dissolve Tool* will combine *Selected Mesh Elements* as opposed to *Deleting* them. The result is an *Ngon*. The result depends on the *Mesh Elements* in the current *Selection*.

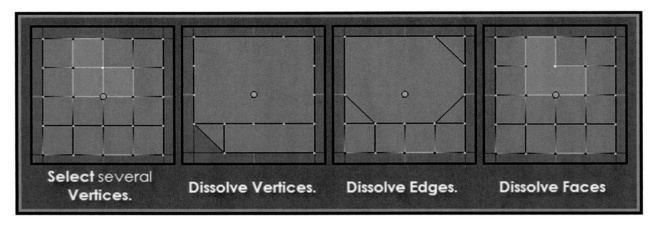

Notice in the above illustration that all 3 *Dissolve* options create *Ngons*. *Dissolve Vertices* and *Dissolve Edges* also create *Triangles*. The *Dissolve Vertices* removed all *Selected Vertices* without removing any *Faces*. Instead, an *Ngon* or *Triangle* was created. *Dissolve Edges* exhibits a similar behavior. The *Selected Edges* are removed at the cost of *Ngons* and *Triangles*. *Dissolve Faces* will also result in the creation of *Ngons*. One way to think of it is the *Dissolve Tool* allows you to remove *Mesh Elements* without removing any *Faces* and thus leaves no holes in your *Mesh*.

Dissolve can be useful for adding or removing geometry in a non-destructive way. You maintain the shape of your *Mesh* without removing any *Faces* or creating holes. I would just caution you to ensure you fix you *Ngons* and *Triangles* after doing a *Dissolve*.

Limited Dissolve

Limited Dissolve is similar to *Dissolve* in terms of the final result but there are rules around which *Selected Mesh Elements* are removed. Essentially, the angle of the *Edges* / *Vertices* determines which *Mesh Elements* get *Dissolved*. You set the *Angle* on the *Operator Panel* after initiating a *Limited Dissolve* operation. To access the *Limited Dissolve Operator Panel*, press F6 after initiating a *Limited Dissolve* operation. The *Operator Panel* also appears in the *Tools Shelf* if you have it open.

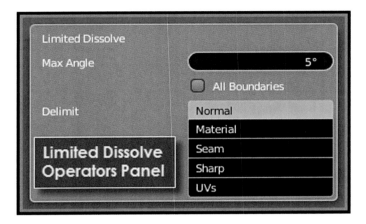

To demonstrate *Limited Dissolve* I will start with a *Subdivided Plane*. I enabled the displaying of *Angles* for the *Selected Edges* in the *Mesh Display* section of the *Properties Shelf* (see **Chapter 3 – Mesh Display**). I use *Edges* to demonstrate *Limited Dissolve* for this example.

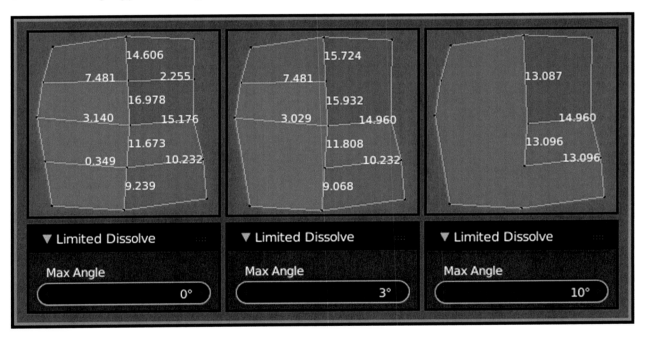

The angles listed for the *Edges* in the first panel have a value of 0.349 degrees or higher. The *Max Angle* is set to 0 and consequently no *Edges* have been *Dissolved*. When I increase the *Max Angle* to 3 degrees, any *Edges* whose angle is less than 3 degrees are *Dissolved*. In this example, only 1 *Edge* had an angle less than 3 degrees and consequently only that *Edge* was *Dissolved*. I then changed the *Max Angle* to 10 degrees which caused all *Edges* that had an angle of less than 10 degrees to be *Dissolved*.

You may have noticed that the angles for some of the *Edges* changed after the *Dissolve* operation. When you perform a *Dissolve Limited* operation, the angle of the surrounding *Edges* will change as other *Edges* are *Dissolved*. The change in angle can cause *Edges* that initially had an angle that was above the *Max Angle* to change to an angle that is below the *Max Angle* causing them to also be *Dissolved*.

Edge Collapse

Edges Collapse works the same as the *Collapse* option when performing a *Merge* operation (See **Chapter 8 – Merge**).

Edge Loops

I talk about creating and deleting *Edge Loops* in the **The Loop Cut Tool** section. The *Edge Loops* option allows you to remove *Edge Loops* in a non-destructive way. You can remove an entire *Edge Loop* without affecting the surrounding *Geometry*. This is very handy for removing *Geometry* without having to rebuild the *Mesh*.

The Extrude Tool

There is a reason why *Extrude* is the first tool I am talking about in this chapter. You will use a variety of tools when *3D Modeling* but it's a safe bet that you will use the *Extrude Tool* more than any other tool. When you think of the term *Extrude* you think of forcing something through a die to help shape it. *Extrude* in *Blender* is slightly different. One way to think of it is to create a <u>connected copy</u> of a *Mesh Element* to the original *Selection*. Here is a basic example.

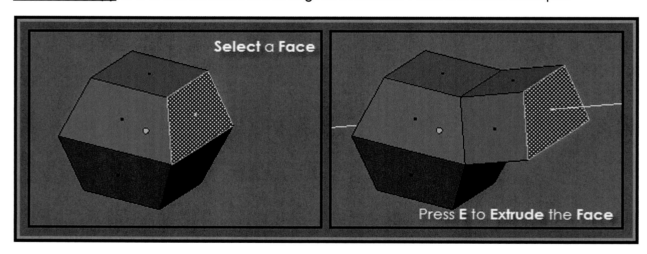

In the above illustration the single *Face* is *Extruded* by pressing E on the keyboard. The direction of the *Extrusion* is constrained along the *Face Normal* (for more on *Normals* see **Chapter 3 – Normals** and **Chapter 5 – Normal Transform Orientation**). After the *Extrude* operation is initiated, you then use the Mouse to position the *Extruded Mesh Element* by moving it along the *Face Normal*. Once you are happy with the *Location* of the *Extruded Mesh Element*, press the LMB to confirm the operation. You could also constrain the *Extruded Face* to any *Axis* by pressing X, Y or Z after initiating the *Extrude*. If you hit Escape or press the RMB after initiating the *Extrusion* operation, (i.e. don't press LMB to confirm the operation) the *Extruded Mesh Element* will *Snap* back to its original *Location*. This will not cancel the *Extrude* operation, it will only cancel the *Transform* portion of the *Extrude* operation. You can then perform any *Transform* operations on the *Extruded Mesh Element* you like.

You can *Extrude* more than one *Mesh Element* and the result will depend on whether or not the *Mesh Elements* are connected. If 2 or more *Mesh Elements* are connected, they will be *Extruded* as 1 *Mesh Element*, if they are not connected, they will be *Extruded* individually.

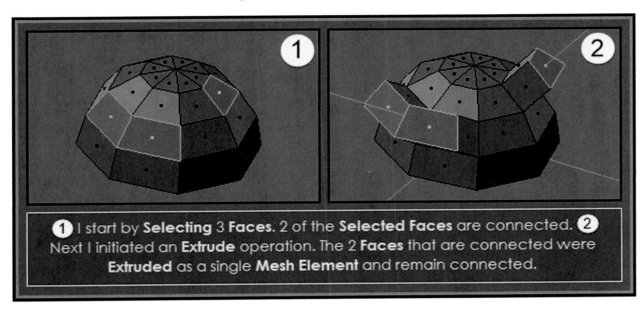

① I start by **Selecting** 3 **Faces**. 2 of the **Selected Faces** are connected. **②** Next I initiated an **Extrude** operation. The 2 **Faces** that are connected were **Extruded** as a single **Mesh Element** and remain connected.

I have been using *Faces* in my examples so far but you can *Extrude Edges* and *Vertices* as well.

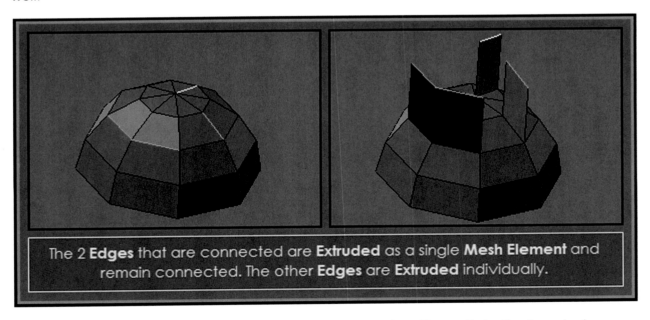

The 2 **Edges** that are connected are **Extruded** as a single **Mesh Element** and remain connected. The other **Edges** are **Extruded** individually.

It doesn't really matter what *Mesh Select Mode* you are using. If your *Selection* is a single un-connected *Vertex*, it will be extruded as a single *Vertex*. If your *Selected Mesh Elements* form one or more *Edges* or *Faces*, they will be *Extruded* as *Edges* and *Faces* accordingly.

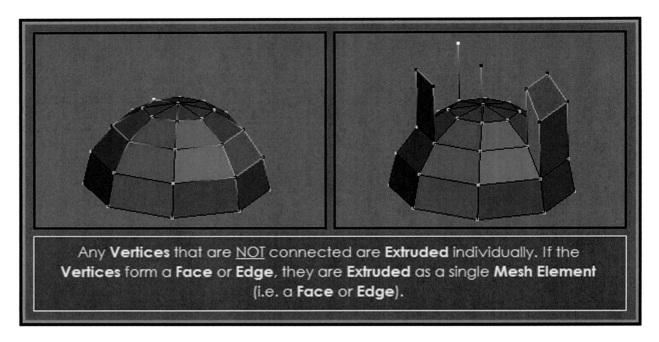

Any **Vertices** that are <u>NOT</u> connected are **Extruded** individually. If the **Vertices** form a **Face** or **Edge**, they are **Extruded** as a single **Mesh Element** (i.e. a **Face** or **Edge**).

There is also a way to *Individually Extrude* <u>connected</u> *Mesh Elements*. For example, If you were *Modeling* a hand, you would want to *Extrude* the fingers individually .

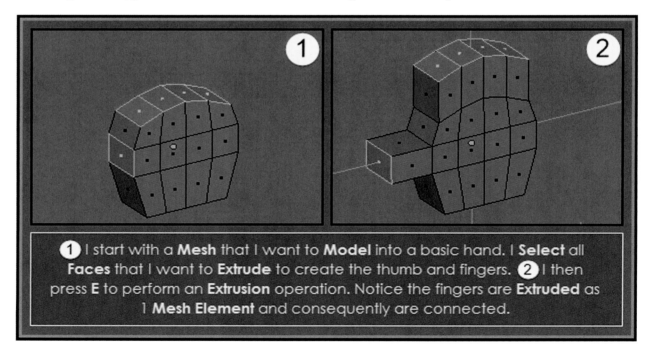

① I start with a **Mesh** that I want to **Model** into a basic hand. I **Select** all **Faces** that I want to **Extrude** to create the thumb and fingers. **②** I then press **E** to perform an **Extrusion** operation. Notice the fingers are **Extruded** as 1 **Mesh Element** and consequently are connected.

You can see in the above illustration that I didn't get exaclty what I wanted. I *Extruded* the 4 *Faces* that will become the fingers of the hand, but they are connected. In this case, I would have to find some way to separate the fingers. I could also *Select* and *Extrude* 1 *Face* at a time which could be time consuming depending on the number of *Faces* you need to *Extrude*. Fortunately, there is an option to *Extrude* each *Face* individually. It can be found in the *Extrude Menu* which can be accessed by pressing Alt + E in *Face Select Mode*.

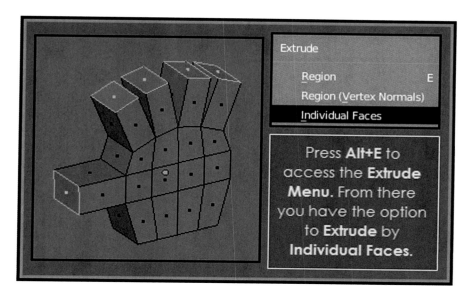

In the above illustration, I performed the *Extrude* operation using the Alt + E shortcut which gave me access to the *Extrude Menu*. By selecting *Individual Faces* from the *Extrude Menu* I was able to *Extrude* each *Face* individually to achieve the desired result.

Notice the first option in the *Extrude Menu* is *Region*. The *Region* option is essentially what you get when you use the E shortcut to perform an *Extrude* operation. It's the default mode for *Extrusion*. There is also a *Region (Vertex Normals)* option.

Using Alt + E to perform *Extrusion* operations will give you access to the *Extrude Menu* regardless of the current *Mesh Select Mode*. The options that are available in the *Extrude Menu* will depend on your current *Mesh Select Mode* and your current *Selection*.

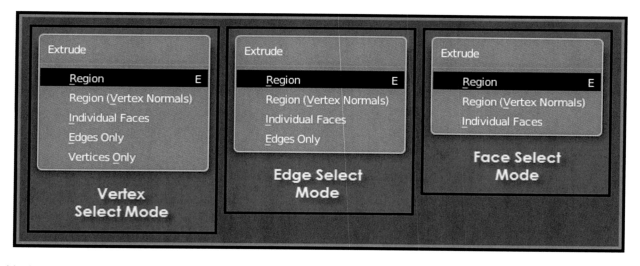

Notice in the above illustration that the options avaialble in the *Extrude Menu* vary depending on your current *Mesh Select Mode*. The options available in the *Extrude Menu* will also depend on your current *Selection*. If, for example, you are in *Vertex Select Mode* and your current *Selection* consists of 1 *Vertex*, the only option you will see when you access the *Extrude Menu* is *Vertices Only*. If you add a 2nd *Vertex* to your current *Selection* and that *Vertex* is connected to the 1st

Vertex forming an *Edge*, you will have 2 options when accessing the *Extrude Menu*. You could then choose from *Edges Only* or *Vertices Only*. In order to generate the above screenshot for *Vertex Select Mode* I had to have a single *Vertex Selected* as well as *Vertices Selected* to form an *Edge* and *Face*. Once again, your current *Selection* determines which options are aviailable in the *Extrude Menu*.

You can perform an *Extrusion* operation by *Selecting* a *Mesh Element*, holding *Ctrl* on the keyboard and clicking the *LMB* in the *3D View*. Each time you click the *LMB* you will *Extrude* the current *Selection*. I don't use this option very often as it tends to lack precision. I find it most useful in *Vertex Select Mode* in *Front*, *Side* and *Top View*. It allows you to easily add *Vertices* to a flat *Mesh* like a *Plane*. I encourage you to try it and keep it in mind as a possible option to the many *Modeling* challenges you will face.

As is the case with many other tools in *Blender*, there is a *UI* option for *Extrusion* operations. I prefer keyboard shortcuts but you can also initiate an *Extrusion* operation from the *Tools Tab* on the *Tools Shelf*.

If you have any experience at all with *Blender* you are probably already very familiar with the *Extrude Tool*. If you are new to *Blender*, expect to use it frequently from the moment you start your first *Modeling* tutorial.

The Loop Cut Tool

The *Loop Cut Tool* allows you to add *Edge Loops* to a group of *Faces*. It's used almost as often as *Extrude* during the *Modeling* process. The *Loop Cut Tool* is often referred to as the *Loop Subdivide Tool*. Here is a basic example.

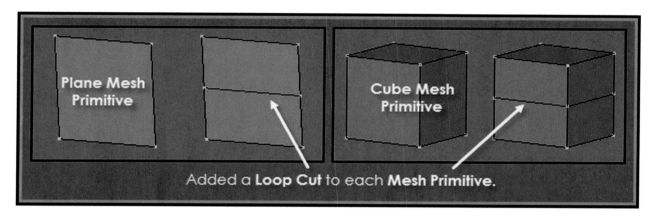

Added a **Loop Cut** to each **Mesh Primitive.**

I started out with 2 *Mesh Primitives*. I then added a *Loop* Cut to each *Mesh*. As you can see, the *Loop Cut* introduced new geometry in a non-destructive way. The *Loop Cut* performed on the *Cube* actually extends all the way around the *Cube* and we refer to the end result as an *Edge Loop*.

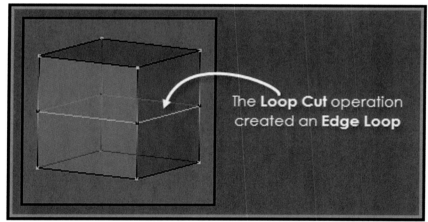

The **Loop Cut** operation created an **Edge Loop**

The keyboard shortcut to perform a *Loop Cut* is Ctrl + R. After initiating a *Loop Cut* you go into a kind of preview mode where you choose the desired location of the *Loop Cut* by moving your *Mouse* over the *Mesh*. As you move your *Mouse* over the various *Edges* of the *Mesh*, *Blender* will display the final location of the *Loop Cut* should you confirm the *Loop Cut* at that time. The location of the *Loop Cut* is displayed with a colored line (which is magenta by default). For example, when you perform a *Loop Cut* on a *Cube Mesh Primitive*, there are 3 options available.

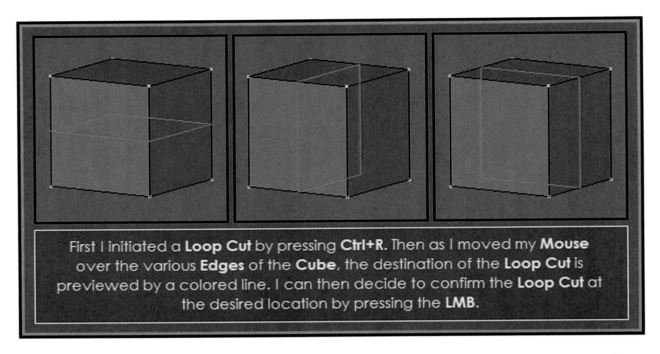

First I initiated a **Loop Cut** by pressing **Ctrl+R**. Then as I moved my **Mouse** over the various **Edges** of the **Cube**, the destination of the **Loop Cut** is previewed by a colored line. I can then decide to confirm the **Loop Cut** at the desired location by pressing the **LMB**.

Once you are happy with the location of the *Loop Cut* you can confirm it by pressing the LMB. Once confirmed, you enter *Edge Slide Mode* (for more on *Edge Slide* see **Chapter 5 – Edge Slide**). You can then use *Edge Slide* to fine tune the final position of the *Loop Cut* before confirming it again with the LMB. As an alternative, once in *Edge Slide Mode* you can press the RMB which will set the *Loop Cut* at the exact center of the cut. This is very handy when you want to cut a *Cube* or *Plane* exactly in half or you want to ensure the *Loop Cut* is distributed evenly which can help ensure the end result is as smooth as possible. This is especially noticeable on a *Mesh* with a *Subdivision Surface Modifier*. Placing a *Loop Cut* too close to another *Edge Loop* can create a noticeable line. This is fine when you want to *Sharpen* an *Edge* but can be problematic on a portion of the *Mesh* that you want to remain *Smooth*. I cover the *Subdivision Surface Modifier* in the next chapter but here is an example of the effect of placing an *Edge Loop* too close to a neighboring *Edge Loop*.

I added a **UV Sphere Mesh** and then added a **Subsurface Modifier**. I performed a couple of **Loop Cut** operations. I placed the **Loop Cuts** very close one of the adjacent **Edges Loops**.

In the above example, the *Loop Cuts* produced undesired artifacts as I wanted the *Mesh* to remain *Smooth*. *Loop Cuts* are one of the primary tools used to *Sharpen* and *Smooth* the *Edges* of an *Object*. See **Chapter 8 – Smoothing** for more info.

You can create multiple *Loop Cuts* at once using the *Loop Cut Tool*. After confirming the location of the *Loop Cut* you can increase the number of *Loop Cuts* to create using the Mouse Wheel. If your mouse doesn't have a Wheel, you can use Numpad + and Numpad -.

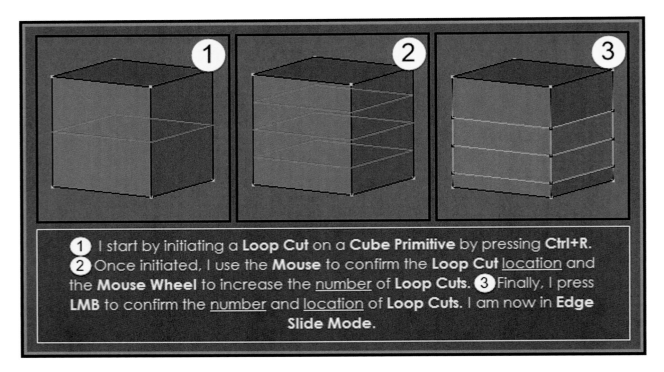

① I start by initiating a **Loop Cut** on a **Cube Primitive** by pressing **Ctrl+R**.
② Once initiated, I use the **Mouse** to confirm the **Loop Cut** location and the **Mouse Wheel** to increase the number of **Loop Cuts**. ③ Finally, I press **LMB** to confirm the number and location of **Loop Cuts**. I am now in **Edge Slide Mode**.

If you choose to add multiple *Loop Cuts*, the distance between each *Edge Loop* will be distributed evenly. After confirming the *Location* and number of *Loop Cuts*, you will be in *Edge Slide Mode* with all *Edge Loops Selected*. You can then *Slide* all *Edge Loops* to the desired *Location* or press the RMB to center and evenly distribute all *Edge Loops*. Once the *Edge Loops* are in the desired location, press LMB to confirm the *Loop Cut* operation (unless you already used RMB to center the *Edge Loops* which also confirms the operation). Here is another example showing multiple *Loops Cuts*. This example better demonstrates the distance between *Edge Loops* when performing a *Loop Cut* operation with multiple *Loop Cuts*.

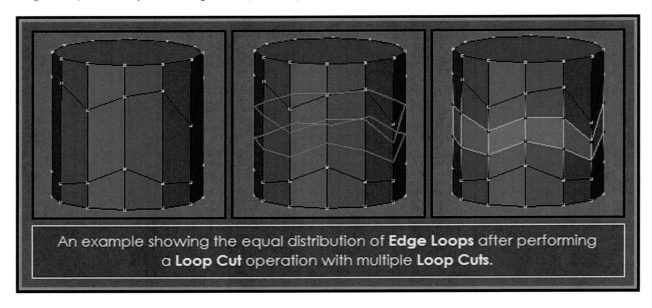

An example showing the equal distribution of **Edge Loops** after performing a **Loop Cut** operation with multiple **Loop Cuts**.

You can see in the above illustration that the *Loop Cuts* are distributed evenly based on the location of the neighboring *Edge Loops*.

You can *Select* an existing *Edge Loop* by hovering the *Mouse Cursor* over an *Edge* that is part of the *Edge Loop* you want to *Select* and pressing Alt + RMB (for more info see **Chapter 6 – Select Edge Loop**). Once *Selected*, you can press G, G to enter *Edge Slide Mode* allowing you to reposition an *Edge Loop* at any time (for more info see **Chapter 5 – Edge Slide**). You can also *Delete* an *Edge Loop* by pressing X to bring up the *Delete Menu* and selecting *Edge Loops*. The advantage of *Deleting Edge Loops* by *Selecting Edge Loops* in the *Delete Menu* is that the *Edge Loop* is removed without affecting the surrounding *Geometry*. If you were to just *Delete* the *Selected Edge Loop*, it would *Delete* several *Face Loops* and you would be required to rebuild the geometry.

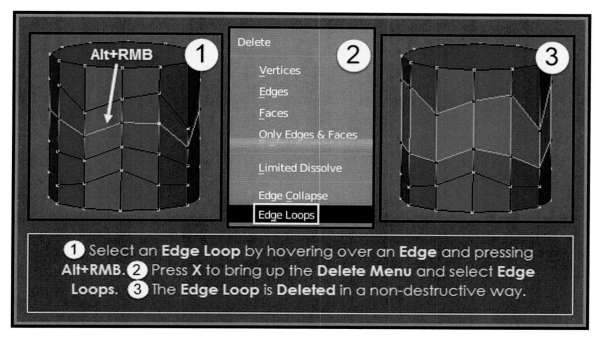

① Select an **Edge Loop** by hovering over an **Edge** and pressing **Alt+RMB. ②** Press X to bring up the **Delete Menu** and select **Edge Loops. ③** The **Edge Loop** is **Deleted** in a non-destructive way.

There are times when you attempt a *Loop Cut* operation and the preview appears to indicate that no *Loop Cut* is possible at that *Location*. This can happen with certain *Topology*. *Triangles* can be an issue when performing *Loop Cuts*. To see an example, add a *Cone Mesh Primitive* and attempt to add a *Loop Cut*. After initiating the *Loop Cut* operation you will notice that no preview line appears. This indicates that no *Loop Cut* is possible given the *Topology* of the *Mesh*. Here is another example.

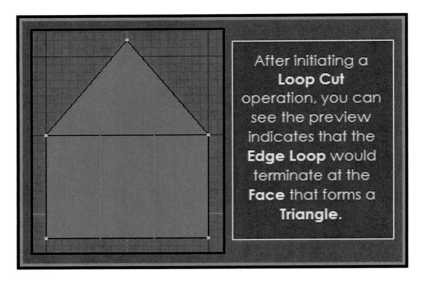

After initiating a **Loop Cut** operation, you can see the preview indicates that the **Edge Loop** would terminate at the **Face** that forms a **Triangle**.

Most of the time performing *Loop Cuts* works as expected but if you don't see the result you want you should check you're *Mesh* to see if it might be related to the *Mesh Topology*.

The *Loop Cut Tool* is used constantly during the *Modeling Process*. I listed the *Extrude Tool* and the *Loop Cut Tool* as the first 2 tools I discussed in this chapter for a reason. They are the most common way to introduce new *Geometry*.

The Inset Tool

The *Inset Tool* creates a connected copy of the *Selected Mesh Elements* that lies within the boundaries of the *Selection*. In many ways it behaves like the *Extrude Tool*. In some cases, it's hard to tell the 2 tools apart.

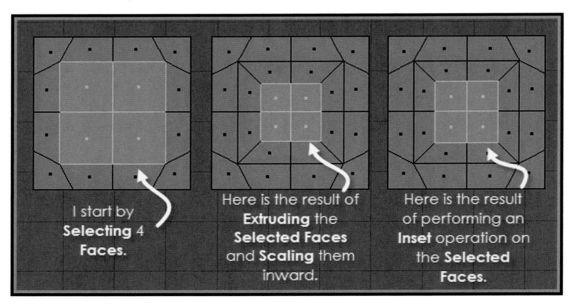

I start by **Selecting 4 Faces**.

Here is the result of **Extruding** the **Selected Faces** and **Scaling** them inward.

Here is the result of performing an **Inset** operation on the **Selected Faces**.

In the above example the *Extrude* operation yielded identical results to the *Inset* operation. In some situations, they are practically interchangeable. I put the result of the *Inset* operation next to the result of the *Extrude* operation to make a point but *Extrude* is not generally used this way. The *Inset* Tool is a more recent tool and it has many benefits over the *Extrusion Tool* in specific situations. It also comes with a multitude of options.

To start an *Inset* operation simply *Select* 1 or more *Faces* and press I to initiate the *Inset* operation. Once initiated, you can adjust the result of the *Inset* operation by sliding your *Mouse*.

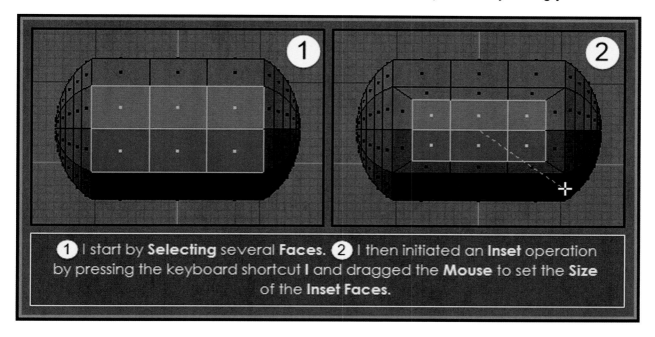

1 I start by **Selecting** several **Faces**. **2** I then initiated an **Inset** operation by pressing the keyboard shortcut **I** and dragged the **Mouse** to set the **Size** of the **Inset Faces**.

You can also access the *Inset Tool* from the *Faces Menu* (press Ctrl + F to access the *Faces Menu*). After initiating an *Inset* operation, you can cancel it by pressing Escape or clicking the RMB.

I mentioned above that the *Inset Tool* comes with numerous options. After initiating an *Inset* operation press F6 to bring up the *Operator Panel*. Here you will find all the options available to modify the result of the *Inset* operation. The *Operator Panel* is also visible on the *Tools Shelf* if you have it open. Here is what the *Operator Panel* looks like for the *Inset Tool*.

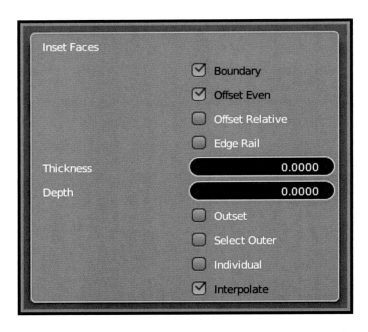

As you can see the *Inset Tool* has many options. I will discuss several of them below.

The *Boundary* option determines if any *Faces* with open *Edges* will be included as part of the *Inset* operation. In other words, if the *Edge* of a *Face* is not connected to another *Face*, it will be affected by this setting.

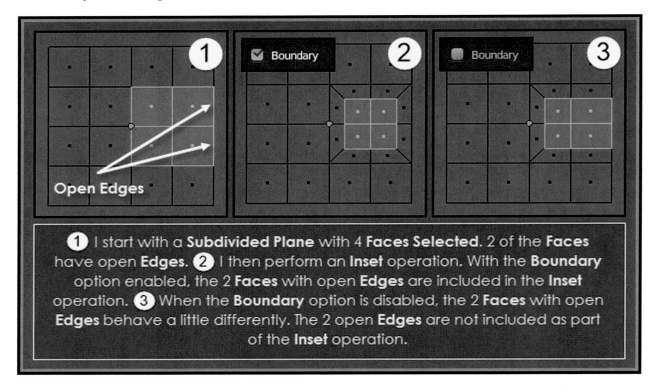

① I start with a **Subdivided Plane** with 4 **Faces Selected**. 2 of the **Faces** have open **Edges**. **②** I then perform an **Inset** operation. With the **Boundary** option enabled, the 2 **Faces** with open **Edges** are included in the **Inset** operation. **③** When the **Boundary** option is disabled, the 2 **Faces** with open **Edges** behave a little differently. The 2 open **Edges** are not included as part of the **Inset** operation.

The *Boundary* option comes in handy when *Modeling* a *Mash* that has a *Mirror Modifier* (see **Chapter 9 –The Mirror Modifier**). Consider the following basic *Mesh* that has a *Mirror Modifier*.

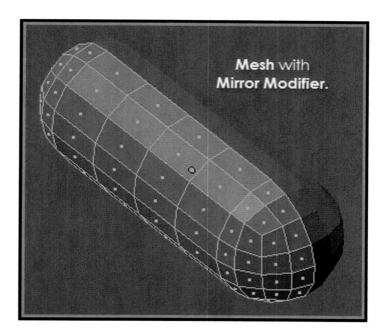

I have a couple of *Faces Selected*. The *Faces* have open *Edges* even though there is a *Mirror Modifier*. The *Mirror Modifier* isn't applied yet so to *Blender* the 2 *Selected Faces* have open *Edges*.

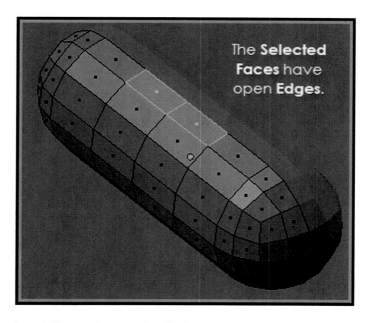

Next I will perform an *Inset Operation* on the *Selected Faces*.

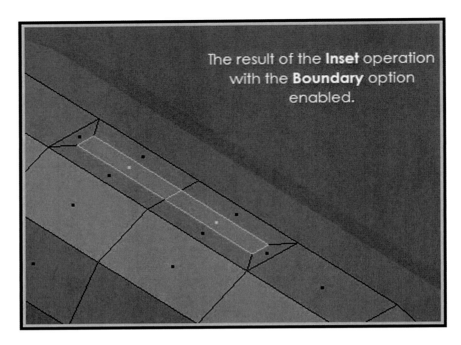

The result of the **Inset** operation with the **Boundary** option enabled.

That isn't the result I wanted ☹. I wanted the *Faces* that are *Selected* and *Mirrored* to be included as part of the *Inset* operation. In the above illustration, we can see the result is 2 separate *Inset* operations (one on each side of the *Mirrored Mesh*). Let's disable the *Boundary* option.

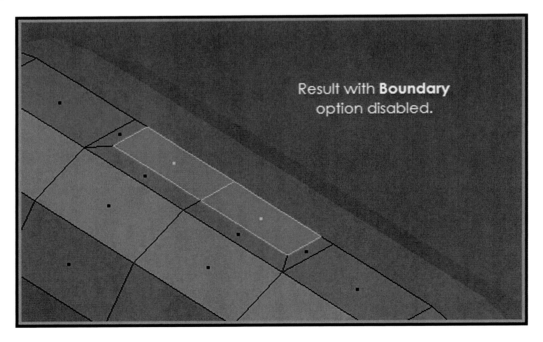

Result with **Boundary** option disabled.

That's the result I was looking for. Keep the *Boundary* option in mind when using the *Inset Tool* on open *Edges* including open *Edges* that are at the boundary of the *Mirror Modifier*.

The *Offset Even* option will attempt to even out the thickness of *Faces* surrounding the *Inset* result.

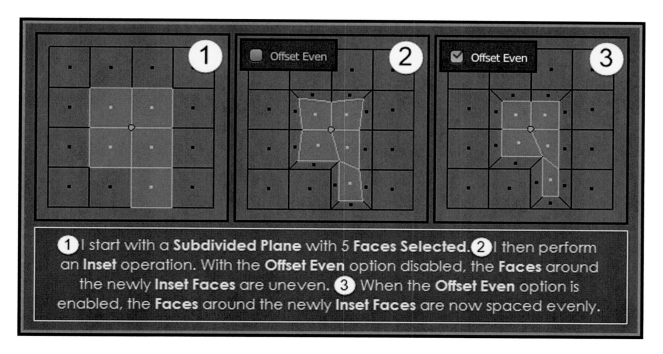

1 I start with a **Subdivided Plane** with 5 **Faces Selected.** **2** I then perform an **Inset** operation. With the **Offset Even** option disabled, the **Faces** around the newly **Inset Faces** are uneven. **3** When the **Offset Even** option is enabled, the **Faces** around the newly **Inset Faces** are now spaced evenly.

Most of the time you will probably want this option enabled as it produces a cleaner result.

The *Offset Relative* option will *Scale* the *Faces* around the *Inset* result based on the surrounding geometry. Here is an example.

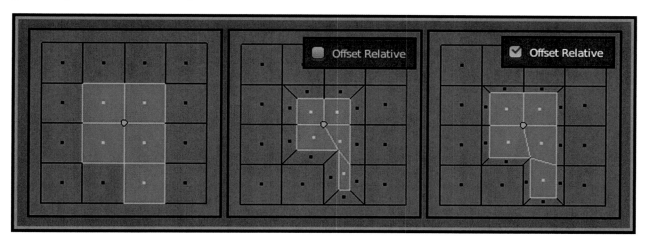

The *Edge Rail* option will align the *Edges* of the *Faces* that result from the *Inset* operation with the *Edges* of the *Faces* that surround the results of the *Inset* operation. That's a mouth full. An illustration is in order.

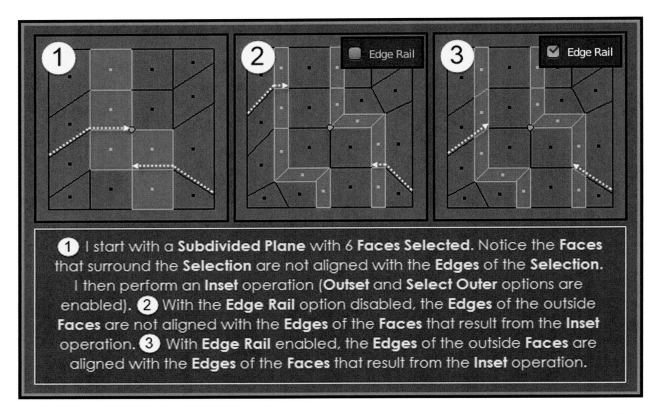

1 I start with a **Subdivided Plane** with 6 **Faces Selected**. Notice the **Faces** that surround the **Selection** are not aligned with the **Edges** of the **Selection**. I then perform an **Inset** operation (**Outset** and **Select Outer** options are enabled). **2** With the **Edge Rail** option disabled, the **Edges** of the outside **Faces** are not aligned with the **Edges** of the **Faces** that result from the **Inset** operation. **3** With **Edge Rail** enabled, the **Edges** of the outside **Faces** are aligned with the **Edges** of the **Faces** that result from the **Inset** operation.

After you initiate an *Inset* operation you use your mouse to determine the size or thickness of the *Inset Faces*. After you set the desired *Thickness*, you press the LMB to confirm the operation. After you confirm the *Inset* operation, you can still modify the *Thickness* using the *Thickness* slider. You can either drag the slider or input a value if you require more precision. This option is pretty straightforward and the results are what you would expect.

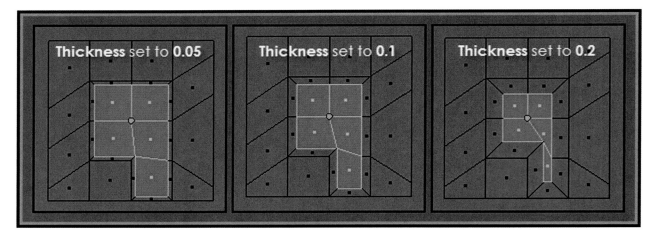

The *Depth* slider allows you to move the *Faces* that result from the *Inset* operation inward or outward. The result is similar to an *Extrude* operation. You can add depth after you initiate the *Inset* operation by holding the Ctrl key and using the Mouse to set the depth. You can press Ctrl at any time to enable / disable setting the *Depth*. So after initiating an *Inset* operation, you can use the Mouse to set the *Thickness* and press Ctrl and use the Mouse to set the *Depth*. Similar to the *Thickness* slider, the *Depth* slider allows you to change the *Depth* after you confirm the *Inset* operation. You can either drag the slider or input a value if you require more precision.

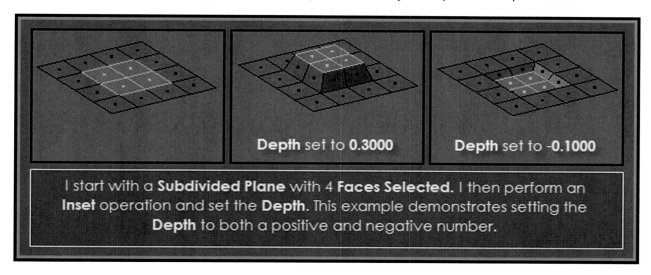

Depth set to 0.3000   Depth set to -0.1000

I start with a **Subdivided Plane** with 4 **Faces Selected**. I then perform an **Inset** operation and set the **Depth**. This example demonstrates setting the **Depth** to both a positive and negative number.

The *Outset* option can be enabled so that the *Faces* generated as part of the *Inset* operation are created outside the *Selection* instead of inside the *Selection*.

The *Select Outer* option lets you toggle which *Faces* are *Selected* after the *Inset* operation.

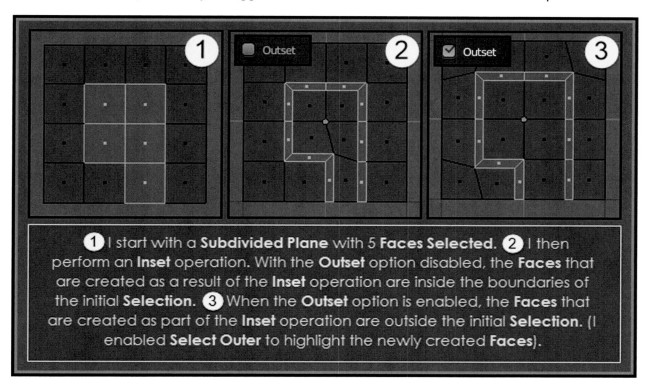

❶ I start with a **Subdivided Plane** with 5 **Faces Selected**. **❷** I then perform an **Inset** operation. With the **Outset** option disabled, the **Faces** that are created as a result of the **Inset** operation are inside the boundaries of the initial **Selection**. **❸** When the **Outset** option is enabled, the **Faces** that are created as part of the **Inset** operation are outside the initial **Selection**. (I enabled **Select Outer** to highlight the newly created **Faces**).

The Individual option will cause the *Selected Faces* to be *Inset* individually as opposed to a single entity or group.

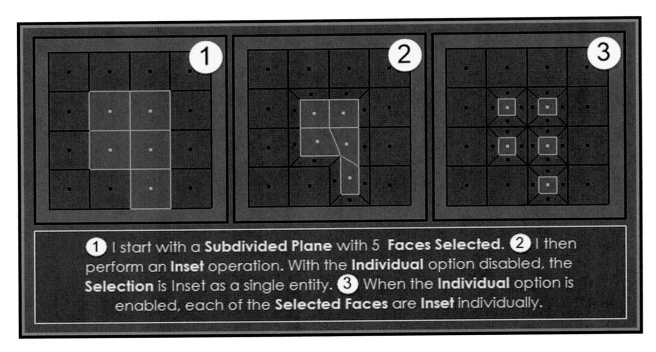

① I start with a **Subdivided Plane** with 5 **Faces Selected**. ② I then perform an **Inset** operation. With the **Individual** option disabled, the **Selection** is Inset as a single entity. ③ When the **Individual** option is enabled, each of the **Selected Faces** are **Inset** individually.

With all of its options the *Inset Tool* is very powerful. You will quickly learn when to use *Inset* versus using *Extrude*. There are no hard and fast rules on which tool to use when but here are some examples of how I might to approach certain *Modeling* tasks.

- If I plan to model a fish, I use *Extrude* to create the body and *Inset* to create the mouth and fins.
- If I am modelling an air plane, I use *Extrude* to create the plane body and *Inset* for the wings and cockpit.
- When *Modeling* a human head, I use *Inset* for the eyes, nose and mouth.
- If I am *Modeling* a tire, I use *Extrude* to create the tire and *Inset* to create the tire tread.

I think you get the idea. Think of it as creating new (*Extrude*) versus add to existing (*Inset*). *Inset* has the advantage of not distorting the surrounding geometry. Performing an *Inset* operation on a curved surface will create fewer artifacts than if you attempted the same operation with *Extrude*.

The Knife Tool

The *Knife Tool*, as the name implies, allows you to introduce *Geometry* to your *Mesh* by making cuts. The *Knife Tool* has come a long way and now has several options that make it very versatile. To activate the *Knife Tool* press K in *Edit Mode*. You can also access the *Knife Tool* on the *Tools Shelf*. The *Knife Tool* is located on the *Tools* tab in the *Mesh Tools Panel*.

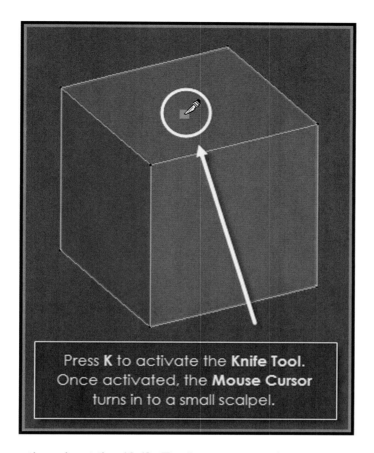

Press **K** to activate the **Knife Tool**.
Once activated, the **Mouse Cursor**
turns in to a small scalpel.

Once activated, information about the *Knife Tool's* current settings is displayed in the *3D Window Header*. There is so much information that I decided to split the screenshot in half as I was worried it would be illegible otherwise. Can you read this?

Enter/PadEnter/Space: confirm, Esc/RMB: cancel, LMB: start/define cut, dbl-LMB: close cut, E: new cut, CtrlL/CtrlR: midpoint snap (OFF), ShiftL/ShiftR: ignore snap (ON), C: angle constraint (OFF), Z: cut through (OFF), MMB: panning

Is this a little better?

Enter/PadEnter/Space: confirm, Esc/RMB: cancel, LMB: start/define cut, dbl-LMB: close cut, E: new cut, CtrlL/CtrlR: midpoint snap (OFF),

ShiftL/ShiftR: ignore snap (OFF), C: angle constraint (OFF), Z: cut through (OFF), MMB: panning

Once activated, you simply move the *Scalpel* to the desired *Location* and press the LMB to create a *Cut*. Performing a *Cut* on an *Edge* will simply add a new *Vertex* to the *Edge*. The result is the same as you get when *Subdividing* an *Edge*.

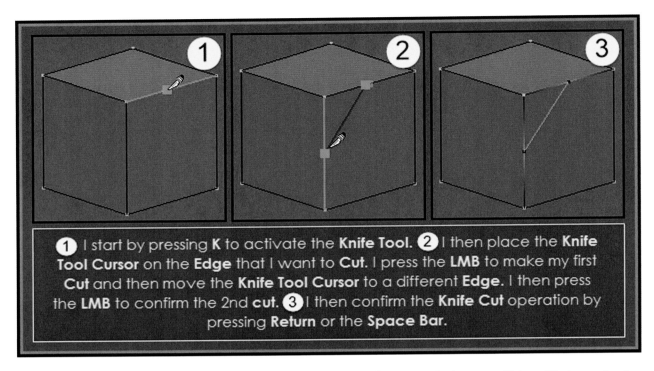

1 I start by pressing **K** to activate the **Knife Tool**. **2** I then place the **Knife Tool Cursor** on the **Edge** that I want to **Cut**. I press the **LMB** to make my first **Cut** and then move the **Knife Tool Cursor** to a different **Edge**. I then press the **LMB** to confirm the 2nd **cut**. **3** I then confirm the **Knife Cut** operation by pressing **Return** or the **Space Bar**.

You can see in the above illustration that performing 2 *Cuts* created a new *Edge*. It's important to note that the *Knife Cut* operation also resulted in one of the Faces being split in to a *Triangle* and an *Ngon*. 2 other *Faces* are now *Ngons* as well.

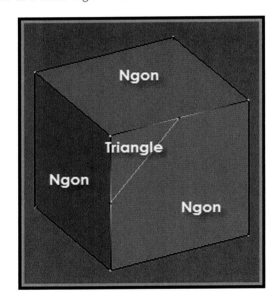

That, in my opinion, is one of the side effects of using the *Knife Tool* that requires a little diligence. If you are aware that you could produce undesired geometry with the *Knife Tool*, you can attempt to plan your *Knife Cuts* ahead of time. This isn't always easy to do but you will start to get a feel for it. Personally, as I add each *Cut*, I look at the surrounding geometry and decide if another *Cut* in the same area would help keep the geometry clean. Having said all that, you can still easily fix any problems in your topology after you have confirmed a *Knife Cut* operation. It's just a good habit to keep it in mind when using the *Knife Tool*. As I have mentioned several times, I try to ensure my *Mesh* is composed entirely of quads and the *Knife Tool* can easily result in the creation of *Triangles* and *Ngons*. I am not encouraging you to avoid such a powerful tool, just making you aware of its strengths and weaknesses.

I think calling this *Tool* the *Knife Tool* is appropriate because all it really does is create new *Edges*. You are creating new *Edges* by splitting *Existing Edges* or by drawing and connecting new *Vertices* on a *Face*. The *Knife Cut* operation will result in new *Vertices* and *Faces* but you are really only creating new *Edges*. When you click on an existing *Vertex* with the *Knife Tool*, it doesn't create a new *Vertex*. The *Vertex* is simply now a starting point for a new *Cut*, which is the start of creating a new *Edge*. If you were to initiate a *Knife Cut* operation and click on 1 *Vertex* and then press *Return* to confirm the *Knife Cut* operation, nothing would happen. You would get the same result if you used a single click on an *Edge* or in the middle of a *Face*. If you clicked on a *Face* and then clicked on another *Location* on the same *Face*, then pressed *Return*, you would also get no result. The *Edges* created by the *Knife Cuts* need to be closed or connected to existing geometry achieve a result.

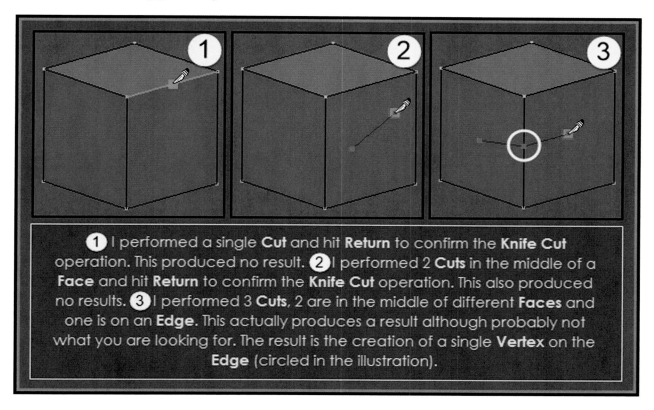

1 I performed a single **Cut** and hit **Return** to confirm the **Knife Cut** operation. This produced no result. **2** I performed 2 **Cuts** in the middle of a **Face** and hit **Return** to confirm the **Knife Cut** operation. This also produced no results. **3** I performed 3 **Cuts**, 2 are in the middle of different **Faces** and one is on an **Edge**. This actually produces a result although probably not what you are looking for. The result is the creation of a single **Vertex** on the **Edge** (circled in the illustration).

You can create *Cuts* on a face to create a hole, as long as they are connected.

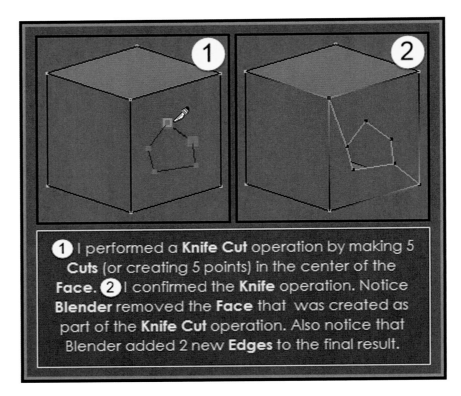

1 I performed a **Knife Cut** operation by making 5 **Cuts** (or creating 5 points) in the center of the **Face**. **2** I confirmed the **Knife** operation. Notice **Blender** removed the **Face** that was created as part of the **Knife Cut** operation. Also notice that Blender added 2 new **Edges** to the final result.

As the above illustration demonstrates, creating a hole using the *Knife Tool* can be problematic but only when used on a single *Face*. In the above example, an *Inset* operation would have been a better choice. Let's try the same thing on multiple *Faces*.

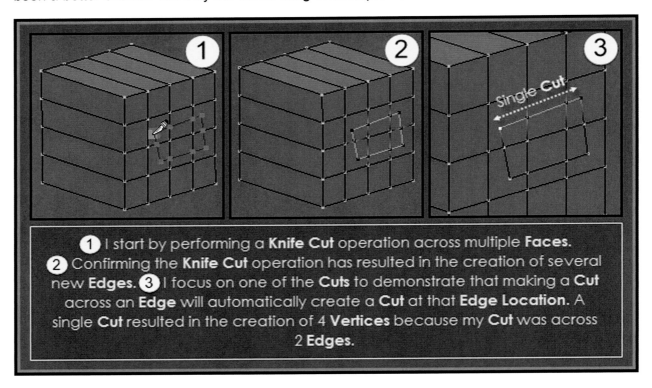

1 I start by performing a **Knife Cut** operation across multiple **Faces**. **2** Confirming the **Knife Cut** operation has resulted in the creation of several new **Edges**. **3** I focus on one of the **Cuts** to demonstrate that making a **Cut** across an **Edge** will automatically create a **Cut** at that **Edge Location**. A single **Cut** resulted in the creation of 4 **Vertices** because my **Cut** was across 2 **Edges**.

As I mention above, if your current *Cut* falls across an existing *Edge*, a *Cut* will be done on that *Edge*. In the above illustration we see that a single *Cut* resulted in 4 *Vertices*. You could also argue that a single *Cut* resulted in the creation of 3 new *Edges*.

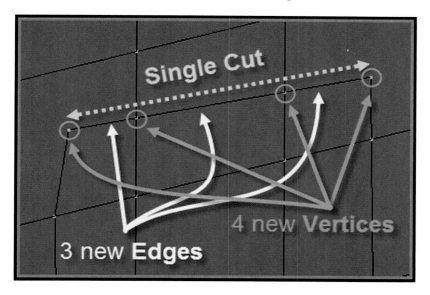

The *Knife Tool* may seem like it has a lot of complex rules and nuances but like any other tool in *Blender*, the more you use it the more you will know what to do and when to do it.

As I mentioned earlier in the section, there are several options available to help when using the *Knife Tool*. The options are <u>not</u> available on an *Operator Panel* like many of the other *Tools*. Instead, the options are toggled via the keyboard the moment you activate the *Knife Tool*.

Here is a breakdown of the available options:

- LMB - to create the *Cuts* or more accurately, the points that define the *Cuts*.
- Space Bar or Return - confirm the *Knife Tool* operation.
- Escape or RMB - cancel the *Knife Tool* operation.
- E - start new *Cut*. Once you are happy with a set of *Cuts* you can initiate a new set of *Cuts* without applying the current *Cuts* by pressing E. The small line that is connected to the last *Cut* point will disappear allowing you to start a new *Cut* operation.
- Ctrl - snap *Knife Tool Cursor* to midpoint. Hold Control while hovering the *Knife Tool Cursor* over an *Edge* and it will *Snap* to the exact center of that *Edge*.
- Shift - turns off *Snapping*. During the course of a *Knife Tool* operation, the *Knife Tool Cursor* will automatically *Snap* to any nearby *Edges* or *Vertices*. This can be handy but there are times when you want to make *Cuts* close to an *Edge* or *Vertex* without *Snapping*. Simply hold Shift to disable *Snapping*.
- C - constrains the *Cuts* to an angle. Once enabled, any *Cuts* will be constrained to the view in 45 degree increments.

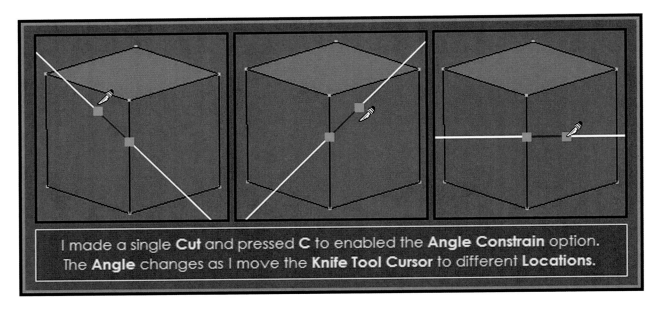

I made a single **Cut** and pressed **C** to enabled the **Angle Constrain** option. The **Angle** changes as I move the **Knife Tool Cursor** to different **Locations.**

- Z - enables *Cut Through*. Any *Cuts* will not only be on visible *Faces*, but also any *Faces* that aren't visible. This can often produce odd results.

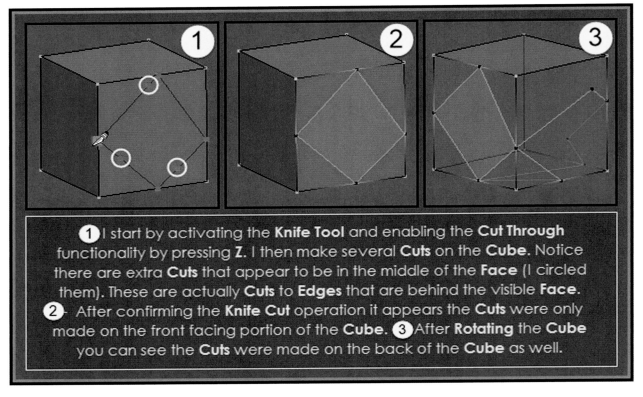

1 I start by activating the **Knife Tool** and enabling the **Cut Through** functionality by pressing **Z**. I then make several **Cuts** on the **Cube**. Notice there are extra **Cuts** that appear to be in the middle of the **Face** (I circled them). These are actually **Cuts** to **Edges** that are behind the visible **Face**. **2** After confirming the **Knife Cut** operation it appears the **Cuts** were only made on the front facing portion of the **Cube**. **3** After **Rotating** the **Cube** you can see the **Cuts** were made on the back of the **Cube** as well.

- Hold LMB - by holding down the LMB and dragging the Mouse you can create *Cuts* on any *Edge* the *Knife Tool Cursor* crosses. It essentially allows you to create *Cuts* in freehand mode. Your results will depend on your skill with a Mouse and the steadiness of your hand.

The *Knife Tool* works on *Mesh Elements* whether they are *Selected* or not. You can, however, limit *Cuts* to only *Selected Faces*. To activate the *Knife Tool* so it only makes *Cuts* to *Selected Faces* press Shift + K. Once activated, the *Knife Tool Cursor* will still appear over *Faces* that aren't part of the *Selection* but the little *Dot* that indicates the *Location* of the next *Cut* will disappear.

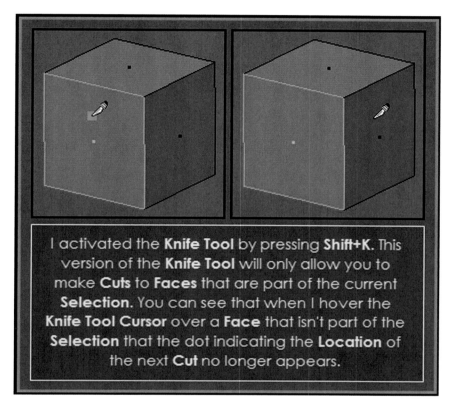

I activated the **Knife Tool** by pressing **Shift+K**. This version of the **Knife Tool** will only allow you to make **Cuts** to **Faces** that are part of the current **Selection**. You can see that when I hover the **Knife Tool Cursor** over a **Face** that isn't part of the **Selection** that the dot indicating the **Location** of the next **Cut** no longer appears.

I have seen the *Knife Tool* used often in some tutorials and not as much in others. A recent tutorial I watched used it often and it opened my eyes to its versatility. It's great for performing surgery on a *Mesh* allowing you to cut holes or for slicing off pieces of a *Mesh*.

You can use the *Knife Tool* to *Cut* a *Mesh* in half.

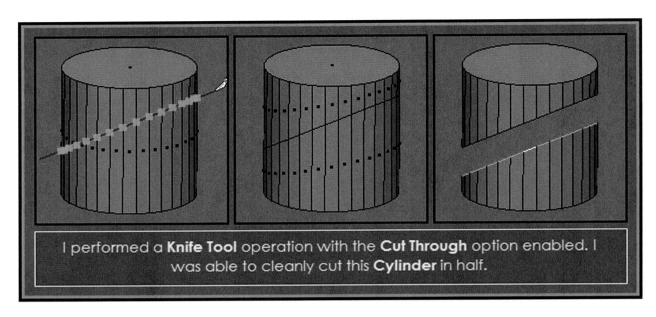

I performed a **Knife Tool** operation with the **Cut Through** option enabled. I was able to cleanly cut this **Cylinder** in half.

Cut out the beginnings of an ear (a crude example but you get the idea).

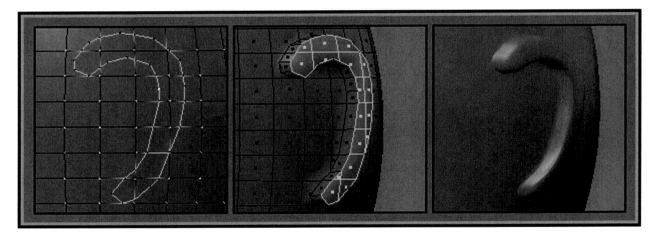

Make a key hole.

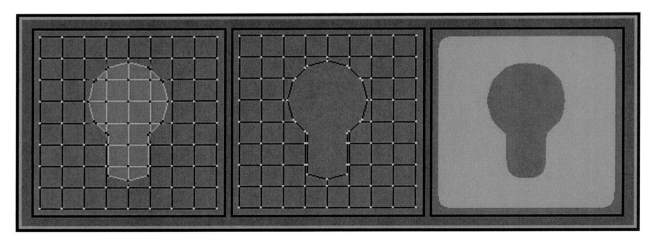

You may be thinking that the key hole I *Cut* out is nice and clean. You may be thinking "this guy has a pretty steady hand". You may be thinking "it almost looks like he created the key hole as a separate mesh and used it to make the *Cuts*". You may be right!! Ok, I didn't make the *Cuts* freehand; I used *Knife Projection* which I talk about next.

Knife Projection

With *Knife Projection* you can make *Cuts* to one *Mesh* using the *Geometry* of another *Mesh*. In other words, one *Mesh* determines where to make *Cuts* on a target *Mesh*. I will refer to the *Mesh* that defines the *Cuts* as the *Cutter Mesh* and the *Mesh* to be *Cut* as the *Target Mesh*. I am not sure what the proper terms are or if any even exist so I came up with my own. Let's start with a basic example. Here are a couple of basic *Meshes*.

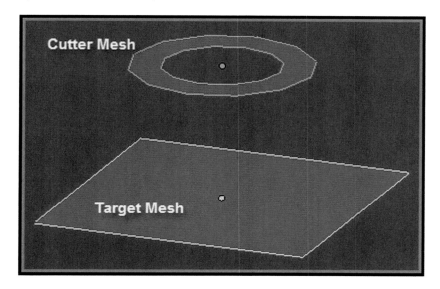

I will use the *Cutter Mesh* to define the *Cuts* on the *Target Mesh*.

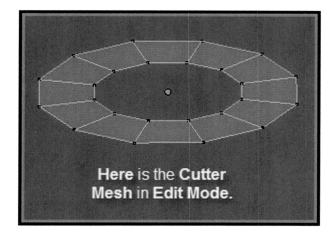

To perform the *Knife Projection* operation, I first go into *Object Mode*. Next, I *Select* the *Cutter Mesh*, hold down *Shift* and *Select* the *Target Mesh* to add it to the current *Selection*. I align the *View* so the *Cutter Mesh* is placed over the *Target Mesh* in the *3D View*. Remember, you are *Projecting* one *Mesh* on to another so the position of the *Meshes* determines where the *Cuts* are made. Finally, I go in to *Edit* mode and press the *Knife Project* button located on the *Tools Shelf*. Look for it on the *Mesh Tools Panel* on the *Tools* Tab.

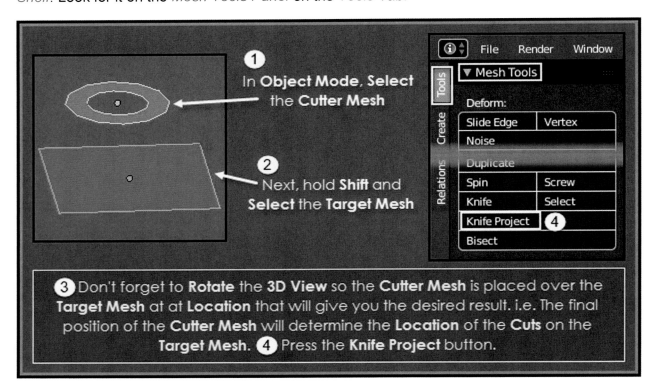

As I mention in the above illustration, I need to *Rotate* the *3D View* so the *Cutter Mesh* is aligned with the *Target Mesh* in such a way that I get the *Cuts* I want in the *Location* I want.

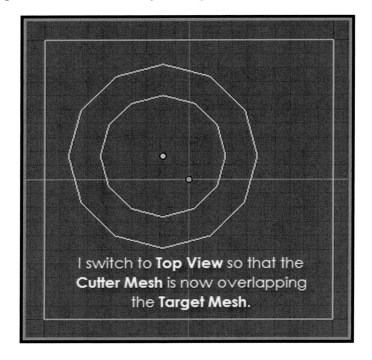

Once completed, the *Target Mesh* should now have several *New Edges* based on the same shape of the *Cutter Mesh*.

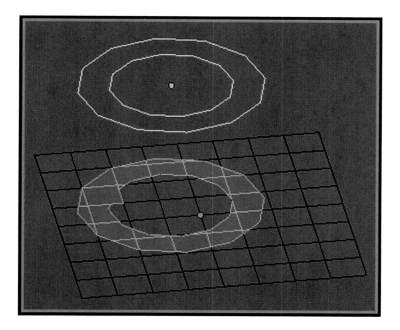

In the above illustrations I *Rotated* the *3D View* so you could see the result of the *Knife Project* operation. As you can see the result isn't perfect. You can achieve a better quality result by adding *Geometry* to *Cutter Object* and / or the *Target Object*. Here is the result after I *Subdivide* both the *Cutter* and *Target Objects* (once again, I performed the *Knife Project* operation with the *Cutter Mesh* positioned over the *Target Mesh*. I then *Rotated* the *3D View* to show the result).

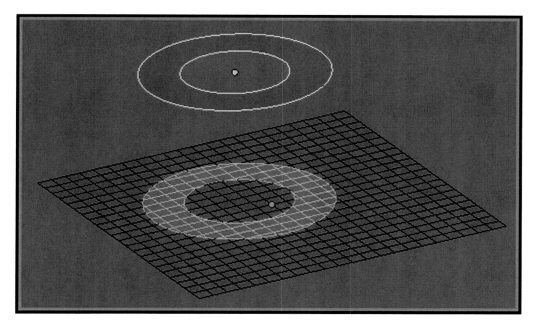

As you may have guessed by now, you can *Rotate* the *3D View* to get all sorts of results from a *Knife Project* operation. In the next example, a portion of the *Cutter Object* is outside the boundary of the *Target Object*.

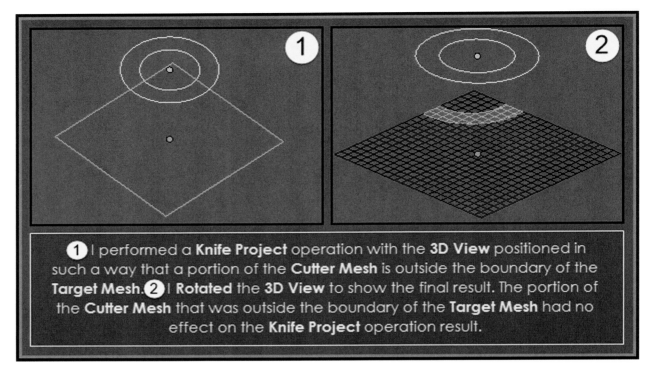

① I performed a **Knife Project** operation with the **3D View** positioned in such a way that a portion of the **Cutter Mesh** is outside the boundary of the **Target Mesh.② I Rotated** the **3D View** to show the final result. The portion of the **Cutter Mesh** that was outside the boundary of the **Target Mesh** had no effect on the **Knife Project** operation result.

Up to this point the examples I used to demonstrate *Knife Projection* have had a flat *Target Mesh. Knife Projection* works pretty well on *Meshes* of all shapes and sizes.

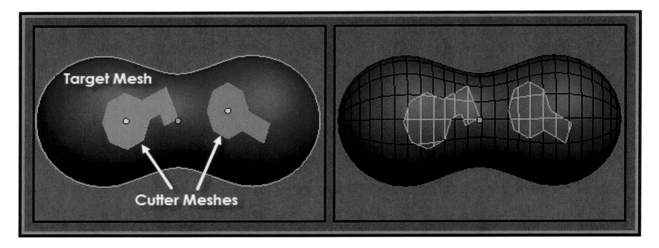

The *Knife Projection* functionality is an excellent tool for making precise *Cuts* in a *Mesh*. The ability to create a *Cutter Mesh* and tweak it until you get it just right is invaluable to making such precise *Cuts*. I have seen it used in many tutorials for a variety of *Modeling* tasks.

I must once again remind you to check your *Mesh* with *Mesh Lint* (see **Chapter 4 – MeshLint Add-On**) after using the *Knife* or *Knife Projection Tools*. Chances are pretty good you ended up with some *Triangle* or *Quad Faces* in the final result.

The Bevel Tool

The *Bevel Tool* can be used to smooth *Edges* and corners. The *Bevel Tool* creates a *Bevel* by subdividing any *Selected Edges*. Only the *Selected Edges* will be affected by a *Bevel* operation. To initiate a *Bevel* operation, *Select* 1 or more *Edges* and press Ctrl + B.

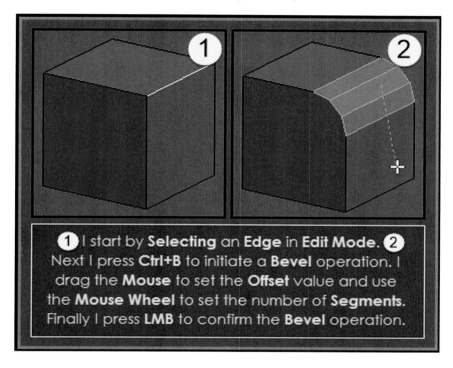

1 I start by **Selecting** an **Edge** in **Edit Mode**. **2** Next I press **Ctrl+B** to initiate a **Bevel** operation. I drag the **Mouse** to set the **Offset** value and use the **Mouse Wheel** to set the number of **Segments**. Finally I press **LMB** to confirm the **Bevel** operation.

Press F6 after confirming a *Bevel* operation to can gain access to the *Bevel Operator Panel* (the *Bevel Operator Panel* is also visible on the *Tools Shelf* if you have it open). There you can change several options related to the *Bevel* operation.

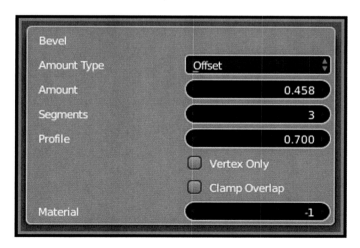

The options on the *Operator Panel* are as follows:

Amount Type - The *Amount Type Menu* determines how the *Size* of the *Bevel* is calculated (the *Size* is set by the *Amount* setting). I will let *Blender* describe each option for you.

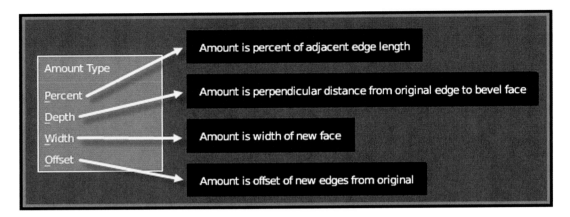

Despite the informative description for each menu option, you can also just try each setting to see how it will affect the *Bevel* result.

Amount - the size of the *Bevel* effect. You set the amount by dragging the Mouse after initiating a *Bevel* operation. After confirming the *Bevel* operation you can change the *Amount* numerically using the *Amount Slider*. To change the amount, either click and drag the *Slider* with the LMB or click on the slider and enter a number. Setting the *Amount* by entering a value allows you to set precise values.

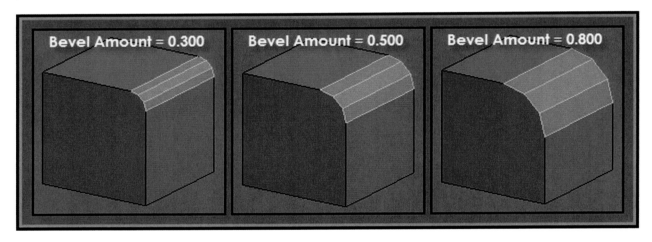

Segments - the number of new *Edges* that are created as part of a *Bevel* operation. Increasing the *Segments* results in a smoother result but comes at the cost of more geometry. The number of *Segments* can be set after initiating a *Bevel* operation and scrolling the Mouse Wheel up or down. After confirming the *Bevel* operation you can change the *Segments* using the *Segments Slider*. To change the number of *Segments*, either click-drag the slider with the LMB or click on the slider and enter a number.

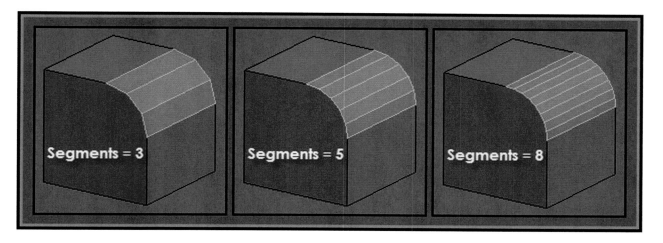

Profile - changes the *Shape* or *Profile* of the *Bevel*. The *Profile* field accepts a value between 0 and 1. The default value it 0.5.

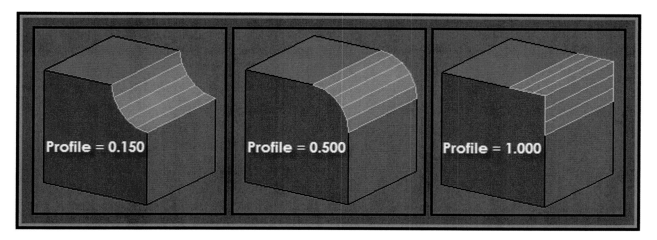

Vertex Only - once enabled, *Vertex Only* mode will cause all *Bevel* operations to only affect the *Vertices* of any *Selected Edges*. The *Edges* themselves will be unaffected.

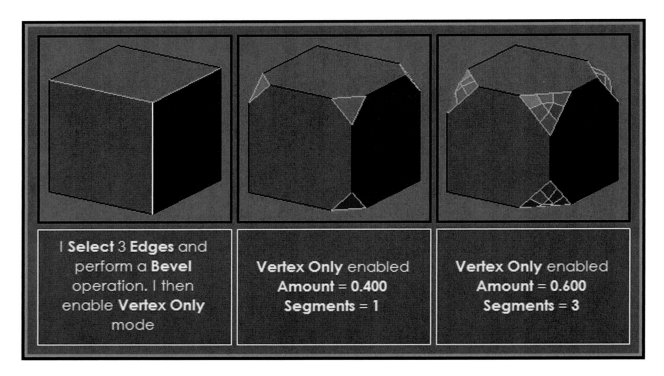

You can initiate a *Bevel* operation in *Vertex Only* mode using the shortcut Ctrl + Shift + B.

Clamp Overlap - prevents *Edges* that result from a *Bevel* operation from overlapping with each other. *Clamp Overlap* only affects *Edges* that are close together.

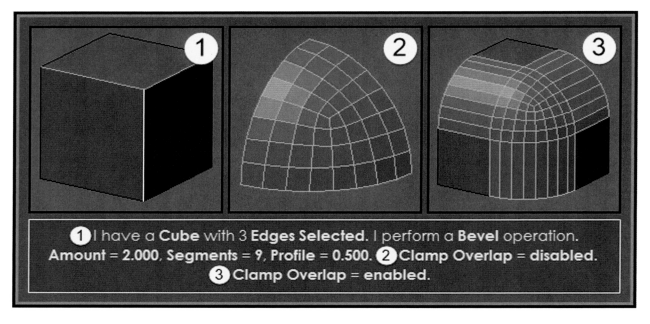

Material - the *Material* setting allows you to define what *Material* will be assigned to any new *Faces* that result from the *Bevel* operation. The default is -1 which essentially turns the option off. When set to -1, any new *Faces* that result from the *Bevel* operation will inherit the *Material* from the closest *Face*.

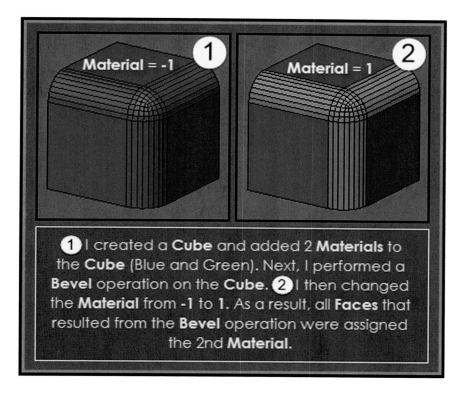

Beware that the *Bevel Tool* can result in the creation of *Triangles* and *Ngons*.

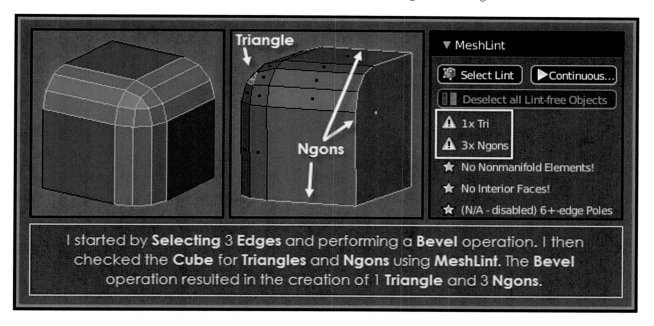

I prefer to use the *Bevel Tool* on *Edge Loops* and *Face Loops* as it generally will not create *Triangles* or *Ngons* in either case.

I performed **Bevel** operations on several **Edge Loops**. The **Faces** created as a result of the **Bevel** operation did not produce any **Triangles** or **Ngons**.

I have seen the *Bevel Tool* used heavily in some tutorials and rarely in others. They are used to both smooth out sharp *Edges* and introduce new geometry. I tend to use them selectively as I try to keep on top of bad geometry as much as possible. In many cases, like in the above illustration, I could have accomplished the same thing with *Loop Cuts*. The advantage with the *Bevel Tool* is I performed the *Bevel* operation on all *Selected Edges* simultaneously.

Here is an example of using *Bevel* and *Inset* to quickly create an airplane tire.

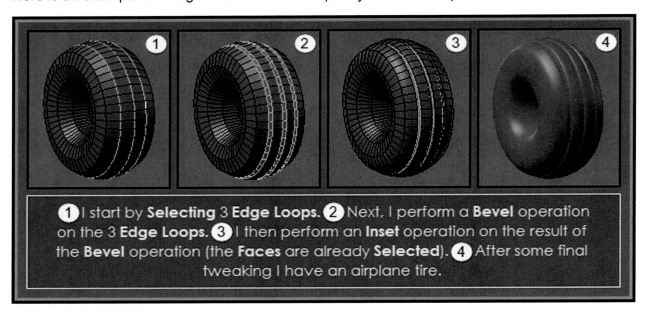

1 I start by **Selecting** 3 **Edge Loops**. **2** Next, I perform a **Bevel** operation on the 3 **Edge Loops**. **3** I then perform an **Inset** operation on the result of the **Bevel** operation (the **Faces** are already **Selected**). **4** After some final tweaking I have an airplane tire.

As you can see in the above illustration, I was able to introduce 3 new *Loop Cuts* and distribute them evenly using a single *Bevel* operation. For this type of *Modeling* task, the *Bevel Tool* was a good choice.

There is also a *Bevel Modifier* that can be used as an alternative to the *Bevel Tool*. See **Chapter 9 – The Bevel Modifier** for more info.

Subdivide Tool

The *Subdivide Tool* can be used to add geometry by splitting or slicing your *Mesh*. Think of it like dividing up a *Birthday Cake*. After you blow out the candles, you need to make *Cuts* to the *Cake* so everyone gets a piece. You are, essentially, *Subdividing* the *Cake*. The *Subdivide Tool* may initially seem simple but the results are determined by several rules.

To initiate a *Subdivide* operation, press W to access the *Specials Menu* and select *Subdivide*. You can also access the *Subdivide Tool* on the *Tools Shelf*. The *Subdivide Tool* is located on the *Tools* tab in the *Mesh Tools Panel*. Here is a basic example.

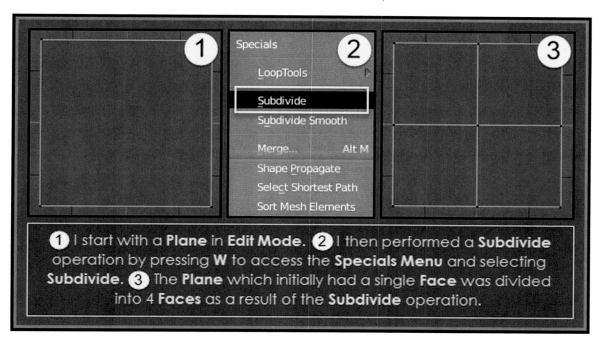

① I start with a **Plane** in **Edit Mode**. **②** I then performed a **Subdivide** operation by pressing **W** to access the **Specials Menu** and selecting **Subdivide**. **③** The **Plane** which initially had a single **Face** was divided into 4 **Faces** as a result of the **Subdivide** operation.

Press F6 after confirming a *Subdivide* operation to can gain access to the *Subdivide Operator Panel* (the *Subdivide Operator Panel* is also visible on the *Tools Shelf* if you have it open). There you can change several options related to the *Subdivide* operation.

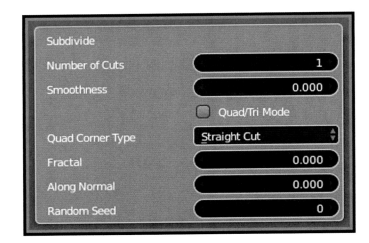

The options on the *Operator Panel* are as follows:

Number of Cuts - number of *Cuts* to make as part of the *Subdivide* operation. The behavior of the *Subdivide Tool* is such that a value of 1 in the *Number of Cuts* field will result in 1 *Cut* being made on <u>ALL</u> *Selected Edges*.

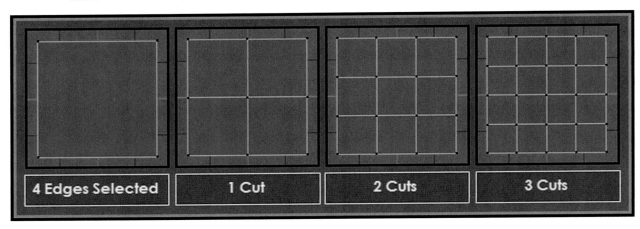

Notice in the above illustration that I start with 4 *Selected Edges*. I start with a value of 1 for *Number* of *Cuts*. This results in each *Selected Edge* being *Cut* once and any needed *Vertices* are also added. When I increase the Number of *Cuts* to 2, each *Selected Edge* is *Cut* twice and so on.

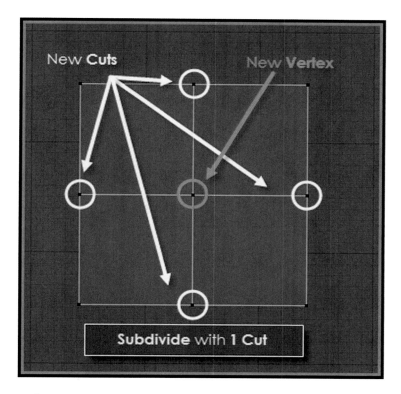

Looking at the above diagram you get the impression that the *Subdivide* operation created 5 new *Vertices* and you would be right. When it comes to *Subdivision*, you have to look at it in terms of *Edges*. The *Plane* had 4 *Selected Edges*. With the number of *Cuts* set to 1, each *Selected Edge* gets 1 *Cut*. The *Subdivide* operation resulted in 4 new *Cuts*, 1 for each *Selected Edge*. A 5th *Vertex* was created as it was required to complete the *Subdivide* operation. The alternative is an *Ngon* with 8 *Vertices*.

Smoothness - The *Smoothness* slider can be used to generate a *Smoother* result when performing a *Subdivide* operation. You can set a value between 0 and 1 by clicking and sliding your Mouse on the *Smoothness* slider or you can manually input a value to set the *Smoothness*. A value of 0 will result in no *Smoothness* and a value of 1 will result in maximum *Smoothness*.

You may have noticed there is a *Subdivide Smooth* option in the *Specials Menu*. Selecting this option will perform a *Subdivide* operation with the *Smoothness* set to 1.0

Quad / Tri Mode - Attempts to prevent the creation of *Ngon Faces* during a *Subdivide* operation. When enabled, any *Ngons* will be created using *Triangles*.

Quad Corner Type - used to define the behavior of a *Subdivide* operation when 2 adjacent *Edges* are *Selected*.

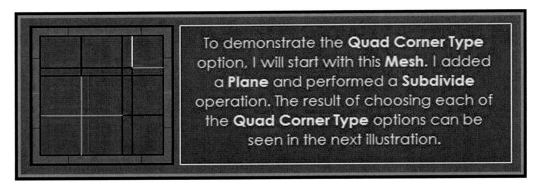

Here are the results for each *Quad Corner Type*.

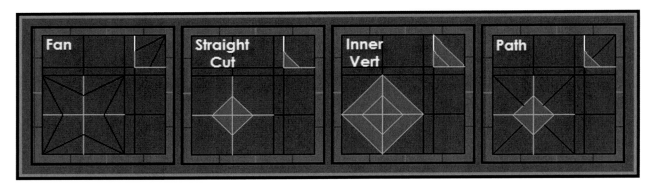

Although the *Quad Corner Types Menu* is interesting, I can't imagine committing the rules for each menu option to memory and knowing which to choose to achieve a particular result. Also, it's important to keep in mind that all 4 options produce *Triangles*.

Fractal - randomly scatters the *Vertices* that are both *Selected* and that result from the *Subdivide* operation in random directions. It is in many ways the opposite of the *Smoothness* setting. Despite that, you can use the *Fractal* and *Smoothness* settings together to get what I would describe as a *Smooth Fractal* effect ☺.

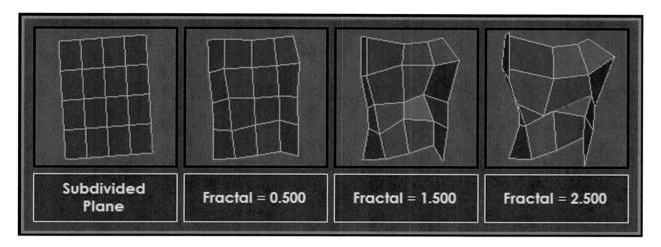

Along Normal - used in conjunction with the *Fractal* setting and causes the *Vertices* to move along their *Normals* as opposed to being scattered randomly. The *Along Normal* slider accepts a value between 0 and 1. The *Along Normal* option has a *Smoothing* effect and you may need to increase the *Fractal* value if you want more noise.

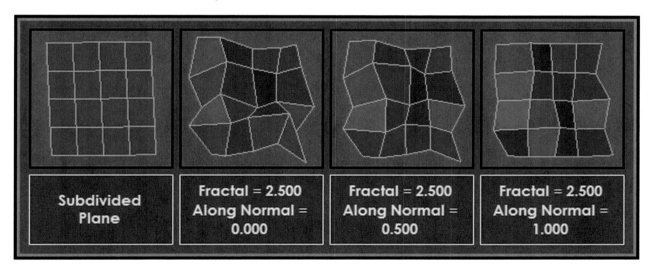

Random Seed - used in conjunction with the *Fractal* setting and is used to change the seed value that is used to generate the *Fractal* results. When you change the *Fractal* value a formula is used to generate the random directions for the *Vertices*. The formula is calculated using a seed value and by changing this value you can change the result of the *Fractal*. The *Random Seed* slider accepts a value between 0 and 50.

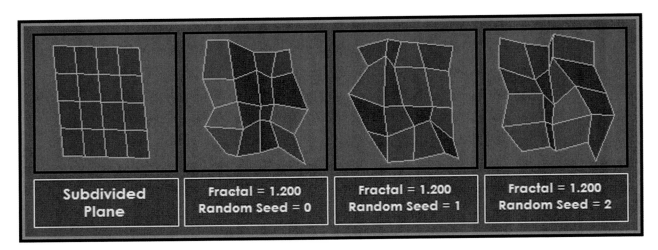

There are many rules that affect the outcome of a *Subdivide* operation. It isn't practical to learn them all and you will know what to expect with experience.

I personally don't use the *Subdivide Tool* very often. I usually use it to *Subdivide* a *Mesh Primitive* immediately after I add it. I find it useful for creating geometry on a small portion of a mesh but most of the time I introduce new geometry using *Extrude*, *Inset* and *Loop Cuts*. I don't recommend *Subdividing* your entire *Mesh*. Doing so will make it difficult to work with. There is a far better solution when it comes to *Subdividing* a *Mesh* (see **Chapter 9 – The Subdivision Surface Modifier**).

Subdivide Smooth

Subdivide Smooth and *Subdivide* produce identical results with the only difference being that with *Subdivide Smooth* you get a *Smoother* result. You can of course use the *Smoothness* setting when performing a *Subdivide* operation to achieve a similar result. Subdivide Smooth Is also initiated from the *Specials Menu* (press W to access the *Specials Menu*).

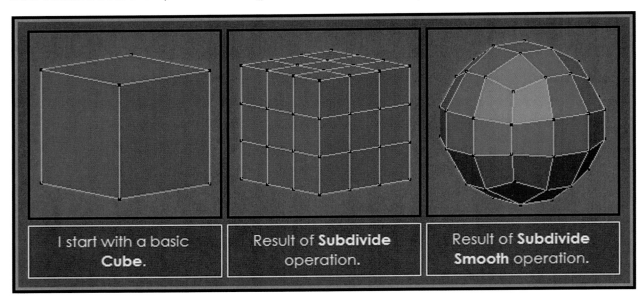

Merge

The *Merge Tool* allows you to *Merge* all *Selected Vertices* into 1 *Vertex*. You initiate a *Merge* operation by pressing Alt + M after *Selecting* 2 or more *Vertices*. Once initiated, a menu will appear allowing you to choose a *Merge* option. The options on the *Merge Menu* are as follows:

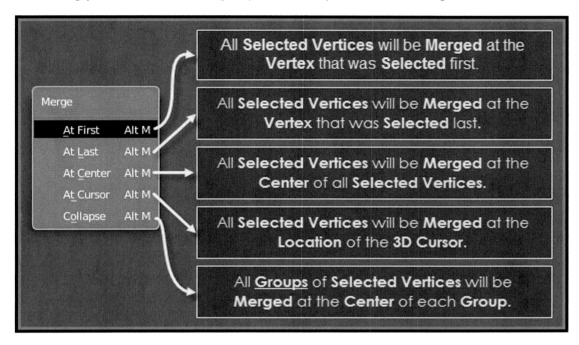

The first 4 options are pretty self-explanatory. The *Collapse* option will collapse *Groups* of *Selected Vertices* into their individual group center.

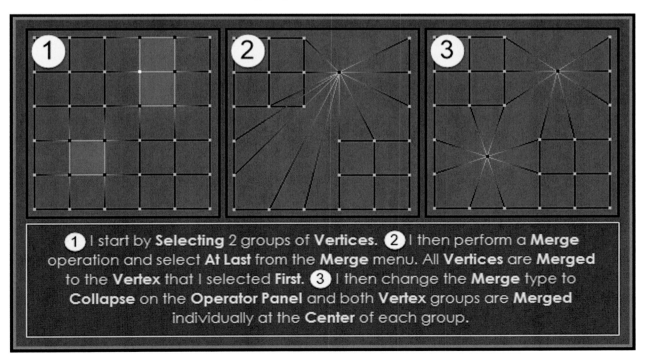

1 I start by **Selecting** 2 groups of **Vertices**. **2** I then perform a **Merge** operation and select **At Last** from the **Merge** menu. All **Vertices** are **Merged** to the **Vertex** that I selected **First**. **3** I then change the **Merge** type to **Collapse** on the **Operator Panel** and both **Vertex** groups are **Merged** individually at the **Center** of each group.

Performing a *Merge* operation will result in the deletion of some *Edges / Faces*. *Blender* does it's best to intelligently remove *Edges / Faces* during a *Merge* operation but you could end up with topology issues depending on the number and *Location* of *Selected Vertices* you are trying to *Merge*.

I see the *Merge Tool* used all the time in tutorials. It comes in very handy when you are fixing or modifying *Mesh Topology*.

AutoMerge

The *AutoMerge* setting will allow you to *Merge Vertices* by *Snapping* one *Vertex* to another using the *Snap To Mesh Tool* (see **Chapter 8 – The Snap To Mesh Tool**). When *Auto Merge* is enabled, any time a *Vertex* is *Snapped* to another *Vertex* using the *Snap To Mesh Tool* they will automatically be *Merged*. To enable *AutoMerge*, click on the *AutoMerge* icon on the *3D View Window Header*.

Remove Doubles

The *Remove Doubles Tool*, once initiated, will *Merge* any *Selected Vertices* that are close to each other. To initiate a *Remove Doubles* operation (with 2 or more *Vertices Selected*) press W to access the *Specials Menu* and select *Remove Doubles*. You can set the distance that *Blender* uses to decide whether or not to *Merge* any of the *Selected Vertices*. The setting can be changed on the *Remove Doubles Operator Panel* which can be accessed by pressing F6 after initiating a *Remove Doubles* operation. The *Remove Doubles Operator Panel* also appears in the *Tools Shelf* if you have it open. The result of the *Remove Doubles* operation is displayed in the info bar at the top of the *3D View Window*.

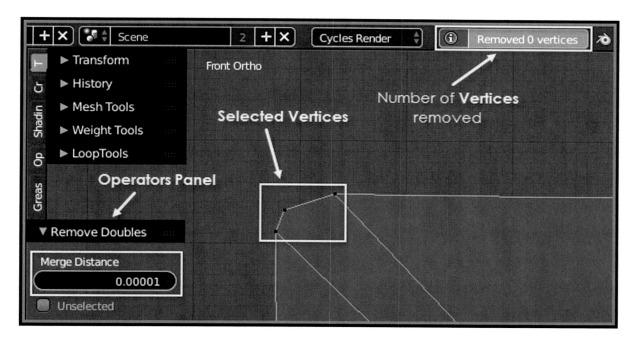

In the next illustration I show the result of performing a *Remove Doubles* operation based on the *Selected Vertices* in the above illustration. The *Selected Vertices* may seem very far apart but they are actually fairly close. I zoomed in on the *Vertices* to help demonstrate the *Remove Doubles* operation.

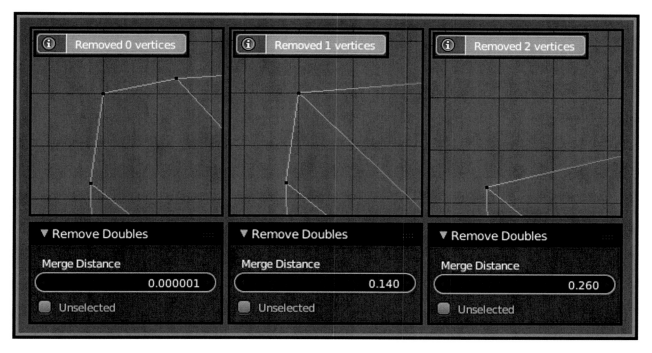

You can see in the above illustration that the number of *Vertices* removed as part of the *Remove Doubles* operation increases as I increase the *Merge Distance*. This is both good and bad. It's good when the *Vertices* you want to *Merge* aren't very close to each other. It's bad when you accidentally *Merge Vertices* that you didn't intend to *Remove*. Often times you will introduce geometry that results in *Vertices* that are very close to each other. *Loop Cuts*, for example, often end up very close to other *Edges / Vertices* if they are being used to *Sharpen Edges*. Doing a *Remove Doubles* operation on an entire *Mesh* could easily lead to you unintentionally removing more *Vertices* than you originally intended. *Selecting* only the *Vertices* that you want to be affected by the *Remove Doubles* operation is the best way to ensure you get the desired results when performing a *Remove Doubles* operation. I always keep a close eye on how many *Doubles* are *Removed* after initiating a *Remove Doubles* operation. If the number seems abnormally high, I double check the *Selected Vertices* to ensure I haven't accidentally included *Vertices* that I don't want to be affected by a *Remove Doubles* operation.

There is also a checkbox on the *Operator Panel* labeled *Unselected*. When enabled, the *Remove Doubles* operation will be performed on all *Vertices*, both *Selected* and *Unselected*. This is the equivalent of performing a *Remove Doubles* on the entire *Mesh* which as I mentioned above, isn't usually a good idea.

The Bridge Tool

The *Bridge Tool* allows you to connect or *Bridge* 2 or more *Groups* of *Selected Vertices*. Think of it as a way to quickly create *Faces* between *Groups* of *Selected Vertices*. It's truly a time saver. Let's start with a basic example using *Edge Loops*.

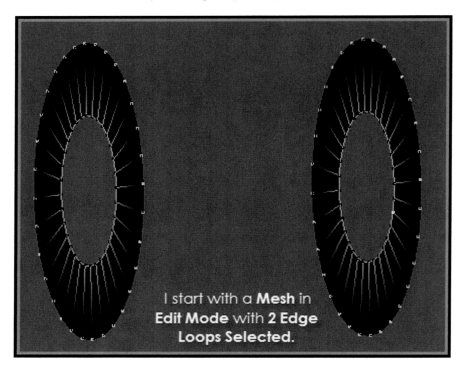

I start with a **Mesh** in **Edit Mode** with **2 Edge Loops Selected.**

I can now *Bridge* the *Selected Edge Loops* by pressing W to access the *Specials Menu* and selecting *Bridge Edge Loops*. **Note:** The above *Mesh* will be the starting point for many of the examples below.

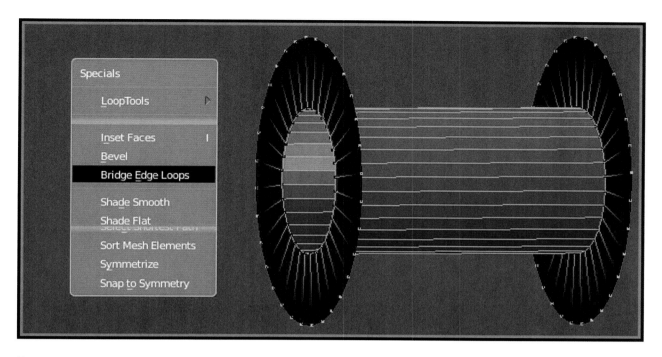

Press F6 after selecting *Bridge Edge Loops* from the *Specials Menu* to can gain access to the *Bridge Edge Loops Operator Panel* (the *Bridge Edge Loops Operator Panel* is also visible on the *Tools Shelf* if you have it open). There you can change several options related to the *Bridge Edge Loops* operation.

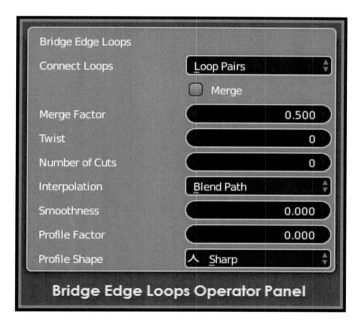

The options on the *Operator Panel* are as follows:

Connect Loops - allows you to choose which method is used to *Connect* multiple *Edge Loops*. To demonstrate I start by Selecting 4 *Edge Loops*.

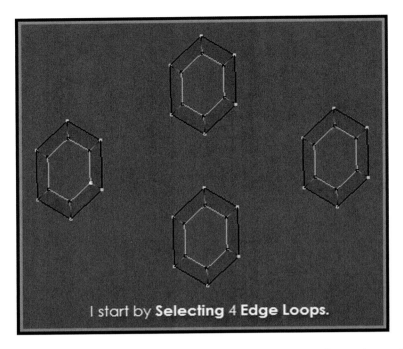

Next I perform a *Bridge Edge Loops* operation. I start by selecting *Open Loop* from the *Connect Loops Menu*.

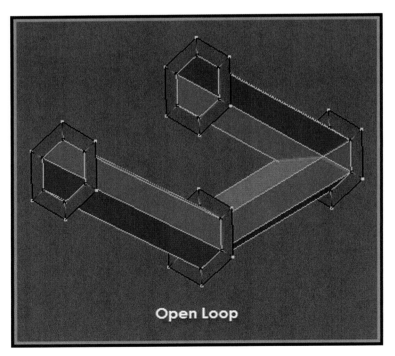

All 4 *Edge Loops* are *Connected* except for the *Edge Loop* that was *Selected* first and the *Edge Loop* that was *Selected* last. Next I select *Closed Loop* from the *Connect Loops Menu*.

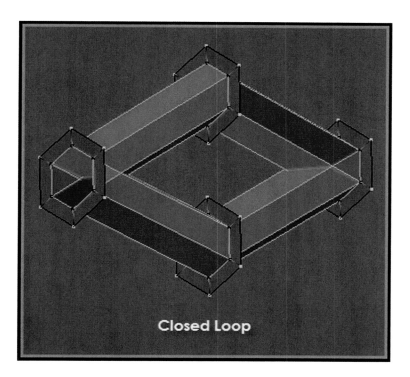

Closed Loop

All 4 *Edge Loops* are *Connected* including the *Edge Loop* that was *Selected* first and the *Edge Loop* that was *Selected* last. Finally I select *Loop Pairs* from the *Connect Loops Menu*.

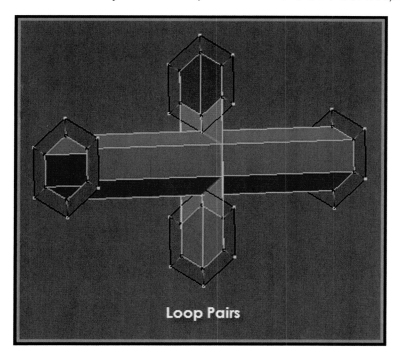

Loop Pairs

The *Loop Pairs* option will bridge *Pairs* of *Edge Loops*. This option requires an even number of *Edge Loops* to be *Selected*. Attempting to use this option with an odd number of *Edge Loops Selected* will produce an error.

Merge and Merge Factor - enabling *Merge* will cause the *Selected Edge Loops* to be *Merged* as opposed to being connected. The *Merge Factor* field accepts a value between 0.000 and 1.000 and determines the *Location* of the *Merged Vertices*.

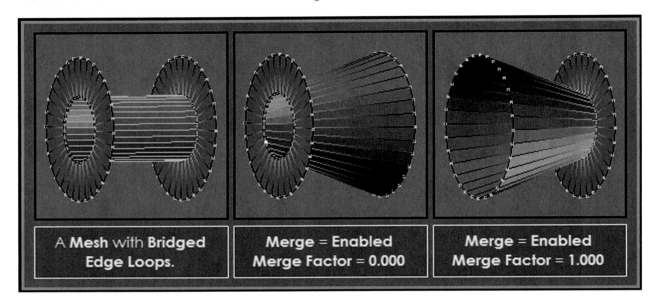

Twist - allows you to *Twist* or *Rotate* the *Edge Loops* used in the *Bridge Edge Loops* operation.

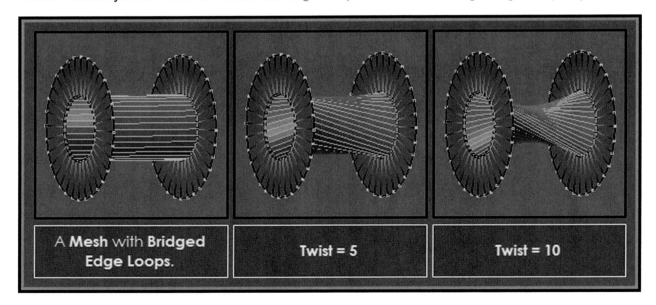

Note: *Twist* only works with closed *Edge Loops*.

Number of Cuts - allows you to add *Loop Cuts* to the *Faces* created by the *Bridge Edge Loops* operation.

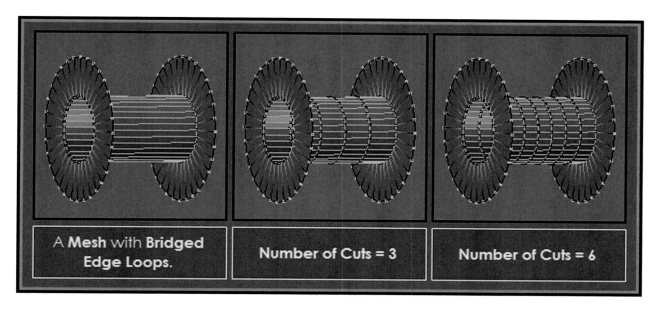

All of the remaining options work in conjunction with the *Number of Cuts* setting.

Interpolation - used to determine how the *Cuts* are distributed. There is math involved here so I will avoid looking silly by going right to an illustration.

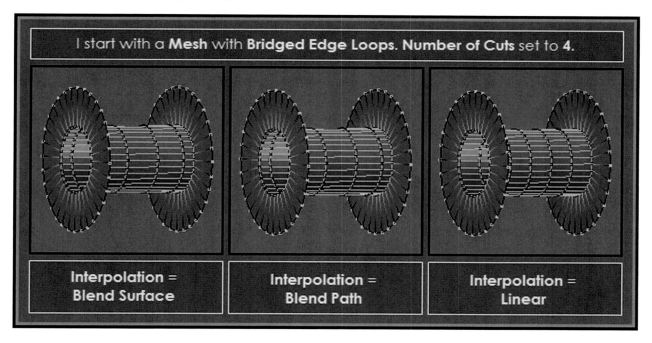

The *Smoothness* option plays a role in the result of the *Interpolation* setting as we will see next.

Smoothness - allows you to *Set* the *Smoothness* of any *Cuts* you add. The result you get will depend on your *Interpolation* setting. The *Smoothness* field accepts a value between 0.000 and 0.200.

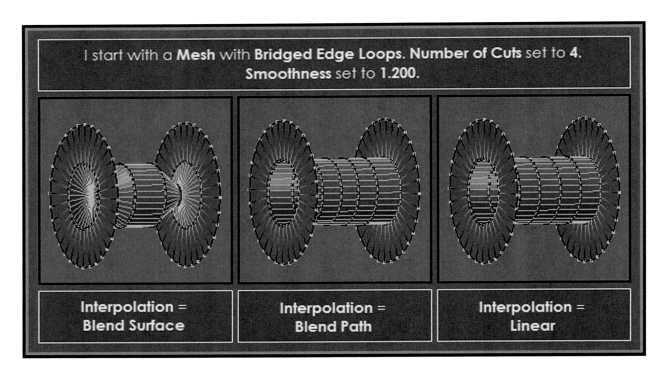

As you can see in the above illustration, the *Smoothness* setting used in conjunction with *Interpolation* set to *Blend Surface* makes for some interesting results.

Profile Factor - the *Profile Factor* setting essentially allows you inflate or deflate the *Faces* created as part of the *Bridge Edge Loops* operation. *Interpolation* is set to *Linear* for the next 2 illustrations.

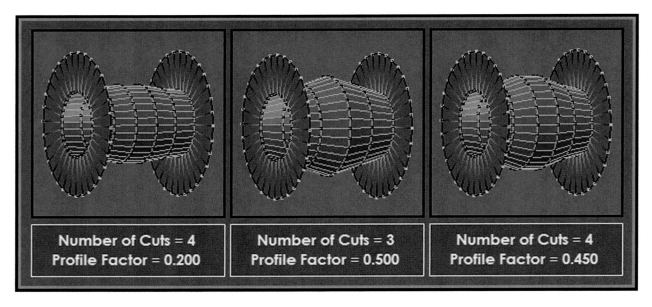

Here are a few more examples using a negative value for the *Profile Factor*.

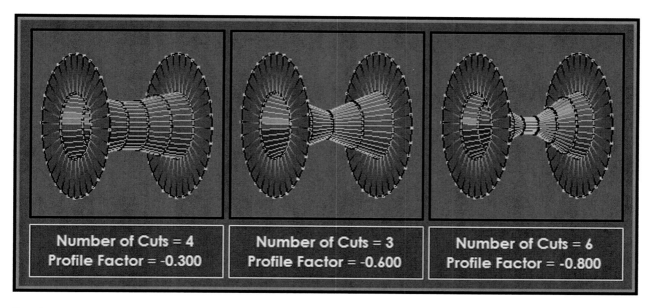

| Number of Cuts = 4 | Number of Cuts = 3 | Number of Cuts = 6 |
| Profile Factor = -0.300 | Profile Factor = -0.600 | Profile Factor = -0.800 |

Profile Shape - the *Profile Shape* setting works in conjunction with the *Profile Factor* value. Were *Profile Factor* inflates / deflates the *Faces*, the *Profile Shape* determines the *Shape* of the inflated / deflated *Faces*. There are a variety of *Profile Shapes* to choose from which results in a large variety of results.

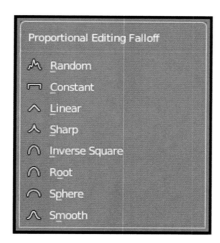

Here is a small sample of the results of changing the Profile Shape.

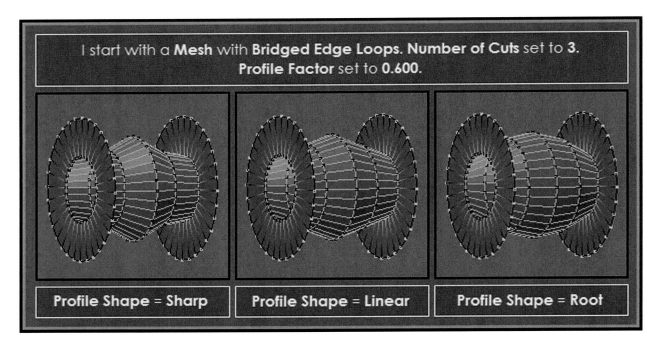

Up until now I have mostly shown examples using *Selected Edge Loops*. The *Bridge Edge Loops Tool* is not limited to *Edge Loops*. You can perform a *Bridge Edge Loops* operation on as few as 2 *Edges*.

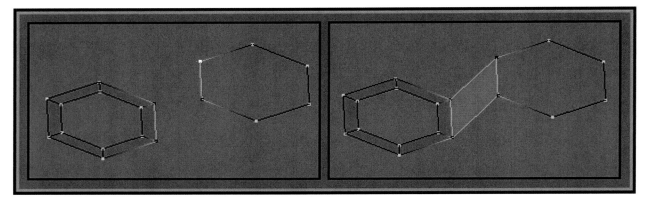

You can also connect an uneven number of *Edges*. Keep in mind that the result will probably result in *Triangles*.

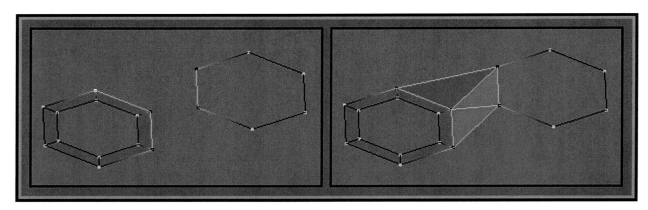

The *Selected Vertices* don't have to be on separate *Mesh Elements*.

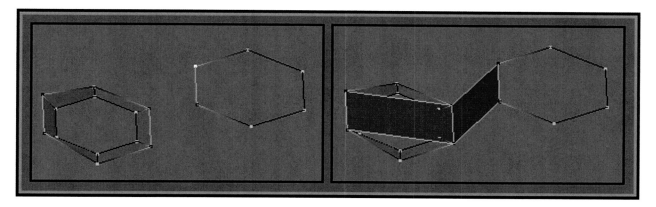

Thanks to all the options, you can use it to help you quickly add geometry to your *Mesh*.

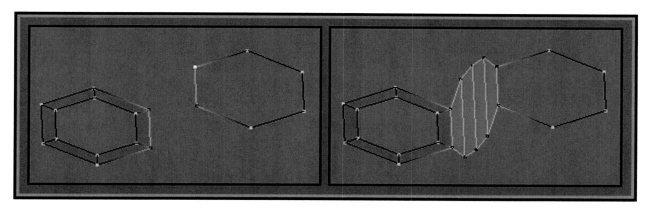

You can also use the *Bridge Tool* to create holes in your *Mesh* without having to *Delete* and re-add *Faces*.

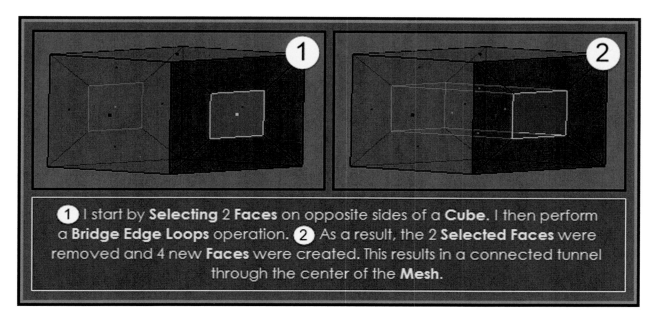

1 I start by **Selecting** 2 **Faces** on opposite sides of a **Cube**. I then perform a **Bridge Edge Loops** operation. **2** As a result, the 2 **Selected Faces** were removed and 4 new **Faces** were created. This results in a connected tunnel through the center of the **Mesh**.

The *Bridge Tool* was a welcome addition to the *Blender Modeling* tool box. I remember the first time I saw it and thought - "that is going to be a huge time saver". With so many options the *Bridge Tool* is not only a time saver but extremely versatile as well.

The Rip Tool

The *Rip Tool* allows you to *Rip* your *Mesh* much like you would a piece of paper. When you *Rip* a piece of paper you create 2 *Edges*, one on each side of the *Rip*. You can kind of think of it the same way when you perform a *Rip* operation in *Blender*. Each *Edge* in *Blender* can be attached to 2 or more *Faces*. When you perform a *Rip* operation on an *Edge* in *Blender*, you essentially *Split* the *Selected Edge*(s) so there is an *Edge* for each *Face*. This of course only applies to *Edges* that are connected to 2 or more *Faces*. To initiate a *Rip* operation press ∨ on the keyboard.

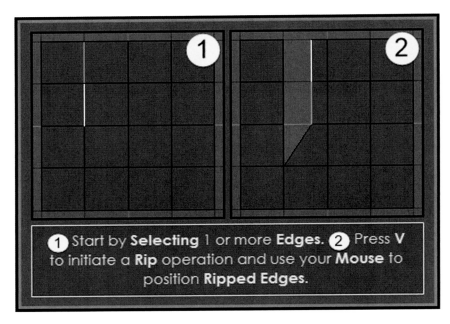

1 Start by **Selecting** 1 or more **Edges.** 2 Press **V** to initiate a **Rip** operation and use your **Mouse** to position **Ripped Edges.**

3D Cursor placement plays a role when performing *Rip* operations. The direction of the *Rip* is determined by the position of the *3D Cursor*.

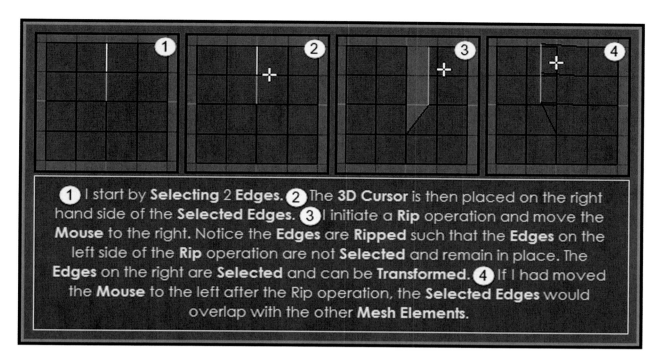

① I start by **Selecting** 2 Edges. ② The **3D Cursor** is then placed on the right hand side of the **Selected Edges**. ③ I initiate a **Rip** operation and move the **Mouse** to the right. Notice the **Edges** are **Ripped** such that the **Edges** on the left side of the **Rip** operation are not **Selected** and remain in place. The **Edges** on the right are **Selected** and can be **Transformed**. ④ If I had moved the **Mouse** to the left after the Rip operation, the **Selected Edges** would overlap with the other **Mesh Elements**.

As you can see in the above illustration, you always want to be aware of your *3D Cursor* position before initiating a *Rip Tool* operation. If I had wanted to *Rip* the *Edges* so that the left hand *Edges* that resulted from the *Rip* operation were *Selected* after the *Rip* operation, I would have to place my *3D Cursor* to the left of the *Selected Edges* before initiating the *Rip* operation.

You can make multiple *Rips* on groups of *Selected Edges* at the same time.

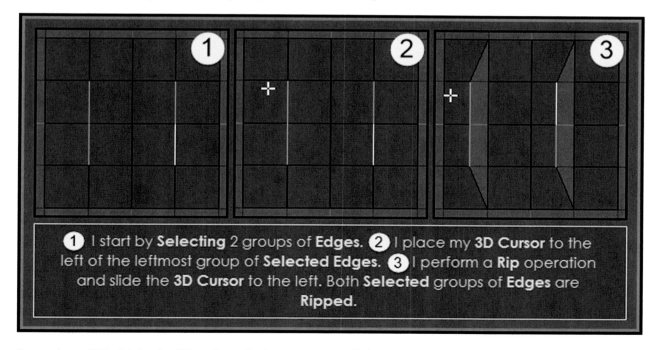

① I start by **Selecting** 2 groups of **Edges**. ② I place my **3D Cursor** to the left of the leftmost group of **Selected Edges**. ③ I perform a **Rip** operation and slide the **3D Cursor** to the left. Both **Selected** groups of **Edges** are **Ripped**.

It can be a little tricky to *Rip* edges that are not parallel to each other. Determining the best *Location* for the *3D Cursor* may initially involve some experimentation.

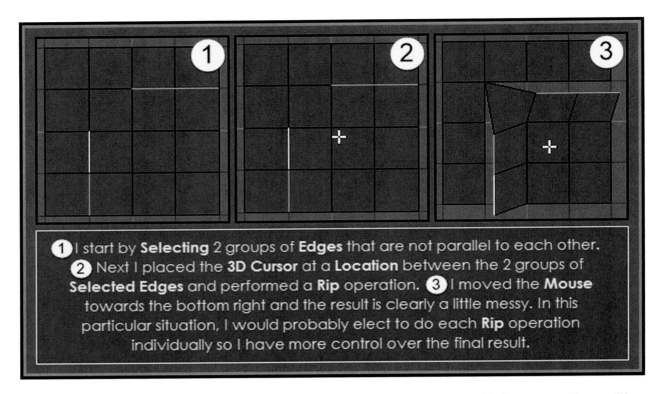

1 I start by **Selecting** 2 groups of **Edges** that are not parallel to each other. 2 Next I placed the **3D Cursor** at a **Location** between the 2 groups of **Selected Edges** and performed a **Rip** operation. 3 I moved the **Mouse** towards the bottom right and the result is clearly a little messy. In this particular situation, I would probably elect to do each **Rip** operation individually so I have more control over the final result.

I mentioned above you can perform a *Rip Tool* operation on an *Edge* with 2 or more *Faces*. It's possible to have multiple *Faces* attached to a *Single Edge*. The only difference when *Ripping* an *Edge* with more than 2 *Faces* is that after the *Rip* operation none of the *Edges* that were *Ripped* will be *Selected*. You will have to *Select* and *Transform* each *Edge* individually.

You can also hit *Escape* after performing a *Rip* operation to cancel the *Transform* operation. A situation where I might want to cancel the *Transform* operation after performing a *Rip* operation is when creating a door for a house. To demonstrate, I will start with a very basic house. I first *Select* the *Edges* that I want to *Rip* in order to create the door.

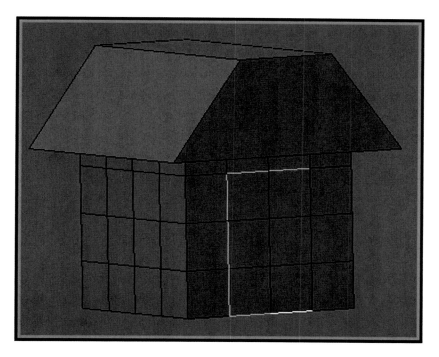

Next I perform a *Rip* operation and immediately hit *Escape* to cancel the *Transform* operation on the *Selected Edges*. Now I want to place the *3D Cursor* at the *Location* that I want to act as a *Pivot Point* when opening and closing the door. It's essentially where the door hinges would be. To do this, I select the *Edges* that I want to *Pivot* around and *Snap* the *3D Cursor* to that *Location*.

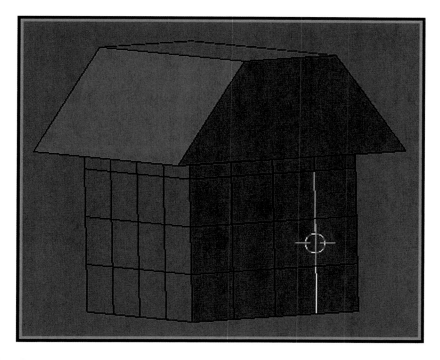

Now that the *3D Cursor* is in the right *Location*, I set the *Pivot Point* to *3D Cursor*, switch to *Face Select Mode* and *Select* the *Faces* that represent the door. Now I can simply *Rotate* the

Selected Faces around the *3D Cursor* to open and close the door. In this example, I constrained the *Rotate* operation along the *Z-Axis* as I was in *Front View*. (Note: I cover *Pivot Point* and *Mesh Select Mode* earlier in the book).

There you have it, a quick and easy door thanks to the *Rip Tool*.

The *Rip Tool* is often used to change *Mesh Topology* as you can easily introduce new geometry to change *Edge Flow*, among other things (see **Chapter 4 – Edge Flow** for more info). Here is a small example of changing *Edge Flow* using the *Rip Tool*.

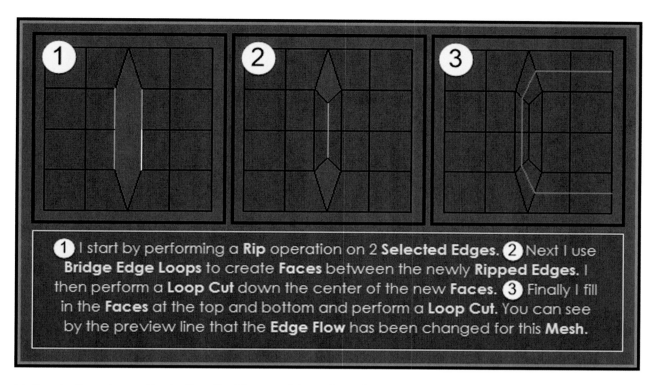

① I start by performing a **Rip** operation on 2 **Selected Edges**. **②** Next I use **Bridge Edge Loops** to create **Faces** between the newly **Ripped Edges**. I then perform a **Loop Cut** down the center of the new **Faces**. **③** Finally I fill in the **Faces** at the top and bottom and perform a **Loop Cut**. You can see by the preview line that the **Edge Flow** has been changed for this **Mesh**.

Notice in the above illustration that I was able to introduce new geometry to the middle of a *Mesh* without producing any *Triangles* or *Ngons*.

The Rip Fill Tool

The *Rip Fill Tool* works the same way as the *Rip Tool* with the only difference being it doesn't leave a hole in your *Mesh*. The *Rip Fill Tool* will fill the hole created by the *Rip* operation with *Faces*. To initiate a *Rip Fill Tool* operation press Alt + V on the keyboard.

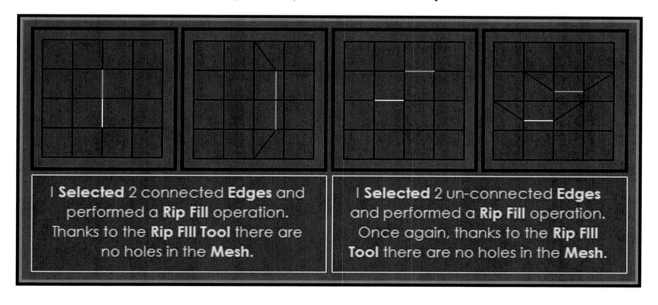

I **Selected** 2 connected **Edges** and performed a **Rip Fill** operation. Thanks to the **Rip Fill Tool** there are no holes in the **Mesh**.

I **Selected** 2 un-connected **Edges** and performed a **Rip Fill** operation. Once again, thanks to the **Rip Fill Tool** there are no holes in the **Mesh**.

I find the end result of using this tool to often be a little odd or unexpected. Also keep in mind that using this variation of the *Rip* tool will usually introduce several *Triangles* and *Nonmanifold Elements* to your *Mesh*.

The Split Tool

The *Split Tool* can be used to *Split* or *Separate* a *Mesh Element* from its *Mesh*. The behavior of the *Split Tool* differs based on your current *Mesh Select Mode*. Using the *Split Tool* to *Split Vertices* / *Edges* will result in the *Selected Vertices* / *Edges* being duplicated. The originally *Selected Mesh Elements* are not removed. To perform a *Split* operation *Select* 1 or more *Mesh Elements* and press Y. Once initiated, the *Mesh Elements* that were *Split* will be *Selected* and can be *Transformed*.

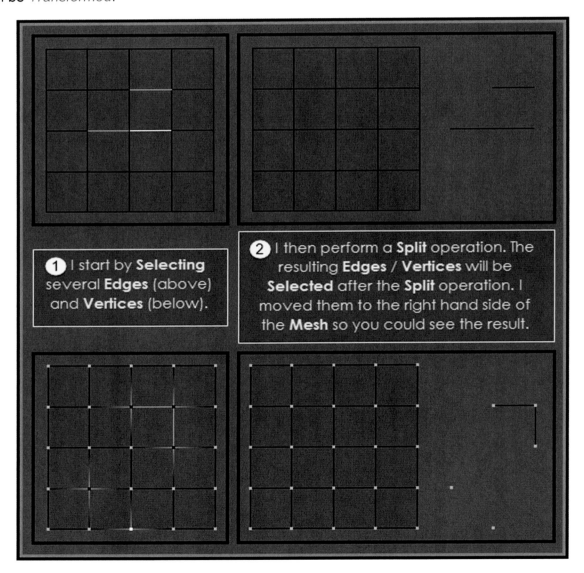

1 I start by **Selecting** several **Edges** (above) and **Vertices** (below).

2 I then perform a **Split** operation. The resulting **Edges / Vertices** will be **Selected** after the **Split** operation. I moved them to the right hand side of the **Mesh** so you could see the result.

As you can see from the above illustration, the *Split Tool* acts very much the same way as the *Duplicate Tool*. Using the *Split Tool* in *Face Select Mode* will produce a different result. The

Selected Face(s) will be detached from the *Mesh* and the originally *Selected Face(s)* will be removed.

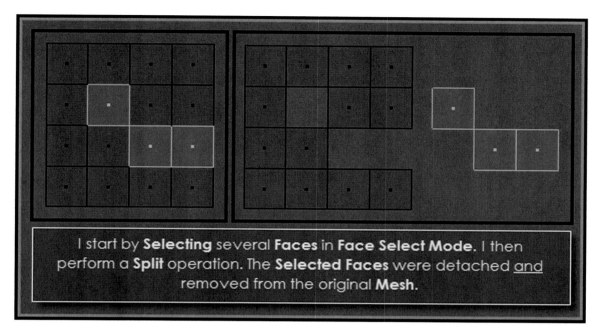

I start by **Selecting** several **Faces** in **Face Select Mode**. I then perform a **Split** operation. The **Selected Faces** were detached <u>and</u> removed from the original **Mesh**.

I find the *Split Tool* far more useful in *Face Select Mode*. It's useful for situations where you want to detach a *Face* but leave it in its original position. A good example might be creating a windshield on a car or a panel on a space ship.

The Separate Tool

See **Chapter 7 – Separating a Mesh into Objects**.

The Spin Tool

The *Spin Tool* works like the *Extrude Tool* except that it *Extrudes* around a *Pivot Point*. The *Pivot Point* used by the *Spin Tool* is the *3D Cursor*. Your current *View* also plays a role in the result of a *Spin Tool* operation.

The *Spin Tool* can be used to make anything from tires to wine glasses. I will start with a basic example.

Start in *Top View*. Center the *3D Cursor* (Shift + C). Add an 8 point *Circle*.

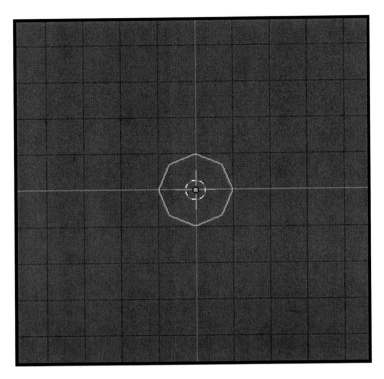

Go in to *Edit Mode*. *Rotate* the *Circle* 90 degrees along the *Y-Axis*. Move the *Circle* along the *Y-Axis* so it appears above the *3D Cursor* in the *3D View*.

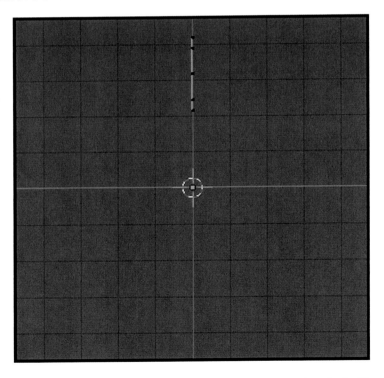

Initiate a *Spin* operation by pressing Alt + R. You can also access the *Spin Tool* on the *Tools Shelf*. The *Spin Tool* is also located on the *Tools Tab* in the *Mesh Tools Panel*.

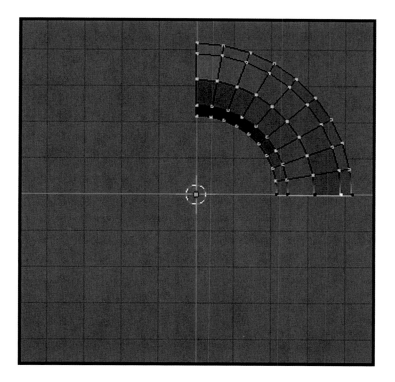

You can see from the above illustration that the *Spin Tool* essentially *Extruded* the *Selected Vertices* in a circle around the *3D Cursor*.

Press F6 after performing a *Spin Tool* operation to can gain access to the *Spin Operator Panel* (the *Spin Operator Panel* is also visible on the *Tools Shelf* if you have it open). There you can change several options related to the *Spin* operation.

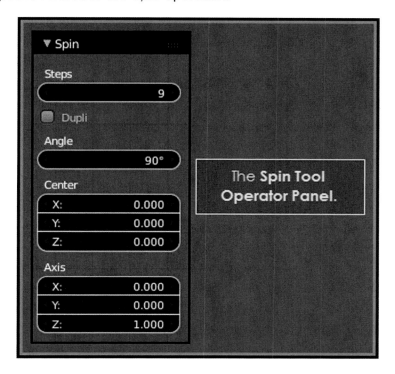

The **Spin Tool** Operator Panel.

The options on the *Operator Panel* are as follows:

Steps - Think of *Steps* as the number of times the *Vertices* are *Extruded* during the *Spin* operation.

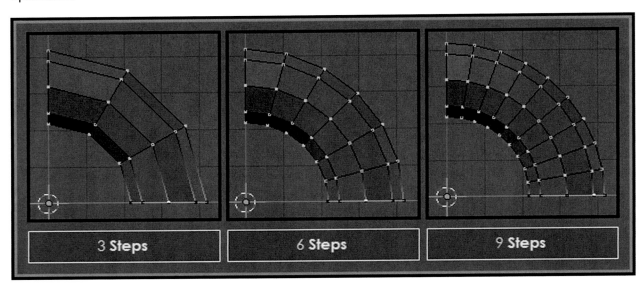

Here is a different viewing angle.

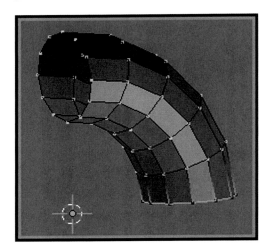

Dupli - short for *Duplicates* (not sure why they decided to remove half the word). Enabling *Dupli* after a *Spin Tool* operation will result in *Duplicates* of the *Selected Vertices* being created with no connecting *Faces*.

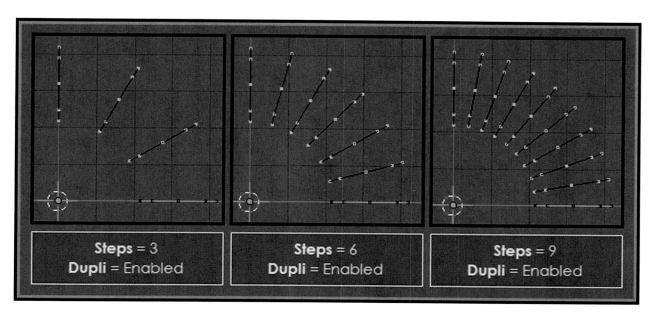

| **Steps** = 3 **Dupli** = Enabled | **Steps** = 6 **Dupli** = Enabled | **Steps** = 9 **Dupli** = Enabled |

Here is a different viewing angle.

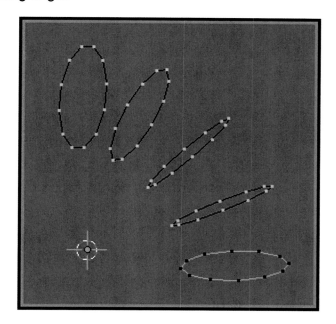

Angle - The *Angle* setting determines how far the *Vertices* will be *Extruded* in terms of degrees. The *Angle* setting essentially allows you to create a ¼ *Circle*, a ½ *Circle* or a full *Circle* etc. by setting the degrees. You can set any angle between 1 and 360. You can even enter decimal values like 182.3 or 344.56.

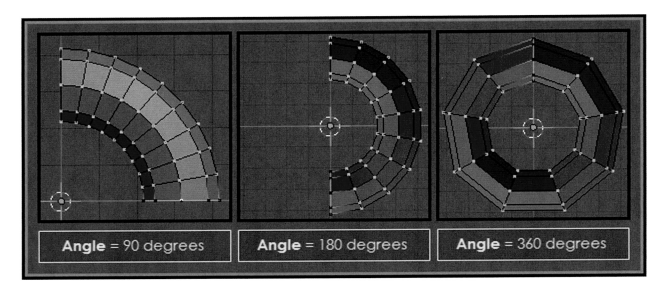

| Angle = 90 degrees | Angle = 180 degrees | Angle = 360 degrees |

You may have noticed that once a *Spin* operation is complete the *Vertices* that result from the final *Extrusion* are *Selected*. When the *Angle* is set to 360 degrees you end up with the final set of *Vertices* at the same *Location* as the original *Selection*. It's important to remember to perform a *Remove Doubles* operation to ensure the *Mesh* is closed. Ensure *Limit Selection to Visible* is disabled before *Selecting* the *Vertices* for the *Remove Doubles* operation (see **Chapter 6 – Limit Selection** and **Chapter 8 – Remove Doubles**).

Center - The *Spin Tool* will *Extrude Vertices* in a *Circle* around the *3D Cursor*. If you don't like the result you can undo the operation, move the *3D Cursor* and try again. With the *Center* settings, you can change what the *Spin Tool* considers to be the *3D Cursor* coordinates without moving the *3D Cursor* itself. The results can often be interesting and possibly unexpected.

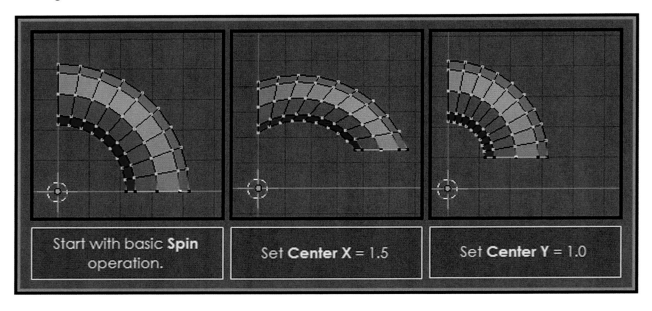

| Start with basic **Spin** operation. | Set **Center X** = 1.5 | Set **Center Y** = 1.0 |

Axis - The *Axis* settings allow you to bend your *Mesh* after performing a *Spin Tool* operation. It offers great flexibility and often requires a little experimentation to get right. Each of the *Axis* settings accepts a value between 1.0 and -1.0.

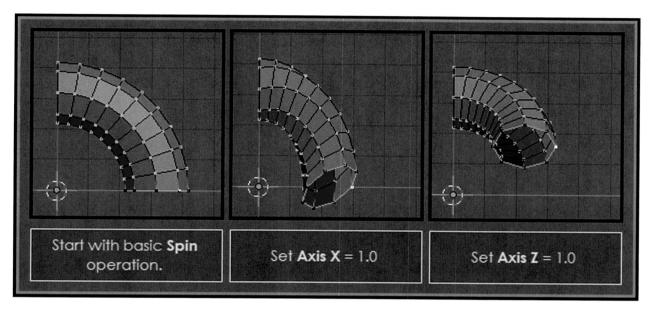

| Start with basic **Spin** operation. | Set **Axis X** = 1.0 | Set **Axis Z** = 1.0 |

The *Spin Tool* can be used to create an egg, a glass, a chess piece or a car tire and that's just the tip of the iceberg. In a lot of ways you can think of it as a 3D lathe.

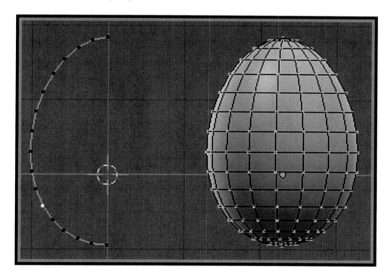

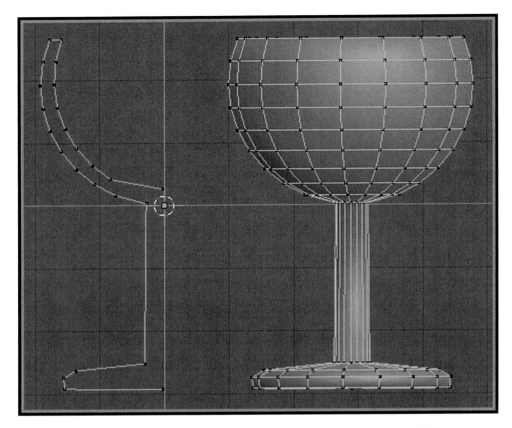

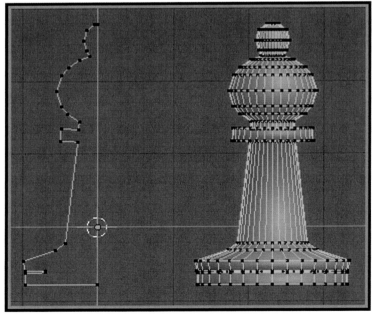

The Screw Tool

The *Screw Tool* is similar to the *Spin Tool* in that it *Extrudes* in a circle around the *3D Cursor*. The difference is you can also use a *Mesh Element* as a sort of offset that will also allow the *Extruded Mesh Elements* to be *Extruded* upwards at various angles. The *Screw Tool* allows you to create things like screws, springs and other interesting shapes.

The *Screw Tool* has several rules that must be followed to get a result. The first is that you must have 1 open ended *Mesh Element*. The *Mesh Element* can have numerous *Vertices* but must end in 2 open or disconnected *Vertices*. You can only have 1 open ended *Mesh Element* when performing a *Screw* operation. If you *Select* more than 1 open ended *Mesh Element* you will get an error. I will refer to the open ended *Mesh Element* as the *Vector Mesh* for the rest of this section. The two open *Vertices* of the *Vector Mesh* are used by *Blender* to calculate the height and angle that will be used when performing the *Screw* operation. So you get a regular *Spin* plus height and angle when using the *Screw Tool*. After creating a *Vector Mesh* you can then add other closed *Mesh Elements* which are referred to as *Profiles*. The *Profiles* can be *Circles*, *Squares* as well as *Mesh Elements* with open or closed *Faces*.

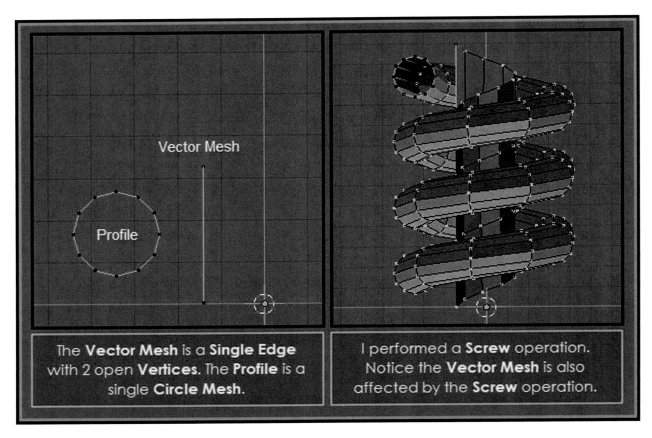

The **Vector Mesh** is a **Single Edge** with 2 open **Vertices**. The **Profile** is a single **Circle Mesh**.

I performed a **Screw** operation. Notice the **Vector Mesh** is also affected by the **Screw** operation.

The *Vector Mesh* in the above illustration is a simple *Edge*. It's comprised of 2 open *Vertices* or *Vertices* that are not connected to any other *Mesh Elements*. The *Profile Mesh* is a simple *Circle*. As I mentioned above, you can have as many *Profile Mesh Elements* as you want as long as they are closed. I also show the result of a *Screw* operation. Notice both the *Profile* and *Vector Mesh* are affected by the *Screw* operation. The *Vector Mesh* is used to calculate the height and angle of the *Screw* operation and is also affected by the *Screw* operation. You will often want to delete the *Vector Mesh* after performing a *Screw* operation as it's used to determine characteristics of the *Screw* operation and is often not wanted in the final result.

Press F6 after performing a *Screw Tool* operation to gain access to the *Screw Operator Panel* (the *Screw Operator Panel* is also visible on the *Tools Shelf* if you have it open). There you can change several options related to the *Screw* operation.

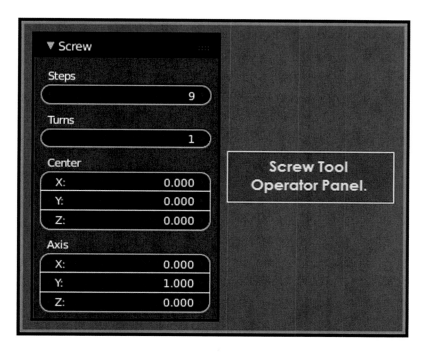

The options on the *Operator Panel* are as follows:

Note: all illustrations used when discussing the *Operator Panel* will start with the following *Mesh Elements*. All operations are done in *Front View*.

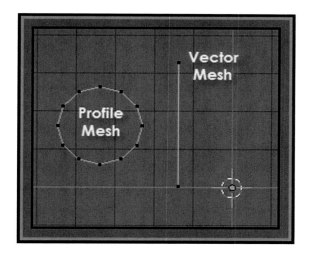

Steps - the *Steps* setting is used to determine how many times the *Selected Vertices* are *Extruded* for <u>each</u> full turn. By 1 turn I mean 360 degrees. The value can be anywhere between 3 and 256 and the *Steps* are distributed evenly over the 360 degrees. The more *Steps* you have the smoother the result but it can also become quite taxing on your computer very quickly.

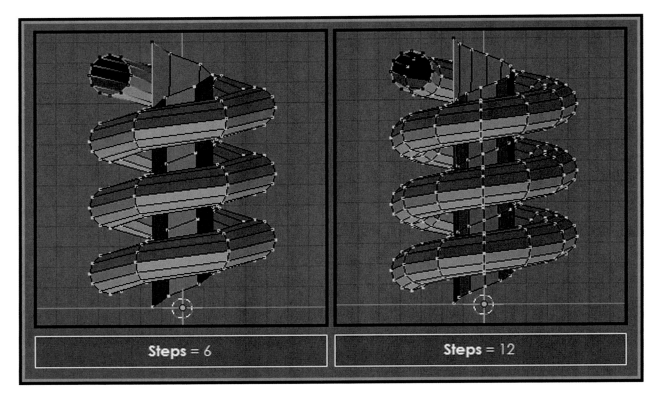

Turns – number of *Turns* in the *Screw Operation* were 1 *Turn* is equal to 360 degrees. The *Turns* option accepts a value between 1 and 256.

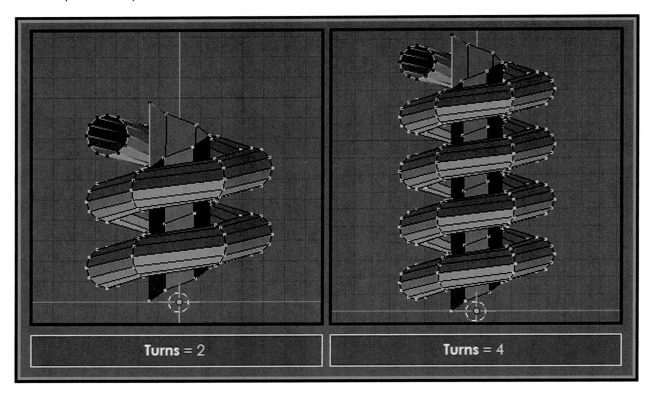

Center - The *Center* settings for the *Screw Tool* behave similarly to the *Center* settings on the *Spin Tool Operator Panel*. During a *Screw* operation, *Blender Extrudes* the *Selected Vertices* in a *Circle* around the *3D Cursor*. With the *Center* settings, you can change what the *Screw Tool* considers to be the *3D Cursor* coordinates without moving the *3D Cursor* itself.

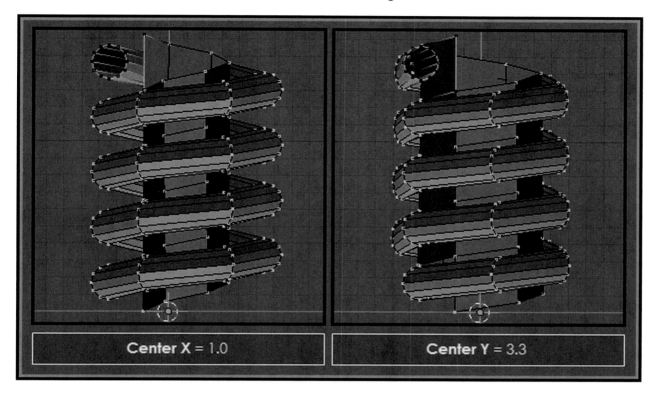

Axis - Similar to the *Axis* settings on the *Spin Tool Operator Panel*, the *Axis* settings allow you to bend your *Mesh* after performing a *Spin Tool* operation. It offers great flexibility and often requires a little experimentation to get right. Each of the *Axis* settings accepts a value between 1.0 and -1.0.

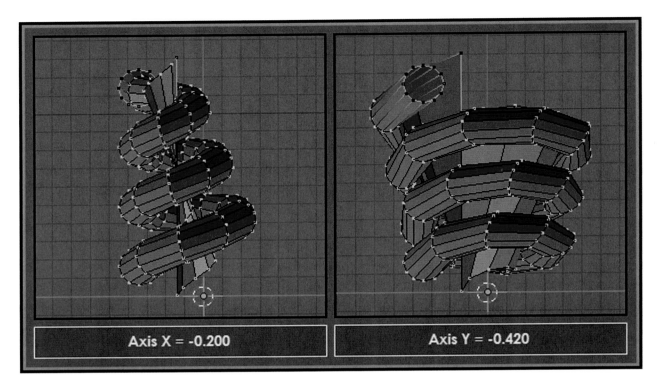

There is a more detailed explanation of the *Axis* setting for both the *Spin* and *Screw Tool* on the net. The truth is, I don't think anyone can memorize the rules or math behind this type of setting. My explanation of the *Axis* setting was at a very high level. I find the best practice for this type of setting is experimentation and trial and error. You will eventually get a feel for how it behaves.

If you notice that the result of a *Screw* operation is going in the wrong direction, you can fix it by flipping the *Vector Mesh*. By wrong direction I mean the direction of the *Extruded Vertices* is downwards instead of upwards (unless you wanted the direction of the Extrusion to be downwards). Flipping the *Vector Mesh* will change the *Extrusion* direction. To flip the *Vector Mesh* in *Front View*, you can simply highlight all *Vertices* and *Mirror* them along the *Z-Axis* (Ctrl + M then press Z).

The best way to understand the *Screw Tool* is to experiment with it. As I mentioned above, all you need is a *Vector Mesh*. Here is a basic example using just a *Vector Mesh*.

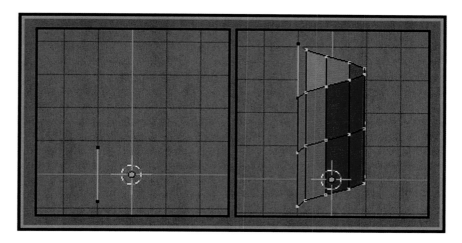

I performed a *Screw* operation on a basic *Vector Mesh*. The result was a basic tube. Now I will modify the *Vector Mesh* by moving the top *Vertex* along the *X-Axis*.

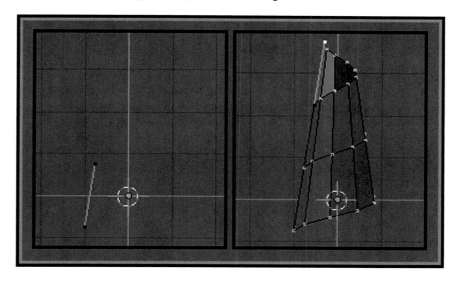

The result of modifying the *Vector Mesh* in the above illustration is a cone shaped *Mesh*. Next I will add 1 *Vertex* to the *Vector Mesh*.

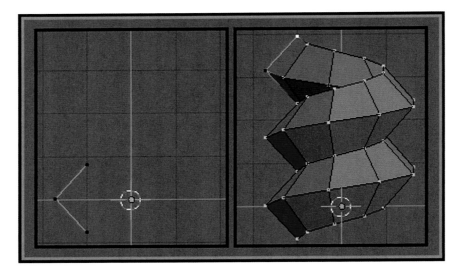

The result of a *Screw* operation is a screw shaped *Mesh*. Watch what happens when I move the top *Vertex* slightly to the left.

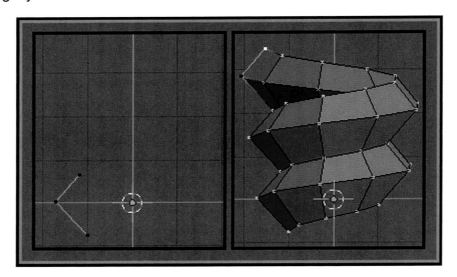

As you can see, even slight variations to the *Vector Mesh* can have a big effect on the result of a *Screw* operation. The *Vector Mesh* is also used to determine the result of a *Screw* operation on one or more profile *Meshes*.

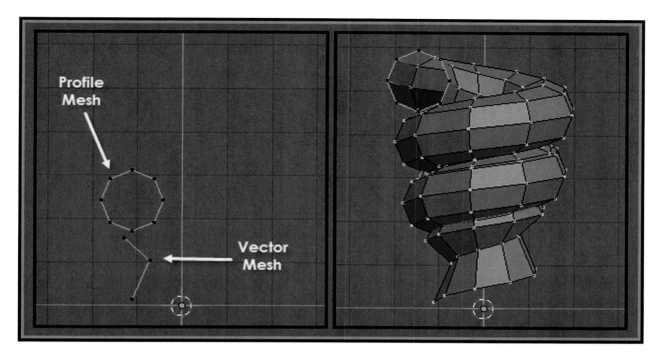

You can see in the above illustration that both the *Vector* and *Profile Mesh* were included in the *Screw* operation. As I mentioned above, you can always *Delete* the *Vector Mesh*. I *Selected* the *Vector Mesh* and moved it so you can see the individual results.

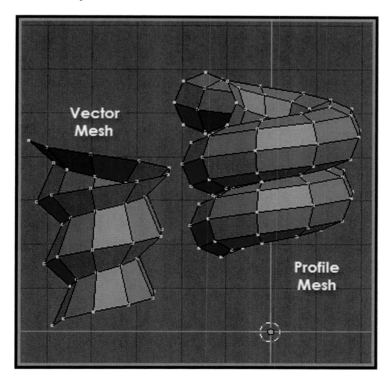

As I mentioned previously, you can have multiple *Profile Meshes*.

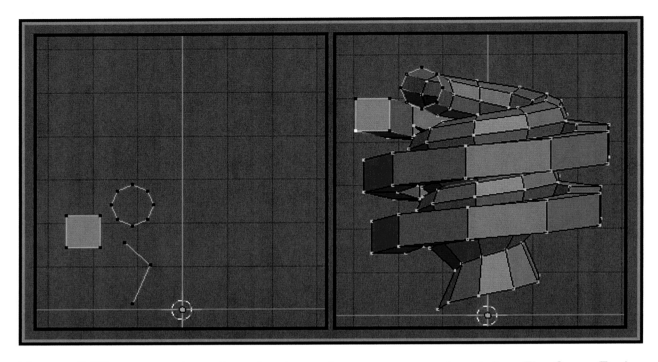

The possibilities are nearly endless. As always, I encourage experimentation. The *Screw Tool* came in handy for me fairly recently when I was *Modeling* a basic snail.

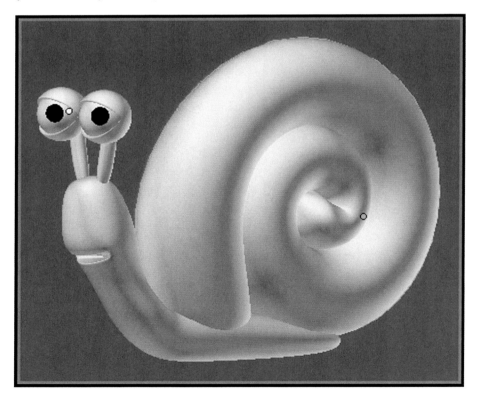

There is also a *Screw Modifier* that makes performing some types of *Screw* operations much easier with the added bonus of being able to go back and change the *Screw Modifier* options at any time. (See **Chapter 9 – The Screw Modifier**)

Proportional Editing

With *Proportional Editing* enabled, any *Transformation* of *Selected Mesh Elements* will affect the surrounding *Un-Selected Mesh Elements*. This allows you to *Transform Mesh Elements* in such a way that the end result isn't so pronounced. In other words, it helps the keep the area between *Selected Mesh Elements* and *Un-Selected Mesh Elements* nice and smooth.

Let's start with a *Subdivided Plane* added in *Top View*. I will *Select* the *Vertex* in the center and *Move* it along the *Z-Axis*.

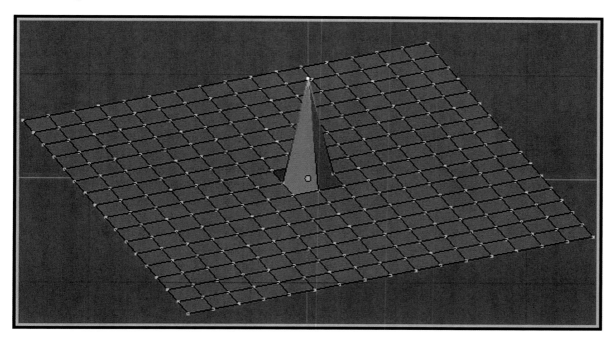

The result of the *Grab* operation is what you might expect. The *Selected Vertex* was moved along the *Z-Axis* and did not influence any surrounding *Un-Selected Vertices*. The result is not smooth and looks like a spike. If I wanted to make a nice smooth bump I would have to *Select* each of the surrounding *Vertices* one at a time and move them up slightly and so on. The alternative of course is the *Proportional Editing Tool*.

I will perform the same operation except that I will first press ○ to enable *Proportional Editing* before I move the *Selected Vertex*.

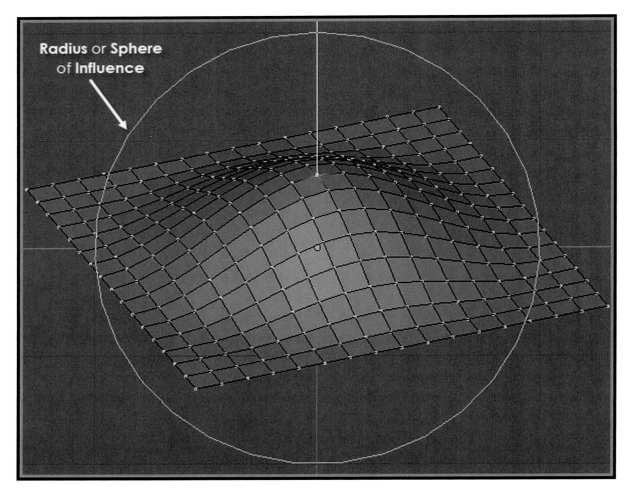

That is quite a different result. Moving a single *Selected Vertex* with *Proportional Editing* enabled has resulted in the surrounding *Vertices* being moved as well. The *Circle* that you see in the above illustration is the *Radius* or *Sphere of Influence*. As you might have guessed, it determines which *Un-Selected Vertices* are affected by the *Transform* operation with *Proportional Editing* enabled. The *Sphere of Influence* appears after you start a *Transform* operation when *Proportional Editing* is enabled. You can change the *Sphere of Influence* using the Mouse Wheel or the PageUp and PageDown keys.

Here is an example where I decreased the *Sphere of Influence.*

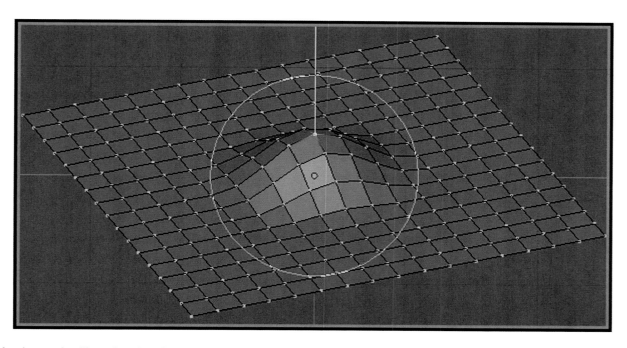

And now I will make the *Sphere of Influence* larger than the actual *Mesh*.

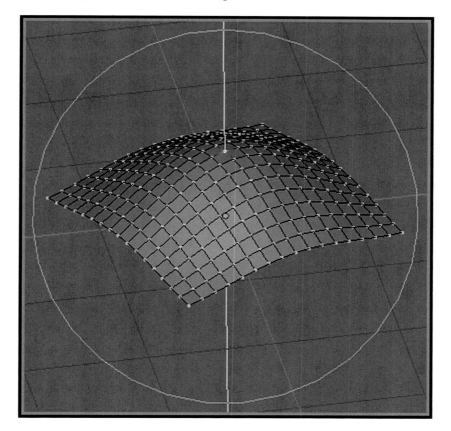

Press F6 after performing a *Transform* operation with *Proportional Editing* enabled to can gain access to the *Transform Operator Panel* (the *Transform Operator Panel* is also visible on the *Tools Shelf* if you have it open). There you can change several options related to the *Transform*

operation including various options related to *Proportional Editing*. As you can see in the next illustration, you can actually perform any *Transform* operation with *Proportional Editing* disabled and then choose to enable or disable it on the *Transform Operator Panel*.

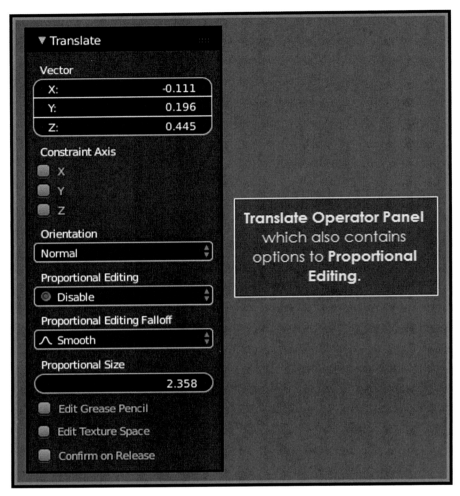

I won't cover the *Vector* or *Constraint Axis* options as they are covered in the *Transform Operations* chapter. The options related to *Proportional Editing* on the *Translate Operator Panel* are as follows:

Proportional Editing - this menu allows you to enable and disable *Proportional Editing*. As I mentioned above, you can enable and disable the tool after you complete the *Transform* operation. There are a couple of other options including *Project (2D)* and *Connected*.

The *Project (2D)* option will enable *Proportional Editing* but will ignore depth along the *View*. This option is rather new and one of the best ways to see the difference is to perform a *Translation* operation with regular *Proportional Editing* enabled and the same operation with *Project (2D)* enabled.

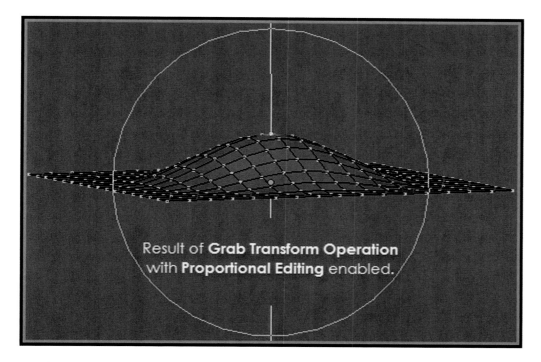

Now I will perform the same *Transform* operation with *Proportional Editing* enabled using the *Project (2D)* option.

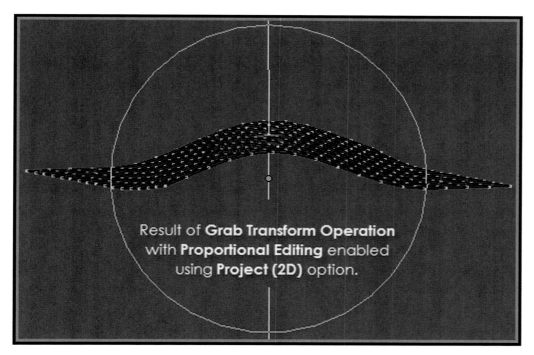

The *Project (2D)* option doesn't *Transform* the *Vertex* and surrounding *Vertices* in a uniform fashion like the regular *Proportional Editing* option does. Here is a different angle of the same operations.

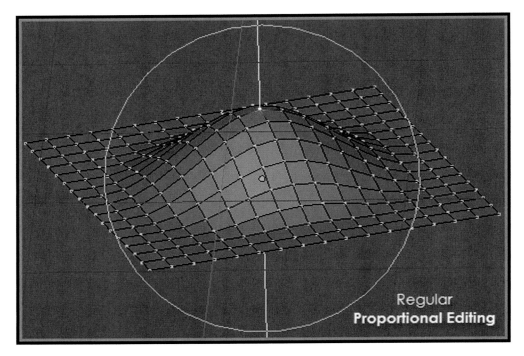

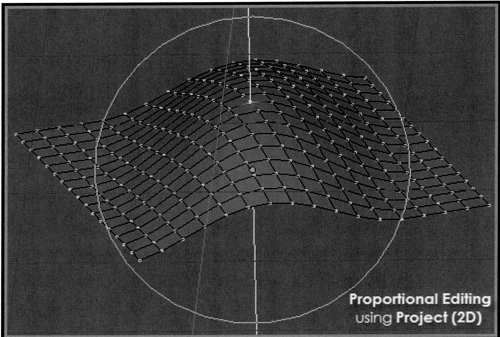

The *Connected* option will enable *Proportional Editing* but *Vertices* not connected to the *Selected Mesh Elements* will be unaffected. For the next example I will use the same *Plane* I have used for all the previous illustrations but I will disconnect portions of the *Mesh* before I perform the *Grab* operation with the *Connected* option enabled.

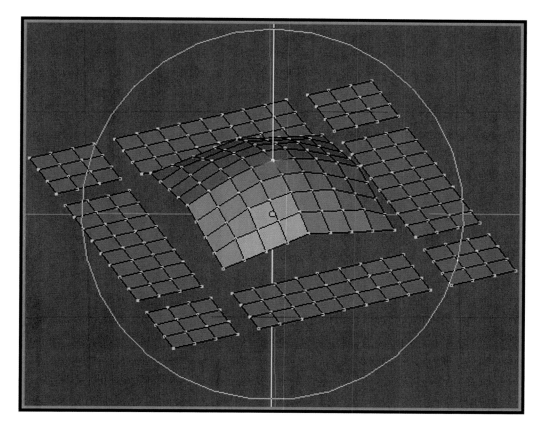

You can see in the above illustration that even though some of the *Vertices* fall within the *Sphere* of *Influence* they are not affected by the *Proportional Editing* operation when the *Connected* option is used. Only the *Vertices* that are connected to the *Selected Vertex* are affected.

Proportional Editing Falloff - the *Falloff Menu* allows you to choose the shape or profile of the *Mesh Elements* that are affected by the *Proportional Editing Translation* operation. There are several profiles to choose from that can help you deal with all kinds of *Modeling* challenges.

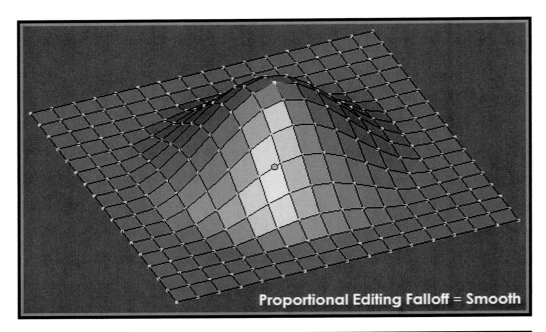

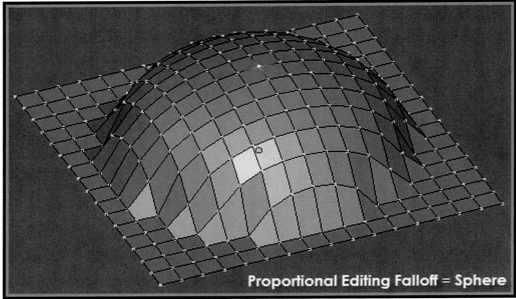

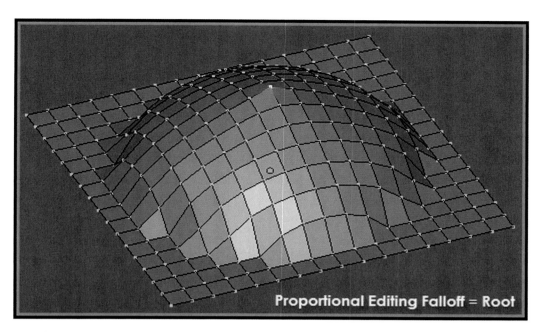

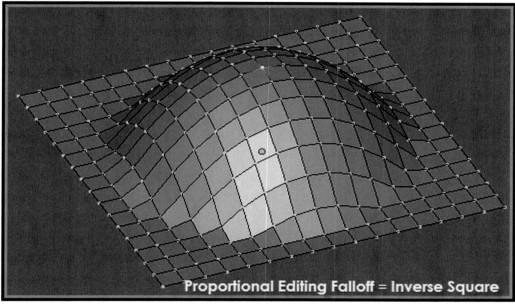

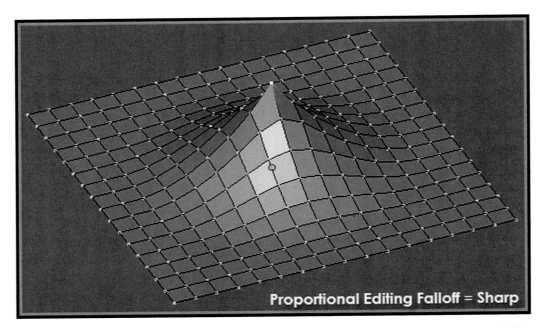

Proportional Editing Falloff = Sharp

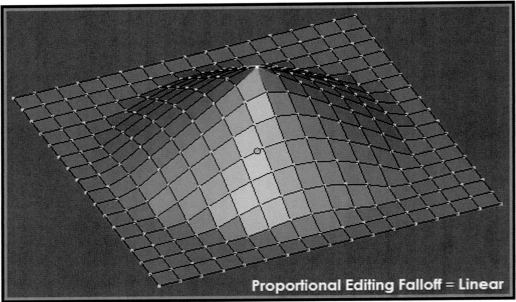

Proportional Editing Falloff = Linear

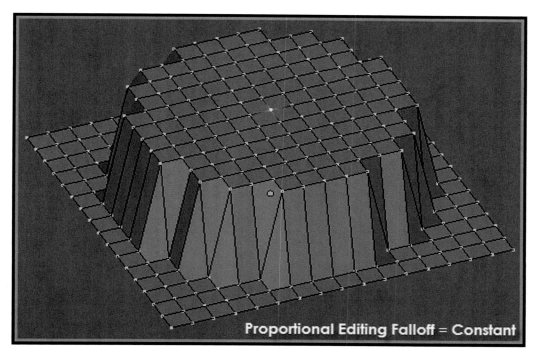

Proportional Editing Falloff = Constant

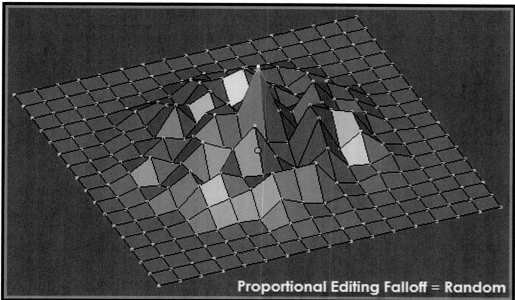

Proportional Editing Falloff = Random

Proportional Size - Use this setting to precisely change the *Sphere of Influence*. The disadvantage is the circle representing the *Sphere of Influence* isn't visible on the screen.

You can perform *Transform* operations using *Proportional Editing* on *Mesh Elements* that aren't connected to each other. Each *Mesh Element* will be affected individually.

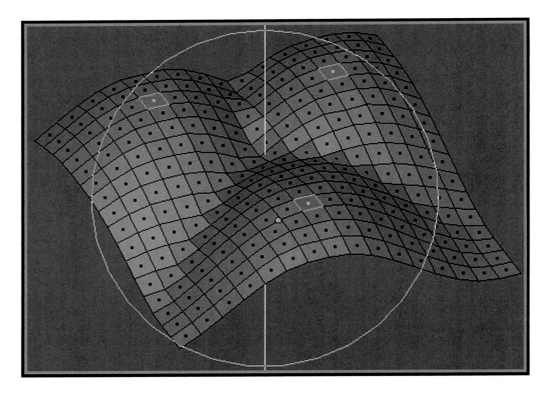

You can also hide *Mesh Elements* so that they are unaffected by any type *Transform* operations. This can be useful to perform *Transform* operations with *Proportional Editing* enabled on isolated parts of your *Mesh*. In the next example, I start with a basic *Sphere*. First I *Select* 1 *Face* and perform a *Grab* operation with *Proportional Editing* enabled. Here is the result.

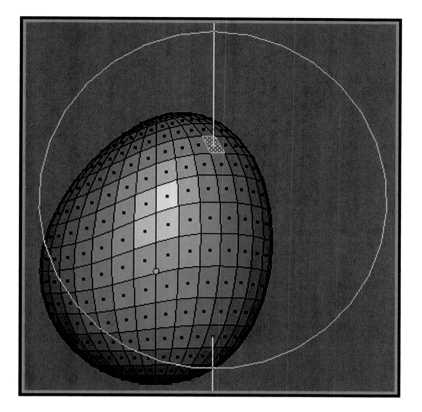

All *Faces* within the *Sphere of Influence* are affected. I will perform the same operation again but this time I will *Hide* the bottom half of the *Sphere*.

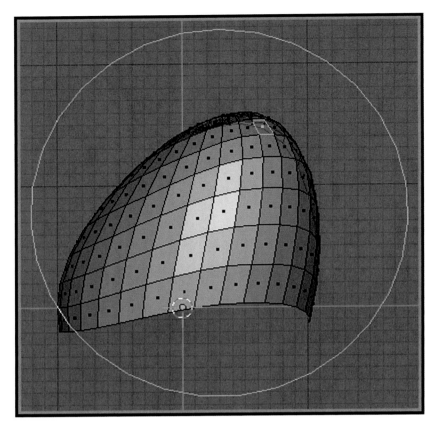

Now that the *Grab* operation using *Proportional Editing* is complete, I can *Un-Hide* the hidden *Vertices* to see the result.

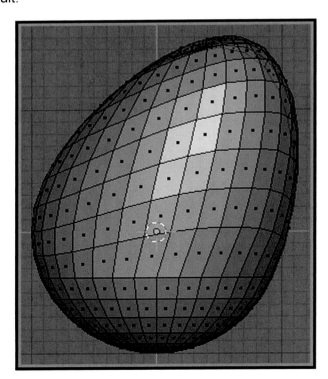

Notice the bottom half of the *Sphere* (the *Faces* that were hidden) weren't affected by the *Grab* operation. Isolating *Mesh Elements* before performing *Translation* operations using *Proportional Editing* gives you greater control over the behavior of the operation and consequently the final result.

You can also get interesting results when performing *Scale* and *Rotation* operations using *Proportional Editing*.

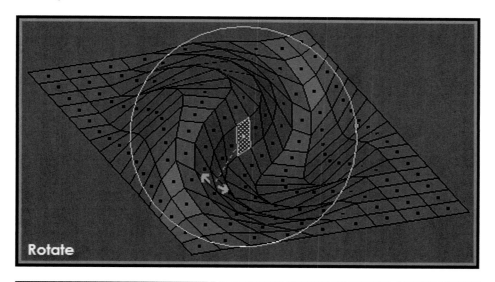

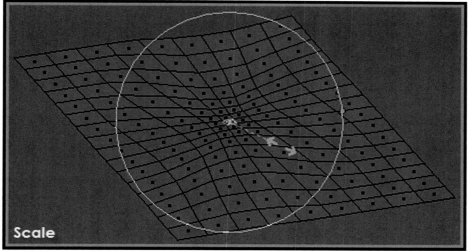

Anytime you see a wiki page or tutorial on *Proportional Editing* you mostly see an example of how to make a quick set of hills / mountains.

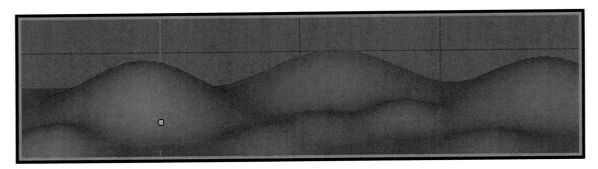

Watching or reading tutorials on *Hard Surface Modeling* will reveal that *Proportional Editing* is useful for so much more. I remember watching a tutorial that started with a basic *Plane* that was *Subdivided* several times. *Proportional Editing* was then used to mold the *Plane* in to a panel for a *Motorcycle*. *Proportional Editing* can be used for very subtle tweaking or for molding a *Model* into just about any shape while maintaining a smooth result. I should also mention that *Proportional Editing* also works in *Object Mode*. Any *Objects* within the *Sphere of Influence* will be affected by any *Transform* operations performed on the *Selected Objects*. This might be if you want to smoothly distribute a *Group* of *Objects*.

The Snap To Mesh Tool

The *Snap to Mesh Tool* (sometimes referred to as the *Magnet Tool*) allows you to *Snap Objects* or *Mesh Elements* to a *Vertex*, *Edge* or *Face* during *Transform* operations. The *Snap To Mesh Tool* and all of its options are located on the *3D Window Header*

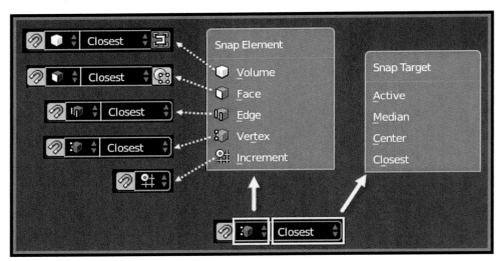

The *Snap To Mesh Tool* can be enabled with the little *Magnet* icon (actually there are other ways as you will see below). Once enabled, you can use the *Snap Element* and *Snap Target* *Menus* to set the options for the *Snap To Mesh Tool*. Certain options will appear / disappear depending on what you choose in the *Snap Element Menu*. Notice above that choosing *Face* or *Volume* results in the appearance of a new icon next to the *Snap Target*. Also notice that when *Increment* is selected, the *Snap Target Menu* is no longer available. The *Mesh Select Mode* also plays a role in how *Blender* performs *Snap* operations.

I will start by discussing the *Snap Element Menu* options. I will set the *Snap Target* to *Active* for this discussion. The only exception of course is the *Increment* option in the *Snap Element Menu* which has no *Snap Target* option (more on that below).

You can enable the *Snap to Mesh Tool* one of 3 ways. You can enable and disable the *Snap to Mesh Tool* by pressing the little *Magnet* icon or by pressing Shift + Tab. You can also enable the *Snap to Mesh Tool* by holding down the Ctrl key after you initiate a *Transform* operation. I find the 3rd choice the easiest as I can basically toggle the *Snap Tool* on and off during any *Transform* operation.

I will start with the last option in the *Snap Element Menu* which is *Increment*. As it turns out, I have already discussed this option in detail in **Chapter 5** in the **Precise Transformations** section, specifically the **Ctrl Key** section so I won't discuss it further here.

The next *Snap Element Menu* option is *Vertex*. Selecting *Vertex* as the *Snap Element* will cause the *Selected Mesh Elements* to be *Snapped* to any *Vertex* that is close to the *3D Cursor*.

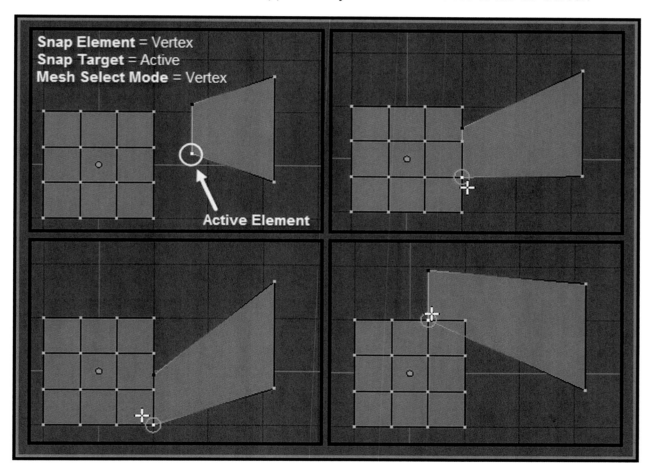

Before I discuss the *Transform* operation in the above illustration, let me first talk about the various settings used to demonstrate the *Snap to Mesh Tool*. I set the *Snap Element* to *Vertex* indicating I want to *Snap* the *Selected Mesh Elements* to a *Vertex*. I set the *Snap Target* to *Active* indicating that I want to *Snap* the *Active Element* in my *Selection* to a *Vertex*. This setting is a bit ambiguous to me as I would think the *Target* is the *Object* or *Mesh Element* I want to *Snap* to. In this case, it actually refers to the *Selected Mesh Elements* that I want to *Snap* to a new *Location* as part of a *Transformation* operation. In other words, which of the *Selected Mesh Elements* do you want to *Snap* to another *Mesh Element*. Finally, I set the *Mesh Select Mode* to *Vertex*.

Now that I've discussed all the settings, I will discuss the actual *Transform* operation in the above illustration. I started by *Selecting* 2 *Vertices*. Remember that the *Vertex* I *Selected* last is the *Active Element*. I then initiated a *Grab* operation by pressing G. After initiating the *Grab* operation I held down the Ctrl key to enable the *Snap to Mesh* functionality. I then moved my *3D Cursor* close to various *Vertices* causing the *Active Element* to *Snap* to the *Vertex* that is closest to the *3D Cursor*. I could then click the LMB to complete the *Grab* operation. In this case, once the *Grab* operation is completed, I probably want to perform a **Remove Doubles** operation.

I could have released the Ctrl key at any time to disable the *Snap to Mesh* functionality. Again, that's why I find using the Ctrl key to enable / disable the *Snap to Mesh Tool* to be the most convenient option.

Now I will perform the same *Grab* operation but I will set the *Mesh Select Mode* to *Edge*. I will *Select* 2 *Edges* and *Snap* the *Active Element* to the closest *Vertex*.

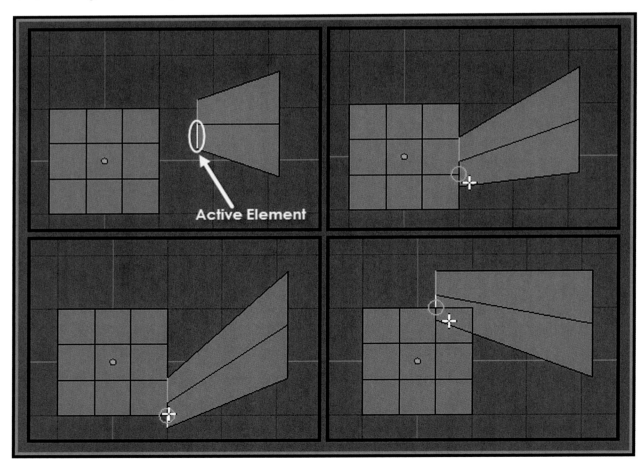

Active Element

As you can see we get a very different result in *Edge Select Mode*. Instead of the *Active Vertex* being *Snapped* to the closest *Vertex*, the *Active Edge* is *Snapped* to the closest *Vertex*. More accurately, the center of the *Active Edge* is *Snapped* to the closest *Vertex*.

Now here is the same *Grab* operation in *Face Select Mode*.

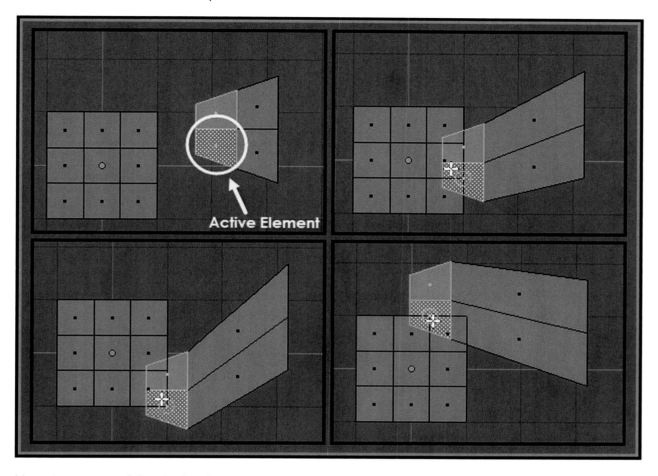

Now the center of the *Active Face* is being *Snapped* to the closest *Vertex*. Simply changing the *Mesh Select Mode* has had a big effect on the result.

Next I will set the *Snap Element* to *Edge* and perform *Snap to Mesh* operations similar to what I did above. I will perform a *Grab* operation in all 3 *Mesh Select Modes*.

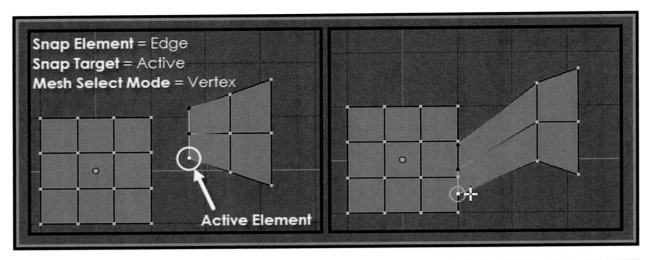

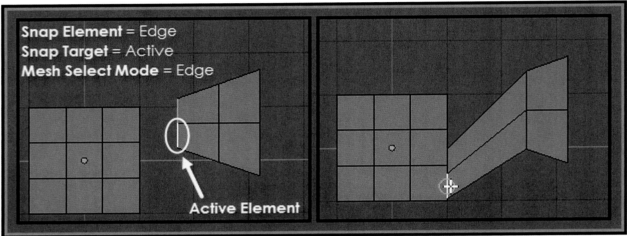

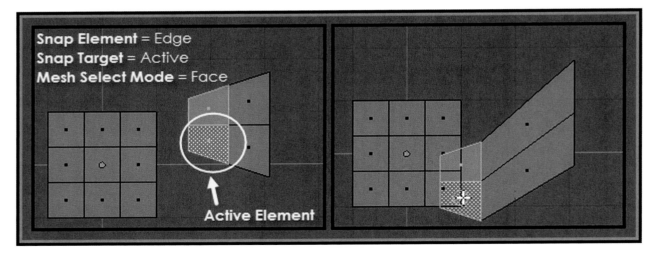

All 3 *Mesh Select Modes Snap* the *Active Mesh Element* to the *Edge* closest to the *3D Cursor*. Unlike a *Vertex* which occupies 1 position in *3D Space*, an *Edge* spans between 2 *Vertices*. When *Snapping* to an *Edge* you can slide the *Active Mesh Element* along the closest *Edge*. In other words, you initiate a *Grab* operation, press and hold Ctrl to enable *Snapping*, move your *3D Cursor* close to an *Edge* causing it to *Snap* to that *Edge* and at that point you can slide the

Snapped Mesh Element along the *Edge* to position it. This offers less precision than *Snapping* to a *Vertex*.

Now for some examples with the *Snap Element* set to *Face*.

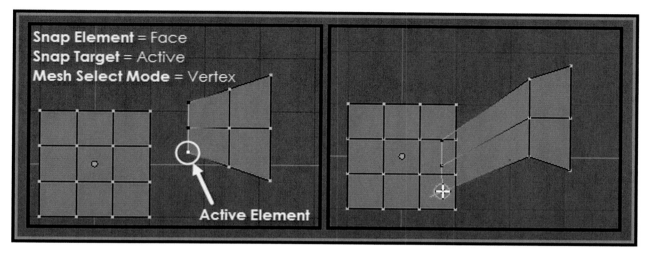

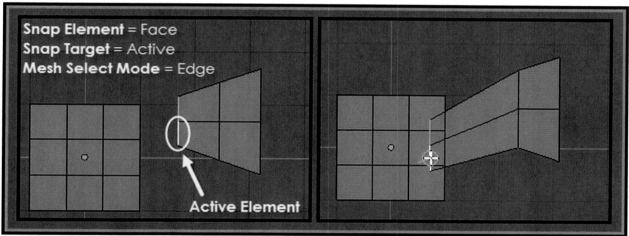

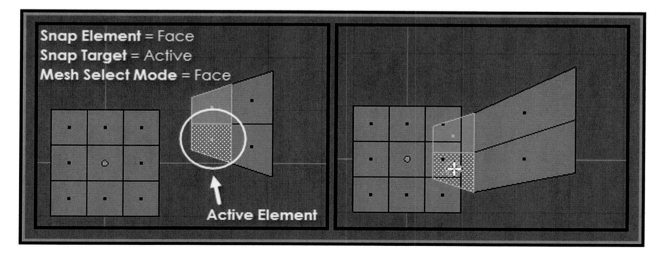

With *Snap Element* set to *Face* you can *Snap* any *Active Vertex / Edge / Face* to any *Face*. Once the *Active Mesh Element* is *Snapped* to a *Face* you can move the *Mesh Element* to any *Location* on the Face. You can see in the above illustrations that the active *Mesh Element* is *Snapped* to various locations on the *Face* and not to the center of the *Face*. Setting *Snap Element* to *Face* (or *Edge*) lacks the precision of setting it to *Vertex*, at least when the *Snap Target* is set to *Active*.

The final option in the *Snap Element Menu* is *Volume*. I have never used this option and very little information exists on its functionality. Feel free to play with the *Volume* option to see if you can gain any insight on its characteristics.

Next we have the *Snap Target Menu*. This menu allows you to set which part of your *Selection* will be *Snapped* to the closest *Mesh Element*. There are 4 options to choose from.

Closest - with this option enabled, the *Mesh Element* in your current *Selection* that is closest to a *Mesh Element* will be *Snapped* to that *Mesh Element*.

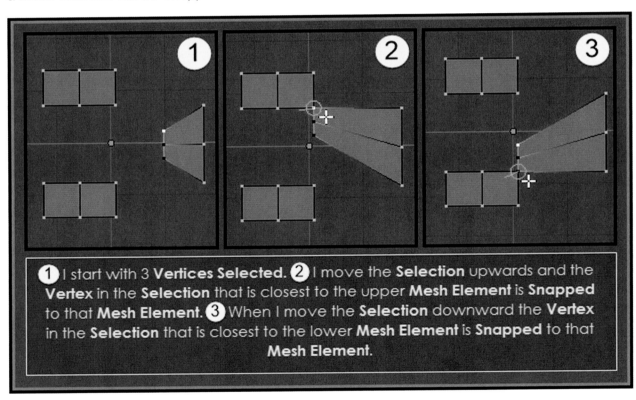

① I start with 3 **Vertices Selected.** ② I move the **Selection** upwards and the **Vertex** in the **Selection** that is closest to the upper **Mesh Element** is **Snapped** to that **Mesh Element**. ③ When I move the **Selection** downward the **Vertex** in the **Selection** that is closest to the lower **Mesh Element** is **Snapped** to that **Mesh Element**.

Notice in the above illustration that the *Selected Mesh Element* that is being *Snapped* changes based on the location of the *Mesh* being *Snapped* to.

Center - this option will *Snap* the *Center* of you current *Selection* to the closest *Mesh Element*.

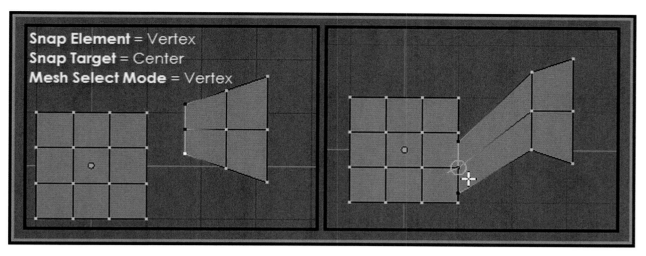

Snap Element = Vertex
Snap Target = Center
Mesh Select Mode = Vertex

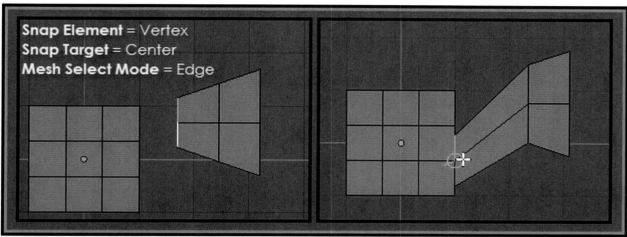

Snap Element = Vertex
Snap Target = Center
Mesh Select Mode = Edge

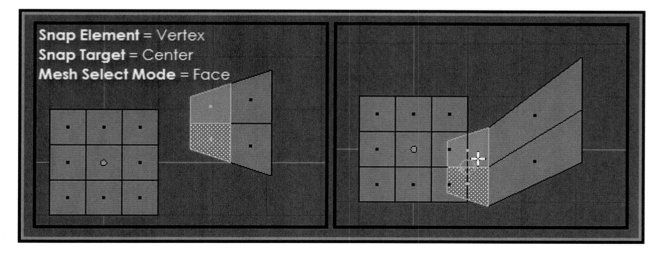

Snap Element = Vertex
Snap Target = Center
Mesh Select Mode = Face

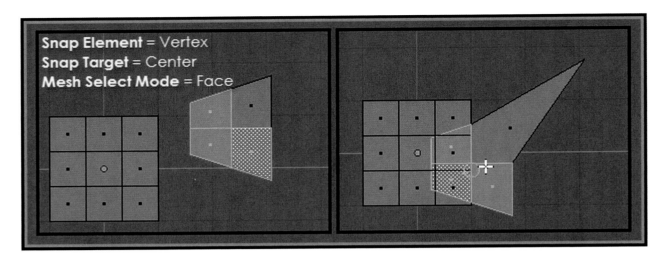

The above illustration shows examples with the *Snap Target* set to *Center*. In all 3 *Edge Select Modes* the *Center* of the *Selection* is *Snapped* to the closest *Mesh Element*.

Median - this option will *Snap* the *Median Point* of the *Selected Mesh Elements* to the closest *Mesh Element*. Remember the *Median* is different than the *Center* in that the concentration and *Location* of the *Vertices* plays a role in what *Blender* considers the *Median* (see **Chapter 5 – Median Point**).

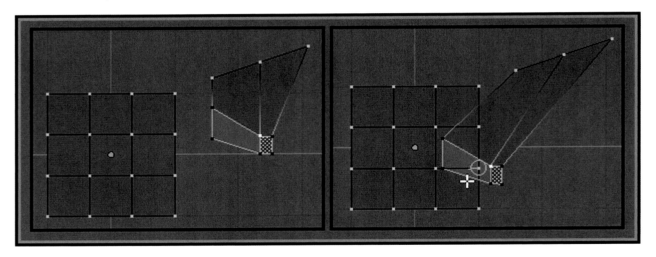

Notice the *Median Point* in the above *Selection* is close to the concentration of *Vertices* and that *Location* (considered the *Median* by *Blender*) is *Snapped* to the closest *Vertex*.

Active - this option *Snaps* the *Active Element* in the current *Selection* to the closest *Mesh Element*. I used this option several times already so I won't elaborate on it any further.

It should be obvious by now that the various combinations of setting the *Snap Element*, *Snap Target* and *Mesh Select Mode* makes for numerous possibilities when using the *Snap To Mesh Tool*. I personally use the following settings most of the time:

- **Snap Element** = *Vertex*

- **Snap Target** = *Active*
- **Mesh Select Mode** = *Vertex*

I find the above settings give me the most control when performing *Snap to Mesh* operations. Now some examples of where the *Snap to Mesh Tool* can come in handy.

The *Snap to Mesh Tool* is an excellent way to move a row of *Vertices* so they are aligned with another *Mesh Element*.

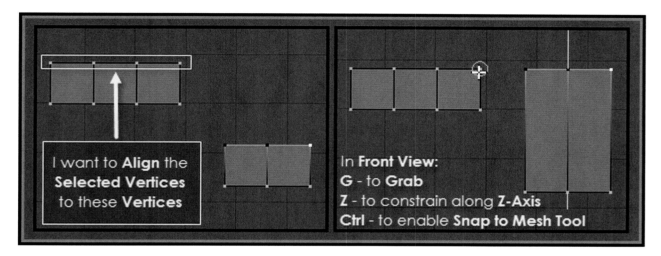

You can see in the above illustration how easy it was to align 1 row of *Vertices* to another row of *Vertices*. In *Front View*, I *Selected* a row of *Vertices*, I pressed *G* to perform a *Grab* operation, I pressed *Z* to constrain the *Grab* operation along the *Z-Axis* and finally I press *Ctrl* to enable *Snapping*. All I need to do at that point is move the *3D Cursor* to any *Vertex* in the row of *Vertices* I want to align my *Selection* to and the *Selected Vertices* will *Snap* to the desired *Location*. It was important to constrain the *Grab* operation along the *Z-Axis* or I would have ended up with this.

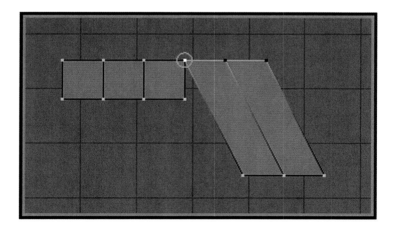

Not the result I was looking for in this particular example.

The *Snap Mesh Tool* is also great for fill in a hole in a *Mesh*. For example, consider the following *Mesh*.

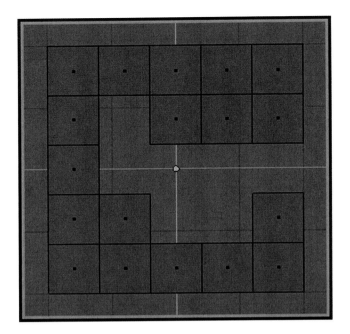

For this example, I want to re-construct the missing *Faces* in this *Mesh*. There are a couple of ways we can do this and the *Snap* to *Mesh Tool* is a good choice. For this example I have the *Mesh Snap Element* set to *Vertex*, the *Snap Target* set to *Active* and the *Select Mode* set to *Vertex*.

I start by *Selecting* a row of *Vertices*, I then *Extrude* the *Selection* and *Snap* them to the desired target.

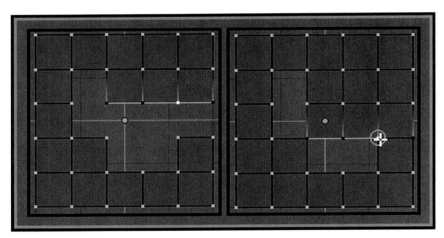

With 1 set of actions I have already created 3 *Faces* and positioned them perfectly. I will do similar operations for the remaining 2 holes.

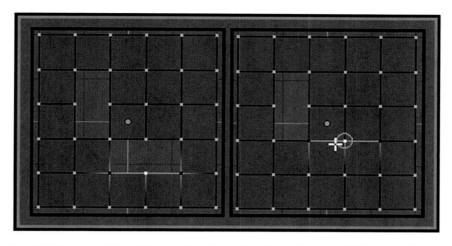

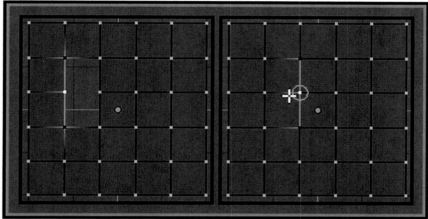

Now that the *Mesh* has been reconstructed, I can perform a *Remove Doubles* operation which will give me the final result I want.

You can also *Snap Mesh Elements* at various angles. For example, I was *Modeling* a gingerbread house and I wanted to put some candy on the roof. I wanted the candy to match the angle of the roof exactly. Here is how I did it.

- **Snap Element** = Face
- **Snap Target** = Active
- **Mesh Select Mode** = Face
- In the *3D Viewport Header*, next to the *Snap Target Menu* you'll see two icons, make sure the first one, *Align rotation with the snapping target* is selected
- The second icon, *Project individual elements on the surface of other objects* should be deselected.

It should look like:

Now by *Selecting* the candy, holding down *Ctrl* and moving it close to the gingerbread house roof, I can have the candy *Snap* to the *Faces* on the roof at the proper angle.

You can tweak the result by moving the *Object Origin* and changing the *Snap Target* but you can see that it allowed me to quickly add candy at the proper angle to my gingerbread house. Blender basically aligns the *Z-Axis* of the *Selected Object* with the *Normal* of the *Face* that is being *Snapped* to.

The Smooth Vertex Tool

The *Smooth Vertex Tool* will *Smooth* out any *Selected Mesh Elements*. Simply *Select* several *Mesh Elements* and hit the *Smooth Vertex* button one or more times to *Smooth* out the *Selected Mesh Elements*. *Blender* attempts to *Smooth* out the *Selected Mesh Elements* by reducing sharp angles that exist between the *Faces* and *Edges*. The distance between each *Vertex* is also distributed more evenly every time you press the *Smooth Vertex* button. You can access the *Smooth Vertex Tool* on the *Tools Shelf*. It's located on the *Tools* tab in the *Mesh Tools Panel*. You can also access *Smooth Vertex* from the *Vertex Menu* (Ctrl + V).

Here is a basic example.

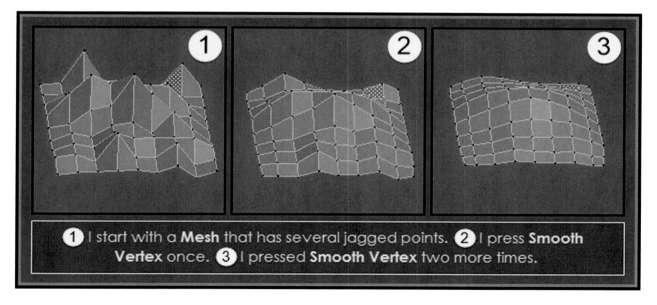

1 I start with a **Mesh** that has several jagged points. **2** I press **Smooth Vertex** once. **3** I pressed **Smooth Vertex** two more times.

You normally wouldn't use *Smooth Vertex* to *Smooth* out an entire *Mesh*. I do find the *Smooth Vertex Tool* useful for small problem areas. Often when I go into *Edit Mode* I notice a crease or artifact that needs a little attention the *Smooth Vertex Tool* can be a good option. Careful use of the *Smooth Vertex Tool* can be a real life saver.

You always have the option of *Hiding* any *Mesh Elements* you don't want affected by a *Smooth Vertex* operation. Be aware that as the *Smooth Tool* attempts to distribute the *Mesh Elements* more evenly and the end result could be gaps between the *Selected* and *Un-Selected Mesh Elements*.

Be aware that the *Smooth Vertex Tool* tends to flatten any affected *Mesh Elements*. It isn't ideal for curved surfaces like a *Sphere* unless you use a *Shrink Wrap Modifier* (see **Chapter 9 – The Shrinkwrap Modifier**).

The Grid Fill Tool

The *Grid Fill Tool* allows you to quickly fill a hole in a *Mesh*. The hole is filled with a *Grid* of *Quad Faces* (which is fantastic). To use the *Grid Fill Tool* simply *Select* 2 *Edge Loops*, access the *Faces Menu* using Ctrl+F and select *Grid Fill*.

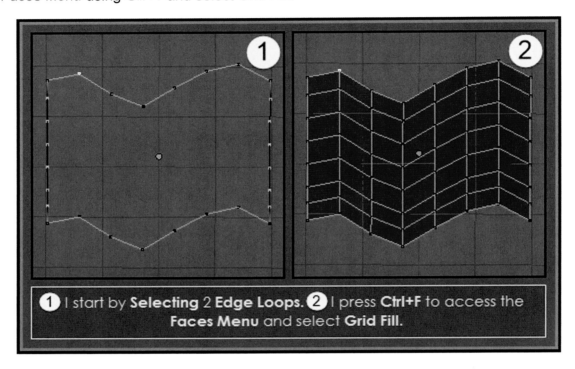

1 I start by **Selecting** 2 **Edge Loops. 2** I press **Ctrl+F** to access the **Faces Menu** and select **Grid Fill.**

As you can see in the above illustration, the *Grid Fill Tool* is a huge time saver.

I could have actually *Selected* the entire *Edge Loop* and the *Grid Fill* operation would have still worked.

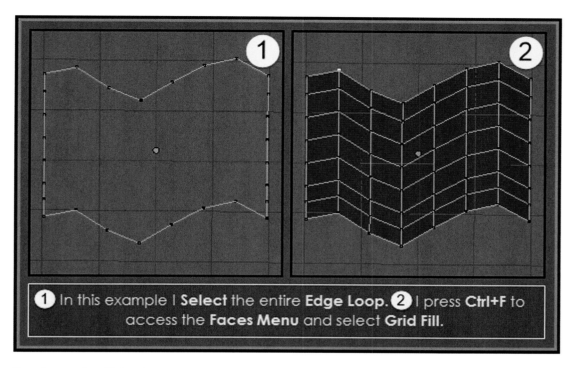

① In this example I **Select** the entire **Edge Loop**. ② I press **Ctrl+F** to access the **Faces Menu** and select **Grid Fill**.

Selecting the entire *Edge Loop* is probably the easier way to perform the *Grid Fill* operation as you don't have to worry about *Selecting* an equal number of *Vertices* in each *Edge Loop*. In *Blenders* eyes you are still *Selecting* 2 separate *Edge Loops*. Selecting 2 separate *Edge Loops* offers some control over the final result but I prefer to use the *Grid Fill Operator Panel* to tweak the final result.

In order to perform a *Grid Fill* operation you must have an even number of *Vertices* in the entire *Edge Loop*. If you attempt a *Grid Fill* operation without an even number of *Vertices* you will get an error. You can always add a *Vertex* to the *Edge Loop* to satisfy the requirements needed to perform a *Grid Fill* operation.

Press F6 after performing a *Grid Fill* operation to can gain access to the *Grid Fill Operator Panel* (the *Grid Fill Operator Panel* is also visible on the *Tools Shelf* if you have it open).

I will explain the options in the *Grid Fill Operator Panel* using illustrations. The options essentially allow you to change the *Geometry* and position of the *Grid Fill* result. Here is the result of changing the *Span* setting after performing a *Grid Fill* operation on a *Circle Mesh* with 32 *Vertices*.

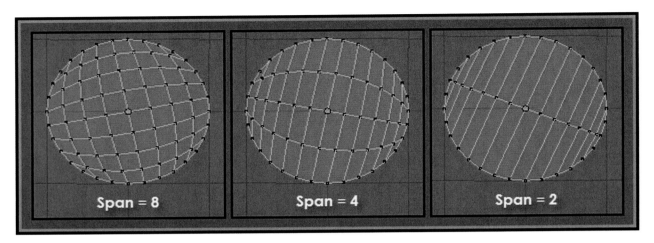

Here is the result of changing the *Offset* setting after performing a *Grid Fill* operation on the same *Circle Mesh*. The *Span* in the next example is set to 8 for all 3 *Meshes*.

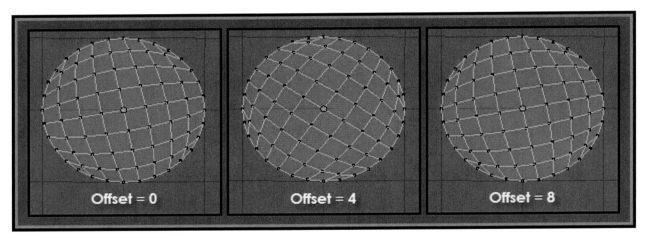

As you can see, you have plenty of control over the final result of a *Grid Fill* operation. Notice the result maintains *Quads* throughout no matter how you modify the result via the *Grid Fill Operator Panel*.

One place I use often the *Grid Fill Tool* to cap a *Cylinder Mesh Primitive*.

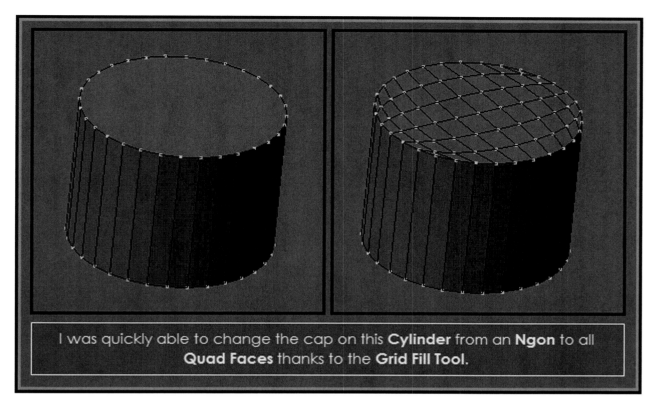

I was quickly able to change the cap on this **Cylinder** from an **Ngon** to all **Quad Faces** thanks to the **Grid Fill Tool.**

As you can see, the *Grid Fill Tool* can help you fill large holes with *Quads* very quickly. What used to be a long and tedious activity can now be accomplished in a matter of seconds.

Vertices, Edges, Faces Menu

There are menus in *Blender* that are specific to *Vertices*, *Edges* and *Faces*. I won't go in to great detail about each menu as I have covered much of the functionality already but I thought I would give them a mention.

- *Vertices Menu* - Ctrl + V
- *Edges Menu* - Ctrl + E
- *Faces Menu* - Ctrl + F

Each menu gives you access to options and operations specific to that type of *Mesh Element*. As I said, I have already covered many items available in each menu often using keyboard shortcuts. I encourage you to have a look at each menu and experiment with any options or operations that haven't been covered in this book.

Sharpening

As I mentioned earlier in the chapter, I always add a *Subdivision Surface Modifier* to any *3D Mesh* I create (see **Chapter 9 – The Subdivision Surface Modifier**). One of the great things about the *Subdivision Surface Modifier* is it produces a *Smooth* result. The only problem is most of the time when you create a *Mesh* you will want to *Sharpen* up 1 or more of *Edges*. There are a few ways you can do this and some are better than others, at least in my opinion.

The majority of the time I will *Sharpen Edges* using the *Loop Cut Tool*. Adding *Loop Cuts* and sliding them towards an *Edge* will *Sharpen* the *Edge*.

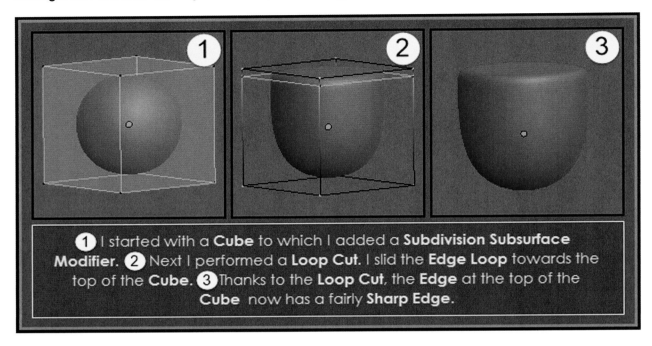

① I started with a **Cube** to which I added a **Subdivision Subsurface Modifier.** **②** Next I performed a **Loop Cut.** I slid the **Edge Loop** towards the top of the **Cube.** **③** Thanks to the **Loop Cut**, the **Edge** at the top of the **Cube** now has a fairly **Sharp Edge.**

I can add several *Loop Cuts* to *Sharpen* the *Edges* of the *Cube* even further.

Adding several **Loop Cuts** has resulted in the **Sharpening** of several **Edges.**

Here is a more realistic use of using *Loop Cuts* to *Sharpen Edges*. In the next illustration we see the beginnings of a *Submarine*. I added a *Subdivision Surface Modifier* and you can see the top portion of the *Submarine* where the hatch is located is in need of some *Sharp Edges*.

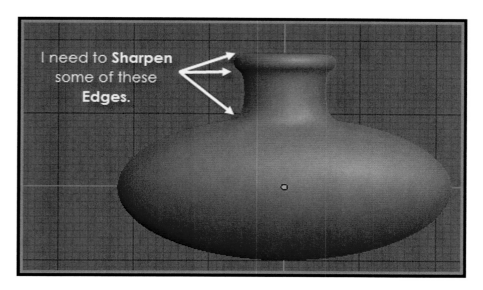

Next I will use *Loop Cuts* to *Sharpen* up some of the *Edges*.

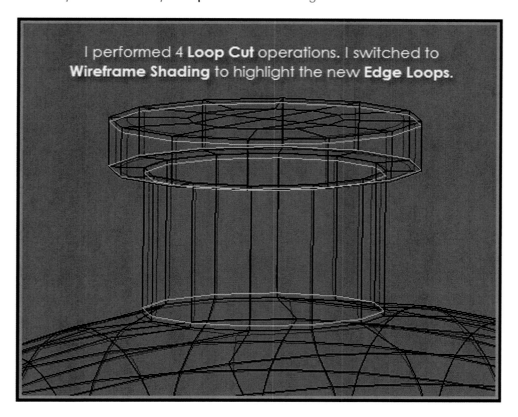

Here is how the *Submarine* looks now with *Sharpened Edges* created by the *Loop Cuts*.

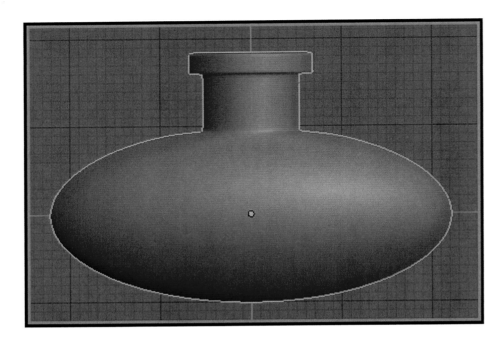

Using *Loop Cuts* is my preferred method when it comes to *Sharpening Edges*. I sometimes use the *Bevel Tool* on *Meshes* with open ends or to *Sharpen* the *Edges* around any holes in my *Mesh*. Most *Edge Loops* can be a good candidate for the *Bevel Tool*.

Another popular technique is to use a combination of the *Bevel Tool* in conjunction with the *Inset Tool*. Start by performing a *Bevel* on an *Edge Loop* and then immediately do an *Inset* operation on the *Face Loop* that resulted from the *Bevel*. You can then *Select* another *Edge Loop* and repeat. This technique is better suited to an *Object* that doesn't have a *Subdivision Surface Modifier*.

Another way to *Sharpen Edges* is to use *Creasing*. To *Crease* an *Edge*, start by *Selecting* 1 or more *Edges*, the press Shift + E and use the *Mouse* to increase or decrease the amount of *Crease* for the *Selected* Edges. You can also set the *Crease* value on the *Properties Shelf*. The *Mean Crease* field is located on the *Transform* tab while in *Edit Mode*. You can set the *Mean Crease* to a value between 0 and 1. I personally don't use *Creasing* to *Sharpen* my *Edges*. I prefer to use *Geometry* to create *Sharp Edges*. I find the result of using *Creasing* to be a little unnatural at times and I feel like it's cheating in some ways. I have seen *Creasing* used in many tutorials so I leave it to personal preference. Here is a comparison between *Creasing* and using *Loop Cuts*.

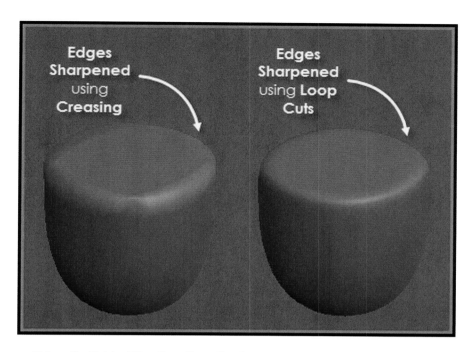

There is also an *Edge Split Modifier* that literally *Splits* or *Separates Edges* to make them appear *Sharp*. I find the *Edge* Split *Modifier* far too destructive for my taste as it affects the entire *Mesh* and I don't like the idea of *Edges* in my *Mesh* being *Split*. I have only seen it used once or twice and haven't found a situation where it was the best solution to *Sharpening Edges*. I leave it to you to give it a test drive if you are so inclined.

Chapter 9 - Modifiers

Blender has several *Modifiers* that help you to quickly perform all kinds of very useful operations. With *Modifiers* you can *Subdivide, Mirror, Wrap, Smooth* and *Bevel* a *3D Mesh* and so much more. The advantage of using *Modifiers* is they are non-destructive. The changes brought about by *Modifiers* are not permanent and can be toggled off and on at any time. You do have the option of applying a *Modifier* to make the operation permanent. Several of these *Modifiers* are extremely useful (I would go as far as calling them indispensable) when creating a *3D Model*. Many of the time consuming and tedious operations that you encounter when *3D Modeling* are made significantly easier thanks to *Modifiers*.

Modifiers appear to modify *Geometry* without actually changing the *Geometry* at all. When you add a *Modifier* you essentially get a preview of what your *Mesh* will look like once the *Modifier* is applied. You can continue to modify the *Mesh* knowing that you are getting an accurate preview of the result of using any added *Modifiers*. Blender *Modifiers* are stackable and the order that the *Modifiers* are stacked affects the result.

The topic of *Modifiers* in *Blender* is HUGE. You could write an entire book on *Modifiers* alone. I will cover the *Modifiers* that I think are the most important when it comes to *3D Modeling*. As always, I encourage you to experiment with each *Modifier* and look for information on the internet about each of the *Modifiers* to get a better idea of how they work and what kind of results can be achieved using *Modifiers*.

The Modifiers Menu

You can add a *Modifier* to a *Mesh* by way of the *Modifiers Menu*. To access the *Modifiers Menu*, go to the *Modifiers Context Window*.

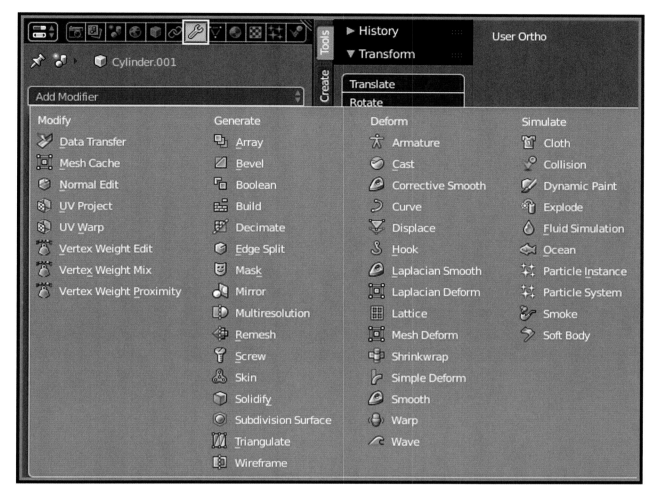

Simply select a *Modifier* from the *Modifier Menu* to add it to the currently *Selected Object*. Once added, the *Modifier* will appear in the *Modifier Context Window* in what is referred to as the *Modifier Stack* (more on the *Modifier Stack* in the next section).

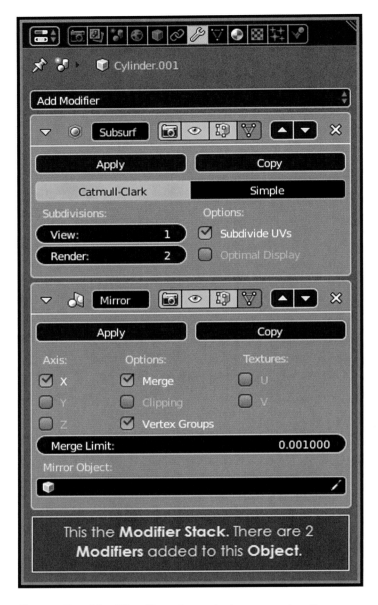

You can expand or collapse the *Modifier Panels* and also re-order them.

You can also rename *Modifiers* to give them a more descriptive name which is especially useful when you're adding several *Modifiers* of the same type. There are also buttons that allow you to set when the *Modifier* is displayed.

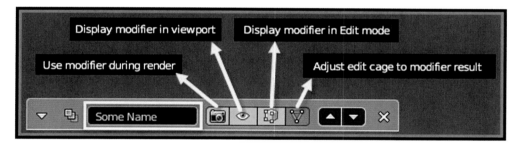

As you can see in the above illustration, options exist that allow you to enable / disable the effect of a *Modifier* during a *Render* operation as well as decide how it's displayed in the *3D View*.

The Modifier Stack

You can add several *Modifiers* to an *Object* and the corresponding *Panels* are listed in the *Modifiers Context Window*. The list of *Modifiers* is referred to as the *Modifier Stack*.

The term *Stack* is fitting and you can think of the *Modifiers* as being *Stacked* on top of each other. The result of each *Modifier* is calculated in order and the result of calculating a *Modifier* is affected by the calculations of any *Modifiers* that came before it.

Using the *Modifier Stack* in the above illustration, the *Subsurface Modifier* would be calculated first. Next the *Mirror Modifier* would be calculated but it's calculated against the *Object* that resulted from the *Subsurface Modifier*. Finally the *Smooth Modifier* is calculated against the *Object* that resulted from the 2 previous *Modifiers* and so on.

The order of the *Modifiers* is important but you can re-arrange them as needed if you don't see the result you want. Using the *Subsurface Modifier* with a *Mirror Modifier* is a good way to demonstrate the effect of the *Modifier Stack* order. In the next example I will add a *Mirror Modifier* and a *Subdivision Surface Modifier* to an *Object*. I will change the order of the *Modifiers* to demonstrate the effect the order of the *Modifiers* has on the result.

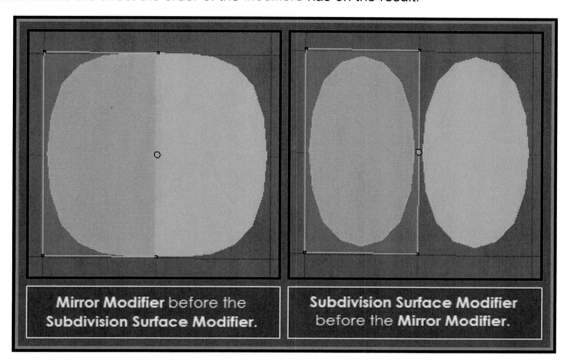

Mirror Modifier before the *Subdivision Surface Modifier.*

Subdivision Surface Modifier before the **Mirror Modifier.**

The result of modifying the *Modifier Stack* isn't always as extreme as the result we see in the above illustration but it's certainly a good idea to be conscious of your *Stack* order and how it might be affecting your *Model*.

The Subdivision Surface Modifier

There is a reason I decided to start with the *Subdivision-Surface Modifier*. I don't believe I have ever created a *3D Model* without adding this *Modifier*. It's indispensable when it comes to creating a detailed model without using too much *Geometry*.

I have already covered the *Subdivide Tool* which allows you to introduce *Geometry* to your *Mesh* by *Subdividing* or splitting it. *Subdividing* your *Mesh* is a great way to make it look *Smooth* but it comes at the cost of making permanent changes to your *Mesh*. The more you *Subdivide* your *Mesh* the *Smoother* it looks but it also makes it significantly more difficult to do any further *Modeling*. With the *Subdivision Surface Modifier* you can *Subdivide* your *Mesh* multiple times without the result being permanent. It essentially lets you see what the *Mesh* will look like once it has been *Subdivided* but then allows you to go back to the basic *Mesh* to continue *Modeling*.

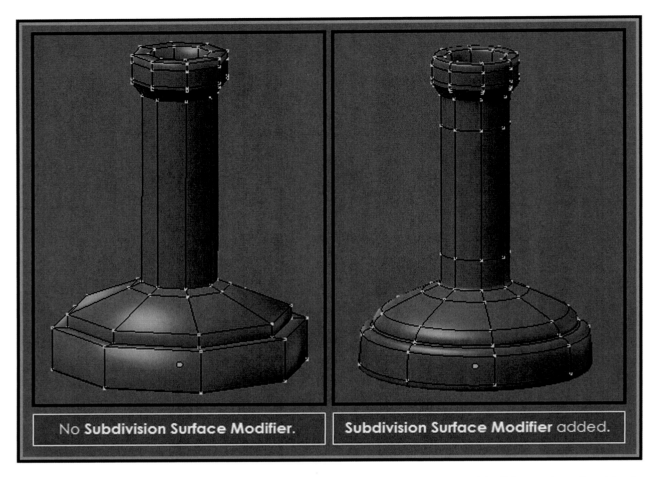

No **Subdivision Surface Modifier.**　　**Subdivision Surface Modifier** added.

As you can see in the above illustration, adding a *Subdivision Surface Modifier* makes the *Mesh* nice and *Smooth*, especially at the base. You can also see that no new *Geometry* was added. You can continue to work with the *Mesh* while getting a preview of how it would look after it was *Subdivided*. Here is what it looks like when the *Mesh* is *Subdivided* twice using the *Subdivide Tool*.

As you might imagine, it would be far more difficult to work with a *Mesh* that was permanently *Subdivided*.

Here are the options available when using the *Subdivision Surface Modifier*.

Apply - applies the *Modifier* so that the *Subdivision* operation is permanent. The *Modifier* is also removed from the *Modifier* Stack.

Copy - make a copy of this *Modifier* and add it to the *Modifier Stack*.

Catmull-Clark / Simple - using these buttons you can choose which algorithm is used to calculate how the *Mesh* is *Subdivided*. You get a *Smooth* result with *Catmull-Clark* were as

Simple does no *Smoothing* at all. Using *Simple* is the equivalent of doing a basic *Subdivide* operation.

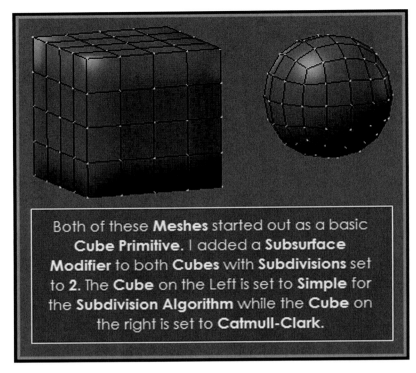

Both of these **Meshes** started out as a basic **Cube Primitive.** I added a **Subsurface Modifier** to both **Cubes** with **Subdivisions** set to **2.** The **Cube** on the Left is set to **Simple** for the **Subdivision Algorithm** while the **Cube** on the right is set to **Catmull-Clark.**

As you can see in the above illustration, both *Cubes* have the same amount of *Subdivisions* after applying the *Subdivision Surface Modifier*. The difference is that the *Cube* that is using *Catmull-Clark* has a much *Smoother* result.

Subdivisions View / Render - set how many *Subdivision Levels* to add to the *Mesh*. The *View* setting sets the number of *Subdivisions* to display on the *Mesh* in the *3D View*. The *Render* setting sets the number of *Subdivisions* to display in any *Renders*. You can set the *View* setting to a low number when you are *Modeling* to avoid slowdown and lag that comes with a complex *Mesh* and then temporarily increase it to see how it will look once *Subdivided* and *Rendered*.

Subdivide UVs - enabling this setting will result in any *UV Maps* associated with a *Mesh* also being *Subdivided*.

Optimal Display - enabling this setting will prevent any wires that result from the *Subdivide* operation from being displayed in the *3D View*. You must be in *Wireframe Shading Mode* to see the effect of this setting.

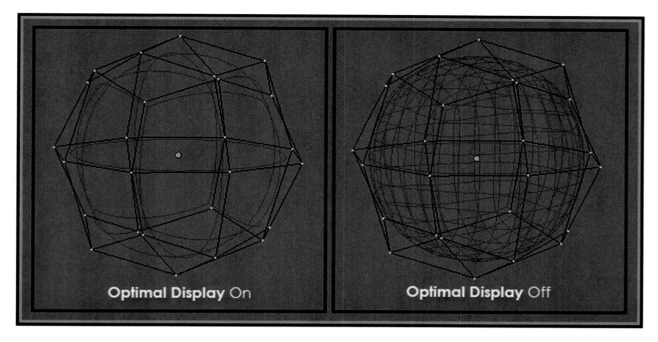

The tactic I like to take with using the *Subsurface Modifier* is to *Model* as much as I can without using the *Subsurface Modifier*. Once I've done all I can, I will add a *Subdivision Surface Modifier* with a *Subdivision Level* of 1. I then continue *Modeling* while I toggle the visibility of the *Modifier* off and on to see how it looks *Subdivided*. Once I have done all I can, I apply the *Subsurface Modifier* (at a Level of 1). I continue the *Modeling* process and attempt to complete a *Model* with as few permanent *Subdivision* operations as possible. In other words, I try to create a *3D Model* by *Subdividing* a total of 2 times and then adding a *Subdivision Surface Modifier* to the final *Model*. It isn't always possible to do it this way but it's the formula I try to stick to.

I like the challenge of trying to create a low polygon *Model* that looks great when it's *Rendered* with a *Subsurface Modifier* added. Just remember to toggle the *Subdivision Surface Modifier* off and on as you *Model* so you can get a preview of the final *Render* and make adjustments to the *Mesh* accordingly. Remember, a low polygon *Model* is easier to modify, results in a smaller file and is ideal for use in video games etc.

Let's see the *Subdivision Surface Modifier* in action. Here is a *Render* of the submarine you have seen from time to time in this book. This *Mesh* has a *Subdivision Surface Modifier* and the *Render Subdivision Level* is set to 1.

Here is a *Wireframe Render* with a *Subdivision Surface Modifier* added with a *Subdivision Level* of 1.

Here is a *Wireframe Render* of the same submarine with no *Subdivision Surface* Modifier. The *Mesh* is still easy to work with.

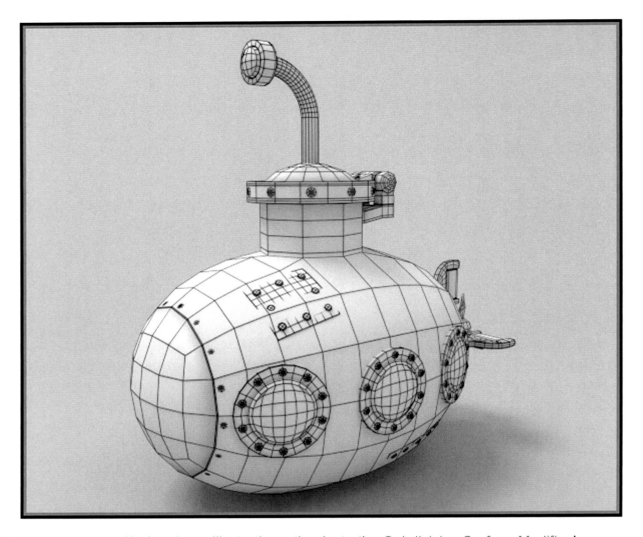

As you can see with the above illustrations, thanks to the *Subdivision Surface Modifier* I can *Render* a *Mesh* with plenty of *Geometry* which results in a nice smooth *Model*. I can then disable the *Subdivision Surface Modifier* which allows me to work with a much more manageable *Mesh*.

The Mirror Modifier

The *Mirror Modifier* allows you to *Mirror* a *Mesh* along any of its *Axes* based on the *Object Origin*. It's a far more flexible option than using the *Mirror Tool*.

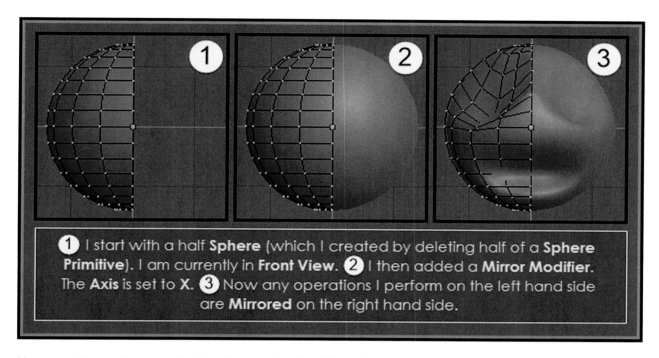

① I start with a half **Sphere** (which I created by deleting half of a **Sphere Primitive**). I am currently in **Front View**. **②** I then added a **Mirror Modifier**. The **Axis** is set to **X**. **③** Now any operations I perform on the left hand side are **Mirrored** on the right hand side.

Here are the options available when using the *Mirror Modifier.*

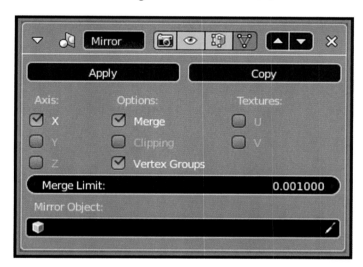

Apply - applies the *Modifier* so that the *Mirror* operation is permanent. The *Modifier* is also removed from the *Modifier Stack.*

Copy - make a copy of this *Modifier* and add it to the *Modifier Stack.*

Axis X, Y, Z - allows you to set which *Axis* is used to *Mirror* your *Mesh.* If you are working in *Front View* for example, you will probably want to *Mirror* along the *X-Axis.* You can also *Mirror* along *Multiple Axis.*

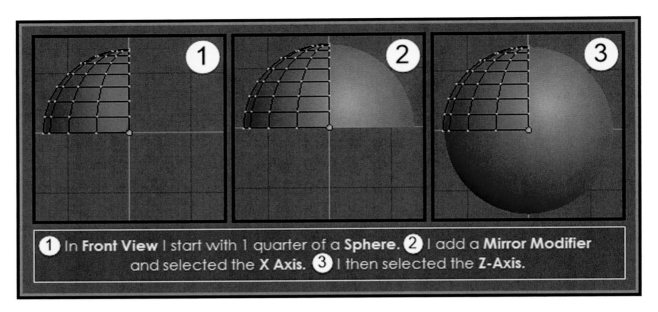

① In **Front View** I start with 1 quarter of a **Sphere**. **②** I add a **Mirror Modifier** and selected the **X Axis**. **③** I then selected the **Z-Axis**.

In the above illustration I enabled both *X-Axis* and *Z-Axis* on a *Mirror Modifier*. This result is a full *Sphere*. If you started with an eighth of a *Sphere* you would have to Mirror along all 3 *Axis* to get a *Sphere*.

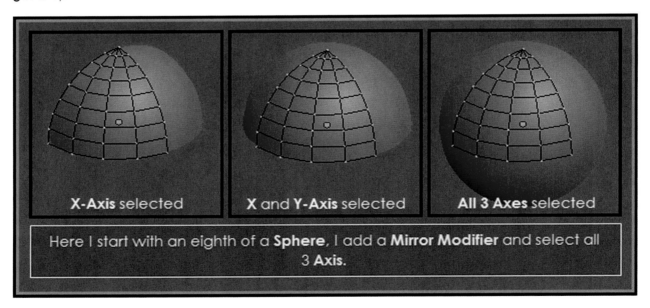

X-Axis selected · **X** and **Y-Axis** selected · **All 3 Axes** selected

Here I start with an eighth of a **Sphere**, I add a **Mirror Modifier** and select all 3 **Axis**.

You can see in the above illustration that the *Mirror* effect is cumulative.

Merge and Merge Limit -this setting determines the distance at which a *Vertex* and the *Vertex* created as part of the *Mirror Modifier* are *Merged*. Once the *Mirror Modifier* is applied, any *Vertices* that are within the *Merge Limit* will be *Merged*.

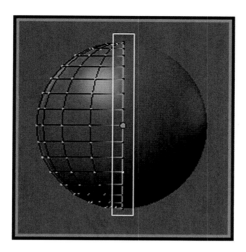

In the above illustration the Vertices that are *Selected* and the *Vertices* that are created by the *Mirror Modifier* will be *Merged*. This isn't a good example of the *Merge* setting in action. Here is an example were all of the *Vertices* along the center *Edge Loop* do not run directly along the *Center* of the *Mesh*.

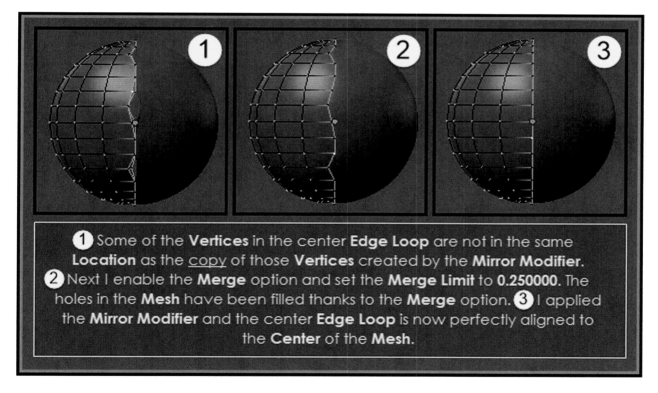

1 Some of the **Vertices** in the center **Edge Loop** are not in the same **Location** as the <u>copy</u> of those **Vertices** created by the **Mirror Modifier**. **2** Next I enable the **Merge** option and set the **Merge Limit** to 0.250000. The holes in the **Mesh** have been filled thanks to the **Merge** option. **3** I applied the **Mirror Modifier** and the center **Edge Loop** is now perfectly aligned to the **Center** of the **Mesh**.

I avoid using the *Merge* option as I prefer to fix the fix the *Geometry* instead of having the *Mirror Modifier* do it for me. You could also inadvertently *Merge* some *Vertices* that you hadn't intended.

Clipping - *Blender* refers to the invisible line where the *Mirror* operation begins as the *Mirror Plane*. The *Clipping* setting prevents you from moving any *Selected Vertices* across the *Mirror Plane*.

I added a *Plane* in the above illustration to help you visualize the *Mirror Plane*. With *Clipping* enabled, you wouldn't be able to *Select* and *Move* any of the *Vertices* across the *Plane*. You probably want to leave *Clipping* on as moving *Vertices* across the *Mirror Plane* can lead to undesirable results. One thing to keep in mind is once *Clipping* is enabled you will not be able to move any *Vertices* that are on the *Mirror Plane* away from the *Mirror Plane*. In other words, you wouldn't be able to *Move* any *Selected Vertices* that are on the *Mirror Plane* over or away from the *Mirror Plane*. You can always temporarily disable *Clipping* if you want to move *Selected Vertices* over or away from the *Mirror Plane*.

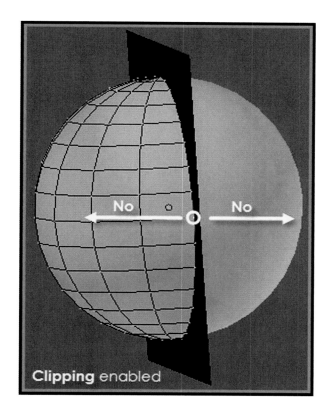

The *Selected Vertex* in the above illustration can't be moved over or away from the *Mirror Plane* while *Clipping* is enabled.

Vertex Group - the *Vertex Group* option will create a *Mirror* of any *Vertex Groups* (see **Chapter 7 – Vertex Groups**). Let's say for example I have a *Mesh* that has a *Mirror Modifier* and I create a *Vertex Group*.

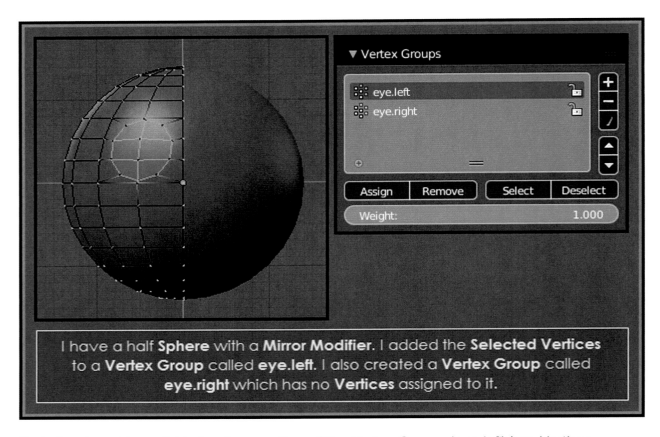

I have a half **Sphere** with a **Mirror Modifier**. I added the **Selected Vertices** to a **Vertex Group** called **eye.left**. I also created a **Vertex Group** called **eye.right** which has no **Vertices** assigned to it.

So to be clear, I have 2 *Vertex Groups*. One of the *Vertex Groups* (*eye.left*) has *Vertices* assigned to it. Specifically, the *Vertices* you see in the above illustration. I also created another *Vertex Group* (*eye.right*) which has no *Vertices* assigned to it.

Next I ensure *Vertex Groups* is selected and I apply the *Mirror Modifier*. *Applying* the *Mirror Modifier* has resulted in *Blender Mirroring* the *Vertex Group* so that the *Vertices* in *eye.left* that were *Mirrored* are now part of the *eye,right Vertex Group*. Now both *Vertex Groups* have *Vertices* assigned to them.

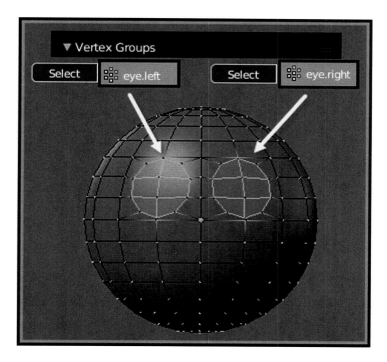

You can see in the above illustration that after applying the *Mirror Modifier* there are now *Vertices* assigned to the *eye.right Vertex Group*.

There are a couple of rules around using the *Vertex Groups* option.

- There is a naming convention you are required to follow. When naming the *Vertex Groups* you must use a left/right pattern as a suffix. So *eye.left / eye.right* or *eye.L / eye.R* are valid.
- You are responsible for creating the empty *Vertex Group*.

To re-iterate, you have to create the *Vertex Group* to be *Mirrored*, it must be empty and it has to be named following the above mentioned naming convention.

Textures - with this option you can *Mirror UV Texture* coordinates similar to *Mirroring Vertex Groups* above. *UV Textures* are outside the scope of this book.

Mirror Object - this setting allows you to use an *Object* as the *Mirror Plane*. The majority of the time an *Empty* is used as the *Mirror Object*. The *Mirror Plane* is usually located at the *Object Origin*. With this setting it can literally be *Located* anywhere.

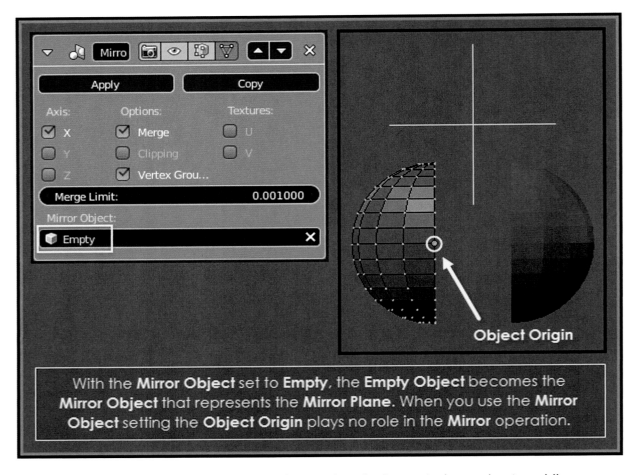

With the **Mirror Object** set to **Empty**, the **Empty Object** becomes the **Mirror Object** that represents the **Mirror Plane**. When you use the **Mirror Object** setting the **Object Origin** plays no role in the **Mirror** operation.

The *Mirror Modifier* is great for *Modeling* a human head, planes, trains and automobiles. Anything symmetric is a good candidate for the *Mirror Modifier*.

The *Mirror Modifier* is not only useful for *Mirroring* half of a *Mesh*, it's also a great option for *Mirroring* entire *Objects*. Here is a covered wagon.

This wagon, like most wagons, has 4 wheels. With the *Mirror Modifier* I can create 1 wagon wheel and *Mirror* it using *Mirror Objects* to create the other 3 wagon wheels. First I create 1 wagon wheel and use an *Empty* as a *Mirror Object* to *Mirror* it to the opposite side of the wagon.

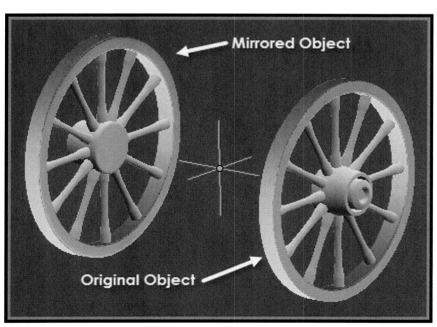

Now I can add a second *Mirror Modifier* and it will not only *Mirror* the *Original Object*, it will *Mirror* the *Mirrored Object*. I mentioned the *Modifier Stack* earlier in this chapter and this is an example of how the *Modifier Stack* works. The first *Mirror Modifier* is added to the *Object* and the result is calculated. Then the 2nd *Mirror Modifier* is calculated and takes in account the result of any *Modifiers* above it. The *Modifiers* are processed in order and their effects are applied in order. So I can use a 2nd *Mirror Modifier* to *Mirror* the 2 front wagon wheels.

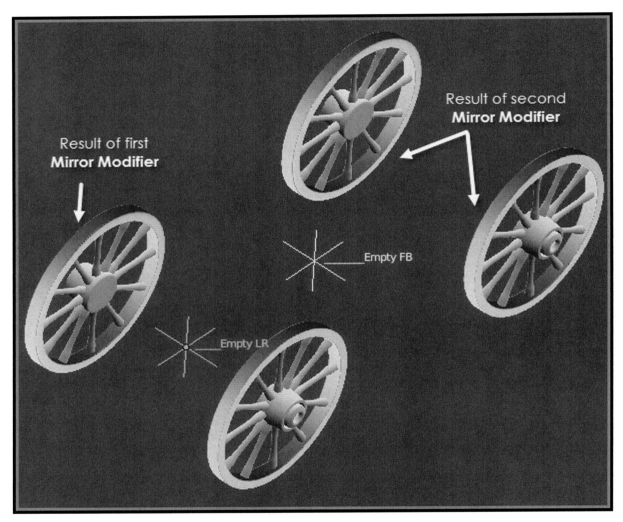

In the above illustration the *Empty* named *Empty.LR* is used as the *Mirror Object* to *Mirror* the front left wheel to the front right of the wagon. The 2nd *Mirror Modifier* is using the *Empty* named *Empty.FB* as the *Mirror Object* to *Mirror* the 2 front wheels to the back of the wagon. Now any changes I make to the front left wheel will be *Mirrored* to all other wagon wheels. You can use this for anything like wheels, car mirrors, dual exhaust and so on.

Remember that the *Object Origin* is used as the *Location* for the *Mirror Plane* when using the *Mirror Modifier* (unless you are using a *Mirror Object*). You may need to reposition the *Object Origin* along what will be the *Center* of the *Mesh* once the *Mirror Modifier* is applied. I talk about how to reposition the *Object Origin* in **Chapter 7 – Object Origins**.

The Shrinkwrap Modifier

The *Shrinkwrap Modifier* allows you to *Shrinkwrap* one *Object* on to the surface of another *Object*. The *Object* being *Wrapped* takes on the shape of the *Target Mesh*. For the rest of the section I will call the *Object* that is being *Wrapped* the *Source Object* and the *Object* that is the destination of the *Source Object* as the *Target*. In other words, the *Source Object* will be *Shrinkwrapped* to or around the *Target Object*.

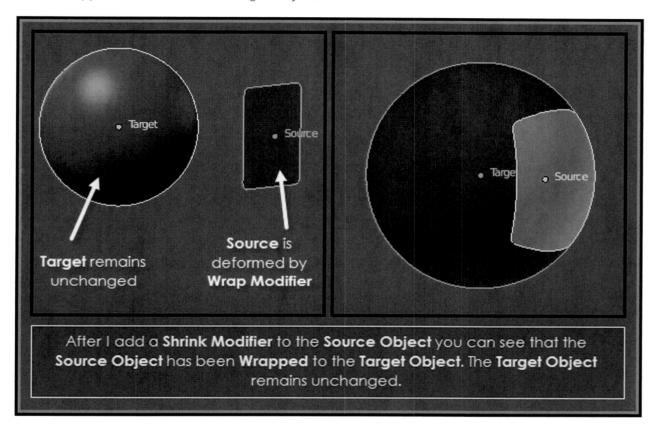

After I add a **Shrink Modifier** to the **Source Object** you can see that the **Source Object** has been **Wrapped** to the **Target Object**. The **Target Object** remains unchanged.

Here are the options available when using the *Shrinkwrap Modifier*. The illustrations to follow show the options for the *Shrinkwrap Modifier* when the *Mode* is set to *Nearest Surface Point*. I discuss the *Mode* option later in the chapter.

Apply - applies the *Modifier* so that the *Shrinkwrap* operation is permanent. The *Modifier* is also removed from the *Modifier Stack*.

Apply as Shape Key - applies the *Modifier* resulting in the creation of a *Shape Key*. The *Modifier* is also removed from the *Modifier Stack*. *Shape Keys* are outside the scope of this book.

Copy - make a copy of this *Modifier* and adds it to the *Modifier Stack*.

Target - choose an *Object* to be the *Target* for the *Source Object*.

Offset - allows you to set a value that represents the distance between the *Source* and the *Target*.

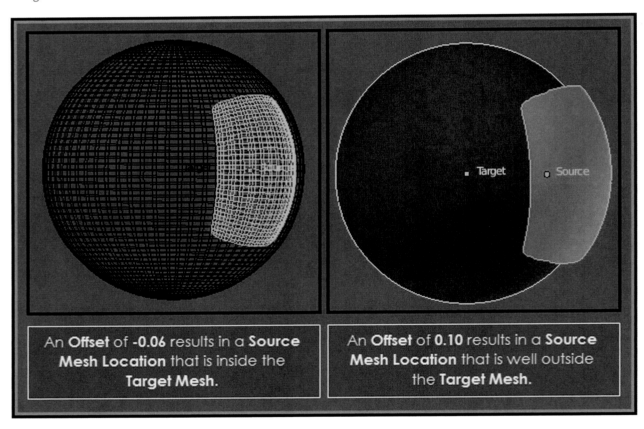

An **Offset** of **-0.06** results in a **Source Mesh Location** that is inside the **Target Mesh**.

An **Offset** of **0.10** results in a **Source Mesh Location** that is well outside the **Target Mesh**.

I personally use an *Offset* of 0.001 most of the time. It keeps the *Source Object* ever so slightly above the surface of the *Target* so that I can at least see it when I am *Modeling*.

Vertex Group - this setting allows you to tell *Blender* that you want the *Wrap Modifier* to be calculated against a specific *Vertex Group* for that *Object*. Any *Vertices* that you want to be affected by the *Shrinkwrap Modifier* can be added to the *Vertex Group*, all others will not be affected. This option is useful when you want to *Extrude* some *Geometry* that is currently *Shrinkwrapped*.

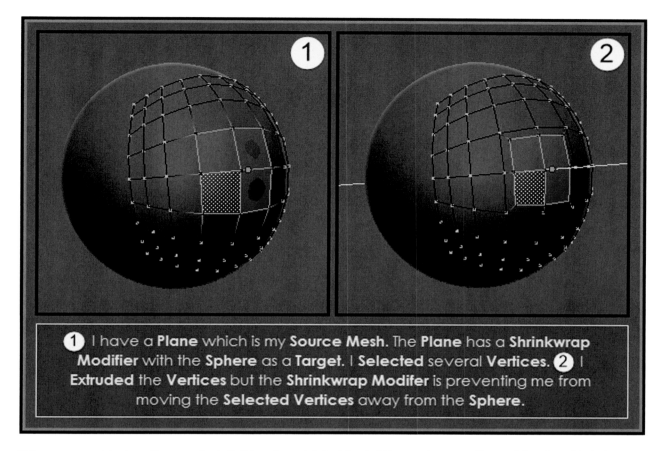

① I have a **Plane** which is my **Source Mesh**. The **Plane** has a **Shrinkwrap Modifier** with the **Sphere** as a **Target**. I **Selected** several **Vertices**. ② I **Extruded** the **Vertices** but the **Shrinkwrap Modifer** is preventing me from moving the **Selected Vertices** away from the **Sphere**.

We can use *Vertex Groups* to tell *Blender* which *Mesh Elements* are affected by the *Shrinkwrap Modifier*. Given the above illustration as an example, the first thing I need to do before the *Extrusion* operation is *Select* all *Vertices* and assign them to a *Vertex Group*.

I created a *Vertex Group* called "Wrap" and assigned <u>all</u> *Vertices* to the *Vertex Group*. Next I selected the "*Wrap*" *Vertex Group* in the *Vertex Group* field on the *Shrinkwrap Modifier Panel*.

Now I can *Extrude* any of the *Mesh Elements* and remove them from the *Vertex Group* which will allow me to *Move* the *Mesh Elements* away from the *Mesh*. I could always add them back to the *Vertex Group* to have them once again be affected by the *Shrinkwrap Modifier*.

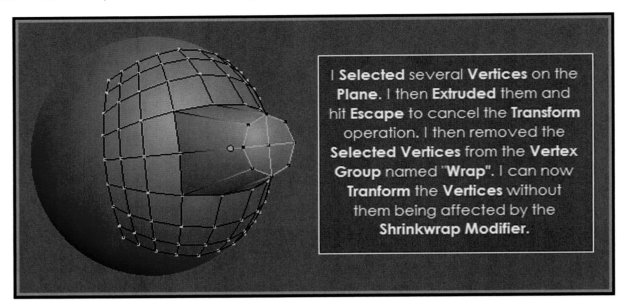

I **Selected** several **Vertices** on the **Plane**. I then **Extruded** them and hit **Escape** to cancel the **Transform** operation. I then removed the **Selected Vertices** from the **Vertex Group** named "**Wrap**". I can now **Tranform** the **Vertices** without them being affected by the **Shrinkwrap Modifier**.

I discuss a more practical example later in this section.

All of the options discussed until now are available no matter which *Mode* you select.

Mode - there are 3 *Modes* you can choose from and the options that appear on the *Shrinkwrap Modifier Panel* will change based on the current *Mode*. The *Mode* determines how the *Shrinkwrap* calculations are made. One way to think of it is that each *Vertex* on the *Source Object* is snapped to a point on the *Target*. The *Mode* determines how that point is determined.

Mode: Nearest Surface Point - this *Mode* will snap each *Vertex* of the *Source Object* to the closest location of the *Target Object*. I find I get the best result with this *Mode*, at least for the type of operations I use the *Shrinkwrap Modifier* for. The only extra option that appears for this mode is the *Keep Above Surface* option. This setting will keep the *Source Vertices* above the surface of the *Target Object*.

Mode: Nearest Vertex - this *Mode* will snap each *Vertex* of the *Source Object* to the closest *Vertex* on the *Target Object*. The amount of Vertices on the *Target Object* plays a role on how much accuracy is available when placing the *Source Object*. This *Mode* can be used to have a *Target Mesh* act as a sort of map to precisely place the *Source Object*. As I mentioned above, *Nearest Surface Point Mode* seems to give me better results.

Mode: Projection - this Mode will *Project* the *Source Object Vertices* until they touch the *Target*. This *Mode* reminds me of the *Knife Project Tool* (see **Chapter 8 – Knife Projection**) but with the flexibility of being able to reposition and tweak the final result before applying it. This *Mode* comes with several options and can require some trial and error compared to the other 2 modes. Here is the *Options Panel* for *Project Mode*.

Mode: Projection->Subsurf Levels - will temporarily *Subdivide* the *Source* object before calculating the *Wrap*. At the time of this writing this setting appears to have no effect.

On a side note, I often add a *Subdivision Surface Modifier* to the *Source Object* above the *Wrap Modifier* as it gives a better result.

Mode: Projection->Limit - you can use the *Limit* option to *Limit* the number of *Vertices* that are affected by the *Wrap Modifier* based on distance. Any *Vertex* over the *Limit* value will be unaffected by the *Wrap Modifier*.

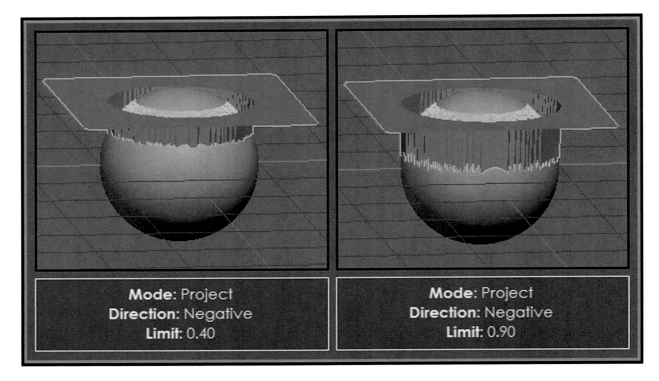

Mode: Project
Direction: Negative
Limit: 0.40

Mode: Project
Direction: Negative
Limit: 0.90

Mode: Projection->Axis X, Y, Z - set the direction of the *Projection* based on the *Local X, Y* or *Z-Axis* of the *Source Object*.

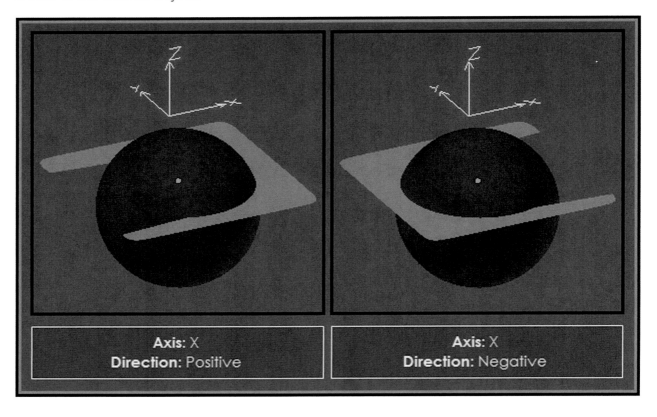

Axis: X
Direction: Positive

Axis: X
Direction: Negative

Mode: Projection->Direction Negative,Positive - Just as the *Axis* allows you to set *Direction*, so does the *Positive* and *Negative Direction* setting. Using the *Direction* option in conjunction with the *Axis* option offers a lot of flexibility when using *Projection Mode*.

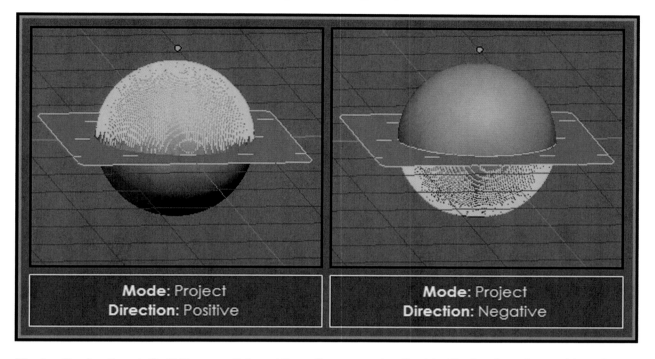

Mode: Projection->Cull Faces - this setting allows you to disable *Projection* along either the *Front* of *Back* of the *Target Faces*. The *Front* or *Back* of a *Face* is determined by the *Face Normal*.

Mode: Projection->Auxiliary Target - allows you to add an additional *Target* for the *Source Object*.

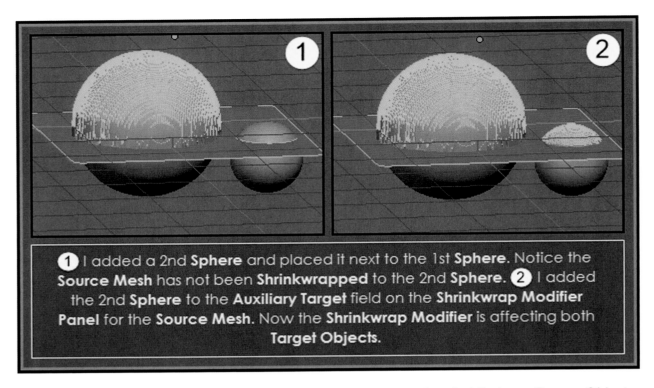

1 I added a 2nd **Sphere** and placed it next to the 1st **Sphere**. Notice the **Source Mesh** has not been **Shrinkwrapped** to the 2nd **Sphere**. **2** I added the 2nd **Sphere** to the **Auxiliary Target** field on the **Shrinkwrap Modifier Panel** for the **Source Mesh**. Now the **Shrinkwrap Modifier** is affecting both **Target Objects.**

As you can see *Projection Mode* offers plenty of options. Keep in mind that any *Source Object Vertices* that are *Projected* but don't touch the *Target* will not be affected by the *Shrinkwrap Modifier.*

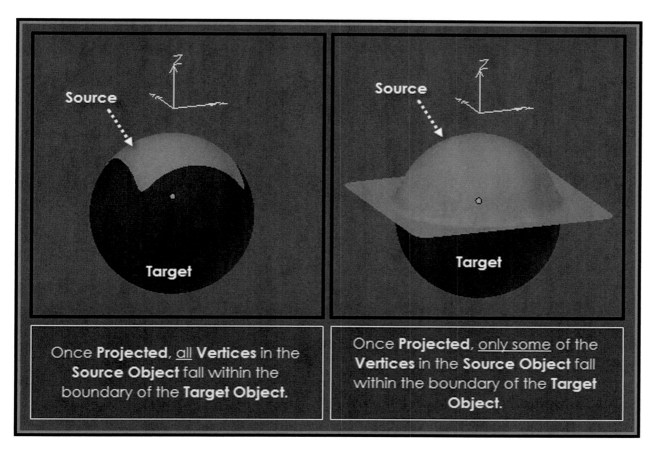

As you can see in the above illustration, the example on right demonstrates that any *Vertices* that do not touch the *Target Object* after being *Projected* are not affected by the *Shrink Wrap Modifier*. The example on the left shows the result when all *Vertices* touch the *Target* after being *Projected*.

One of the reasons I like the *Shrinkwrap Modifier* is it allows me to *Extrude Mesh Elements* in a uniform way. As an example, let's say I want to add a window to a castle and I want the window to be surrounded by stones. I could attempt it without the *Shrinkwrap Modifier* but as we will soon see, it doesn't produce the best result. I will start with a castle tower and the *Mesh* that will eventually become the tower window.

I could simply *Extrude* the individual *Faces* to create the stones and place it against the tower.

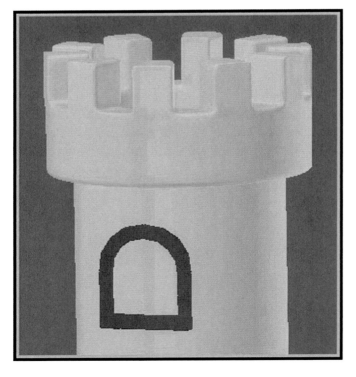

From a distance it just doesn't look right and when we get closer we can see why simply *Extruding* the window *Mesh* didn't produce a good result.

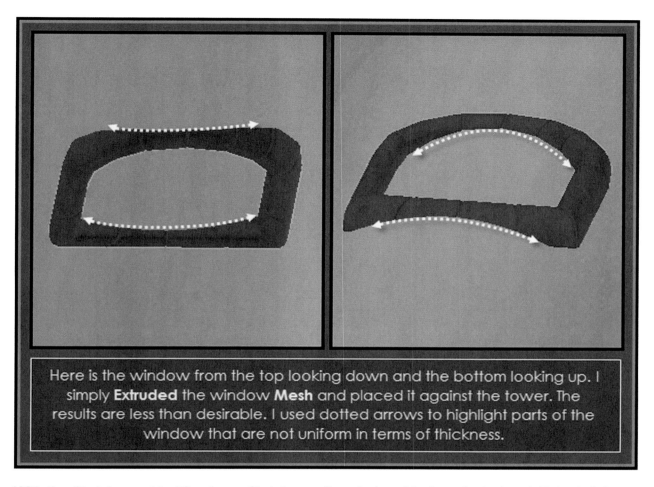

Here is the window from the top looking down and the bottom looking up. I simply **Extruded** the window **Mesh** and placed it against the tower. The results are less than desirable. I used dotted arrows to highlight parts of the window that are not uniform in terms of thickness.

With the *Shrinkwrap Modifier*, I can *Shrinkwrap* the window *Mesh* so that when I *Extrude* it I get a result that is much more uniform as it relates to the tower. First I will *Shrinkwrap* the window *Mesh* before I *Extrude* it.

The result looks better already. Now I can apply the *Shrinkwrap Modifier* and *Extrude* the *Faces* to create the stones. I also need to cut a hole in the tower for the window. Here is the result.

You can see that the *Extruded Faces* that I used to create the stones around the window look much better now that they follow the contour of the tower. I even added a few random bricks using the *Shrinkwrap Modifier* so they are rounded nicely.

I have used a *Model* of a submarine several times in this book. I used the *Shrinkwrap Modifier* when I created the portals and metal plates.

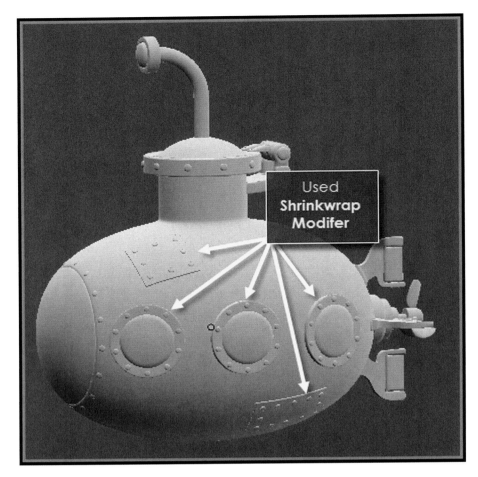

You can move the *Source Object* around once it has been *Shrinkwrapped* to the *Target*. This allows you to fine tune the placement of the *Source Object*. This brings me to the next situation where I frequently see the *Shrinkwrap Modifier*.

Often when *Modeling* a *Plane*, *Train* or *Automobile* you will start with large detail and add in the more intricate detail later in the *Modeling* process. The problem that can arise is if you cut a hole or *Extrude* a *Mesh Element* there is a good chance that you could inadvertently deform the *Mesh*. Let's take a car for example. Once the basic shape of the car is done you may want to add *Mirrors*. If you use an *Extrude* operation to create the *Mirrors* there is a chance that while you are manipulating the mirror that you create an artifact on the car by accidentally pulling or pushing portions of the *Mesh*. Another example is on a *Plane*. If you *Extrude* a wing and decide you want to move the wing up a little, there is a good chance the surrounding *Mesh* will end up with unwanted artifacts.

One technique that is used to keep a base *Mesh* in place while small details are added is as follows:

- Create your base *Mesh* whether it be a car or plane etc. You want the basic form of the *Object* with some detail if possible but nothing too intricate.
- *Duplicate* the base *Mesh* and resize it up ever so slightly. You should now have 2 identical *Meshes*, 1 slightly bigger than the other.

- *Shrinkwrap* the slightly bigger *Mesh* to the smaller *Mesh*. It's a good idea to name everything to keep it all straight and quickly find it in the *Outliner*.

Now you can work on the *Shrinkwrapped Mesh* without worrying about accidentally changing the overall shape. You can *Select* and move *Mesh Elements* around and the *Shrinkwrap Modifier* will ensure they stay *Snapped* to the *Model* and consequently don't lose their shape.

The *Shrinkwrap Modifier* usually requires a little trial and error to get exactly what you want. You need enough *Geometry* on the *Source Object* for it to *Wrap* properly. You don't want to overdo it but you will probably have to *Subdivide* it 1 or more times to get the result you want. I always strive to get a good *Wrapping* result with as few *Subdivisions* as possible.

The Array Modifier

The *Array Modifier* will create copies of the base *Object*. Why is it called the *Array Modifier*? A series of *Objects* is often referred to as an *Array*. The position of each copy is determined by an *Offset* and allows for numerous possibilities and consequently results.

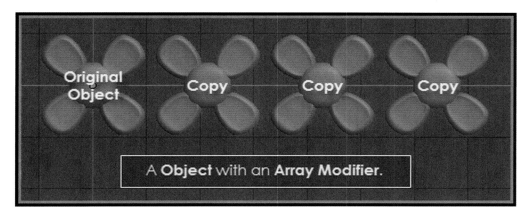

A **Object** with an **Array Modifier**.

Here are the options available when using the *Array Modifier*.

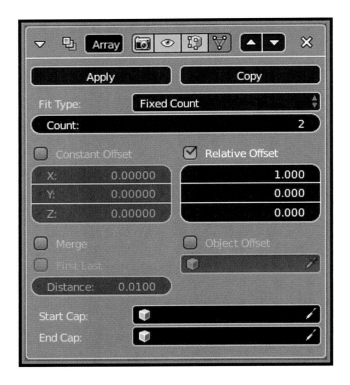

Apply - applies the *Modifier* so that the *Array* operation is permanent. The *Modifier* is also removed from the *Modifier Stack*.

Copy - make a copy of this *Modifier* and add it to the *Modifier Stack*.

Fit Type - lets you set the length of the *Array*. You have 3 options to choose from.

Fit Type -> Fixed Count - set the number of copies based on the *Count* setting. Simply increment the *Count* to add the desired number of Copies.

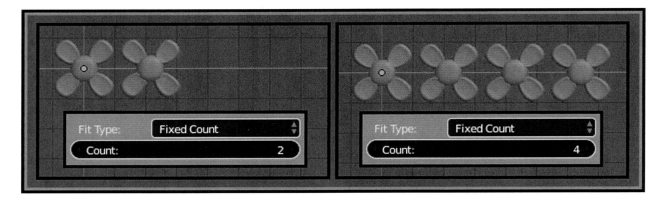

Fit Type -> Fixed Length - This *Fit Type* allows you to set the *Length* of the *Array* based on the value you enter in the *Length* field. Increase the *Length* value to add copies to the Array.

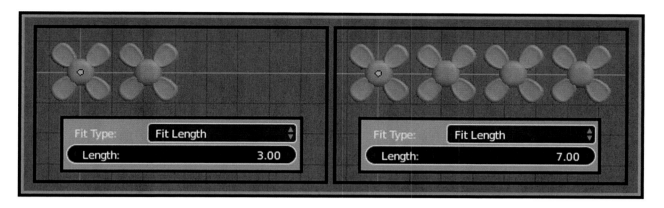

Fit Type -> Fit Curve - the *Length* of the Array is based on the length of a *Curve* that you associate with the *Array Modifier* by way of the *Curve* field.

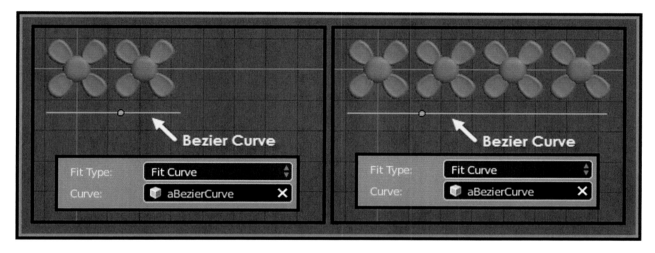

Constant Offset - X, Y, Z - allows you to position the *Copies* along 1 or more *Axes*. Simply enter a positive or negative value to change the *Offset* effectively changing the position of each *Copy*. The value you enter will *Offset* the *Copies* based on *Blender Units*.

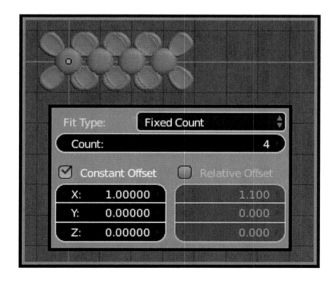

You can see in the above illustration that a *Constant Offset* of 1.0000 on the *X-Axis* resulted in the *Copies* overlapping with each other as each copy is moved 1 *Blender Unit*.

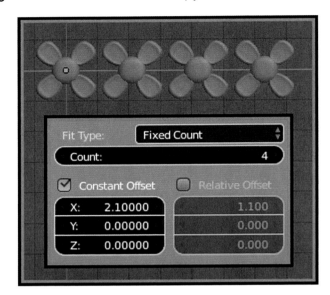

I changed the *Constant Offset* to 2.10000 on the *X-Axis* resulting in spacing between the *Copies*.

You can of course *Offset* along more than 1 *Axis* at the same time.

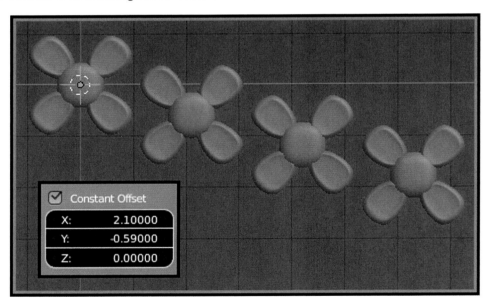

Relative Offset X, Y, Z - allows you to position the *Copies* along 1 or more *Axes*. Simply enter a positive or negative value to change the *Offset* effectively changing the position of each *Copy*. The value you enter will *Offset* the *Copies* based on the *Bounding Box* of the *Object* (as opposed to *Blender Units* used in the *Constant Offset* option).

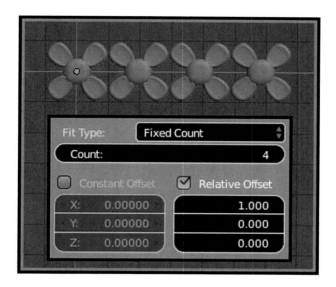

You can see in the above illustration that a *Relative Offset* of 1.0000 on the *X-Axis* resulted in the *Copies* being right next to each other. With *Relative Offset*, a value of 1.000 on the *X-Axis* will move the *Copy* a distance that is equal to the size of the *Objects Bounding Box*. In other words, the *Bounding Box* becomes the unit of measurement.

Object Offset - by far the most interesting *Offset* option, *Object Offset* lets you associate an *Object* with the *Array Modifier* so that any *Transform* operations performed on that *Object* affect the *Copies* generated by the *Array Modifier*. Most of the time an *Empty* is used as the *Offset Object*. The advantage of using an *Object* for *Offset* is you can not only *Move* the *Offset Object*, you can *Rotate* and *Scale* it as well resulting in some interesting or just plain cool results.

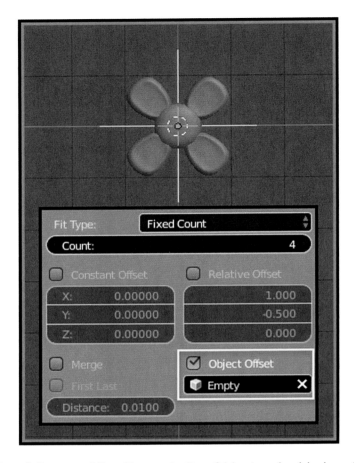

In the above illustration, I *Snapped* the *Cursor* to the *Object* and added an *Empty* at that *Location*. I also added an *Array Modifier* and set the *Object Offset* to the *Empty* I created. All of the *Copies* are in the same *Location* because I haven't *Transformed* the *Empty* yet. Now I will *Transform* the *Empty*.

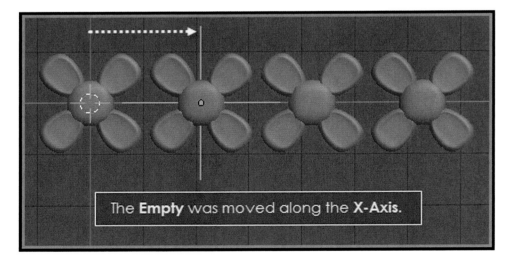

Not an overly interesting example. Next I will *Transform* the *Empty* a little further.

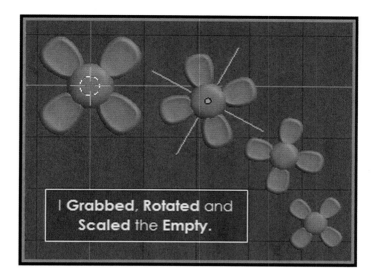

You can see in the above illustration how *Transforming* the *Empty* has affected the *Copies* of the *Array*. The *Object Offset* option is in my opinion the most useful *Offset* option as it offers the most control and flexibility.

The *Offset Object* is also the only option that allows for circular results.

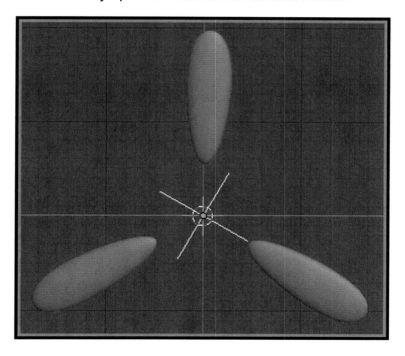

In the above illustration I was able to place *Copies* in a circle around the *Empty*. You can use this technique for everything from flowers to propellers to car wheels.

Here is how I achieved this result.

- Add an *Object* and an *Empty* at the same *Location*.
- Add an *Array Modifier* to the *Object* and set the *Empty* as the *Object Offset*.

- Go in to *Edit Mode* and *Move* the *Object* away from its *Object Origin* (in the above case, I moved it along the *Y-Axis* as I was in *Top View*). The reason I moved the *Object* in *Edit Mode* is I wanted to leave the *Object Origin* in its original *Location*.
- Next I *Rotated* the *Empty* resulting in the *Copies* being *Rotated* around the *Empty*.

Merge - this option will *Merge* any *Vertices* from one *Copy* to the next as long as they are within a given *Distance* (there is an option to set the *Distance* below the *First Last* option). To demonstrate, I will start with a *Cylinder* that has an *Array Modifier*. I will set the *Offset* so that the *Copies* are not touching each other.

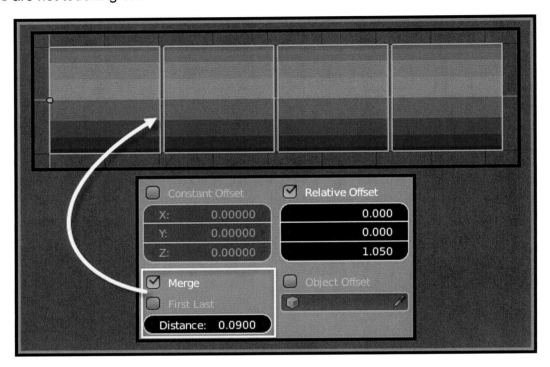

Even after I enable *Merge*, none of the *Vertices* from one *Copy* to the next are *Merged* because all *Vertices* still fall outside the value in the *Distance* setting. Now I will up the *Distance* to 0.1000.

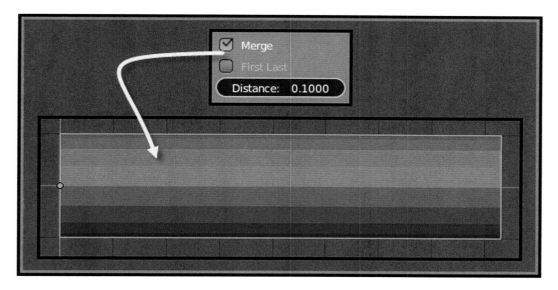

As we can see in the above illustration, *Vertices* from *Copy* to *Copy* that are *Located* within the designated *Distance* are now *Merged*. *Merge* can be used to make the *Copies* of an *Array* look connected or continuous.

This option is also handy if you are using the *Array Modifier* to create a *Circular Object* like a car tire. I started with the following.

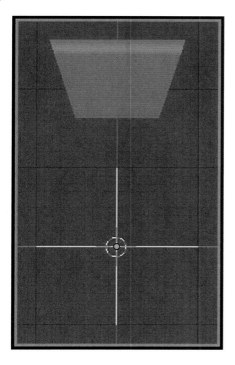

Next I added the following *Array Modifier*.

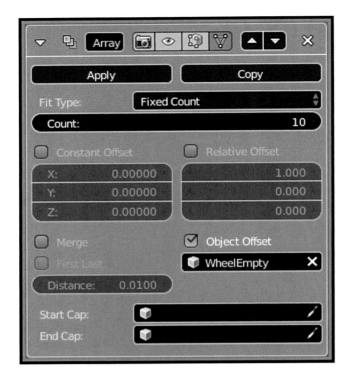

I rotated the *Empty* and added a *Subdivision Surface Modifier.* **Here is the result.**

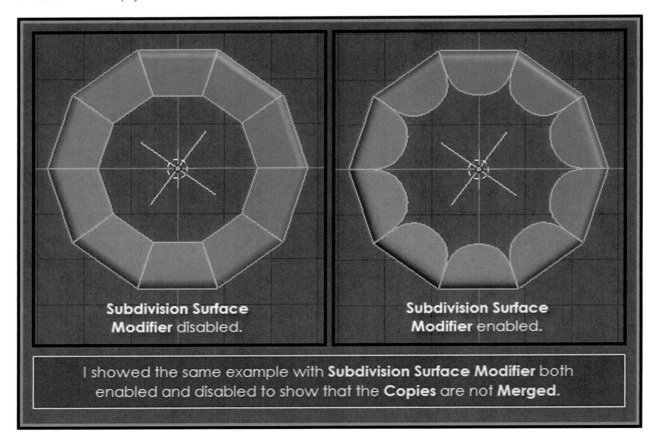

Subdivision Surface Modifier disabled.

Subdivision Surface Modifier enabled.

I showed the same example with **Subdivision Surface Modifier** both enabled and disabled to show that the **Copies** are not **Merged.**

As you can see, my (very rudimentary) tire isn't really road worthy. The *Copies* are not *Connected* together. Now I will enable the *Merge* option.

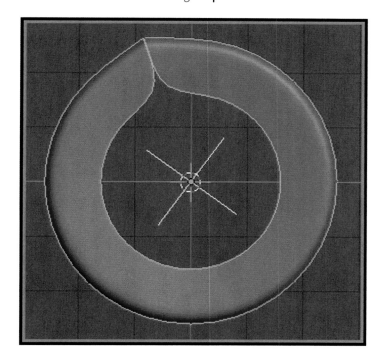

Ok, that's a little closer. I still don't think its road worthy. The final *Copy* is not *Merged* with the original *Object*. Let's move on to the next option to fix that.

First Last - enable this option so that the *Vertices* in the final *Copy* will be *Merged* with the *Vertices* in the original *Object*. I will use this option to fix the issue with our *Tire* in the previous illustration.

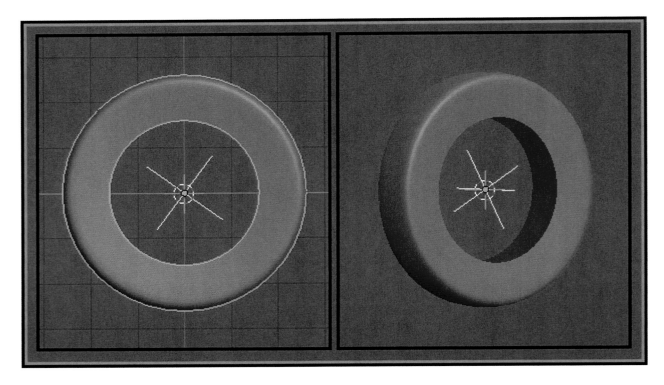

Now I can finally go for a drive.

Start Cap - allows you to designate an *Object* to act as the *Start Cap* for the *Array*. A single copy of the *Object* will be placed at the *Start* of the *Array*.

End Cap - allows you to designate an *Object* to act as the *End Cap* for the *Array*. A single copy of the *Object* will be placed at the *End* of the *Array*.

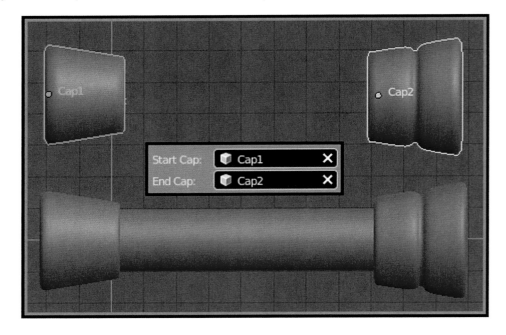

In the above illustration I created 2 *Objects* to be used as *Caps* for the *Array Modifier* added to the main *Object* (the main *Object* is the tube and the *Cap Objects* are named *Cap1* and *Cap2*). I typed the *Object* names in the relevant fields resulting in the *Object* being added to the *Array* as a *Start* or *End Cap*.

You can combine any of the *Offset* types. In other words, you can enable any combination of *Constant*, *Relative* and *Object Offset* at the same time. All of the *Offset* values will be added to calculate the final *Offset* position.

You can easily create some amazing things with the *Array Modifier*. You can stack *Array Modifiers* to quickly create large complicated *Models* in no time. Here is the result of adding 2 *Array Modifiers* followed by 2 *Mirrors* Modifiers. The *Array Modifiers* are using the *Object Offset*.

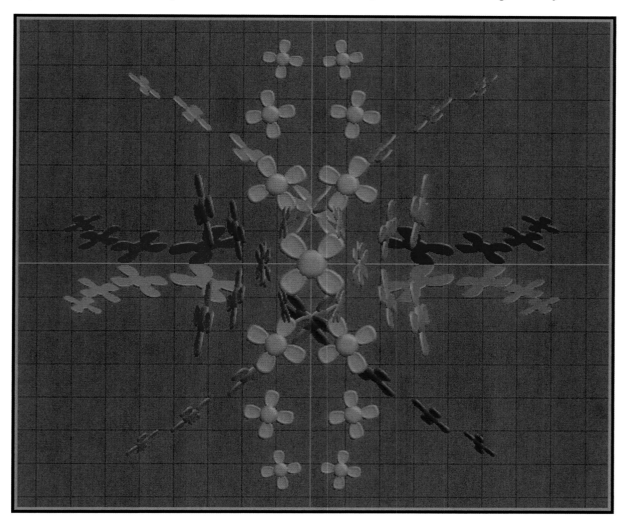

Remember, everything you see in the above illustration started with a single *Object*. It remains a single *Object* as I can disable or remove the *Array / Mirror Modifiers* at any time. That is the power of the *Array Modifier* and *Modifiers* in general.

The Solidify Modifier

The *Solidify Modifier* allows you to add depth or thickness to a *Mesh*. With this *Modifier* you can create a *Mesh* and then give it some depth similar to an *Extrude* operation but with a plethora of options allowing you to tweak the result. Think of it as an *Extrusion* operation but with cleaner results. Consider the following *Mesh*.

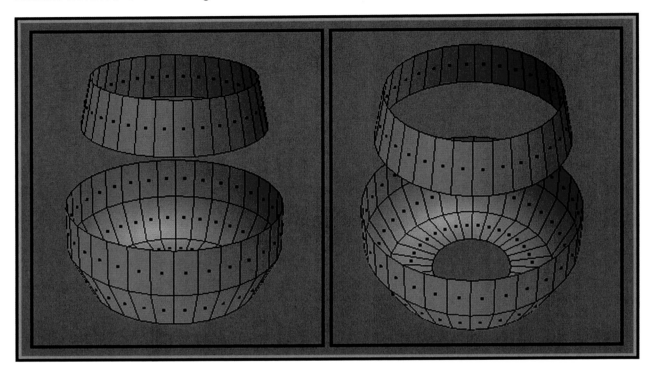

If I wanted to add *thickness* to this *Model* I could use *Extrusion* but it would be hard to get a uniform result. Here is the same *Model* with a *Solidify Modifier*.

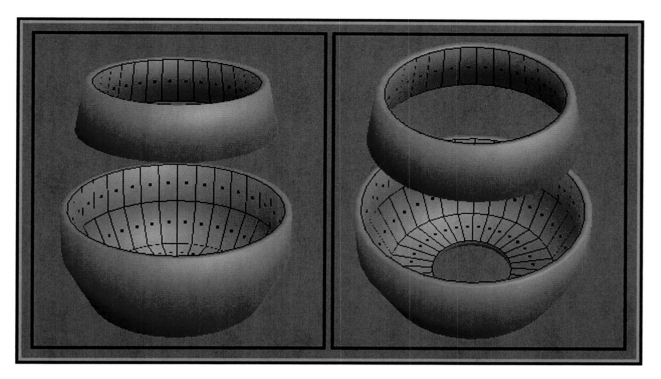

Now if I apply the *Modifier*, I get a nice result.

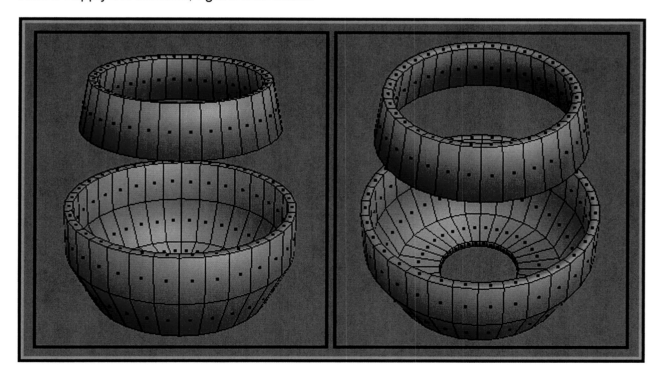

You can get a preview of how the *Mesh* will look without applying.

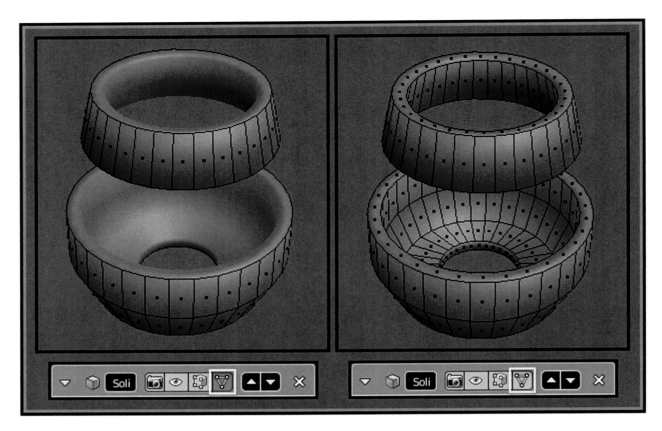

Here are the options available when using the *Solidify Modifier*.

Apply - applies the *Modifier* so that the *Solidify* operation is permanent. The *Modifier* is also removed from the *Modifier Stack*.

Copy - make a copy of this *Modifier* and add it to the *Modifier Stack*.

Thickness - set the thickness of the *Solidify* operation.

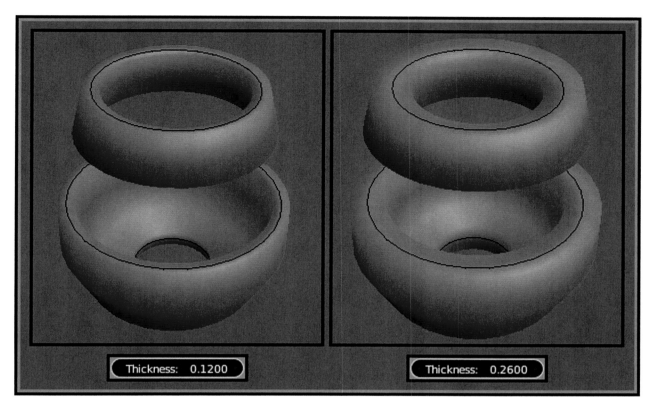

Offset - lets you set the added depth on the inside or outside of the *Mesh*. The *Offset* field accepts a value between 1 and -1 (just set to 0 for no *Offset*).

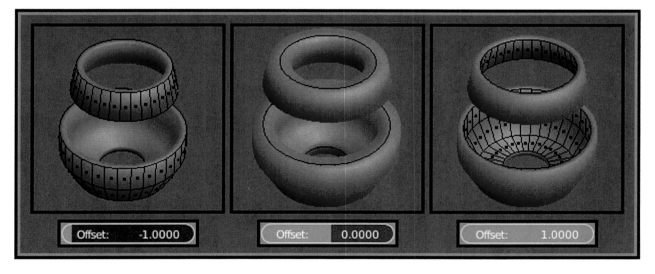

This setting can be useful when used in conjunction with the *Shrinkwrap* Modifier. You could use *Shrinkwrap* to create clothes on a *Mesh* and use the *Solidify Modifier* to give the clothes some *Depth*. You would want to set the *Offset* to a positive number as you would want the clothes to expand out from the *Mesh*.

Clamp - there are times when using the *Solidify Modifier* will result in *Faces* from the inside of the *Mesh* overlapping with *Faces* from the outside of the *Mesh*. The *Clamp* setting accepts a value between 0 and 2 and attempts to prevent the *Mesh* from intersecting with itself.

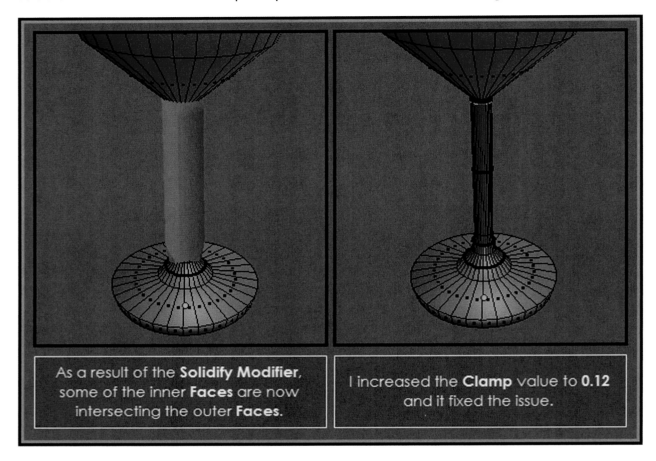

As a result of the **Solidify Modifier**, some of the inner **Faces** are now intersecting the outer **Faces**.

I increased the **Clamp** value to **0.12** and it fixed the issue.

Vertex Group - with this setting only *Vertices* that are part of a *Vertex Group* will be affected by the *Solidify Modifier* (see **Chapter 7 – Vertex Groups**). Start by assigning some *Vertices* to a *Vertex Group* and then select the *Vertex Group* in the *Solidify Modifier Options Panel*.

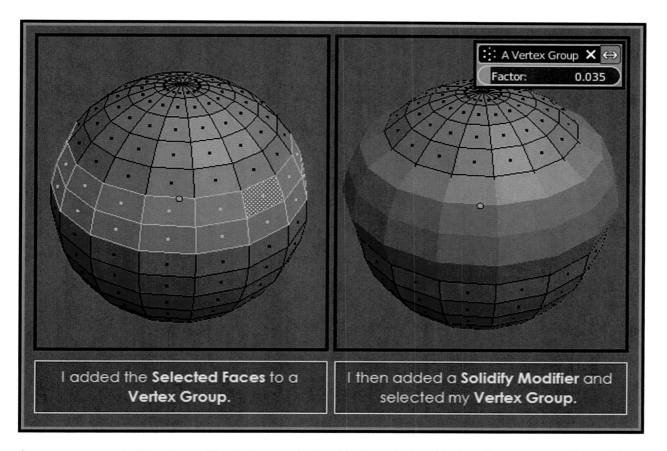

I added the **Selected Faces** to a Vertex Group.

I then added a **Solidify Modifier** and selected my **Vertex Group**.

As you can see in the above illustration, only the *Vertices* in the *Vertex Group* were affected by the *Solidify Modifier*. The small icon next to the *Vertex Group* field allows you to invert how the *Vertex Group* influences the *Solidify Modifier*.

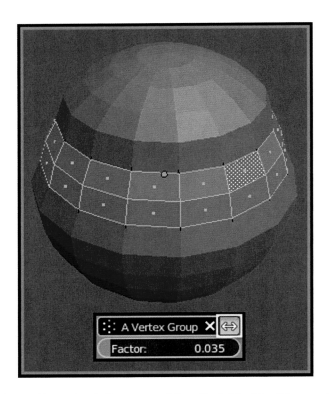

The *Factor* field is used to adjust the influence of the *Solidify Modifier* on the *Vertex Group*.

Crease - the *Crease* setting only works when used in conjunction with a *Subdivision Surface Modifier*. The setting allows you to crease or sharpen the *Edges* created on the original *Mesh* as well as those resulting from the *Solidify Modifier*. In the next example, I started by adding a *Subdivision Surface Modifier* beneath the *Solidify Modifier* (it's important for it to be below the *Solidify Modifier*).

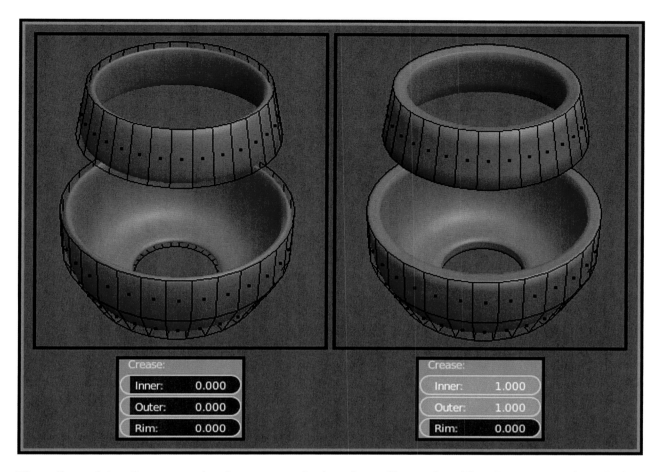

The effect of the *Crease* setting is apparent in the above illustration. The *Edges* went from being rounded and smooth to being sharp.

Flip Normals - allows you to *Flip* the *Normals* for the entire *Mesh*.

Even Thickness - this setting, as the name implies, attempts to keep the depth or thickness that results from the *Solidify Modifier* as even as possible. This can be helpful when your *Model* contains numerous sharp corners but comes at the cost of longer render times.

The result appears subtle but often gives a visibly better result. I personally keep this option enabled the majority of the time.

High Quality Normals - similar to the previous setting, this setting attempts to keep the depth or thickness that results from the *Solidify Modifier* as even as possible. The result is achieved by calculating the *Normals* but can result is slowdown. If you are having issues with thickness, you can enable it to see if it helps, otherwise I would leave it disabled.

Fill Rim - the *Solidify Modifier* results in the creation of inner and outer *Faces*. If some of the *Mesh Elements* are separate from each other, the resulting *Faces* will have gaps between the inner and outer *Edges*. Those gaps can be filled using this setting.

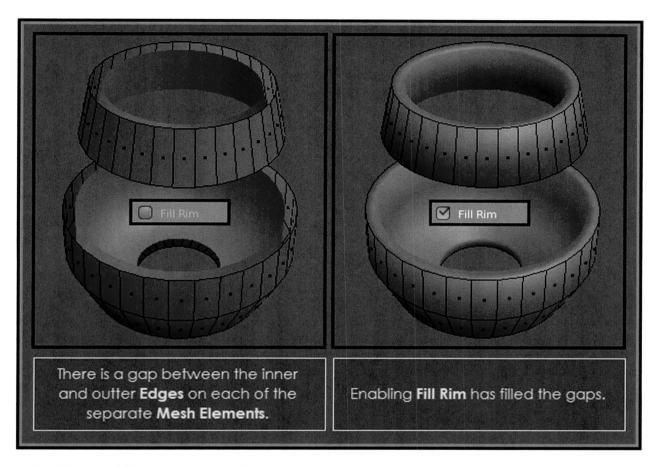

There is a gap between the inner and outer **Edges** on each of the separate **Mesh Elements.**

Enabling **Fill Rim** has filled the gaps.

Only Rim - enabling this setting will result in only the rim being created as part of the *Solidify Modifier* result. This setting appears to only work in conjunction with the *Fill Rim* setting and I was unable to see any difference in the result with it enabled. This setting may be specific to a *Mesh* with a particular *Geometry* layout.

Material Index Offset - this setting allows you to assign a different *Material* to the geometry that results from the *Solidify Modifier*. To use it, add a 2nd *Material* to your *Mesh* and set the *Material Index Offset* to 1. Set *Rim* to 1 to assign a *Material* to the *Rim*. You can also add a 3rd *Material* and so on. First I will start by adding 2 *Materials* to my *Mesh*.

Now I can assign the *Materials* to the result of the *Solidify Modifier*.

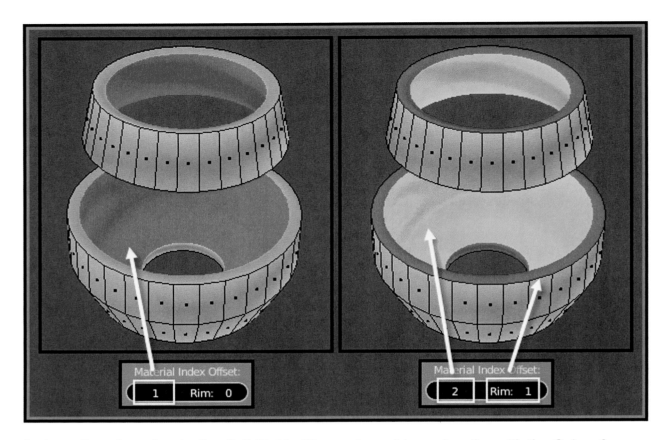

As I mentioned previously, the *Solidify Modifier* works well in conjunction with the *Subsurface Modifier*. I used this combination effectively to create the portals and panels on the submarine I have used in many example illustrations (highlighted in the next illustration).

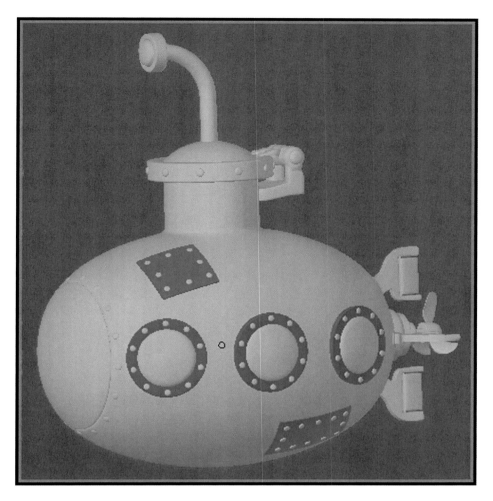

The next illustration is a screen capture of a *Mesh* I created in about 10 minutes using a *Solidify Modifier*, a *Shrinkwrap Modifier* and a *Subdivision Surface Modifier*. I created 2 *Spheres*, I used the *Shrinkwrap Modifier* to *Shrinkwrap* one *Sphere* to the other. I was then able to remove *Faces* without it affecting the shape of the *Sphere*. I then used the *Solidify Modifier* to give it some depth. The whole thing was made quick and easy thanks to *Modifiers*.

The Bevel Modifier

The *Bevel Modifier* allows you to *Bevel* the *Edges* of your *Mesh* and offers extra flexibility not available with **The Bevel Tool**. Like all *Modifiers*, the result of the *Bevel Modifier* is non-destructive and can be enabled and disabled at any time.

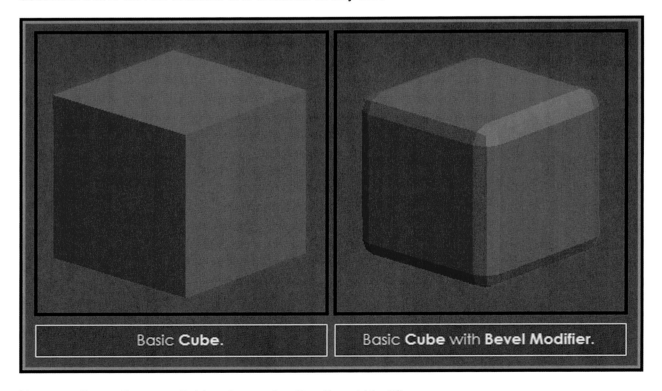

Basic **Cube**.   Basic **Cube** with **Bevel Modifier**.

Here are the options available when using the *Bevel Modifier*.

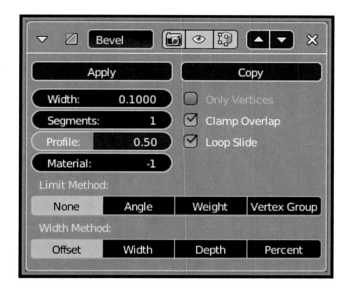

Apply - applies the *Modifier* so that the *Bevel* operation is permanent. The *Modifier* is also removed from the *Modifier Stack*.

Copy - make a copy of this *Modifier* and add it to the *Modifier Stack*.

Width - allows you to set the width or size of the *Bevel*. The *Width Method* options at the bottom of the *Options Panel* will play a role in the result you get from this setting.

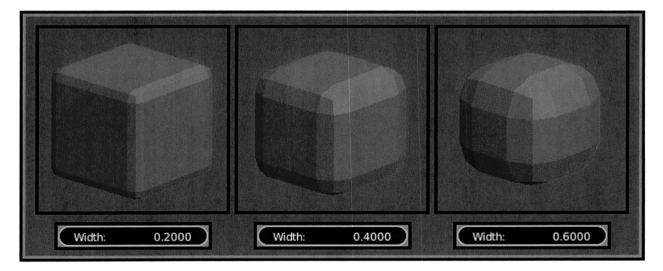

Segments - this setting allows you to set the number of *Edge Loops* to use to create the *Bevel*.

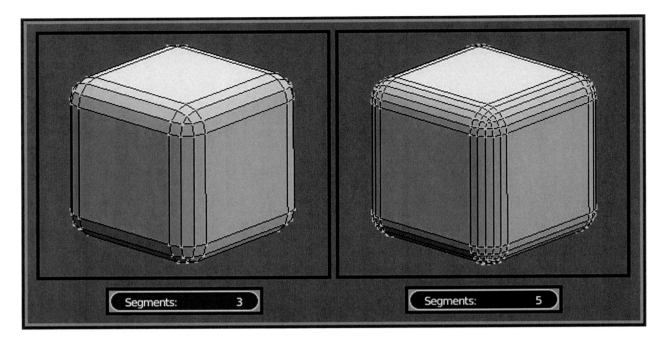

Profile - the *Profile* setting allows you to modify the shape of the *Bevel* result. The default is .5 which is round. This setting allows you to have a *Bevel* that is either concave or convex. You must have 2 or more *Segments* for this setting to have any effect.

Material - the *Material* setting allows you to define what *Material* will be assigned to any new *Faces* that result from the *Bevel* operation. The default is -1 which essentially turns the option off. When set to -1, any new *Faces* that result from the *Bevel* operation will inherit the *Material* from the closest *Face*.

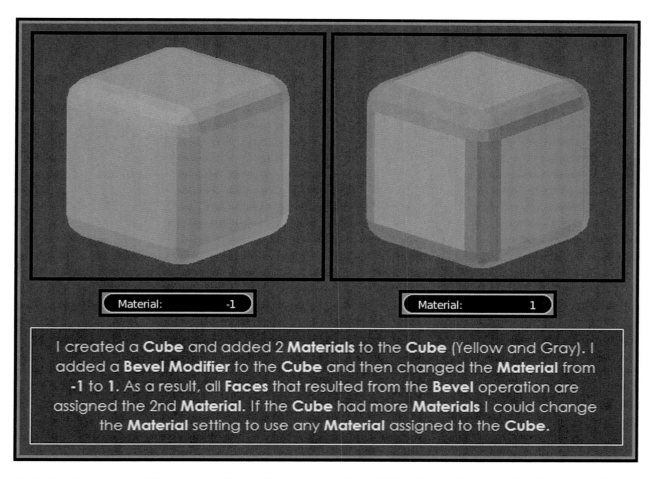

Material: -1

Material: 1

I created a **Cube** and added 2 **Materials** to the **Cube** (Yellow and Gray). I added a **Bevel Modifier** to the **Cube** and then changed the **Material** from -1 to 1. As a result, all **Faces** that resulted from the **Bevel** operation are assigned the 2nd **Material**. If the **Cube** had more **Materials** I could change the **Material** setting to use any **Material** assigned to the **Cube**.

Only Vertices - enabling this option will cause the *Bevel Modifier* to be calculated against the *Objects Vertices* and not its *Edges*.

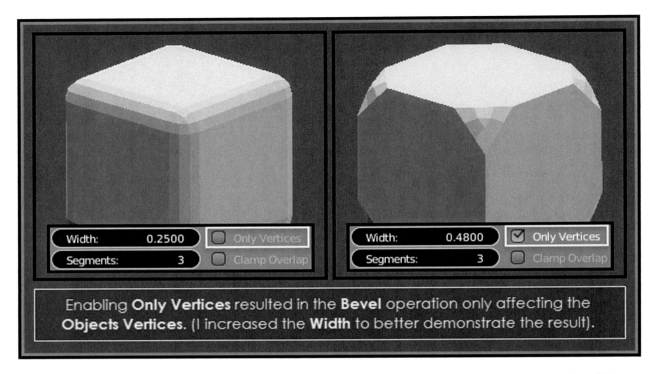

Enabling **Only Vertices** resulted in the **Bevel** operation only affecting the **Objects Vertices**. (I increased the **Width** to better demonstrate the result).

Clamp Overlap - this setting ensures that the *Edges* that are created from the *Bevel Modifier* don't intersect or overlap with each other. Here is a pretty extreme example.

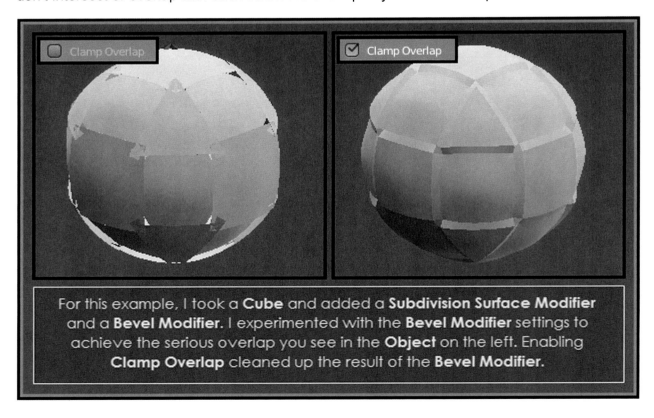

For this example, I took a **Cube** and added a **Subdivision Surface Modifier** and a **Bevel Modifier**. I experimented with the **Bevel Modifier** settings to achieve the serious overlap you see in the **Object** on the left. Enabling **Clamp Overlap** cleaned up the result of the **Bevel Modifier**.

Limit Method - this option provides a group of buttons that allow you to choose where on your *Object* the *Bevel* is added. You can essentially *Limit* the scope of the *Bevel*. The buttons are as follows:

Limit Method ->None - no part of the *Object* is excluded from the *Bevel Modifier*.

Limit Method ->Angle - allows you to use the *Angle* of an *Edge* to *Limit* which *Edges* are *Beveled*. This allows you to have the *Bevel Modifier* only affect *Edges* with *Sharp* angles. Any *Edge* that has an angle that is less than the *Angle* setting will be affected.

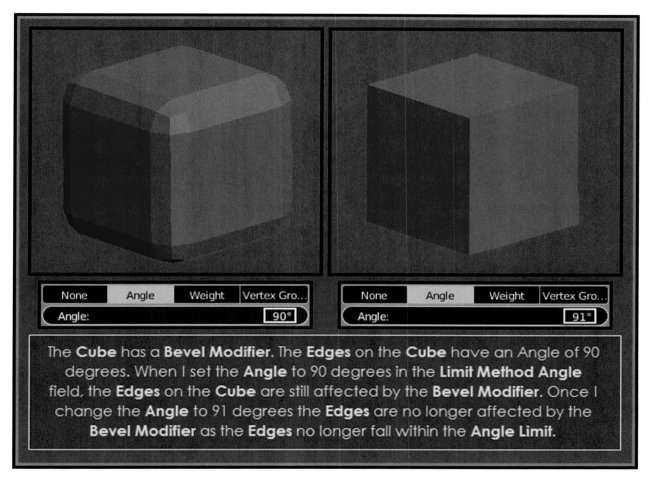

The **Cube** has a **Bevel Modifier**. The **Edges** on the **Cube** have an Angle of 90 degrees. When I set the **Angle** to 90 degrees in the **Limit Method Angle** field, the **Edges** on the **Cube** are still affected by the **Bevel Modifier**. Once I change the **Angle** to 91 degrees the **Edges** are no longer affected by the **Bevel Modifier** as the **Edges** no longer fall within the **Angle Limit**.

With this option, you can ensure that *Smooth* parts of the *Mesh* stay *Smooth* and *Sharp* parts of the *Mesh* are *Beveled*.

Limit Method ->Weight - this option allows you to choose which *Edges* are affected based on the individual *Bevel Weight* of each *Edge*. You can set the *Bevel Weight* of each *Edge* by *Selecting* the *Edge* and changing the *Bevel Weight* value on the *Properties Tool Shelf*. The setting is located on the *Transform Panel* under the *Edge Data*: section.

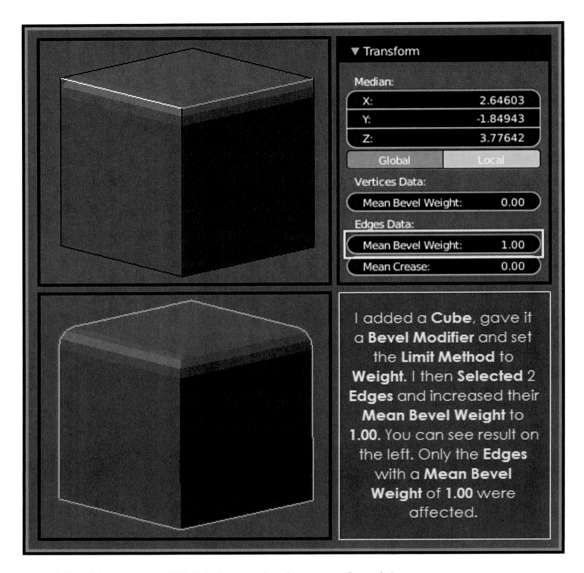

You can set the *Mean Bevel Weight* to a value between 0 and 1.

Limit Method ->**Vertex Group** - this option allows you to have the *Bevel Modifier* only affect the *Edges* that are part of a *Vertex Group* (see **Chapter 7 – Vertex Groups**). In other words, simply add the *Edges* you want affected to a *Vertex Group* and then *Select* the *Group* on the *Options Panel*. Now only the *Edges* in the *Vertex Group* will be affected by the *Bevel Modifier*.

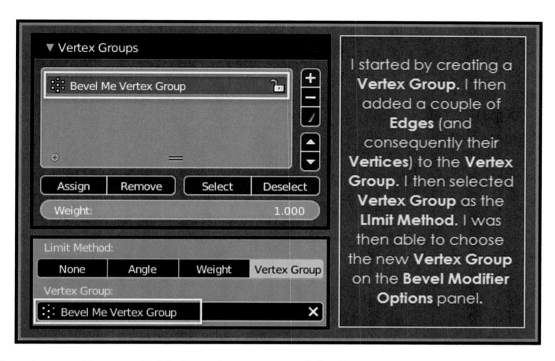

With the above settings, only *Vertices* that are part of the "Bevel Me Vertex Group" will be affected by the *Bevel Modifier*.

Width Method - this setting allows you to choose how the *Bevel Modifier* calculates the *Width*. The *Width Method* works in conjunction with the *Width value* (which was covered earlier). There are 4 options available for the *Width Method*. I usually use *Offset* for the *Width Method*. You can experiment with the other settings but I found they seem to affect the *Width* in different ways but don't offer any variation that I find useful during *3D Modeling* (I will update if I can find specific situations relevant to each setting). If you're interested in what each setting does, here is how they are described by *Blender*.

- **Offset** - Amount is offset of new *Edges* of original.
- **Width** - Amount is width of new *Face*.
- **Depth** - Amount is perpendicular distance from original *Edge* to *Bevel Face*.
- **Percent** - Amount is percent of adjacent *Edge* length.

I generally see the *Bevel Tool* used more often in *Tutorials* than the *Bevel Modifier*. The *Bevel Modifier* offers more flexibility but most of the time I see *Bevel* being used to *Smooth* out *Edges* so the *Bevel Tool* works fine in that type of situation. The *Bevel Modifier* affects the entire *Object* which is often undesirable. As I mentioned when discussing the *Bevel Tool*, I like to use *Beveling* selectively as it can produce *Triangles* depending on the *Edges* you perform the *Bevel* operation on. I find it to be fairly safe on *Edge Loops* but it requires vigilance in most *Modeling* situations to ensure a clean result.

The Wireframe Modifier

The *Wireframe Modifier* lets you convert your *Mesh* in to a *Wireframe*. More importantly (at least to me), it allows you to create a *Wireframe Render* of your *Mesh*. Before the *Wireframe Modifier* came along, there was no standard way to render a *Wireframe* screenshot. Actually, there were plenty of ways to do it, some rather complicated, others fairly simple and all with a wide range of results. Enter the *Wireframe Modifier*. Creating a *Wireframe* render of you *Model* is now simple and the resulting render is excellent.

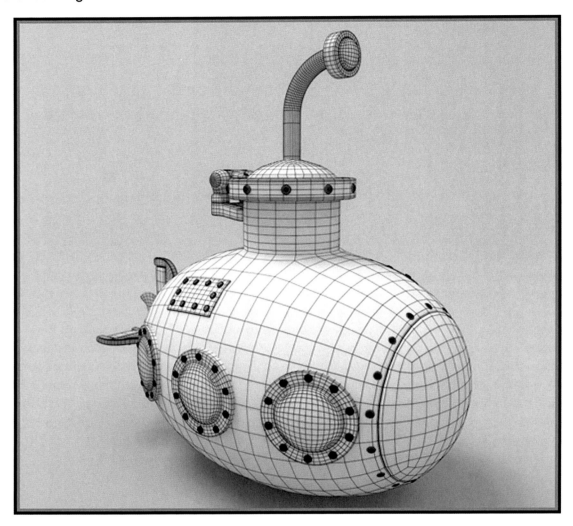

Here is how to set up a *Wireframe* for use in a *Render*.

Add 2 *Materials* to your *Mesh*. The first will be used for the *Mesh* itself and the second will be used to color the *Wireframe*. I use a *Diffuse Shader* for both *Materials*. One is *Light Gray* and the other is *Black*.

Next add a *Wireframe Modifier* to your *Mesh*. I usually also have a *Subdivision Surface Modifier* added to the *Mesh* as well. Use the following settings for the *Wireframe Modifier*.

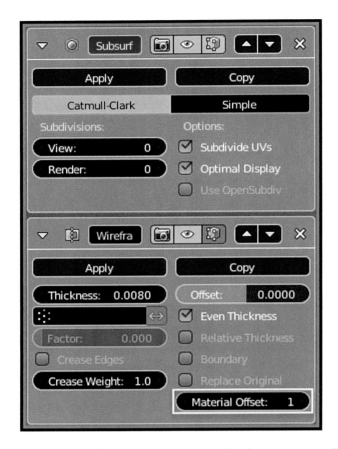

Notice the *Material Offset* is set to 1.This results in the *Wireframe* being displayed using the color of the 2nd *Material.* I also disabled *Replace Original.* Change your *Viewport Shading* to *Material* and you should get something like this.

Now just position your *Camera, Lamps* etc. and you are ready to *Render* a *Wireframe* of your *Mesh*.

You will probably have to play with the *Thickness* setting to get a nice result. There is a fine line between the *Wireframe* being nice and clean vs. the *Wireframe* looking too crowded. You can increase the *Subdivisions* to get a more detailed *Wireframe* but again, you will probably have to tweak the *Thickness* setting on the *Wireframe Modifier Options Panel* to get a nice clean result.

There are other options available for the *Wireframe Modifier*, some of which produce interesting results. I encourage you to play around with the various options to get an idea of the type of things this *Modifier* can do. I only included this *Modifier* in this chapter to show how it can be used to create a *Wireframe Render*.

The Screw Modifier

The *Screw Modifier* gives you similar functionality to that of the *Screw Tool* with all the added benefits that come with using a *Modifier*. As always, the *Modifier* is non-destructive and you can come back and tweak the result at any time. The *Screw Modifier* also has more options than the *Screw Tool*. Here are a couple of quick and easy springs thanks to the *Screw Modifier*.

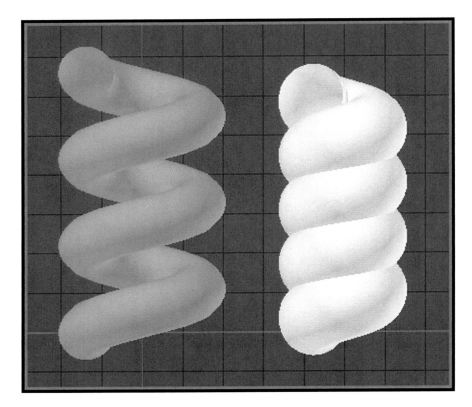

To create the light blue spring in the above illustration, I started with a basic *Circle Mesh Primitive*. When it comes to *Screw* operations, this *Mesh* is often referred to as the *Profile Mesh*. In the above example the *Circle* was added in *Top View*. In *Edit Mode*, I moved the *Circle* away from its *Origin*. Here is what it now looks like prior to adding the *Screw Modifier*.

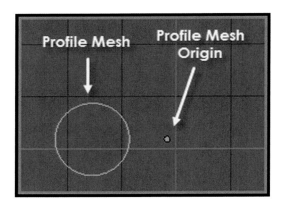

Next I added a *Screw Modifier* and set the *Axis* to *Y* in the *Options Panel*. I tweaked the settings in the *Options Panel* (which I cover next) to get the final result I wanted. I used a similar technique for the white spring on the right in the above illustration. The only difference was the shape of the *Profile Mesh* as well as the *Location* of the *Object Origin*. Here is an illustration showing the *Profile Mesh Location* as well as the result of the *Screw* Modifier. I set the *Viewport Shading* to *Wireframe* so you could see the *Location* of the *Profile Mesh* and its *Origin*.

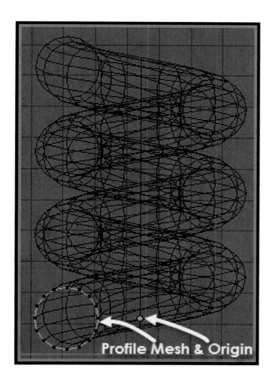

I make a point of showing the position of the *Mesh Origin* because it plays a role in the result of the *Screw Modifier*. *Transforming* the *Profile Mesh* in *Edit Mode* will change the result of the *Screw Modifier*. If you're wondering what type of result I would have got if I hadn't moved the *Mesh* away from its origin, wonder no further. Here is the result in both *Material* and *Wireframe Viewport Shading* mode.

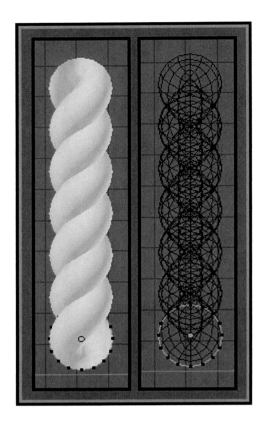

Moving the *Mesh* away from the *Origin* isn't necessary to get the result you want. There is a less destructive option that I will talk about later.

Here are the options available when using the *Screw Modifier*.

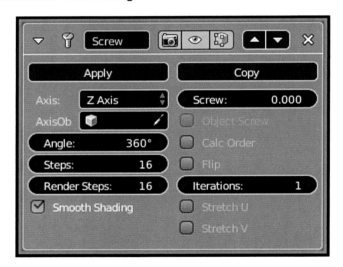

Apply - applies the *Modifier* so that the *Screw* operation is permanent. The *Modifier* is also removed from the *Modifier Stack*.

Copy - make a copy of this *Modifier* and add it to the *Modifier Stack*.

Axis - allows you to choose which *Axis* the *Screw* operation will take place on.

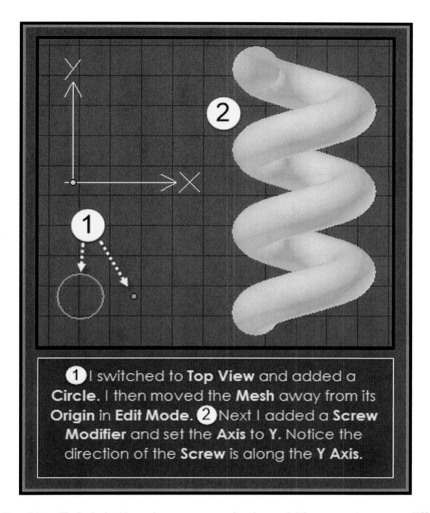

1 I switched to **Top View** and added a **Circle**. I then moved the **Mesh** away from its **Origin** in **Edit Mode**. **2** Next I added a **Screw Modifier** and set the **Axis** to **Y**. Notice the direction of the **Screw** is along the **Y Axis**.

If I had chosen the *X* or *Z-Axis* in the above example, I would have got a very different result. Here is the result for the same *Profile Mesh* on all 3 *Axes*.

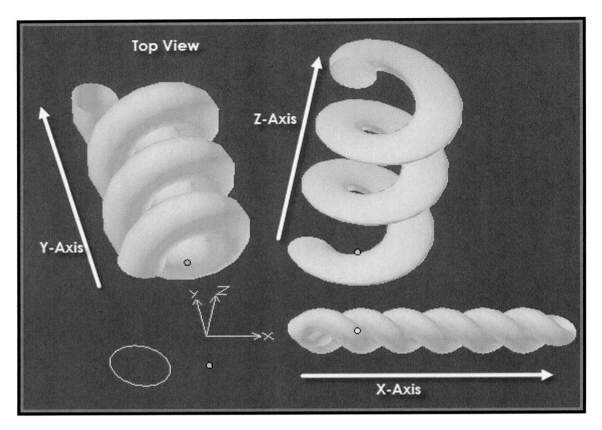

Screw - allows you to set the spacing or height of each revolution in the *Screw Modifier* result (see *Iteration* setting below). You can think of *Iterations* as the number or coils in a spring and the *Screw* value as the distance between each coil. 1 coil or Iteration is essentially a single 360 degree revolution (unless the *Angle* option has been modified - more below).

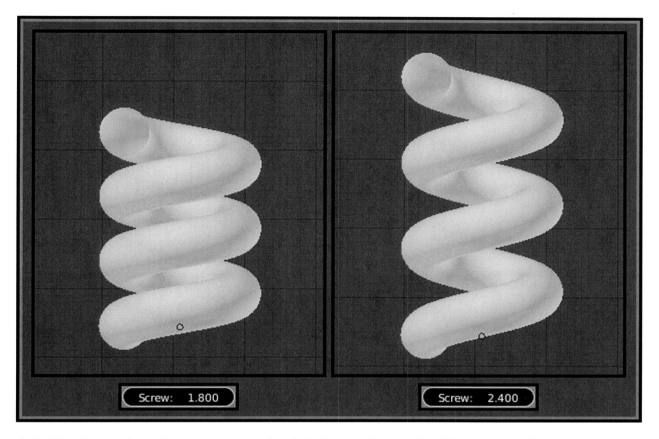

AxisOb - this option allows you to set the *Axis* for the *Screw Modifier* using an *Object*. This setting does not negate the *Axis* setting but it does allow you to change the result of the *Screw Modifier* without moving the *Mesh* away from its *Origin*. An *Empty* is a good choice for the *AxisOb* option.

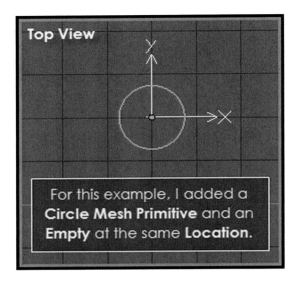

Now I can go ahead and add the *Screw Modifier*. I can then select the *Empty* in the *AxisOb* field.

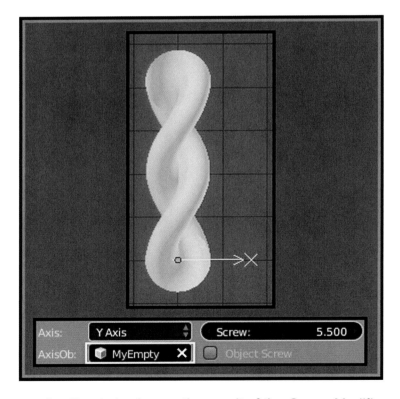

Now I can simply move the *Empty* to change the result of the *Screw Modifier*.

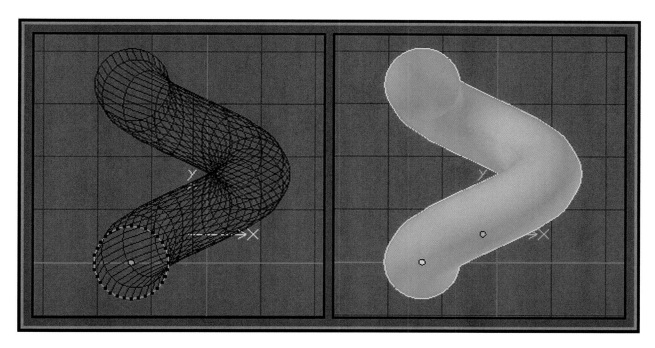

As you can see in the above illustration, moving the *Empty* resulted in the creation of a spring type *Mesh*. Keep in mind that the spacing between the spring coils is still determined by the *Screw* setting (in this example, the value is 5.500). As you will soon see, you can also use the *Empty* to change the *Screw* value.

Object Screw - works in conjunction with the *AxisOb* option. Enabling this option will allow you to use the *Object* selected in the *AxisOb* field to determine the *Screw* value. In other words, you can use the *AxisOb Object* to set the distance between each coil (or *Iteration*) on the spring.

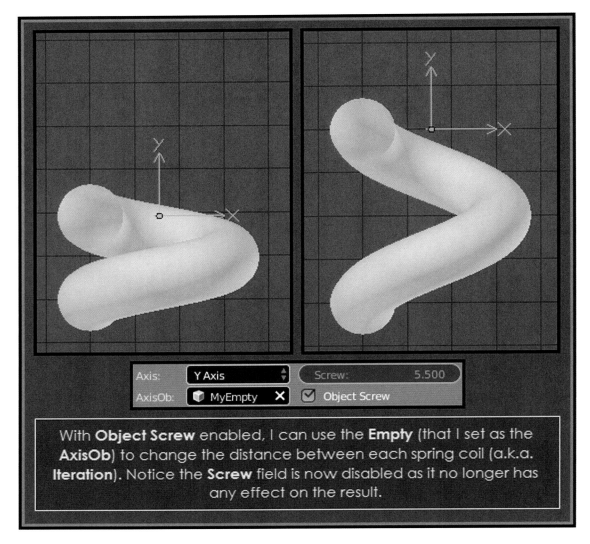

With **Object Screw** enabled, I can use the **Empty** (that I set as the **AxisOb**) to change the distance between each spring coil (a.k.a. **Iteration**). Notice the **Screw** field is now disabled as it no longer has any effect on the result.

I find using the *AxisOb:* option with *Option Screw* enabled to be the best option when using the *Screw Modifier*. It allows me to quickly and easily change the shape and size of the *Mesh* that results from the *Screw Modifier*. You can also *Rotate* the *AxisOb: Object* to quickly change the *Axis*.

Angle - set the distance each spring coil or *Iteration* will travel. I think you will probably want to leave this at 360 degrees most of the time (i.e. 1 full rotation per *Iteration*). To demonstrate, I will modify the *Angle* setting with *Iterations* set to 1.

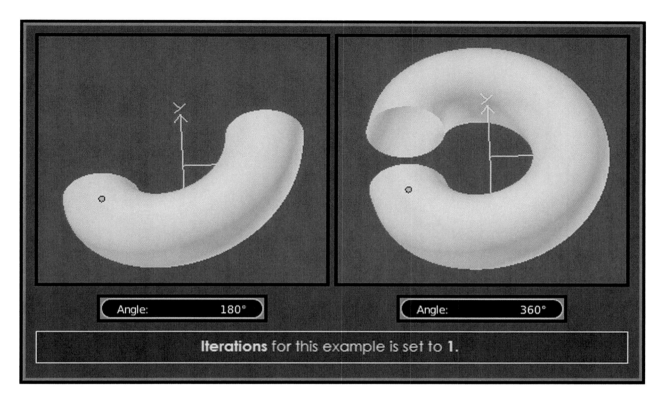

Angle: 180° Angle: 360°

Iterations for this example is set to **1**.

With the *Angle* set to 180 degrees I would need to set *Iterations* to 2 to get 1 full coil in my spring. Again, you will probably want to leave this at 360 degrees unless you have a good reason to change it.

Steps - this option allows you to set how many *Loop Cuts* will be used for each coil or *Iteration*. If, for example, you set it to 10 and you have *Angle* set to 360, you will have 10 *Loop Cuts* for each coil in your spring. If you set the *Angle* to 180 degrees, you will have 10 *Loop Cuts* for each half coil in your spring.

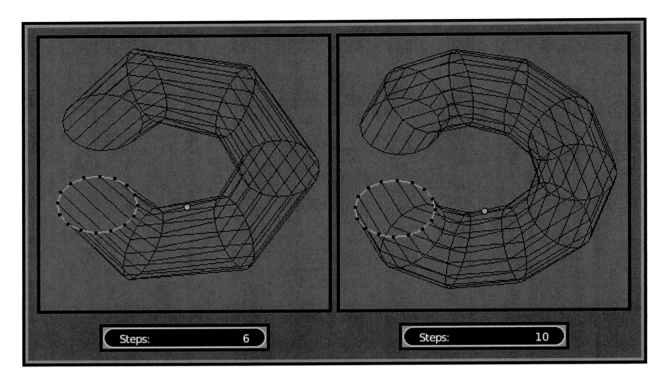

Render Steps - this option is identical to the *Steps* option except that you are setting how many *Loop Cuts* will be used in each *Iteration* at *Render* time. You can keep this value low if you are using a *Subdivision Surface Modifier* in conjunction with the *Screw Modifier*.

Smooth Shading - Allows you to toggle between *Smooth* and *Flat* shading (see **Chapter 3 – Flat vs Smooth**).

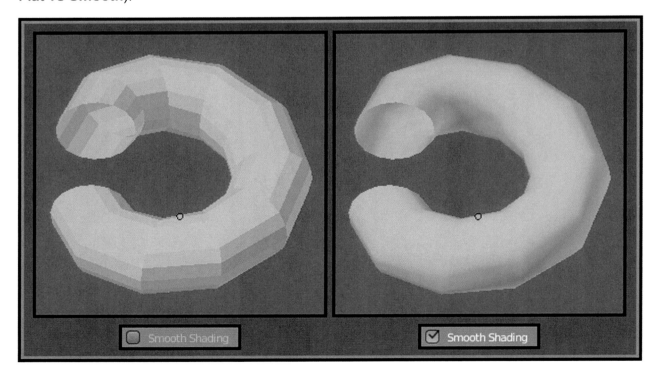

Calc Order - when this setting is enabled the order of the *Edges* are calculated which helps avoid issues with *Normals* and *Shading*. This setting may be needed for *Meshes* but not for *Curves*. The effect of enabling this setting is subtle but it may help fix any issues you may be having with the *Screw Modifier* result.

Flip - this setting simply flips the *Normals* on the *Mesh* that results from the *Screw Modifier*.

Iterations - this setting determines how many times the *Screw Modifier* is applied to the *Profile Mesh*. If the *Angle* is set to 360 degrees, an *Iteration* is basically 1 coil in the resulting spring and adding an *Iteration* will expand the spring by 1 coil.

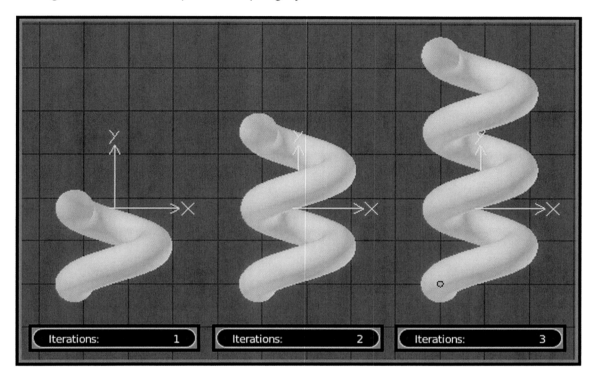

Stretch U / V - this setting, when enabled, will stretch the *UV Coordinates*. *UV Mapping* is outside the scope of this book.

I have presented the *Screw Modifier* as an alternative to the *Screw Tool* as it's non-destructive and its numerous options make it flexible. On the other hand, the *Screw Modifier* doesn't allow you to create a result that is tapered like you can with the *Screw Tool*. In that respect, the *Screw Tool* offers more flexibility as you can create a variety of results that can't be replicated using the *Screw Modifier*.

The Curve Modifier

Curve Modifier allows you to bend your *Mesh* or *Text* using a *Curve Object*.

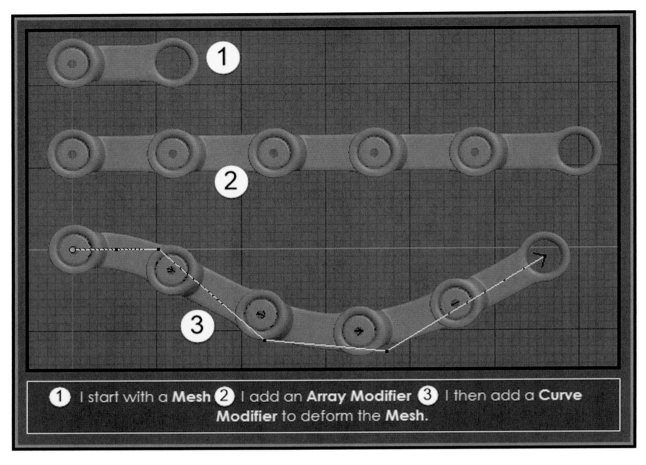

1 I start with a **Mesh** **2** I add an **Array Modifier** **3** I then add a **Curve Modifier** to deform the **Mesh.**

In the above illustration I used two *Modifiers* to create a *Mesh* that resembles a chain. I can simply increase the *Count* on the *Array Modifier* to extend the chain and I can then modify the shape of the *Curve* to bend and shape the chain.

I won't be covering *Curves* in this book but the basics are pretty simple. If they are new to you, there are plenty of beginner tutorials that will get you up and running in no time.

Here are the options available when using the *Curve Modifier.*

Apply - applies the *Modifier* so that the *Curve* operation is permanent. The *Modifier* is also removed from the *Modifier Stack*.

Apply as Shape Key - applies the *Modifier* resulting in the creation of a *Shape Key*. The *Modifier* is also removed from the *Modifier Stack*. *Shape Keys* are outside the scope of this book.

Copy - make a copy of this *Modifier* and add it to the *Modifier Stack*.

Object - here you *Select* which *Curve Object* you want to use to deform your *Mesh*. I will go through a step by step example after the options section.

Vertex Group - with this setting only *Vertices* that are part of a *Vertex Group* will be affected by the *Curve Modifier* (see **Chapter 7 – Vertex Groups**). First, I will add some *Vertices* to a *Vertex Group*.

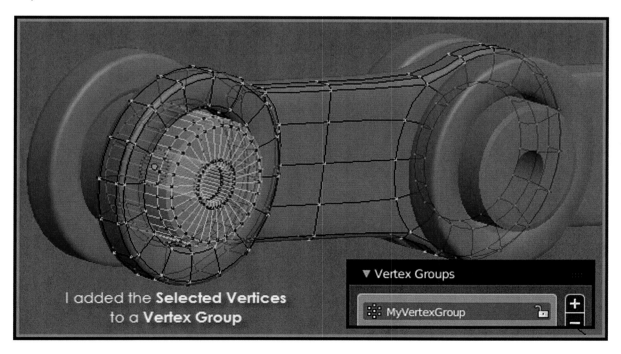

Next I will add the *Vertex Group* to the *Vertex Group* field in the *Curve Modifier* options. Now all *Vertices* in the *Vertex Group* are the only *Vertices* affected by the *Curve Modifier*.

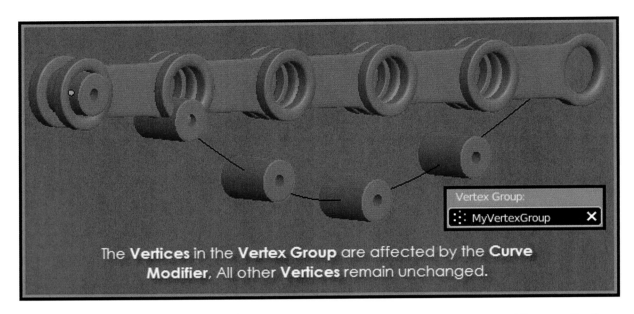

The **Vertices** in the **Vertex Group** are affected by the **Curve Modifier**, All other **Vertices** remain unchanged.

Deformation Axis - here you choose which *Axis* the *Curve* will deform along. The result of switching the *Deformation Axis* can often be unexpected.

I find *Curve Modifier* can be finicky in terms of getting it to work as expected. The result of the *Curve Modifier* can easily give unexpected results as soon as you start *Transforming* your *Mesh* or the *Curve*. I follow a specific set of self-imposed rules when I use the *Curve Modifier*.

Start in *Top View* and add a *Mesh*. Modify the *Mesh* as desired.

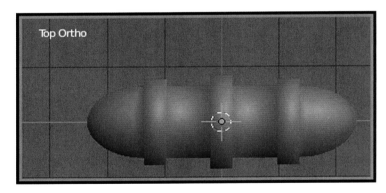

With the *3D Cursor* centered on the *Origin* of the *Mesh* you just created, add a *Path*.

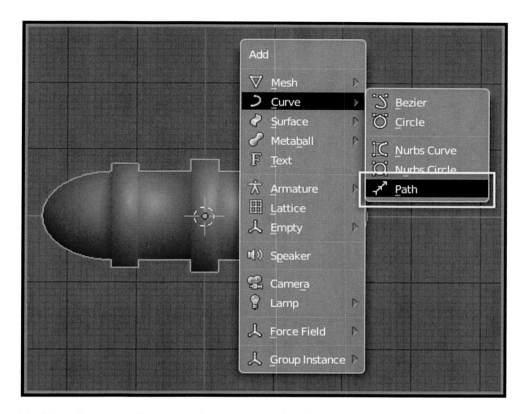

Notice I added the *Curve* at the same *Location* as the *Objects Origin*. If the *Curve* appears to be hidden in the *Object*, switch to *Viewport Shading* to *Wireframe*.

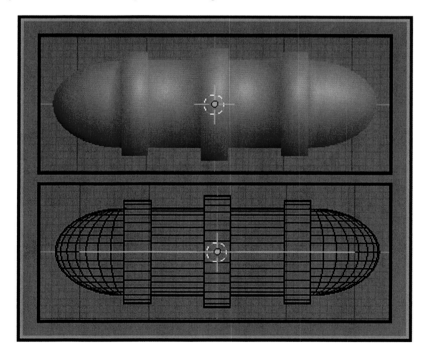

Next I will modify the *Curve* in *Edit Mode* to make it a little more interesting.

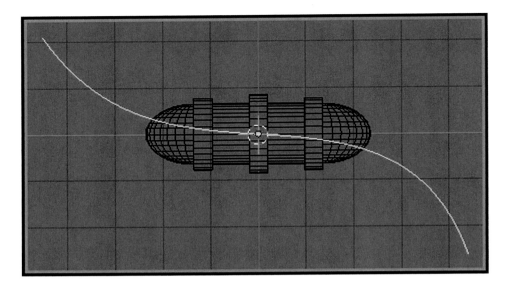

Now I'm ready to add a *Curve Modifier* to the *Object*. Once added, I will go to the *Options Panel* for the *Curve Modifier* and enter the *Name* of my *Curve* in the *Object field*.

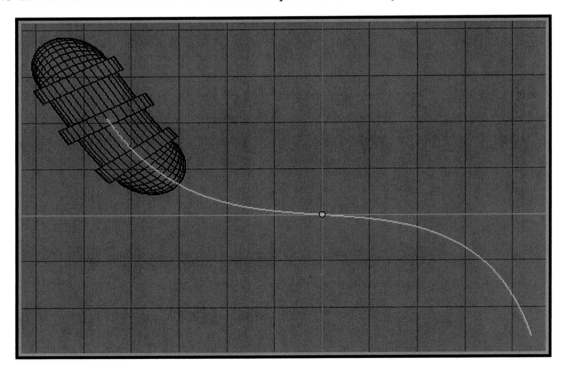

Something interesting happened there. The *Object* moved to the beginning of the *Path* even though its *Origin* has remained unchanged. If you disable the *Curve Modifier* it will move back to its original position. Don't worry when this happens, its normal.

Ok, all done. Now if I move the *Object* along the *X-Axis*, it will follow the *Curve*.

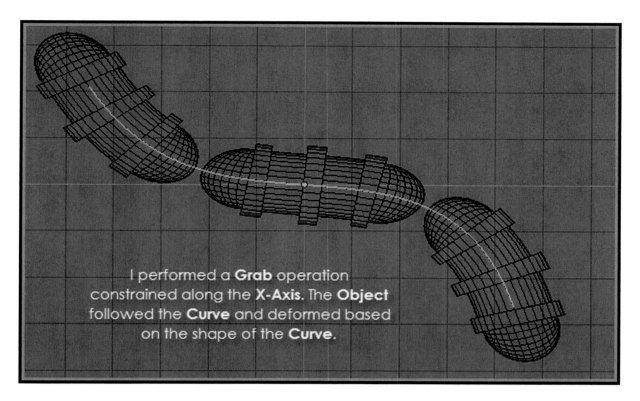

I performed a **Grab** operation constrained along the **X-Axis**. The **Object** followed the **Curve** and deformed based on the shape of the **Curve**.

You can continue to move the *Object* past the end of the *Curve*. It will travel in a straight line at an angle that matches the angle of the *Curve* at the time it moved past the *Curve*.

You can now edit the *Curve* along any *Axis* and the *Object* will deform accordingly.

As I mentioned above, this modifier can be finicky in the sense that it's easy to get undesired results. I find once you start changing *Views* and *Axis* things can suddenly stop behaving as expected.

Up until now, I was careful to do all my work in *Top View* using the *X-Axis* to perform any *Transform* operation based on the shape of the *Curve*. I have found that I have the best luck using this setup. Once you have the *Object* setup the way you like it you can then *Transform* it any way you like. Doing all your work in the *Top View* using the *X-Axis* is a good place to start but eventually you will probably want to reposition your *Object*. I found that I have the best chance of getting the desired result when I perform the same *Transform* operation on both the *Mesh Object* and the *Curve*. In other words, if you need to *Grab*, *Rotate* or *Scale* the *Object*, select both the *Object* and the *Curve* before performing any *Transform* operations so that they are both affected. After performing the *Transform* operation you should still be able to move the *Object* along the *Curve* by constraining the *Grab* operation along the *X-Axis* in *Local Transform Orientation* (G, X, X). If you move the *Object* independently of the *Curve* bad things will happen. I have also found that trying to *Apply Scale* and *Rotation* leads to undesirable results. It's best to apply the *Modifier* before attempting to *Apply* the *Scale* or *Rotation*.

You can also use closed *Curves* with the *Curve Modifier*.

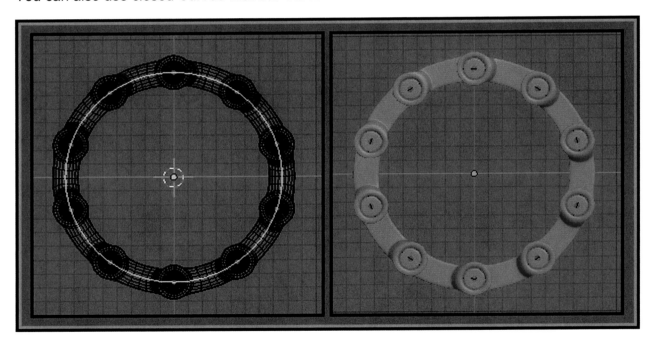

I had to resize the *Bezier Curve* so that the chain would fit together perfectly but it was still quick and easy. Next, I took a single *Object*, added an *Array* and *Curve Modifier* to make a chain that I can resize at any time.

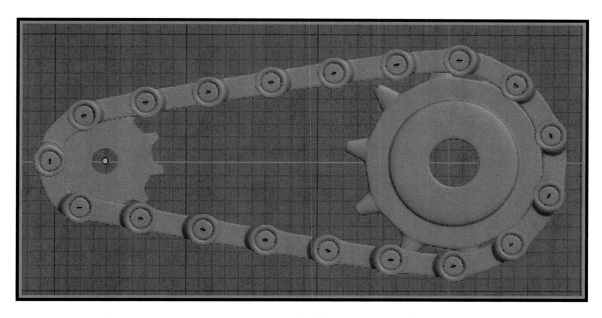

You can also use the closed *Curve* to create cylindrical *Meshes*. For example, you could use it to create a muffler cover.

In *Top View*, *Snap* the *3D Cursor* to *Center* and add a *Bezier Circle* and a *Plain Mesh Primitive*. Resize the *Plane* along the *X-Axis*.

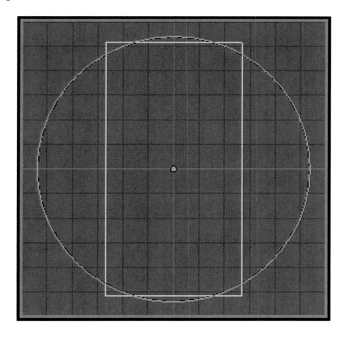

Next add a *Curve Modifier* to the *Plane*. Set the *Bezier Curve* as the *Curve Object* in the *Curve Modifier Options Panel*. Also set the *Axis* to *-X*. You should end up with something very similar to this.

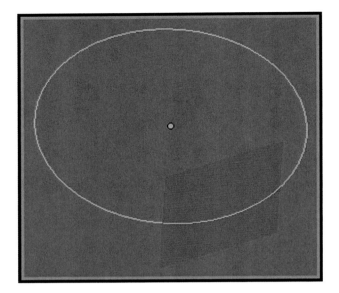

Select the *Plane* and *Subdivide* it. Set the *Cuts* to 4.

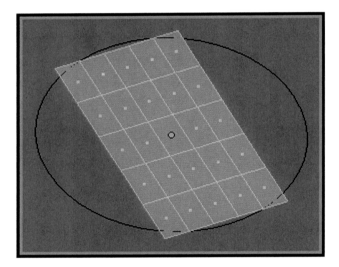

Go back in to *Object Mode*. Thanks to the *Subdivide Tool* the *Plane* is now wrapped around the *Curve* a little more convincingly.

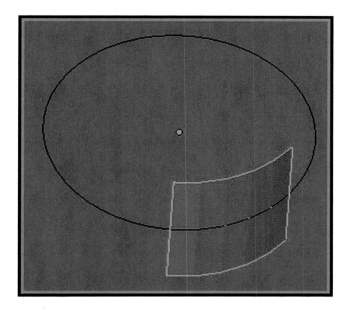

Now add an *Array Modifier* and ensure it's above the *Curve Modifier* in the *Modifier Stack*. I used a *Fixed Count* and set the *Count* to 6 in the *Array Modifier Options Panel*. I then had to slightly resize the *Plane* along the *X-Axis* in *Edit Mode* so that there was no gap between the *First* and *Last Plane*. Here is the result.

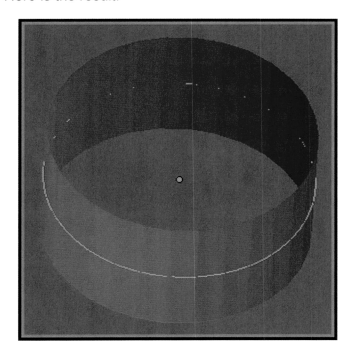

Next I will *Edit* the *Plane* to create holes.

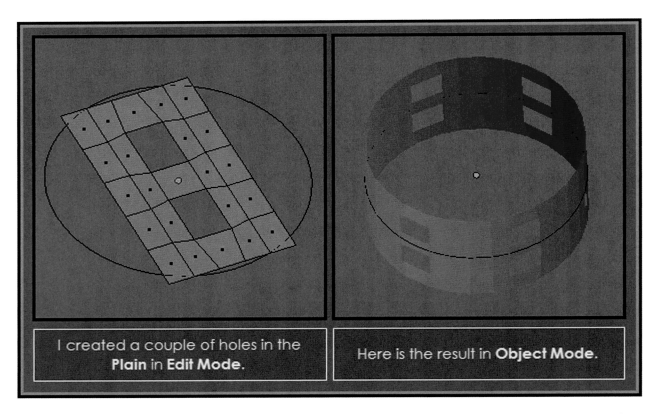

I created a couple of holes in the **Plain** in **Edit Mode.**

Here is the result in **Object Mode.**

Now I can add another *Array Modifier* and a *Subdivision Surface Modifier* to get me close to the final result I am looking for.

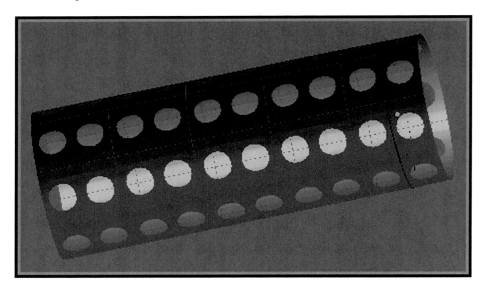

As we near the end of the chapter it should be clear that *Modifiers* offer great power and flexibility. They can make menial *Modeling* tasks quick and simple allowing you to spend less time on the repetitive stuff and more time on the inspirational stuff.

The Chain

Several years ago I watched a tutorial on how to create a chain with several *Modifiers*. The result was a chain that could be extended and deformed very easily in a non-destructive way. It opened my eyes to the power of *Modifiers*.

Fast forward to *Blender 2.5* and the chain is now included as one of the *Blender Add-Ons*. Open *Preferences* (Ctrl + Alt + U), go to the *Add-Ons* tab and search for "chain". Enable the *Add-On* and then press *Save User Settings*.

You should now be able to add a chain by going to the *Tools Shelf*, selecting the *Create* tab and pressing the button labeled "Chain" on the *Add Chain Panel*.

After adding a chain you can now use the associated *Curve* to extend or deform the chain.

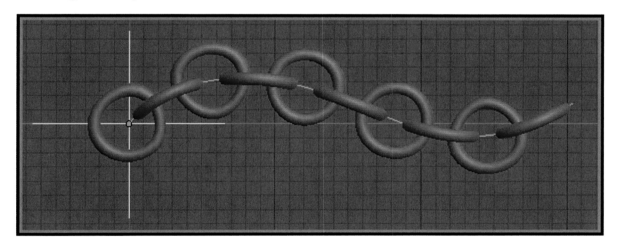

I won't go into details about how to create this chain. You should have enough knowledge by now to figure it out. There are plenty tutorials on creating chains in *Blender* on the internet. It's a popular topic for some reason.

The reason I am mentioning the chain at all is that it can be very convenient for some *Modeling* tasks. Simply *Select* the *Object* in *Edit Mode* (the first link in the chain), then add or remove whatever *Mesh Elements* you like until you get the desired result. You can also take an existing *Mesh*, *Scale* it to approximately the same size as the chain, *Apply Scale* and then *Join* the 2 *Meshes*. You can then go in to *Edit Mode* and *Delete* the original *Mesh*.

Here is an example. I start by *Adding* a chain. I then add a teapot at the same *Location* as the chain (specifically the first link in the chain). I *Scale* the teapot to the size of the first link of the chain. I then *Apply* the *Scale* for the teapot.

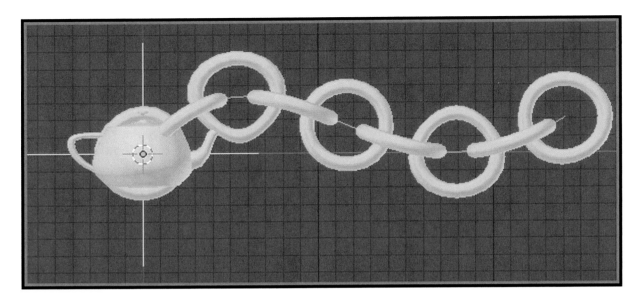

Next I will join the teapot to the chain by *Selecting* both and hitting Ctrl + J.

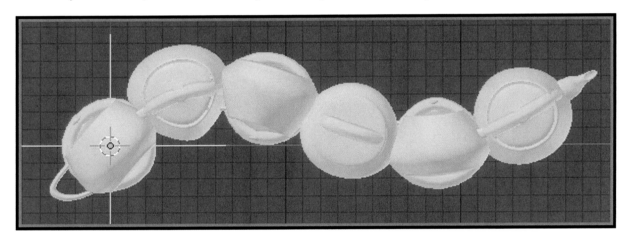

Not exactly what I'm looking for. The first problem is the teapots are *Rotated* because the *Array Modifier* is using the *Empty* as an *Object Offset*. The easiest way to fix this is to *Select* the *Empty* and *Apply* the *Rotation* (Ctrl + A and select *Rotation*). This effectively resets the *Rotation* on the *Empty*.

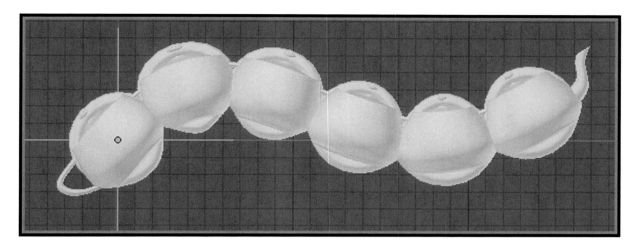

That's a little better. Next I will go in to *Edit Mode* and get rid of the chain link. Simply go in to *Edit Mode*, *Select* a *Vertex* that is part of the chain, hit L to select all *Linked Vertices*, then press X to *Delete* all *Vertices*.

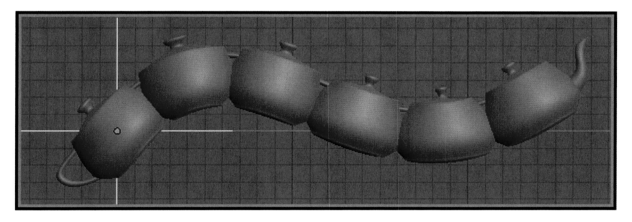

Now all I need to do is change the *Relative Offset* on the *Array Modifier Options Panel* to space the teapots out a little.

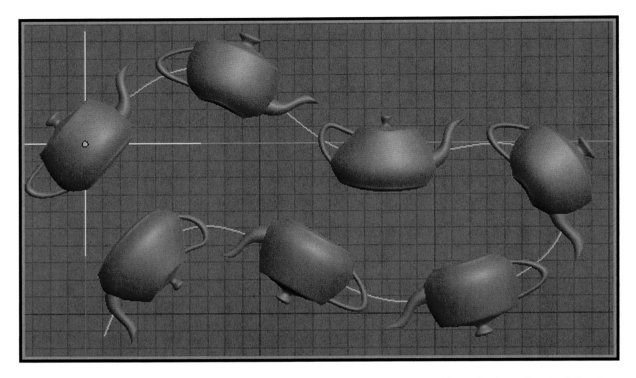

You can also *Transform* the *Empty* to get some interesting results. Here is the effect of *Scaling* the *Empty*.

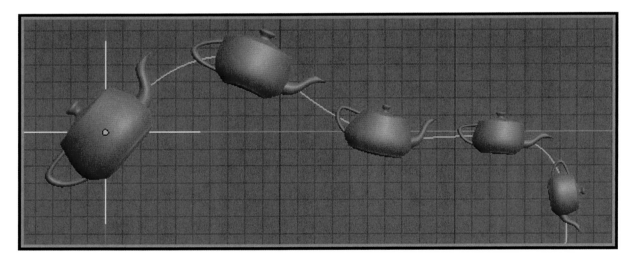

You would be surprised how many times I found the chain to be helpful. Here are a few examples of the kind of result you can get by modifying the chain *Mesh*.

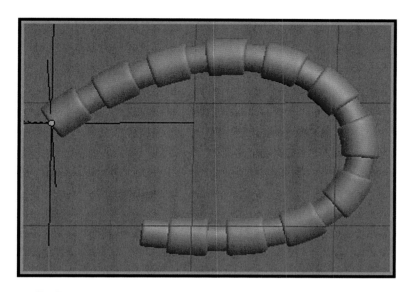

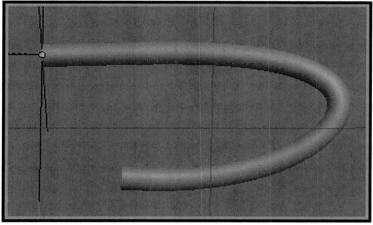

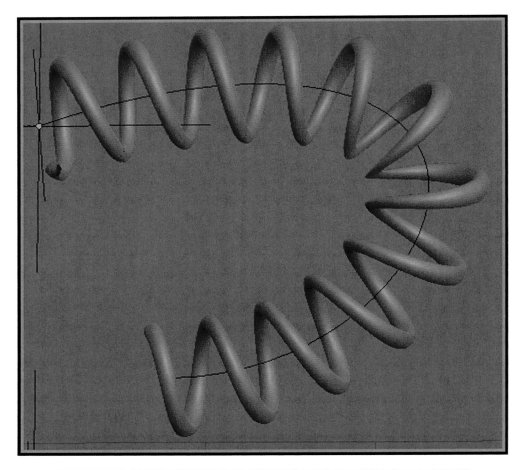

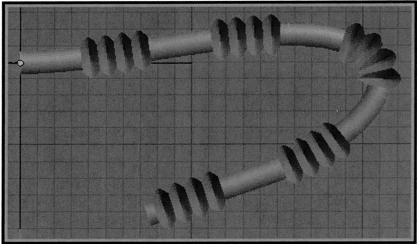

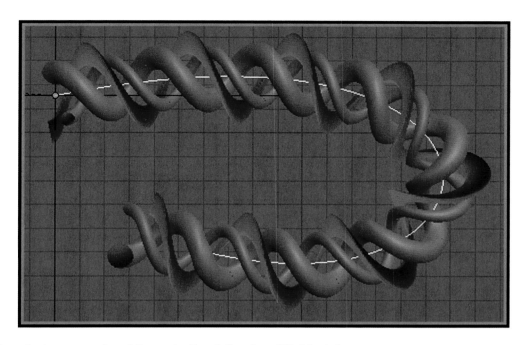

I used the chain a couple of times in the following *3D Model*.

Specifically, the icing along the edge of the roof and the candy path that leads to the door were created quickly thanks to the chain.

There are several other *Modifiers* available in *Blender*. Many are not specific to *Modeling* but I encourage you to experiment and watch tutorials about *Modifiers* so they are at least at the back of your mind when working in *Blender*. You never know when one may come in handy.

Chapter 10 - Advanced Configuration

This section contains information about configuring *Blender* to be more efficient. Some of the topics in this chapter are a little advanced. If you're not careful you could be left wondering why some of your shortcuts are no longer working. I present this information with no guarantees and I am not responsible for any loss of *Blender* functionality that may result from following the instructions in this chapter. If you aren't comfortable with this kind of thing, I recommend reading this chapter for informational purposes only. Having said all that, I believe the type of configuration changes I talk about in this chapter have greatly helped me expedite the process of *3D Modeling*.

Setting up the Keyboard

I am a fan of efficiency, and consequently, a big fan of keyboard shortcuts. They are a big time saver as long as they are within my reach. Unfortunately, some are out of reach. When I model I use my right hand to manipulate the trackball and my left hand is on the keyboard. Many of the keyboard shortcuts I use often are on the right hand side of the keyboard. This means I either have to take my hand off the mouse to use those shortcuts or move my left hand across the keyboard. I know, I know, life is tough.

I decided to try and have as many shortcuts as close to my left hand as possible. Now that *Pie-Menus* come with *Blender*, I was able to refine it even further. Here is my preferred layout.

WARNING: What follows are instructions for modifying some of *Blender's* default shortcuts. Any tutorials you come across will assume the default shortcut configuration so ensure you know which shortcuts were modified and the original keys they were mapped to. I present this section as something that I do to save time but recommend you use caution if you decide to modify any default shortcuts.

Modifying Shortcuts to Help with Workflow

This section involves re-mapping 3 separate shortcuts. I include all 3 in this section as the keys are all mapped in the same area. This is a key configuration I like to use. This section is both an example of re-mapping shortcuts as well as a demonstration of how to set up *Blender* to suit your workflow.

- Open *User Preferences* via the *File Menu* or keyboard shortcut Ctrl + Alt + U and go to the *Input* tab.
- Search for *Local View* and assign it to the 2 key (not the 2 key on the NumPad).

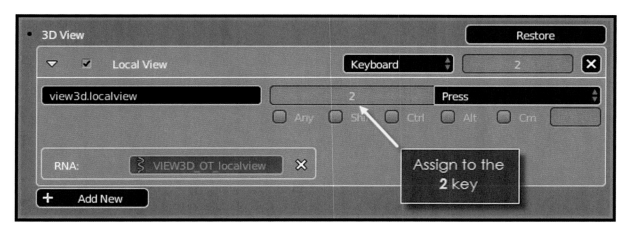

- Search for *View Selected* and assign it to the 3 key.

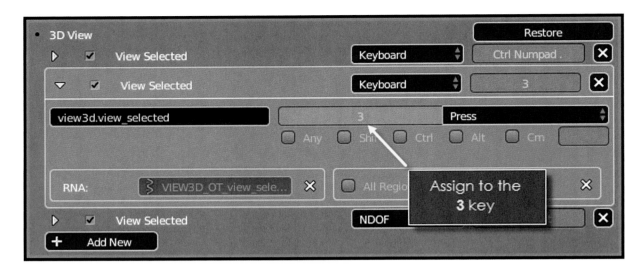

- **Note**: You have to enable *Pie Menus* before you assign a *Pie Menu* to a shortcut (see **Chapter 2 – Pie Menus**).To do this, go to the *Add-Ons* tab and search for **Pie**. Enable the *User Interface: Pie Menus Official* radio button and click *Save User Settings*.

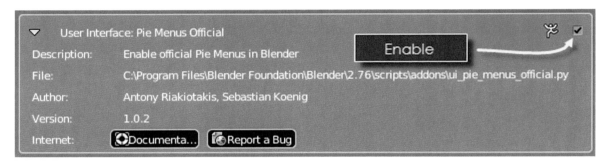

- Now go back to the *Input* tab and search for **Pie**. Open each of the *Call Pie Menu* entries until you find *View3d_Pie_View* and assign it to the 4 key. This now leaves the Q key available which I use for my own custom pop-up menu. More on that later.

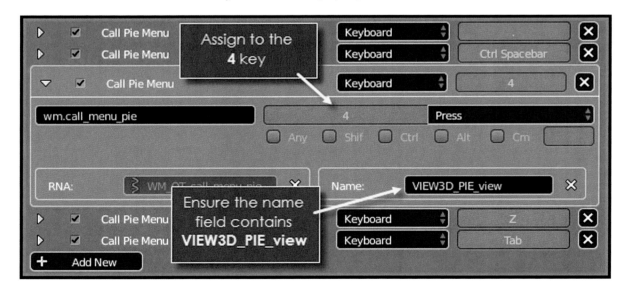

Make sure to save your *User Settings*.

Now you have the ability to change the *3D View*, *Zoom* to an *Object* or *Isolate* it all within easy reach of your left hand (on the *2*, *3* and *4* keys along the top of the keyboard). I believe this configuration has improved my workflow immensely. I change *View* constantly and I also *Zoom* to and *Isolate Objects* on a regular basis. It took me a short time to get used to it but now I can't live without it. If you try it and like it, you can export your *Key Configuration* to a file allowing you to re-import it if you install a new version of *Blender*. Exporting your *Key Configuration* is done on the *Input* tab.

I need to mention again, if you decide to try this *Key Configuration*, you need to be conscious of the fact that all tutorials (including all the examples in this book) will assume you are using the default *Key Configuration*. It may be a good idea to export your current *Key Configuration* before you start.

Snap Element Menu Shortcut

The *Snap Element Menu* is already assigned to Ctrl + Shift + Tab but I find it difficult to press that key combination quickly. If you have *Pie Menus* enabled, the default shortcut will spawn a *Pie Menu*. I re-assign it to Ctrl + Shift + R as follows:

- Open *User Preferences* via the *File Menu* or keyboard shortcut Ctrl + Alt + U and go to the *Input* tab.
- Search for *Wm.Context_Menu_Enum*.
- Expand the *3D View* section.

I map it to Ctrl + Shift + R. I find that key combination much easier to use.

Make sure to save your *User Settings*.

Add Limit Selection to Visible Shortcut

I often toggle the *Limit Selection To Visible* button so I decided to map it as a shortcut so I didn't have to move my mouse cursor to toggle it. I decided to map it to Shift + Z and here is how I did it. The illustration below shows the location of the button.

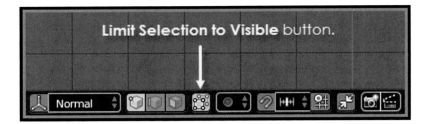

- Go to *File->User Preferences->Input*
- Go to *3D View->Mesh*
- Scroll to bottom and click **add**
- Open it up and in the identifier fields (which currently has a value of **none**), enter :
  Wm.Context_Toggle
- Click on the *Panel* and you should see the Context *Attributes* field. Enter
  Space_Data.User_Occlude_Geometry in that field.
- Use Shift + Z as the shortcut.
- Press *Save User Settings* to save the new shortcut.

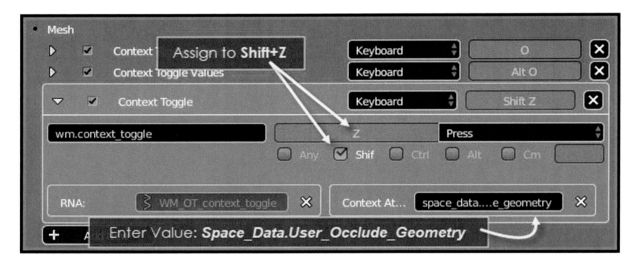

Make sure to save your *User Settings*.

Custom Menu

I came across a video tutorial that explained the basics of creating your own custom shortcut menu. I was immediately intrigued. I watched the video, had a look at the example and created my own custom menu for both *Edit* and *Object Mode*. I won't go into the details of how I wrote both scripts (I have enough programming experience to have eventually figured out just enough to get it done) but I thought I would discuss them as part of the book. I assign the menu to Q on the keyboard. The Q key is usually reserved for the *View Pie Menu* but I re-assign that *Pie Menu* to the 4 key as mentioned in the **Modifying Shortcuts to Help with Workflow** section above.

Object Mode Menu

Here is what the *Object Mode Menu* I created looks like.

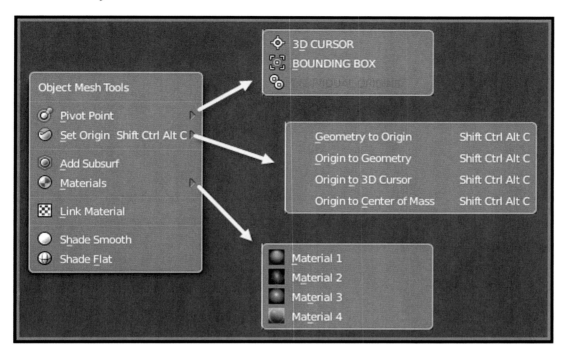

It has changed a little over time but I find the *Pivot Point* and *Set Origin Menu* entries to be especially useful. The *Materials* entry has a sub menu with the values *Material 1*, *Material 2*, *Material 3* and *Material 4*. These entries map to the first 4 four *Materials* in the *Material Properties Window*. The major benefit is you can select several *Objects* in *Object Mode* and assign them all a *Material* at the same time.

Edit Mode Menu

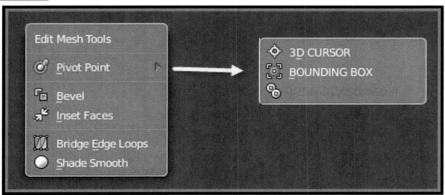

The *Edit Mode Menu* is a little smaller but still useful. Once you get used to using the menu it becomes second nature. Again, the *Pivot Point Menu* item is very hand.

If you're feeling ambitious and have some programming experience I recommend watching a tutorial on creating custom menus and give it a go.

Chapter 11 - Final Thoughts

General Modeling Tips

I thought I would include a section with some general *Modeling* tips. These tips are a collection of general tips I have learned from watching / reading tutorials. I will often stop in the middle of a tutorial to write down a general *Modeling* tip before I forget it. Most of what I mention here has already been mentioned in this book so you can think of this as a high level overview of some of the more important concepts or tips.

You can save time by having a template .blend file. I created a .blend file with my favorite layouts, some *Materials* and a *Light* and *Camera* setup. This .blend is my starting point for any *Modeling* project.

When starting a new *Mesh*, always strive to keep your *Mesh* as simple as possible. Don't start *Modeling* a car and immediately go to work on the headlights. Don't start a plane and immediately start *Modeling* the cockpit. Start with the basic shape and add detail slowly avoiding complexity whenever possible. Once you have blocked out the overall form you can move on to adding detail.

When creating a new model you have to decide how to break up your objects. When I first started *Modeling* I thought the entire mesh and all of its pieces should be contained in 1 *Object*. What I learned from watching / reading tutorials is there is no wrong or right answer to how to break up your model. Do what makes sense. You can always add or remove a part of a *Mesh* from an *Object* if needed.

Strive to keep *Face* distribution as even as possible. Evenly distributed *Faces* is practically impossible for most *3D Models* but keeping on top of it as you go will pay off. The more

Geometry you add, the harder it will be to tweak your *Mesh* so don't wait until the *Mesh* is finished to fix what you can fix now.

Don't forget to *Apply Rotation* and *Scale* on your *Model* often. *Transforming* you *Objects* can affect *Modifiers* so *Applying Rotation* and *Scale* before adding a *Modifier* is always a good idea. Use Ctrl+N to fix *Normals* as you go as well.

Save a copy of your .blend file before you apply any *Modifiers*. I usually apply all *Modifiers* except the *Subdivision Surface Modifier* once I have completed a *3D Model*. I make sure to save my work before applying any *Modifiers*. You never know when you may have to go back and tweak something.

Save often. I try to save every 10 minutes or when I have finished a major portion of a *Mesh*. Being able to go back to a saved *Mesh* after screwing something up is a life saver. I always name my .blend files using a number (e.g. **fast_car_001.blend**). Now when I save, I can simply press F2 followed by the + key on the *NumberPad* and *Blender* will increment the number in the filename for me and I can then just hit Return to save the file.

Final Thoughts

I hope you enjoyed reading this book as much as I enjoyed writing it. In the end, I learned as much about *Blender* while writing this book as I knew when I started the book. I am more amazed than ever that a free piece of software is so feature rich and capable. Keep on *Blending*.

Feel free to send me feedback at BookFeedback@pie-guy.com. Visit my website at http://www.pie-guy.com.

Key Reference

The 3D View

Align View (*Front,Right,Top*) - Numpad 1, 3, 7

Align View (*Back,Left,Bottom*) - Ctrl + Numpad 1, 3, 7

Align View to Selected (*Front,Right,Top*) - Shift + Numpad 1, 3, 7

Align View to Selected (*Back,Left,Bottom*) - Ctrl + Shift + Numpad 1, 3, 7

Center 3D Cursor to World Origin - Shift + C

Hide Selected Objects - H

Hide Non-Selected Objects - Shift + H

Isolate Objects - Numpad /

Maximize Area - Shift + Space, Ctrl + UpArrow , Ctrl + DownArrow

Move Object to Layer - M

Orbit in 3D View - Numpad 2, 4, 6, 8

Pan in 3D View - MMB+Numpad 2, 4, 6, 8

Properties Shelf - P

Quad View — Ctrl + Alt + Q

Shading Solid - Z

Shading Textured — Alt + Z

Shading Wireframe / Rendered — Shift + Z

Tools Shelf - T

View all Objects - Home

View Selected (Zoom to Object / Mesh) - Numpad .

Zoom Border Tool - Shift + B

Zoom In / Out - Mouse Wheel

Edit / Object Mode

Add Menu - Shift + A
Bridge Edge Loops - W (Specials Menu)
Border Region Select - B
Circle Region Select - C
Clipping Border Tool - Alt + B
Delete Menu - X
Magnet Tool (enable) - Shift + M
Merge - M
Mirror Object / Mesh - Ctrl + M
Select Inverse - Ctrl + I
Snap Cursor to 3D World Origin - Shift + C
Snap Element Menu - Ctrl + Shift + Tab
Snap Menu - Shift + S
Specials Menu - W
Transform Grab - G (also G + Axis or G + Axis + Axis)
Transform Orientation Menu - Alt + Space
Transform Rotate - R (also R + Axis or R + Axis + Axis)
Transform Scale - S (also S + Axis or S + Axis + Axis)

Edit Mode

Bevel - Ctrl + B
Crease an Edge - Shift + E
Deselect Linked - Shift + L
Edge Menu - Ctrl + E
Edge Slide - G, G
Extrude - E
Extrude Menu - Alt + E
Face Menu - Ctrl + F
Grid Fill (Faces Menu) + Ctrl + F
Hide Selected - H
Hide Un-Selected - Shift + H
Inset - I
Knife Tool - K
Knife Tool (Selected Faces Only) - Shift + K
Loop Cut Tool - Ctrl + R
Mesh Select Mode - Ctrl + Tab

Proportional Editing (enable) - ○
Separate Mesh Menu - P
Reveal Hidden Mesh Elements - Alt + H
Reverse Normals - Ctrl + N, Ctrl + Shift + N
Rip Tool — V
Rip Fill Tool — Alt + V
Select Edge Loop (*Edge Select Mode*) - Alt + RMB
Select Face Loop (*Face Select Mode*) - Alt + RMB
Select Edge Ring - Ctrl + Alt + RMB
Select Linked - Ctrl + L
Spin - Alt + R
Split - Y
Vertex Group Menu - Ctrl + G
Vertex Slide - G, G

Object Mode

Add Object to Group - Ctrl + Shift + G
Apply Menu - Ctrl + A
Clear Parent - Alt + P
Clear Transformation - Alt + G, Alt + R, Alt + S
Create Group - Ctrl + G
Duplicate Linked - Alt + D
Isolate Object - Numpad /
Join Objects - Ctrl + J
Parenting Objects - Ctrl + P

Index

T

U

V

Made in the USA
Las Vegas, NV
29 December 2023

83699395R00288